The Lost Mining Villages Of Doon Valley

Voices and Images of Ayrshire

"Volunteers aren't paid, not because they are worthless, but because they are priceless"

(Anon)

Barrmill Jolly Beggars Burns Club.
Some of the ever-so-jolly cronies who assisted in research, interviews and a variety of other helpful ways for this book project – *the dream team!*
Top Left and Right: John Moses and David Pettigrew (President).
Back Row Standing (l to r): Willie Black, Willie McDougall, Allan Richardson, David McMillan, Norrie Brown, James R Waite (Past President) and Ronnie Yulle.
Middle row (seated): Willie Edmunds, Tom Irvine (Hon President), Gordon Wilson (Past President), Iain Shaw (Past President), Bob Wark (Past President), Warnock Longridge (Past President), Harry Young (Hon President) and John Simpson.
(Photos (l to r) to end: Bobby Irvine, Duncan Winning OBE, George Anderson, John Waite (Vice President), Archie Brodie, Willie Monahan (Past President), Maurice Hughes (Past President), John Craig, Iain Skene (Hon President), Andrew McCallum, Donald L Reid (Hon President & Secretary), Norman M Henderson (Hon President), Gordon Mabbott and David MacLeod

The Lost Mining Villages Of Doon Valley

Voices and Images of Ayrshire

Hardback: ISBN 978-0-9566343-3-7
(RRP £14.99)
By
Donald L Reid BA FSA Scot
Author of
Doon Valley Memories
Robert Burns' Valley of Doon
Matthew Anderson: Policeman-Poet of Ayrshire
and other Ayrshire local interest books
(see page 199 for full list)

A royalty arising from book sales will benefit:
Dalmellington Band,
Bellsbank Primary School
Dalmellington Scout Group (33rd Ayrshire)
and
Barrmill Jolly Beggars Burns Club

© *Statement: Donald L Reid and Barrmill Jolly Beggars Burns Club, the copyright holders of this work, hereby release it into the public domain. This applies worldwide.*
In case this is not legally possible, permission is granted to anyone the right to use this work for any purpose, without any conditions, unless such conditions are required by law.
2013

This book is dedicated to good friends Archie Hutchison, Hugh Johnstone MBE and Bert Ritchie as a small acknowledgement for their years of outstanding dedication and unstinting loyalty to our wonderful Dalmellington Band.

Of all that may be said of music—that inspiring cheerer of the festive scene, and lightener of the cares of life—it is too often forgotten, (or rather it is not sufficiently realized, even by those who feel the pleasure,) that a fine brass band is capable of giving some of the sweetest developments of the divine art.
                                    Ralph Whitman
          1847 edition of the Brooklyn Daily Eagle

First Published 2013 by
Donald L Reid BA FSA Scot
and
Barrmill Jolly Beggars Burns Club
7 Manuel Avenue
Beith, North Ayrshire,
Scotland KA15 1BJ
Tel: 01505-503801
E: *donaldleesreid@hotmail.com*
Web: *www.jollybeggars.org*

Layout by
Delta Mac Artwork
deltamacartwork@btinternet.com

The publishers gratefully acknowledge financial and other support from:
The Heritage Lottery Fund
Age Scotland
Coal Industry Social Welfare Organisation
Barrmill Jolly Beggars Burns Club
Barrmill Lads & Lassies Burns Club

Printed and bound in Great Britain by
Kestrel Press
25 Whittle Place
Irvine KA11 4HR
www.kestrelpress.com

Contents

Lost Villages o' Doon
– Poem by Rowena M Love 4
Foreword by Craig and Brian
(The MacDonald Brothers) 5
Author's Preface 6
Acknowledgements 7
Introduction 10

Chapters

Poem: Benquhat Memories
(John Relly) 195
Epilogue 196
Poem: Ghaists (Rab Wilson) 197
Bibliography 198
Books by Donald L Reid 199
Author Profile 200
Picture Gallery
– Additional Photographs 201
Appendix
Families of Yesteryear from the Lost
Mining Villages of Doon Valley 210

Chapters

1. Dalmellington and the Upper Doon Valley – An Overview 14
2. Patna 34
3. The Dalmellington Iron Works 43
4. The Hill 48
5. Benwhat and Corbie Craigs 55
6. Auld Craigmark 61
7. Death Knell for Deep Mining 67
8. Bygone Lethanhill (James McFadzean) 71
9. Benwhat – Random Reflections (James 'Jimsy' McPhail) 75
10. Big-hearted Beoch (Andrew Knox Bone) 81
11. Beoch – A Caring Community (Tom Reid) 85
12. Reflections on Beoch (James L Reid) Poem: Benbeoch Memories 95
13. Cairntable Capers (Tom Smith) . 101
14. Tough Times at Corbie Craigs (Bill Bakkom) 106
15. Benwhat – My Hame (Jeannie Mowat or McCreath) ... 110
16. Boyhood Memories of Waterside (John Dinwoodie) 124
17. Tales from Black Rock Glen (Jim McNae) 136
18. The Doon Valley in Retrospect – The 1930s (Anne Joss) 141
19. Childhood Memories of Lethanhill (Ann MacLean) 149
20. A Lethanhill Lad (Hugh Hainey) 153
21. Cairntable Poacher Turned Gamekeeper (Jimmy Dunn) 161
22. Hame at Corbies (Willie McHendry) 166
23. Thoughts on Benwhat (Tom Wilson) 171
24. Dalmellington Memories (Janet C Adams) 175
25. A Wee Boy Remembers Benwhat (John Galloway) 178
26. Benwhat – The Music Plays On (Tom Filson) 181
27. Craigmark – Water of Life (Bill Coughtrie) 185
28. Tongue Row Tales (Sally Robertson or Sampson) ... 186
29. Benwhat Recollections (Andrew Wilson) 189
30. Memories of Cairntable (Janet Grant) 192

Lost Villages o' Doon
Rowena M Love

The author is indebted to Rowena M Love for kindly writing a small poem reflecting the spirit of the Lost Mining Villages of Doon Valley, appropriately titled 'Lost Villages o' Doon'. Great-granddaughter of an Ayrshire miner, Rowena is a writer and poet based in the West of Scotland. She is married with a daughter. Rowena is an experienced tutor and performer. She is currently Writer in Residence for local charity Writability. Her poetry collection *The Chameleon of Happiness* was published in March 2004 by Makar Press, a poetry collective she helped form. The reader can find out more about Rowena and her writing on her website: www.rowenamlove.co.uk.

At Corbie Craigs
hoose nor hut are staunin still,
the space whaur they were teem,
brick an beam as broken
as the mines that fed them.
Benwhat near at haun,
higher up Lethanhill, Burnfoothill,
or Craigmark ablow
are jist as empty.
Beoch, tae, is a lang five mile
frae Da'mellin't'n tae history.

Wreaths are laid
fur the hames that were razed
as if ilka hoose itsel had deed.
Bit bide a wee
in the space whaur they were
and the echoes come real
shapes and sounds mair solid an sure
nor all yer trees an birdsang.

Mither at the mangle, her hauns red raw,
first o her sheets aready snappin wi a guid blaw;
faither scartin last o the coal dust fae his face
wi his well-stropped cut-throat;
a footie gemm, lads efter scuil wi jerseys fur goals
or a sairious team, wi village pride their prod to gie their all;
weans plowterin in the burn, squealin or greetin,
wee Jeannie's ribbon aye at the droop;
windaes flickerin bright wi lowes,
the fires' reek as saft an grey as stags' velvet.

The villages arnae lost,
fur memories o they days
are mortared strang intae that hillside
far above the Doon.

teem = empty, echoing, unoccupied
scartin = scraping
plowterin = splashing
lowes = flames, fires

Foreword
by Craig and Brian
(The MacDonald Brothers)

Like brethren in a common cause,
We'd on each other smile, man;
And equal rights and equal laws
Wad gladden every isle, man.

The Tree of Liberty
Robert Burns

These precious shared memories are recorded with spontaneity and imperfection, and with the inevitable overlapping of topics, but they will, nevertheless, stir fascinating memories of times past, so special to those in whose footsteps we now walk. The stories are compelling and humbling and remind the reader that in the not too distant past, daily life was a real challenge for those living and working in the remote mining villages of Ayrshire's historic Doon Valley. The fact that deep mining is no longer part of daily life, not only in Ayrshire, but the whole of Scotland, makes this book all the more timely.

What shines through strongly about the lost mining villages is the importance of community spirit, with folk knowing everyone else – their strengths and weaknesses – and the willingness to interact with care, consideration and compassion for neighbours in austere times. This is just one example we can all learn from. These important interviews have ensured that many of the influences which have shaped the Doon Valley communities will be more widely known and recognised.

We have been fortunate through our musical career of travelling the world to entertain, singing and playing to audiences who just love all things Scottish. However, we always try to keep our feet firmly on the ground. We are immensely proud of our own roots set in the mining heritage of Ayrshire's Doon Valley. Our dear grandfather, Willie McHendry, was born at Lethanhill and raised at Corbie Craigs. He spent the majority of his working life in the coal mines of Ayrshire. Our mother, Margaret, was raised in Dalmellington where most of the men worked in the local coal mines. We know we have been so fortunate with our family and musical career.

Donald L Reid and his fellow Burnsians from Barrmill Jolly Beggars Burns Club are to be congratulated in providing all of us with the opportunity of remembering a forgotten past through the interviews recorded in this book. As governments wrestle to get to grips with war and the worldwide economic problems of the 21st century, it is also timely for young and old to reflect on yesteryear to better appreciate the real world on our own doorstep, learning from that past. Enjoy a great read!

A this and mair I never heard of,
And, but for you, I might despair'd of
So grateful back your news I send you,
And pray a' guid things may attend you!

To a Gentleman
Robert Burn

The musically talented MacDonald Brothers who have made their career in entertainment. They trace their roots through their maternal grandfather to Lethanhill and Corbie Craigs. (Photo: The MacDonald Brothers)

Author's Preface

The charms o the min', they langer they shine
The mair admiration they draw, man;
While peaches and cherries, and roses and lilies,
They fade and they wither awa, man.
　　　　　　The Ronalds of the Bennals
　　　　　　　　　　　Robert Burns

My parents had experience of life in two of the lost mining villages of Doon Valley. My father, James Lees Reid, born in 1923, lived at Beoch and my late mother, Mary McCulloch Hose, born in 1925, spent her early years at Craigmark. Both moved to Dalmellington around 1938.

My aim in this book is to record and preserve aspects of the social history of the area through the voices of those who lived in the mining communities of the Doon Valley. In doing this I gratefully acknowledge local pensmen including Robert Farrell (1983), Tom Courtney McQuillan (1988) and Alex Johnstone (1995), whose publications provide valuable material about Benwhat, Lethanhill, Corbie Craigs and Craigmark. However, little has been published about Cairntable, Tongue Row, Pennyvenie or Beoch.

I was fortunate and privileged to be able to interview a few former residents of the lost villages and their memories are an important social record. Their stories are the kernel of this book. With the passage of time there are fewer and fewer folk who can recall life as it was in the lost mining villages. The importance of social history – the lived experience of ordinary people – cannot be overstated, because it does give a personal perspective on what life was like.

Without a deep knowledge of the past it is almost impossible to understand and make sense of the present and consequently more difficult to mould the future in a positive way. The older generation who experienced life in the lost villages possessed a largely untapped but enormous fund of knowledge and wisdom, often developed through shared adversity. They were all poor, in relative terms, but as my father often recounted, no pupil ever left Beoch School without being able to read and write. And they also possessed a level of confidence in their skills and ability and aspired to have their place in society, knowing that with a good work ethic and dedication, the world was indeed their oyster.

As this book demonstrates, there are many stories still waiting to be told, if only we have the sense to seek them out while the people are still there to tell them. That is a task the reader can address. Older folk have a special story to tell. Make sure you record their memories of yesteryear before it is too late!

Scotland's national Bard, Robert Burns, immortalised the River Doon, and famously extolled the merits of being able to 'see oursels as ithers see us'. The voices of the past help us to see how others lived and the reader may wish to compare our lifestyle today to that of yesteryear. It may prove very sobering and humbling.

In conclusion, I like to think that in a hundred years' time, someone will pick up this book and enjoy a happy look-back in time and wonder a little about the kindly folk who lived in the lost mining villages of Ayrshire's Doon Valley. I am very grateful that so many remarkable folk shared their precious memories of those halcyon days of yesteryear. Happy reading and remembering!

O' Age has weary days,
And nights o' sleepless pain
Thou golden time o youthful prime,
Why comest thou not again?
　　　　　　　　The Winter of Life
　　　　　　　　　　　Robert Burns

Donald L Reid
Beith, Ayrshire
2013

Acknowledgements

I am taking the old road again;
By the dyke-side, down to the green glen;
And the breezes in the rowans red,
Whisper in trees of my childhood,
'Come you this way again.'

The Old Road
Maureen Henderson

I am indebted to all the interviewees who shared precious memories with me and others. A similar debt of gratitude is owed to those who provided photographs and information. I should like to express my heartfelt thanks to everyone in the Doon Valley and further afield who gave so much help during my research.

This book just seemed to grow and grow, but it was never going to be possible to include extracts of interviews from everyone. There was also a deluge of fascinating photographs; identifying the names of those shown in them was a monumental task, and one we worked very hard on, with a high level of success.

I am grateful to the following for their kind assistance in so many different ways. All reside in the Doon Valley unless otherwise indicated. Age Scotland, David Manion, Chief Executive and the ever-helpful Heather Baillie, Development Officer, East, South and North Ayrshire; Ayrshire newspaper archives: *Ardrossan and Saltcoats Herald*; *Ayr Advertiser*; *Ayrshire Post*; *Cumnock Chronicle and Kilmarnock Standard*; Hon Presidents, Presidents and cronies of Barrmill Jolly Beggars Burns Club, Beith, North Ayrshire; Bellsbank Primary School, with a special mention to Head Teacher Donald Currie, teachers Lynsay Thomson and Kelly McIntyre and all the enthusiastic pupils of P6 and P7; Jim and Margaret Bowie; Katy Clark MP (North Ayrshire and Arran); Angus Cochrane, President of Dunaskin Doon Band; Anthony Collins (Ayr); Bill Coughtrie (Ayr); Dalmellington Local History Group based at Doon Valley Museum; Neil 'Neilly' Dempsey; Councillor Elaine Dinwoodie (EAC Doon Valley); Robert Douglas (Prestwick); Jimmy Dunn (Ayr); Louise Dunn, née Scott (Ayr); Andy Filson; Tom Filson (Ayr); Ian Ferguson (Beith).

Special thanks to the enthusiastic Kennedy Ferguson, a Lethanhill lad, for his wonderful detective work in creating a superb general plan of the lost mining villages and one of Benquhat (Benwhat), Lethanhill and Waterside; Euphemia Galloway; Jean Galloway; John Galloway (Ayr); Libby and Jim Gibson of Ayr Road Garage, Dalmellington for their fantastic support in marketing this and previous Doon Valley books; Kenneth Gibson MSP, Cunninghame North and Arran; Mark Gibson of Craigengillan; Dot Graham (Barrmill) for her support and amazing typesetting skills; Johnnie Graham; Bruce Hainey; Maureen Henderson (Ayr) for permission to quote from her poem, The Old Road; my aunt Agnes Hose who always thinks of others before herself; David Hunter (Dailly); John Hutchison and Giles Hutchison (formerly of Patna); Anne Johnstone; Hugh Johnstone MBE of Dalmellington Band for help in supplying photographs and assisting with a history project with Bellsbank Primary School; Anne B Joss MBE; Dane Love FSA Scot (Auchinleck); Rowena M Love (Scottish poet); George and Penny McCreath; Willie McHendry (Ayr); Frank McHugh of 33rd Ayrshire Dalmellington Scouts; Tom McKnight; Jim McNae (Ayr); Elaine Mackie of Doon Valley Museum for her encouragement and kind assistance with archive material from the museum; Councillor William Menzies (EAC Cumnock); Susan Milligan (Glasgow); Lee Milne (London).

Ellie Swinbank, Keeper, staff and volunteers at the National Mining Museum of Scotland, Lady Victoria Colliery, Newtongrange; Sandra Osborne MP (Ayr, Carrick and Cumnock); Anne and Middleton Park; John Paterson, Chair of 33rd Ayrshire Dalmellington Scouts; David and Margaret Rarity (Patna), very good friends, for their usual fantastic support and encouragement; Ian Riggins (Ayr); Bert Ritchie, President, Dalmellington Band; Elizabeth Ritchie; Stanley Sarsfield, EAC Museums & Arts Department for helpful advice, assistance and encouragement; Flora Scobie; John and Noreen Steele, Ardrossan-based authors and good friends; Linda Stewart (Irvine) for excellent assistance with family history research; Quintin and

Margaret Stirrit; Robert Taylor; Alice and Tom Wallace; Fred Waring (Ramsey, New Jersey, USA); Hugh Wilkie (Paisley); Norma Williamson and all staff at Kestrel Press, Irvine; Andy Wilson (Prestwick); Rab Wilson, poet (New Cumnock); Tom Wilson (Ayr); David Young.

My fellow cronies at Barrmill Jolly Beggars Burns Club also deserve a special mention for their positive help and support of this reminiscence project. In particular, thanks must go to regular companions on visits to the Doon Valley, assistance with the educational element of the project and interviews and research – Norrie and Rose Brown, Norman M Henderson, Warnock Longridge, Iain and Colette Shaw and Harry Young. Special thanks to all the cronies of the club for their support – George Anderson, Archie Brodie, Willie Edmunds, Maurice Hughes, Bobby Irvine, Tom Irvine, Andrew McCallum, Willie McDougall, David MacLeod, David McMillan, Gordon Mabbott, Willie Monahan, John Moses, David Pettigrew, R Allan Richardson, John Simpson, Iain Skene, James R Waite, John Waite, Bob Wark, Duncan Winning OBE, Gordon Wilson and Ronnie Yuille.

A very special word of thanks goes to my father, James L Reid; my dear wife, Kathleen Reid; daughter Elaine Reid; son Fraser Reid and his wife Heather; and my delightful grandchildren, Taylor James Reid and Owen James Reid. Above all, I have to thank Kathleen for her unstinting support and patience working on the manuscript over countless hours.

I take this opportunity to sincerely thank everyone who helped in any way in what was a massive project carried out in a relatively short timescale. It was indeed humbling to learn about many of the happy and sad events which touched the lives of those who were interviewed. I just hope that for those who lived in the lost mining villages of Doon Valley, it helps to awaken long-forgotten memories, and for those too young to have even heard of these lost villages, that they too enjoy learning about the past and endeavour to understand and make sense of what was so special about the small isolated Doon Valley mining communities where their forefathers lived and worked.

This project would not have been possible without the financial assistance provided by the Heritage Lottery Fund and their encouraging staff, with special thanks to Bobbi Campbell, Philippa Clark and Mairi McKee; Barrmill Jolly Beggars Club; Barrmill Lads and Lasses and the Coal Industry Social Welfare Organisation. The support of everyone has been wonderful and very encouraging. It is my hope that this book will be seen as being rather special and timely in capturing the social and industrial history, not only of the lost mining villages, but of the Doon Valley area in general.

Blessings on the old road again,
By the dykeside, down to the green glen;
And the beauty of rowans red,
And the carefree days of my childhood,
Which will not come again

The Old Road
Maureen Henderson

Burnton village was erected near the farm of Burnton, less than 1 mile north-east of Dalmellington. Built *circa* 1924 by the Dalmellington Iron Company, the village comprised of eighty-eight houses. Many of the former residents of Craigmark moved to Burnton and Dalmellington when their old village was eventually demolished as the villagers moved out over a period of several years. This was the Craigmark/Burnton Sunday School cantata *Ali Baba*.
Back row (l to r): Mr Matthew Wilson (Sunday School Superintendent and a highly respected man in the district), Andy Smith, Sadie Calderwood, Annie Carruthers, Mary McCulloch, Mary Beck, David Henderson, William Campbell, Duncan Murphy, John Jackson and Mr J Torbet.

The Bogton Mine aerial skylink ran between Bogton Mine and the coal-washing plant at Minnivey Pit and stretched for just over 1 mile. A similar skylink ran from Minnivey to Chalmerston. The aerial skylink was later removed to the Butlin's Holiday Camp at Heads of Ayr where it was re-erected and used to transport visitors from the camp entrance to the chalets. Bogton Mine was in the process of driving in 1930 and it closed in July 1954. There were four managers during that time, namely Tom Hill, Hugh Anderson, James Lorimer and Tom Kerr. Approximately eighty miners worked at Bogton and they were transferred to Pennyvenie and Beoch in 1954.
(Photo: Courtesy of EAC Doon Valley Museum)

The Lost Mining Villages of Doon Valley

Introduction

From scenes like these, old Scotia's grandeur springs,
That makes her lov'd at home, rever'd abroad;
Princes and lords are but the breath of kings,
'An honest man's the noblest work of God.'
The Cotter's Saturday Night
Robert Burns

The idea for compiling this book was inspired when several members of Barrmill Jolly Beggars Burns Club attended the re-dedication of a lonely, weather-beaten war memorial high up on the side of steep Benwhat Hill on Sunday 12 June 2011.

The remnants of this former mining village sit on the plateau high above Dalmellington in Ayrshire's Doon Valley, made famous by Scotland's Bard, Robert Burns. Deserted around 1953, all that remains today of Benwhat are ruins of the 'new school', the foundations of the rows of miners' cottages and the restored war memorial sitting sentinel above this lost village.

Erected in 1921, this memorial was re-dedicated on that Sunday in June 2011, when around a hundred former villagers, their families and local folk attended a special and very emotional ceremony led in praise by Muriel Wilson, Deaconess at Dalmellington Parish Church. They had gathered to remember those villagers who died in two world wars and more generally the proud folk of Benwhat. The 'Last Post' was played by Dalmellington Junior Band conductor Ian Taylor.

Had we never lov'd sae kindly,
Had we never lov'd sae blindly,
Never met or never parted,
We had ne'er been broken-hearted.
Ae Fond Kiss
Robert Burns

Some junior members of Dalmellington Band played wonderfully well in the packed marquee and this was especially fitting because brass band music was a central feature of village life, the Benwhat Band producing some fine musicians over a hundred years of music making.

The villagers of Benwhat enjoyed working together to make their own entertainment and they regularly held concerts and cantatas and enjoyed many outdoor activities. They had a football team, a silver band, athletics (Doon Harriers), bowling, pigeon racing, and lots of evening classes, concerts and dances. In short it was a really happy and lively community, one which, it is often said, the villagers were loath to leave, even for much improved housing conditions. There was great community spirit and neighbourliness, perhaps not always evident in 21st-century communities. Much of that special community spirit, many villagers said, was left behind in those hills when they left.

Farewell, thou fair day, thou green earth and ye skies,
Now gay with the broad setting sun!
Farewell, loves and friendships, ye dear tender ties –
Our race of existence is run!
The Song of Death
Robert Burns

The re-dedication ceremony was organised by Drew Filson, who arranged the refurbishment of the war memorial with East Ayrshire Council. For this special event the council and others had a large marquee located on the site of the village at the foot of Benwhat Hill. It was nicely decorated with flowers, and there was an intricately decorated cake showing Benwhat, with the words: 'Bricks and mortar may be gone, but Benwhat's spirit lingers on.'

Everyone present agreed that this was a very appropriate sentiment indeed. The council had also arranged for the railings of the war memorial to be replaced, the memorial cleaned and the inscriptions restored, and this was greatly appreciated by all the former residents and their families who came to remember past times, family ties and a former village that was still close to the heart.

Many of those who attended this ceremony were elderly and former villagers of Benwhat or relations of those who lived there. The event brought together folk who had in some cases not met for many years and it was a poignant yet happy event with folk exchanging memories of yesteryear. Despite infirmities, many were able to walk up the steep hill to the memorial and simply reflect and remember, many with a tear in the eye, probably realising that this would be their last visit. Poignantly, Robert 'Robin' Farrell, who loved Benwhat dearly and had written a small booklet about the village, was one who made his very last visit on that June day, passing away a few weeks later.

> *The cruel fate should bid us part*
> *Far as the pole and line,*
> *Her dear idea round my heart*
> *Should tenderly entwine*
>
> The Cruel Fate
> Robert Burns

Benwhat and its sister villages of the Doon Valley such as Lethanhill, Corbie Craigs, Tongue Row, Cairntable, Pennyvenie and Beoch no longer exist, but they were real family communities, occupied by larger-than-life characters, mainly miners and their families.

Benwhat, built between the early 1860s and 1875 with 130 houses in several straight rows, a village school, reading room and pub, was one of several villages or rows of houses created in the Doon Valley of Ayrshire by the Dalmellington Iron Company in the mid to late 19th century. The hill villagers

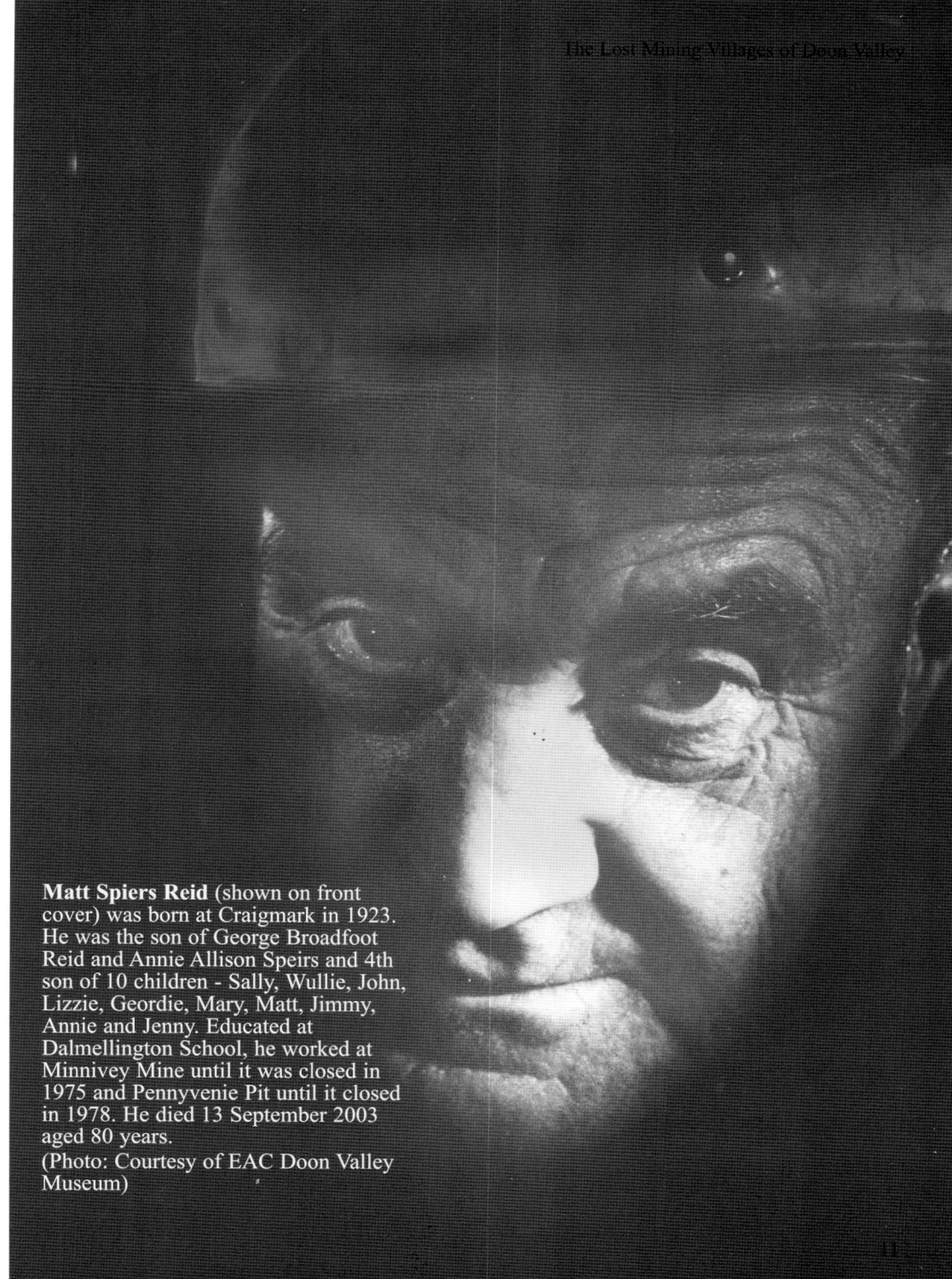

Matt Spiers Reid (shown on front cover) was born at Craigmark in 1923. He was the son of George Broadfoot Reid and Annie Allison Speirs and 4th son of 10 children - Sally, Wullie, John, Lizzie, Geordie, Mary, Matt, Jimmy, Annie and Jenny. Educated at Dalmellington School, he worked at Minnivey Mine until it was closed in 1975 and Pennyvenie Pit until it closed in 1978. He died 13 September 2003 aged 80 years.
(Photo: Courtesy of EAC Doon Valley Museum)

came to the area, in common with families from Ireland, England and elsewhere in Scotland, for work in the rapidly expanding iron workings and the iron and coal mining which supported it.

With the exception perhaps of Beoch and Corbie Craigs, Benwhat was the most isolated community in Ayrshire, yet it was able to boast a brass band, a Burns Club, an excellent harriers club that was well known across Ayrshire and beyond, and Heatherbell, a noted Ayrshire football team that won many honours.

This community was close knit and independent. The villagers, of necessity in the difficult circumstances of hill life, were very hardy, especially in the several periods of decline of the iron industry, when work was scarce. In addition, being situated so high in the hills, the weather in winter was often dire, but this was compensated for by some of the most stunning views across Ayrshire and Galloway.

The miners living in the tied houses of these villages were very much beholden to their employer, because if they lost their job, that invariably meant losing their home. These living quarters were generally cramped and lacking even what today would be described as the most basic facilities. Indeed, the living conditions tolerated by mining families came under severe criticism in reports even before the First World War.

Over the years action was gradually taken to provide more satisfactory housing, but inevitably the poor overall condition of these houses and their remote and inaccessible locations meant that the miners and their families had to be rehoused in more modern dwellings. These were invariably in large council estates or schemes in the Doon Valley built after 1945. The villagers of Benwhat were rehoused mainly in Waterside, Dalmellington or Patna. Beoch was the first village to be abandoned, around 1938, and after the Second World War depopulation gathered speed, so that by 1954 all the remote villages had been abandoned, with the exception of Cairntable, which survived until 1963.

The days of a bustling industrial past in the Doon Valley, with ironstone and coal mining and brick making, are now over. The monument to ironmaking is the large slag bing at Waterside which still dominates the landscape on the A713 at the village despite the fact that the last iron ore slag was tipped there around 1922. Another prominent landmark at Waterside is the tall twin chimneys, known locally as the lums, which dominate the landscape for miles around. These were an integral part of brick production.

Then oh, it was a glorious sight
To see those ironworks so bright
Illuminating darkest night
For miles around Dalmellington.

Dalmellington
Matthew Anderson
(Policeman-poet of Ayrshire)

At Waterside, clay was taken from the quarry at Dunaskin Glen, and brought to the main factory. The clay was crushed and mixed with water and other additives, which included breeze, a very fine anthracite that aided firing. This process, which is also known as pugmilling, improved the consistency, firing qualities, texture, and colour of the brick.

When the bricks were dried, they were then fired or 'burnt' in a kiln, to give them their final hardness and appearance. Brick making at Waterside became the staple industry alongside coal production but the last Dalmellington Iron Company bricks were taken from the kilns in 1976. Bricks from Dunaskin were sent to many places and today you can still find these fine bricks with their DICo mark, treasured by Doon Valley folk and displayed in gardens around the area as a reminder of times past.

Yet sometimes, when a wind sighs through the sedge,
Ghosts of my buried years, and friends come back,
My heart goes sighing after swallows flown
On sometime summer's unreturning track.

From Sunset to Star Rise
Christina Rossetti

The closure of Pennyvenie Colliery in 1978 nicely pinpoints the end of industrial Doon Valley in which large numbers of local men were gainfully employed in the local coal mines. Although opencast mining is still an important feature in the Doon Valley in terms of the sheer amount of coal being extracted, it employs very few local men, the giant earth-moving machines having replaced manual labour.

The Doon Valley is now firmly in a

post-industrial period, bringing new challenges and social change. However, local folk wisely remember their roots and are proud of their rich industrial heritage. It is important to nurture heritage because with the passage of time the social and industrial history of any area can be all too quickly forgotten.

So much of the industrial past has already disappeared almost without physical trace. This is evidenced in the former mining communities of the Doon Valley which no longer exist, other than on old Ordnance Survey maps. With the passing of each generation there is a real danger that these small, vibrant communities – lost villages – will be totally forgotten. Recording some of their social history will help those who follow in our footsteps to remember and better understand how their community of today was shaped by the lives and work activity of those who lived at the sharp end of life, doubtless dreaming of a better tomorrow.

Across the wild moors and quiet valleys, the ghosts of several long-forgotten villages haunt the Doon Valley, in habitations suddenly deserted and left to ruin before being hastily demolished. This book allows a few former villagers to tell their personal stories of yesteryear.

For a' that, an a' that,
It's coming yet for a' that
That man to man, the world o'er
Shall brithers be for a' that.
 A Man's a Man for A' That
 Robert Burns

Dalmellington High School football teams of 1964. Where are they all now and what memories do they have of the High School of Dalmellington?

Back row (l to r): Jim Drysdale, Tom Martin, Charlie Gilbertson, Ian Knox, George O'Neill, John Whiteford, Tom Gilbert, Johnnie Graham and Robert Thompson.

2nd Back row: Mr Samuel 'Yule' Johnson (teacher), Hugh Hose, Robert Stevenson, Tom Donan, Tom Kilpatrick, Adam Watson, David Seawright, Hugh Murphy, Jack Paterson, Joe Donnachie and Mr James Maxwell (teacher).

Second front row: Mr Alex W Scott (PT teacher), Robert Logan, Alan Maxwell, Billy Cullen, Alex Stark, Billy Steele, Robert 'Toady' Sloan, Robert Brand and Mr Sandy McGregor (teacher).

Front : Tom Armour, Alex Yates, Andrew Paterson, George Galloway, Jim McClelland, Malcolm Cullen, Jim Ferguson, Jim McKnight, Jim Clark, Jim McHattie, Stewart Chalmers, Donald Tyson and Billy Chalmers.
(Photo: Courtesy of EAC Doon Valley Museum)

An aerial view of Houldsworth Pit, which operated from 1900 until 1965. After being closed by the NCB it was successfully operated for a number of years by Mr Jim Love, formerly a Scottish cycling champion.
 (Photo: Courtesy of EAC Doon Valley Museum)

Chapter 1

Dalmellington and the Upper Doon Valley – An Overview

Here dwell the lads who do and dare,
And lasses sweet beyond compare,
And kindly wives who tend with care
The miners of Dalmellington.

Craigmark, Benquhat and Burnfoothill,
All give my heart a glorious thrill,
While memories cloud my eyes until
I scarce can see Dalmellington.

Hills over hills lure waves arise
Beneath these health-inspiring skies.
God bless this earthly paradise
My own, my dear Dalmellington.

Dalmellington
Matthew Anderson (1864–1948)
Policeman-poet of the Ayrshire Constabulary

Origins

The upper section of the Doon Valley is an intriguing area with a fascinating industrial and social history stretching far back in time. The village of Dalmellington lies at a height of 600 feet above sea level and some 15 miles south-east of Ayr. It is situated about one mile east of the romantic River Doon, made famous by the world-renowned Bard, Robert Burns, who certainly knew this welcoming corner of Ayrshire.

The origins of the village name can be read in two ways, either as Dal Muilean Tuin, 'the fort on the plain of the mills', or Dal Meallan Tuin, 'the fort on the plain of the hills'. The *New Statistical Account of Scotland* (vol. 5), written in 1837, says that the name can be traced to its Gaelic origin, *Dail*, signifying a field or valley, and *Muileann*, which means a mill, and the common suffix *ton*. It therefore signifies a mill field. There is evidence for all the explanations of the name, as there are castles, hills, valleys, fields and mills. The noteworthy village motte located at the east end of the village is a large smooth eminence proudly rising above the town, where the ancient Pictish inhabitants perhaps met to settle matters of law and custom. At such places matters of concern to all were raised, or 'mooted', for discussion.

The early church

According to William Douglas (*In Ayrshire – 1872*) the history of Dalmellington can be traced as far back as 1003 when it existed in some form at its present location. Mention is also made of the little church in Dalmellington in the records of the Diocese of Glasgow towards the end of the 13th century. It is known that this original church was situated in the old graveyard below the motte in the village, although all traces of it have long ago ceased to exist.

The route to Galloway and persecution in Covenanting times

Dalmellington was strategically located on an ancient route from the south which linked up with the Old Edinburgh Road to Galloway and the pilgrim way to Whithorn. The years 1681–85 are known as the Killing Time because of the atrocities committed, by James Graham, Earl of Claverhouse, Viscount Dundee, among others. He earned his nickname 'Bloody Clavers' by his brutal suppression of the Covenanters. He was regularly in Galloway and indeed is said to have been billeted for a time with Grierson of Lagg and his moss-troopers at Garryhorn Farm at Carsphairn. Accordingly Dalmellington was caught between the Royalist presence at Carsphairn and a very active Covenanting one in Cumnock, which saw the military in large numbers in this part of the county.

In Extracts from *Woodrow's Manuscript Reprint Relating to The Covanantors Who fell In Dalmellington Parish 1666 – 1686*,

Prepared by Hugh Gibson, asserts that 600 troops, armed with cannon, ammunition, iron shackles and fetters, were quartered in the parish in 1685, living off the land. They caused considerable upset to the local population, then numbering only a few hundred, with whom the soldiers would have been billeted. Fines were levied for worship in the open air, people were imprisoned, families dispersed and houses plundered all because local men stood out against Episcopacy.

Quintin Dick, an elder in the parish church, said to have been a wise, well-educated and caring man, suffered terribly during these years. His house was turned into a guardhouse for soldiers in transit to and from Galloway, where many of them served under the notorious Grierson of Lagg, whose local residence was the house of Garryhorn, Carsphairn. Dick was forced to billet twenty of the soldiers, and eventually was sentenced at Ayr to a fine of £1,000 and banished to the plantations of America. He was imprisoned in 1684 and a year later he was taken from Edinburgh to be detained in Dunottar Castle. He would have been deported to America, but was left behind because it was believed he was dying. He recovered and returned to Dalmellington, where he endeavoured to heal the differences that had separated the Presbyterian adherents of the parish.

Another elder of the parish church, Roger Dunne (or Dunn) of Benquhat, was on his way home from Carsphairn Fair in June 1689 when he was ambushed and killed by some rogues who were involved in a local feud of which Dunne had absolutely no part. His grave can still be seen in Carsphairn Kirkyard.

Many other young men, especially those from the farming community, became involved with the Covenanters and the names of Sloss, McAdam, McWhirter and Paterson appear in the Covenanting records.

The Reverend George S Hendrie

Dalmellington is especially precious to its many sons, none more so than those who have left the district. One of the most ardent supporters of the village was the Reverend George S Hendrie, Minister of Dalmellington 1880–1925, chairman of the Parochial Board (1885–95) and a member of the Parish Council (1889–98), who in 1889 penned *The Parish of Dalmellington: History, Antiquities and Objects of Interest*. This booklet was reprinted in 1902 by William Murdoch, a general merchant in Dalmellington, and is still regarded by many as the outstanding historical account of the town and district. In his summing up of Dalmellington he writes:

Here in Dalmellington we have our own share of legend. There is scarcely an epoch in our history that is not represented by some story touched on in this history of the parish. It is an old historic land that lies round our door, a land that has seen brave, and oft-times fierce, contendings for liberty, a land in which industrial peace has had its victories, no less than war. Men have here literally 'beat their swords into ploughshares, and their spears into pruning hooks'. Let us not forget its past, and the lessons we may learn therefrom.

Lord Cockburn

The visitor to the upper reaches of the Doon Valley should take time to explore the village and surrounding area, particularly Loch Doon. One particular visitor was not especially impressed by the village and its environs. Lord Cockburn (1779–1854), the Scottish lawyer, judge and literary figure, visited in 1844, when he had a vision of how Dalmellington could be improved by adapting many of the reforms evident in English villages.

I grieve for Dalmellington. The time will come when English neatness shall be introduced into Scotland, what a village Dalmellington may be. A few trees, irregular ground, tumbling burns, a spire, and a mill – what more is wanted?

Some time later, the noble lord, annoyed at the lack of progress, seems to have damned it with faint praise and was singularly critical of coal miners, describing them as 'black scoundrels'.

It has the appearance, and the reputation of being a singularly virtuous and happy village; and I am told is perhaps the last place in Ayrshire where, with a good deal of old primitive manufacture, rural simplicity and contentment still linger. But the village is now to taste manufacture in an improved state.

> *The devil has disclosed his iron and speculation has begun to work it. There seems to be about a dozen pits sinking within half a mile of the village, and before another year is out those now solitary and peaceful hills will be blazing with furnaces, and blighted by the presence of the vices of a new population of black scoundrels. They were already lying snoring and, I presume, drunk, on many indignant knolls.*

Of course the ironworks and coal mines have long since made their special mark on the valley and its people of yesteryear and sadly are now part of folklore. There are still many former miners living locally but the only remnants of an industry so long at the heart of the Doon Valley villages are a few jobs in opencast mining in the hills to the north-east. What would Lord Cockburn make of Dalmellington today?

Robert Hettrick (1769–1849)

The old cemetery contains a Covenanting memorial and a plaque to the blacksmith-poet of the village, Robert Hettrick. The plaque was placed over his grave in 1888, partly at the expense of a relative, and partly by public subscription, a mural tablet with the following inscription:

> ROBERT HETTRICK, Blacksmith,
> Author of 'Poems and Songs'
> Born at Dalmellington, 1769 – Died, December, 1849.

Sadly, the old cemetery has been neglected and extensively vandalised over the years and many interesting headstones have been lost.

Similarly, St Barbara's RC Church (built 1959–61), octagonal in shape and copper-roofed, used to sit aloft on the edge of the medieval village motte, but was the subject of ongoing and extensive vandalism from its earliest days. The chapel was closed for several years and demolished in July 2003, a sad legacy to the power of mindless vandals.

The parish church

Dalmellington Parish Church sits on a commanding position overlooking the village. Designed by Patrick Wilson of Edinburgh and built by McCandlish of New Galloway in 1846, the building is of neo-Norman style with a distinctive tower. Nearby is the 1766 harled church hall, formerly the old church built by James Armour. Recent renovations have been effectively carried out by a dedicated and enthusiastic small band of older church members at a time when the national church is struggling with falling membership.

The parish church has a very valuable collection of Covenanting silver. The small cups dating from 1637 and 1650 are reputed to have been taken into the nearby hills around Benbeoch Craig, where they were used to give communion, by the Reverend Alexander Stevenson. In 1869 communion cards were introduced at the church in place of metal tokens. In the parish magazine of November 1909 a Dalmellington exile, Thomas H Wallace of Brisbane, Australia wrote:

> *Like a Sentinel guarding the little town,*
> *Stands the old grey church on the hill*
> *Though it's many a year since I saw it last,*
> *It is dear to memory still.*
>
> *There are many who have played within its shade,*
> *Now scattered the world o'er*
> *Who have made their homes in other lands*
> *To return again no more.*

The former Lamloch Church (1851) in Low Main Street built by David Millar, is also a notable building and is now the headquarters of the 33rd Ayrshire Dalmellington Scouts, who celebrated their centenary in 2010. The Doon Valley Museum at Cathcartston, which boasts a date stone of 1744 and was formerly weavers' cottages, also reveals much of the extensive industrial and social history of the village.

Craigengillan

The house of Craigengillan (*c.* 1780) is seen at its best looking across the valley from the road to Loch Doon which leaves the A713 at Mossdale. John McAdam of Craigengillan, who made his fortune as a drover, enlarged or built the house in what has been described as 'an unadventurous Georgian manner'. About 1820 a manorial entrance was added to the east wing. There is also a spectacular domed tower and a square tower with impressive Georgian stables.

The house and its extensive grounds are private and the current owner is the indefatigable Mr Mark Gibson, who has dedicated himself to maintaining and improving Craigengillan and its extensive and beautiful policies, including upgrading the pathway in Ness Glen, building bridges over streams and creating new pathways around the magnificent Dalcairney Linn. A more recent innovation was building a night observatory to enable visitors to enjoy the night skies of Ayrshire.

Quintin McAdam

An earlier laird of Craigengillan, Quintin McAdam, was remarkable in that his widow, Elizabeth Walker, raised a famous action for declarator of marriage, which was based on the following (very brief) circumstances that occurred at Craigengillan on 22 March 1805. He is said to have called three menservants into the hall one day, and holding the hand of Elizabeth Walker, who in 1800 he 'took into keeping', said, 'I take you three to witness that this is my lawful married wife, and the children by her are my lawful children.' He then immediately left the hall and shot himself dead. It is of his forebear, John, a celebrated agricultural improver, that Burns wrote in 1786/87:

An God bless young Dunaskin's Laird,
The blossom of our gentry,
An may he wear an auld man's beard,
A credit to his country!

The old laird's son, also Quintin McAdam, with whom Elizabeth Walker was pregnant at the time of the demise of his father, was responsible for building the romantic walk up the Ness Glen which today has been given a new lease of life and once again attracts visitors interested in walking or canoeing. He would doubtless have been very proud of the work carried out in Ness Glen in recent years through the unstinting efforts of Mark Gibson, Laird of Craigengillan.

Perkelly Burn and trips

In boyhood days when life seemed so happy and simple, the writer has many happy memories of walks through Ness Glen to Loch Doon and trudging down the 'Hungry Brae' to enjoy picnics at Perkelly Burn, often thronged with local folk and happy children paddling in the sunlit summer stream. This was a regular feature of the summer months in the 1950s and early 1960s for folk who lived in Bellsbank. Others will recall, with a twinkle in the eye, the bus trips organised from Bellsbank by John 'Shigs' Coughtrie, taking locals on outings to the seaside at Girvan and Prestwick. These are indeed happy memories.

Local scenes

Those with time to spare would enjoy a walk to the Pickan's Dyke, located above the new cemetery. About 1.5 miles south of the Straiton Road at the Doon Brig, there is the dramatic waterfall at Dalcairnie (OS77: 466 043) which can be seen at its best when the Dalcairnie Burn is in spate. In recent years it has regularly frozen over with dramatic effect, even providing challenges for brave-heart ice-climbers.

A classic photo of Dalcairnie Falls frozen over in 1947 when there was a severe winter. The four boys silhouetted against the gleaming ice wall are (l to r): Hugh Hainey, George Auld, Robert Auld and Tom Leitch. Having been sent to attend Sunday School in Dalmellington, they heard about the frozen falls and decided a visit there was more appealing. (Photo: Courtesy of EAC Doon Valley Museum)

On the Cumnock Road two miles from the village, Ben Beoch Craig (OS77: 498 084), at a height of 1,522 feet above sea level, is seen in spectacular fashion from above Pennyvenie. It has been described as a miniature Giant's Causeway and one can easily picture it as a place of sanctuary for the Covenanters, with many caves on its lower slopes. However, due to opencast working in the area and the danger of ongoing surface mining operations it is best not to approach this hill without permission.

Loch Muck

The Muck Water streams through Dalmellington and on many occasions, particularly 17 July 1927 and again in 1934, the centre of the village has been brought to a standstill by severe floods, vividly remembered by a diminishing number of the oldest residents. Interestingly, the commonly held view that the Muck Water rises in Loch Muck (OS77: 514 007) on the borders of Ayrshire and the Stewartry of Kirkcudbright is in fact spurious. This water actually rises to the north of Campbell's Hill (OS77: 530 027) just over 1 1/2 miles from the loch. Loch Muck, which sits in a basin some 300 yards above sea level, is good for trout fishing. It has only one exit and drains into nearby Loch Doon, and marks the boundary between Ayrshire and the Stewartry of Kirkcudbright.

The Co-op

Formed in 1879, the Dalmellington Co-operative Society became one of the largest employers in the village. By 1950 it had a workforce of seventy-one, with a membership of 1,455 and an annual turnover of £144,000. Forty-eight were employed in shop retailing and it had one mobile shop and eight horse-drawn vans. The bakehouse employed ten bakers and the butchers did their own killing in the slaughterhouse at the Crofts every Wednesday, which was also a half-day shop holiday.

The drapery department supplied all goods in clothing, including ladies' and gents' outfits as well as carpets and furniture. The grocery department was particularly busy and supplied all home provisions as well as selling mining tools such as picks, shovels, hammers and boring equipment. In every respect Dalmellington Co-operative was able to fulfil all the material needs of the villagers.

Dalmellington men endeavouring to clear the Dalmellington to Carsphairn Road in 1948 using manual labour only. The snow is some 8 feet in depth and it must have been exhausting work. Despite this the men can manage a smile for the photographer. Apparently a lorry carrying a load of whisky had been trapped in the drifting snow between Carsphairn and Dalmellington and they were attempting to reach the lorry so that it could be recovered to Dalmellington Police Station for safekeeping. Frank Bunyan is third from the left and to his right at the front is John Cameron. A light aircraft was used to drop food supplies to the workers.
(Photo: Courtesy of Hugh Hainey)

Loch Doon – molten granite and ice cap

For many people Dalmellington is synonymous with the 6-mile-long Loch Doon, the largest of all the Southern Upland lochs, located 3 miles south of the village. Geological studies reveal that it was some 450 million years ago that the Loch Doon hills were created. The Galloway hill group to the south of Loch Doon was then being formed by the molten granite, dramatically erupting through the sandstone rocks of the land. The hot liquid granite baked the surrounding rocks to form a ring of hills, a ring we now call the Rhinns of Kells and the Merrick – Galloway's highest hill. But it was between fourteen thousand and two million years ago that Loch Doon was formed.

As the climate gradually grew colder, an ice cap developed on top of Merrick. This ice cap swelled over the land around it. The monstrous glacier gouged out the rock beneath it and carried massive boulders far away. For how else could boulders of Loch Doon granite have been found as far away as North Wales and Northern Ireland? What you see now, the forests, the plants, the remains of homes where people once lived, even the valley itself, is less than the blink of an eye in the life of this land. One can only speculate, in fourteen thousand years from now, how this beautiful land will have changed, but much depends on the way the people of today treat our fragile environment.

Macnabstone

Several hundred years ago the area around Loch Doon was not as deserted as it now seems. For instance, a few minutes' walk from Loch Doon an ancient farmstead is situated on the west side of the loch, 930 yards north of Beoch, in the area named 'Macnabstone' (OS: NS 475 008). It comprises what would probably have been two rectangular buildings (16.7 metres and 8.5 metres respectively in length within stone wall-footings) adjacent to an enclosure and a possible kiln. What may be another building (3.3 metres by 2.3 metres within stone wall-footings) lies in the north-west corner of the enclosure. Pont's map depicts the farmstead of 'Macknabston' and Armstrong's map records 'McNabbs', but on Thomson's map 'Beoch & McNabston' is recorded as a single farmstead.

Archaeologists speculate that this was once the home of a large family living close to the shores of the loch. They would have lived an almost entirely self-sufficient lifestyle. If you think that no one could ever have grown crops like wheat and rye, barley and oats on the wild moors above this ancient loch, then why did they have a kiln?

Hunter-gatherers

But these hardy folk were not the first to settle on the shores of Loch Doon, not by at least 8,000 years. The earliest inhabitants of Loch Doon were small groups of Mesolithic hunter-gatherers, who lived off the rich wild resources – the plants, fish and animals – of the valley around them.

All they left behind as evidence of their presence were the flint blades, scrapers and arrow points that have been found by the loch over the years. Today the land around the loch is suitable only for forestry and rough grazing, but the tourists who flock to Loch Doon would be wise to remember that it was not always so and the fragile ecology of the area has to be guarded jealously to preserve it for future generations.

Site of Special Scientific Interest

Loch Doon, surrounded by rivers, mountains, forests and moors, is recognised as an area of exceptionally high landscape value. In 1993 the Scottish Office included the loch in the designation of the wider Western Southern Uplands Environmentally Sensitive Area (ESA), in recognition of its landscape, natural history and historical features. It supports a wide range of wildlife, including several important species. Loch Doon is scientifically important for its indigenous population of Arctic char, a relative of the salmon. In 1986 the loch, the only location in southern Scotland where the Arctic char is still found, was recognised as a Site of Special Scientific Interest (SSSI). The naturally occurring char share the loch with brown trout and Atlantic salmon that spawn in the shallow gravel beds on the water's edge. The char are threatened by the increasing acidification of the water due to land use practices and Scottish Natural Heritage have put in place a management plan for the fish, which includes the monitoring of numbers and health of the species and monitoring of the condition of the water in Loch Doon.

Loch Doon is also home to a wide range of bird and plant life. The loch is the largest and best example of an oligotrophic (nutrient-poor) standing water body in south Strathclyde. It supports a number of rare plant species, including slender parsley-piert, round-leaved crowfoot and osier.

The incessant trilling and fluty song that can be heard along the length of the loch belongs to skylarks. Listen out also for the distinctive and haunting 'coor-lee' of the curlew, which abound in the hinterland of the loch on the wild moorland leading from Doon to Girvan Valley. There is something haunting and memorable about the call of the curlew. Look carefully and catch a glimpse of the common sandpiper, mainly between April and August, as they fly in groups a few feet above the surface of the loch. Circling high above the southern end of the loch, buzzards float on the thermals. A few miles further south is the stronghold of the peregrine falcon and the elusive red kites, recently re-introduced into Galloway from Wales. In fact they are absolutely thriving, to the extent that they are already regularly to be seen at Loch Doon. Whooper swans visit the loch's waters in winter and the surrounding area is also home to black grouse, stonechat, meadow pipit, and reed bunting.

Deer are plentiful, and entering the Galloway hills you may encounter wild goats, the mountain fox or perhaps even a golden eagle.

The loch is surrounded by some of the most dramatic and beautiful scenery in Scotland, with the Kells Range on its eastern flank, the Dungeon Range on its southern edge and all of these dominated by the majestic Merrick (2,764 ft) and neighbouring hills to the south-west. This area now abounds with tourists and the lochside was in the past, unfortunately, often littered with caravans all year round, which detracted from the outstanding scenic beauty of the area. In recent years the caravans have been removed from the loch, restoring to the area its natural beauty and, it is said, a consequent increase in wildlife. The narrow road to Loch Doon Castle can be busy with traffic, especially when the weather is good, but because of its historic, scenic beauty and biodiversity, it perhaps does need to be 'light-touch' regulated and protected for future generations to enjoy.

Ness Glen

At the Loch Doon dam the River Doon descends dramatically into Ness Glen, with its sheer rocky sides making it a somewhat inhospitable area, and thunders for about a mile before it settles into 'the bonny banks and braes' through the lower Craigengillan lands. The first mile of the River Doon is arguably the finest and most picturesque of its course, but sadly the overgrown glen makes access almost impossible for the casual visitor. Robert Hettrick, the blacksmith poet of Dalmellington describes it thus in his poem 'Craigs of Ness':

Where from the Doon her silver torrents pour;
With wonder and surprise we here behold
The yawning glen its dizzy steeps unfold;
And art and nature here we see combined.

Loch Doon Castle

Castles in Scotland were built and strategically placed as symbols of power and authority. However, they were also places of refuge to protect those who lived in fear through years of invasion, raids, wars and political intrigue and treachery. Scotland's history is littered with reminders of our uncivilised past, so most castles have an interesting history.

Loch Doon Castle, the ancient seat of the Lords of Carrick, was built after 1275 on an island at the southern end of the loch. David Wilson MacArthur, in his book on the River Doon (1951), states that the Galloway Picts had used Castle Island to fight off invasion by the Cambrian Celts in the fourth century. In 1823 nine ancient Pictish canoes, of hollowed oak 23 feet long, 2 feet 6 inches deep and 3 feet 9 inches broad, were discovered. Three of the canoes were recovered, and one was sent to the Hunterian Museum in Glasgow, while the other two were placed in shallow water at the foot of the loch.

The castle's shape followed that of the islet, which gave it eleven sides. It was a formidable fortress – surrounded by deep water and outwith the range of siege engines. The castle was besieged at least three times, changed hands and was destroyed and rebuilt in its turbulent history. Legend has it that Robert the Bruce took shelter from the English army within its walls during the Wars of Independence. In 1306 Sir Christopher Seaton, a follower and brother-in-law of Bruce, fled here after the defeat of Bruce at the Battle of Methven. The castle was held by the hereditary governor, Sir Gilbert de Carrick, who fearing Bruce to be a lost cause, surrendered to the English without apparently even trying to fight. Sir Christopher was taken prisoner to Dumfries and hanged as a traitor, while Sir Gilbert escaped with his life. In 1319 the castle was besieged by the English, who periodically invaded southern Scotland for some time after Bannockburn. However, it was said that the castle remained impregnable.

Around 1446 Loch Doon was again besieged and eventually surrendered to a force sent by William, 8th Earl of Douglas, whose power in the region was clashing with that of the infamous Kennedy clan. On this occasion the castle appears to have been seized by the MacLellans of Dumfries, who opposed the Douglas attempts to gain control of Carrick. By 1510 Loch Doon Castle was in Kennedy hands, when it was besieged a third time, by William Crawford of Lochmores. These were indeed dark days at Loch Doon.

During the reign of James V, who endeavoured to curb the

powers of the Barons, the castle was burned down and the immense oak roof was thrown into the loch.

Galloway Hydro-Electric Scheme

In the mid-1930s when the Galloway Hydro-Electric Scheme was being created, the loch was used as a reservoir and a tunnel was created, requiring the level of the loch to be raised, with the building of the Loch Doon dam. The castle would have been submerged and it was decided to remove it stone by stone to the western fringe of the loch, where it stands today. The remains of the castle on its island location can still be seen when the water level of the loch is low.

Creating a dam at the northern end of loch Doon resulted in the loch's water level rising by almost 10 metres, expanding its size and changing its shape. The 1.9 km Doon–Deugh Tunnel running through Culledoch Hill on the east side of the loch was built to divert water from the loch to the River Dee to power the stations that make up the hydro scheme.

The Galloway Hydro-Electric Scheme consists of six stations and eight dams, plus tunnels, aqueducts and pipelines. Drumjohn power station was built in 1986 to capture power output from the water released from the needle valve at Carsphairn Lane. In 2009 the scheme generated 260 GW-h of clean, renewable electricity to power homes and businesses. None of this could have happened without the water supplied from Loch Doon.

Caravan Land

The area was once described as an 'enormous free caravan park' with, at times, more than a hundred caravans pitched along the access road. It is acknowledged that many responsible caravanners have been visiting the loch for decades but there have been very real concerns about litter and abandoned caravans, pollution, vandalism and antisocial behaviour which were affecting the ecology of the loch, its resident population and visitors.

In 2008 the members of the Dalmellington Partnership put in place a number of large boulders and signs along the loch road to stop unauthorised roadside caravan parking which had blighted the area for so many years. Together with the appointment of a part-time warden, this has proved to be very successful.

Meanwhile, the Partnership in conjunction with stakeholders including Scottish Power plan to establish a regulated seasonal caravan site at Loch Doon near to the dam. Planning permission was approved for this in mid-2011 and groundwork had begun in August 2011, with a planned finishing date within three years.

Whether such a park, once complete, is financially sustainable in the long term is questionable, but the Doon Valley Caravan Club, who are taking the project forward, with considerable financial support from the council, the Mineral Trust and others, have chosen to go ahead with this major project, presumably having researched and planned for long-term financial sustainability.

One can only hope it proves to be a success and does not have a negative impact on the loch and its environs. One thing is agreed by everyone who genuinely cares about the area: it would be an unmitigated disaster if there was ever a return to open season caravan parking at picturesque Loch Doon.

School of Aerial Gunnery

In August 1916, in support of the war effort, the War Department authorised the spending of £150,000 to build a specialist School of Aerial Gunnery at Loch Doon, using flying boats to shoot at rail-mounted targets in an effort to replicate dogfights. Despite the warnings and concerns of local people, the planners went ahead with this ill-advised scheme. Hangars, roads and jetties were built and the level of the loch was raised 6 feet by building a dam. The School of Aerial Gunnery was the brainchild of Colonel W S Brancker, later to become Air Vice-Marshal Sir Sefton Brancker; he died in the R101 disaster, when the R101 airship crashed in France on its maiden voyage, on 5 October 1930.

As part of the scheme, a railway line was laid from the Bogton Airfield on the northern edge of Dalmellington, running through Craigengillan Estate to Dalfarson about one mile from Loch Doon. All the materials required for the construction were brought to Dalfarson by rail, and were then transferred by lorry for the short journey to the loch. Constructing the rail link right to Loch Doon would have been very expensive as the physical features of the land would have necessitated digging a large tunnel from Dalfarson southwards, hence the decision to use a combination of rail and road transport.

Meanwhile at Loch Doon the concrete piers along the eastern

side of the loch had been built to carry the monorail. Buildings erected included a sewage plant to meet the needs of the population of 1,500 and – strangely enough – a 400-seat cinema, complete with rising seats and a pay-box. This clearly indicated that it was intended that the military presence would be long-term. By May 1917 more than £350,000 had reportedly been spent at Loch Doon, but the real figure must have been substantially more.

Following an inspection visit to Loch Doon by the Duke of Connaught on 1 October 1917, the expenditure on this project began to raise serious questions from the Director of Fortifications and Works, and this was exacerbated by a request from McAlpine, the main contractor, for more funds to blast a 1,150-foot tunnel through the solid granite in order to extend the light railway from the railhead at Dalfarson to the southern end of the loch.

In January 1918 the Parliamentary Under-Secretary of State, Major J L Baird, was sent to Loch Doon to inspect the works, accompanied by Sir John Hunter, the Administrator of Works and Buildings. On receipt of their report the government halted all further work and instituted an inquiry.

And so, after much work with some 1,500 navvies and 500 German prisoners of war involved and a huge amount of money being expended, it was finally realised that Loch Doon was not a suitable location for this enterprise and their plans were indeed fatally flawed.

The subsequent Parliamentary Inquiry concluded that 'Loch Doon will be remembered as the scene of one of the most striking instances of wasted expenditure (in excess of £3m) that our records can show.' The report continued: 'Loch Doon and the country around it will soon return to the solitude and silence from which it was aroused by the introduction of thousands of men over a period of 15 months on an enterprise which was misconceived from the beginning, and which, even if once begun ought never to have been continued.'

The local airfield, covering some 88 acres, constructed at Bogton on the north-western edge of Dalmellington remained an operational airfield until the end of the war. It had two centrally heated hangars, stores and eighteen brick-built barrack blocks to accommodate 500 men. The remains of the hangars and extensive foundations can still be seen on this site.

As with most things in public life, cost is always a key factor. In his book, *Ayrshire 1745–1950*, James E Shaw reveals that more than £3 million had passed from the small bank in Dalmellington during the building period at Loch Doon. The many fine buildings constructed at Loch Doon were simply abandoned and after the war they were demolished. Much evidence remains today of these massive construction works. The track of the light railway can still be followed all the way from the Craigengillan entrance at Bogton Airfield to Dalfarson. This was indeed a folly of monumental proportions, but the visitor today can still enjoy the wonderful scenery of Loch Doon and be intrigued by its industrial past in the dark days of the Great War.

Weaving

As in many other Ayrshire towns in the 17th and 18th centuries, handloom weaving was one of the staple cottage industries and the current Doon Valley Museum was actually occupied by local weavers. However, as the 19th century progressed, this trade went into a long and gradual decline, to be replaced by the growth of the mining industry, with which the Doon Valley villages are proudly associated.

Mining

From the late 1840s the Dalmellington Iron Company and its successors operated dozens of pits and drift mines in the Doon Valley extracting coal and ironstone. Pits such as Bowhill, Polnessan, Dalharco, Houldsworth, Jelliston, Burnfoot, Drumgrange, Dunaskin, Corbie Craigs, Craigmark, Minnivey, Bogton, Sillyhole, Chalmerston, Pennyvenie, Clawfin, Benbain and Beoch had many underground workings until deep mining ceased in 1978 with the closure of Pennyvenie.

The records of the Dalmellington Iron Company and its successor, Bairds and Dalmellington, show a total of forty-three pits were in the area from 1845 until the present day. All that remains today are the extensive Chalmerston opencast mining operations overlooking and to the north-east of the village. This began production in 1987 with the first coal extracted in June of that year. Incredibly, since then some 8 million tons of coal have been extracted by this method and regularly two trains per day, pulling up to forty wagons, remove this mountain of coal from Chalmerston. In June 2001 a total of ninety-two men were employed on this site and some 16,000 tons of coal are extracted every week.

The car park at Minnivey Colliery in the 1960s. Minnivey was sunk in 1955 and its short life ended with closure in 1975.
(Photo: Courtesy of EAC Doon Valley Museum)

The Dalmellington Iron Company

Dalmellington's ironworks came into being in 1845, and totally changed the character of this section of the upper Doon Valley. The ironworks quickly flourished and increased. Sometimes as many as seven furnaces were in blast at one time, the blast engine requiring to be doubled in 1866. A hardworking and poorly paid workforce varied from 900 to almost 2,000.

Besides miners, the Dalmellington Iron Company employed all sorts of craftsmen who cast hundreds of tons of metal in a day, and sent the name Dalmellington stamped upon its bars to all parts of the world where pig iron was used. The blast engine house still stands today and bears the date 1847. David L Smith, in *The Dalmellington Iron Company: Its Engines and Men*, records that when the great beam for the blast engine house was brought by road from Ayr, twenty-four pairs of horses were provided to haul it up the Asylum Brae.

Waterside and the ironworks

Three miles north of Dalmellington, Waterside sits on the edge of Green Hill and was once a thriving industrial village. There was a dramatic growth in the workforce of the Dalmellington Iron Company and by the end of the 1850s Waterside had grown exponentially, with 237 houses and a local economy which was booming.

As the visitor approaches, the view is dominated by two massive chimneys, at 143 and 160 feet. These 'lums', as they are known locally, dominate the surroundings. They dwarf the massive ironstone bing and bear testimony to the extensive mining and iron producing activities of the Dalmellington Iron Company.

The *Ayr Advertiser* of 15 May 1847 issued a word of caution: 'The proprietors of Dalmellington Ironworks intend erecting houses for their workers adjacent to their mines. We hope that the causes of disease, especially smallpox and measles, reported in the newspapers, will cause the proprietors to see that the site chosen is properly drained and the houses, when built, of sufficient size and well ventilated.'

In a report of 17 June 1847 it was highlighted that smallpox and measles were prevalent in Dalmellington and district, although few deaths had occurred. However, it did go on to explain that 'general complaints are on the increase and are considered by many to arise from the poor diet used by the poor, who are unable to purchase suitable food at such high prices that prevail.'

Dunaskin

The ironworks village had a singular confusion of names. It was called Waterside after the name of the nearby farm and this was the name adopted by the Glasgow and South Western Railway for their station. However, the postal authorities called it Dunaskin, after the address of the Dalmellington Iron Works, although Dalmellington was actually three miles further up the valley. Hence even today Waterside and Dunaskin are interchangeable terms for the village. The fascinating history of Waterside is recorded in considerable detail by David L Smith in his book about the Dalmellington Iron Company mentioned above. This excellent and rare book is a factual and entertaining account of the industrial development of the area and is recommended to the reader.

Today only two rows of houses remain at Waterside, one at

either end of the village. However, anyone passing this way might enjoy learning about the industrial heritage of the area at the open-air museum which aims to preserve the industrial and social history of Waterside.

Nearby, high above Dunaskin Burn, is the site of Laight Castle. David Wilson MacArthur, in his book on the River Doon, tells us that according to tradition it was here that Alpin, King of Scots, after landing at Ayr, met the men of Strathclyde, in a fierce and bloody battle which ended with the death of the Scots king. Whilst this may be somewhat fanciful, it certainly has been part of local tradition.

Dalmellington Band

Dalmellington Band in February 1952 on the evening of the annual Slow Melody Competition in Dalmellington Church Hall.
Back row (l to r): John Tyson, William Hainey, William Hill, David Torbet, William Parker, William Currie.
2nd back row: John Smith, David Smith, Edward Kerr, Duncan Wells, Archie Hutchison, Peter Scobie, Jimmy Dick, Robert Boyd, Robert Hill, Andrew Parker (father of William Parker in back row) and Tom 'TP' Park.
2nd front row: Jimmy Ireland, Jimmy Graham, James McPhail, Tom Wilson, Gordon Hunter, William Oughton (bandmaster), John Paulin, John McLeod, Tom Paul (brother of John Paulin) and William Greig.
Front row: William Kennedy, James Hose, Robert Peters, Bert McRoberts.

Dalmellington is proud to be able to boast one of the finest brass bands in the United Kingdom. Formed in 1864 and having won the Scottish Championships on three occasions, 1969, 1976 and 1978, they now boast a first-class youth band which will feed into the senior band, providing continuity of players for the future. Hugh Johnstone MBE and Ian Taylor, with support from other band members, have played a key role in mentoring the youth band, in the process delivering regular competition success at Scottish and UK level.

After tremendous efforts by the band committee, under the outstanding leadership of its President, Bert Ritchie, a new band hall was opened on Ayr Road within the grounds of Dalmellington Community Centre on 2 November 2005.

New Cumnock-based poet Rab Wilson, who mainly writes in Scots, penned a poem after visiting the band hall and enjoying the many photo exhibits of banding down through the years. It is appropriately titled 'Dalmellington Baun'.

Dalmellington Baun

This room, lik a works canteen; stark, functional,
brichtly lit, austere, fit fir ae purpose –
tae fix these players minds anely oan music.
Nae clock hings oan the wa, there's nae distraction,
juist the muckle banners; 'Scottish Champions',
clear mindin o their pridefou pedigree.
The piece they're warkin oan's bi Gilbert Vinter,
bound fir the 'Nationals', comin up in Mairch,
(a wit declares 'a swatch o Arban's Tutor'!).
'Salute to Youth' is technically demandin,
fierce chromatic rins o semi-quavers,
pushin principle players tae their leemits;
concentration etcht upon their faces.
While Airchie, their baun-maister, teases oot
abeelities they thocht they nevir hud;
'A braw wee trio – when ye hear the pairts!'
'Gin thon judge hus goat lugs – best bet, he's listenin!'
an repetition o some fykie pairt
draws frae thaim honed an purposefou perfection.

Ae meenit, saftly, pianissimo,
Syne, stabbin fiercely his conductor's wand,
A snarlin Sforzando, thunderous in its micht!
Oan Airchie's score, 'Eroico' unnerlined,
'Heroically'! juist listen, an ye'll hear,
that smeddum wrocht frae ither generations.
Likesay, the bluid o heroes' in their veins;
whaes faither's faithers wrocht at Pennyvenie,
in Minnivey, at Burnton, an the Beoch,
the huddlet group in thon auld photiegraph,
wi miners cap-laumps, playin Christmas carols,
a history that's leevin, breathin yet.
The Silver Baun, a muckle great machine,
whaes pairts must wark in harmony thegaither,
lik some vast Winding Engine, cast frae bress,
raisin tae the licht its praicious cargo.

Dalmellington Band in 1922 with the Reverend George S Hendrie in the back row, extreme right. The conductor was Robert Thomson, conductor from 1911, who died suddenly September 1927 and the band played at his funeral. The first, handwritten, constitution of the band states as its aim in the latter part of the document: 'To nurture the tuition of brass instruments to youths. To assist charitable causes where and when possible. To provide a cultural activity which can only be good for the community.' The band have achieved this in abundance! (Photo: Courtesy of Hugh Johnstone MBE, Dalmellington Band collection)

Hugh Johnstone MBE

For many folk with Doon Valley origins, the Dalmellington Band is synonymous with the village and many of the leading players have travelled throughout the UK and abroad to play in bands. Importantly, they have always remembered with pride their roots in the Doon Valley. Literally hundreds of players over the years will have fond memories of Hugh Johnstone MBE, the best-known former player, conductor and stalwart worker and trainer of young players. His contribution to Dalmellington Band and the brass band movement in Scotland is legendary.

Other Dalmellington institutions

The Dalmellington Curling Club is believed to be the oldest surviving organisation in the village, having been established in 1841. Several villagers are office-bearers in the club, which remains active and healthy.

Lodge St Thomas (Kilwinning) Dalmellington No. 433 was formed following a meeting on 1 April 1864 in David McBlane's pub (at the end of the close between Dalmellington Inn and Dale's Butcher shop). The lodge now has its own premises in Low Main Street.

Matthew Anderson, policeman-poet

Matthew Anderson, born in Waterside, was known as the policeman-poet of the Ayrshire Constabulary where he served for thirty-six years, working at places such as Dalmellington, Symington, Ardeer, Barrmill and Kilmarnock. He was born at Waterside, Ayrshire, on 7 June 1864 at No. 60 Truffhill Row. Life must have been quite difficult as he had thirteen of a family. After retiring he served as beadle of Martyrs' UF Church, Kilmarnock from 1 January 1925 till 31 January 1927. He wrote some wonderful poetry, which by its sheer simplicity and sincerity was enjoyed by ordinary folk in Ayrshire and indeed much further afield. In retirement he lived at 5 Fairyhill Road, Kilmarnock, where he died on 14 November 1948.

Like Dalmellington with Robert Hettrick, Waterside also boasts a poet of note. Matthew Anderson, the policeman-poet of the Ayrshire Constabulary, was born in Waterside on 7 June 1864 at 60 Truffhill Row. Like his world-renowned counterpart, Anderson began his working life as a farm hand. He abandoned this work at an early age, however, and put his energies to good use in the Royal Marines where he spent three years as a gunner. He later joined the ranks of the Ayrshire Constabulary, where he served in such far-flung places as Dalmellington, Symington, Barrmill, Kilwinning, Coylton, Drongan and Irvine.

Matthew Anderson, like many of his peers, was well educated and held strong views which did not always make him popular with higher ranking officers in the constabulary. Anderson had a great knowledge and understanding of people and a strong interest in nature which is reflected in his poems. His output was prolific and includes *Poems and Songs* (1891) and *Poems of a Policeman* (1898) which were very popular in the county of Ayr. In retirement he lived in Kilmarnock and died there on 14 November 1948 aged eighty-four. He often wrote poems about the villages where he worked. Of Waterside, his birthplace, he wrote:

This happened a' at Waterside,
As braw a place as ony, O,
Where dark, and deep, and smooth, and wide
The river Doon rins bonnie, O;
Where nicht is no like nicht ava,
For aye sae cheerie; aye sae braw,
The furnaces they bleeze awa'
An' licht up every crannie, O
Oh, 'tis a lovely countryside
When flowers are a' in blossom, O;
An' kindness there is beautified
In mony a manly bosom, O;
'Twas there I grew to be a boy,
An' felt my first, my purest joy
At Muckleholm when herdin' kye
'Mang broomy knows sae bonnie, O.

Lethanhill

On the hill to the east of Patna, 900 feet above sea level, there was also a minor miracle at work. The new mining communities of Lethanhill and Burnfoothill – known simply as the Hill – were born in this harsh environment in the mid-1800s at the behest of the Dalmellington Iron Company (sometimes shortened to DICo), who wanted their workers to live close to the ironstone and coal pits where they would work.

Lethanhill remains now hidden in trees creating a ghostly atmosphere. (Photo: Lee Milne of London)

The mining folk on this plateau developed a strong sense of community, exemplified by a willingness to help each other, despite the grimness of life and occupation and the hostility of the environment. This shared sense of community and togetherness was greatly valued and indeed is today often found lacking.

The Hill

By the end of the 1860s, 190 houses had been erected a mile above and east of Patna. There was some confusion about the name of the village. The larger part was known officially as

Lethanhill on the Ordnance Survey maps and all the amenities were located there. However, the row to the north and slightly apart from the others and ultimately comprising over ninety houses, was called Burnfoothill, and the whole village was more commonly called by this name. After a time, however, the folk of the district shortened the title to the simpler one of 'the Hill'.

At its peak, the Hill consisted of ten rows of cottages in the Lethanhill part and three rows forming a long front at Burnfoothill looking down on Patna. The village was built by the Dalmellington Iron Company to house the miners who would work the numerous ironstone pits all over the Knockkippen Plateau between 1849 and 1919. These ironstone pits generally went under the names of the farms whose land they were on, or that of a nearby landmark. The prominent ironstone mines, normally not very deep, included Bowhill, Kerse, Polnessan, Downieston, Burnfoot, Drumgrange and Corbie Craigs.

The immediate area around the Hill was saturated with ironstone pits and in seven cases, namely Burnfoot pits Nos. 1, 2, 3, 6 and 8 and Drumgrange Nos. 2 and 4, the pits were actually sunk in the middle of the village between 1847 and 1860. Later additions to the village were built over these expired workings.

Access to the Hill seems to have been a secondary consideration for the Dalmellington Iron Company, for it was only in 1923, and only after a long campaign of lobbying and tireless letter-writing, that the village got its proper metalled road, replacing what had been little more than a heavily potholed dirt track, which was well-nigh impossible at certain times for motor vehicles or horse-drawn carts to climb or descend safely.

By 1954 Burnfoothill was totally deserted, all the families having moved out, mainly to Patna. However, the village school remained intact and children were bussed up from Patna until 1959, when the school too was demolished.

All that remains of the Hill is the plantation which hides the foundations of many of the cottages, the drumhead at the top of the Drumgrange incline, the war memorial and a concrete memorial to the Hill village.

The Drumgrange incline
The remains of the immense double-track Drumgrange incline can still be seen just north of Waterside, east of the A713. This Dalmellington Iron Company line took the railway from Waterside up to the high-level iron ore lines running between Benwhat and the Hill and out to Houldsworth Pit, Benbranigan Pit and the extensive Corbie Craigs pit networks high above the valley of the River Doon.

This incline had a double track, with pulleys set between each pair of rails for the support of the wire rope. At the top, supported by two large brick-built buttresses, was an iron drum, some 5 feet in diameter. This was fitted with a handbrake, operating large wooden blocks set round the perimeter of the drum. The buttresses are still extant and known as the drumhead. This also included a brick-built shelter for the brakeman. The shelter was important because of the wild weather often experienced on the face of this west-aspect incline and the incline could be operating day and night. Rail wagon traffic moving up and down the incline was removed from the incline and shunted into sidings.

The standard wagons using the incline were of 8, 10, 12 and finally 15 ton capacity. Local historian David L Smith (*The Dalmellington Iron Company: Its Engines and Men*) records that on many occasions, despite the braking system, there were wild runaways even in the days of the small wagons. Although he says there was no record of the wire ropes breaking, couplings on the wagons broke from time to time. The runaway was a dramatic event, the wagon contents scattered widely and on one occasion the wagon actually took to the air on its thrilling descent from top to bottom. Fortunately, there are no records of anyone being hurt.

The Corbie Craigs incline operated on a similar basis to its close neighbour at Drumgrange. It ran from the south end of Waterside from the extensive railway sidings there, across a dramatic and impressive wooden viaduct (no longer in existence) which carried it across Dunaskin Glen and upwards along the southern edge of Dunaskin Burn until joining the Hill rail network on the plateau at Corbie Craigs.

The war memorial
The Lethanhill war memorial is a fine obelisk of grey polished granite, approximately 15 feet tall. The monument now stands high on the deserted hillside where the village once stood. The dedication reads:

> ERECTED
> BY PUBLIC SUBSCRIPTION
> AND
> DEDICATED BY THE INHABITANTS
> OF LETHANHILL AND BURNFOOTHILL
> TO THE REVERED MEMORY
> OF THEIR GLORIOUS DEAD WHO
> IN MAKING THE SUPREME SACRIFICE
> DURING THE GREAT WAR
> 1914–1918
> NOBLY SUSTAINED FREEDOM'S CAUSE
>
> WWI ROLL OF HONOUR:
> BLAIN JOHN PRIVATE
> FERGUSON WILLIAM PRIVATE
> FINLAY ROBERT PRIVATE
> HYNDS HUGH PRIVATE
> LAFFERTY IVY
> LAFFERTY THOMAS PRIVATE
> McCLELLAND DAVID PRIVATE
> McCLYMONT ROBERT PRIVATE
> McCORMICK JOHN PRIVATE
> MILLER ROBERT PRIVATE
> MUIR ROBERT PRIVATE
> NUGENT CHARLES SERGEANT
> NUGENT DENIS PRIVATE
> PYPER SAMUEL PRIVATE
> TALMAN JAMES McG. SERGEANT
> TALMAN WILLIAM PRIVATE
>
> WWII ROLL OF HONOUR:
> FINLAY WILLIAM J. CORPORAL
> GILMORE JAMES PRIVATE
> STEVENSON ALEXANDER TROOPER

The concrete foundations of the vanished buildings can be seen in the grass around the monument and at the time of writing (2012) the opencast workings were moving mountains of earth, extracting rich seams of coal that the miners of yesteryear could only dream of.

Benwhat

A mile to the east yet another mining village was constructed by the Dalmellington Iron Company and quickly grew from forty houses to eighty-four. It was called Benwhat. Built on the 1,000-foot contour line, it was ranked as one of the highest and most remote villages in Scotland. Strangely, although both Lethanhill and Benwhat had roads leading down to the valley, there was no road connecting these hill villages. However, they were connected by railway, which also acted as a path for locals travelling between them.

The dominant feature of Benwhat remains the war memorial located on the side of Benwhat Hill. Erected in 1921, it is a grey granite obelisk approximately 15 feet high and standing on three rustic sandstone steps. The monument is surrounded by a wrought iron fence and was fully refurbished in 2011. The dedication reads:

Readers wishing to explore more about these villages are referred to local books by T Courtney McQuillan and Robert Farrell listed in the Bibliography.

> BENWHAT 1921
> ERECTED BY THE PEOPLE
> OF THIS VILLAGE WITH
> PRIDE AND AFFECTION
> TO THE MEMORY OF
> GALLANT SONS WHO LAID
> DOWN THEIR LIVES FOR
> THEIR KING AND COUNTRY
> IN THE GREAT WAR 1914–1919
> 'GREATER LOVE
> HATH NO MAN THAN THIS'
>
> WWI ROLL OF HONOUR:
> BRYAN W. ROYAL SCOTS FUSILIERS PRIVATE
> HILL W. ROYAL SCOTS FUSILIERS PRIVATE
> HODGSON D. ROYAL SCOTS FUSILIERS PRIVATE
> MILLAR E. ROYAL SCOTS FUSILIERS PRIVATE
> MORRISON R. ROYAL SCOTS FUSILIERS PRIVATE
> NEVILLE G. ARGYLL & SUTHERLAND HIGHLANDERS PRIVATE
> NEVILLE W. ROYAL SCOTS PRIVATE
> PARKER G. ROYAL SCOTS FUSILIERS SERGEANT
> PARKER T. ROYAL SCOTS FUSILIERS PRIVATE
> SCALLY B. SEAFORTH HIGHLANDERS PRIVATE
> WILSON A. ROYAL SCOTS FUSILIERS PRIVATE
> WILSON W. ROYAL SCOTS FUSILIERS PRIVATE
>
> WWII ROLL OF HONOUR:
> BUNYAN T. GORDON HIGHLANDERS PRIVATE
> McMAHON R. GORDON HIGHLANDERS PRIVATE
> ROBERTSON J. BLACK WATCH PRIVATE

Pennyvenie

In 1912 the last of the Dalmellington Iron Company villages was built in the Doon Valley, called Pennyvenie. This village, no longer extant, was located some 11/2 miles north-east of Dalmellington on the B741 road to New Cumnock. The village was built to house miners, at the same time as the Dalmellington Iron Company was developing what was called locally the Big Mine or, more formally, Pennyvenie No. 4.

An earlier colliery had been opened by the Company in 1872 and finally closed in 1978. At its peak there were 725 men working here and it comprised seven separate pit shafts, the last sunk in 1945.

There were around seventy single and double apartment houses in Pennyvenie, stretched out in small rows ranging from four to ten houses per row along the New Cumnock Road (B741). Although the village had a small primary school, it had no store, church, institute or any form of shopping facility. Villagers had to walk the almost two miles on foot into Dalmellington for their provisions and entertainment. They did, however, have regular vans from Dalmellington Co-op, which provided a range of foods.

The closure of Pennyvenie No. 4 in 1961 considerably reduced the nearby employment prospects for men from the village, and many of the mining families left to live in nearby Dalmellington, eventually leaving only a few houses which had not been evacuated or demolished. The last remaining row of houses was known as Sighthill and for many years it sat forlornly on the west side of the B741. It was abandoned in 2011 and demolished in early 2012.

The railhead for the Big Mine ran behind what was known as High Pennyvenie and it, too, was swallowed up by massive opencast mining that took place between Beoch and Pennyvenie for many years.

Today the playground for the old school, which closed in the 1960s, having in later years been used as a school for children with learning difficulties, is just about all that remains of Pennyvenie, except for the massive coal spoil bing that dominates and stands sentinel over Dalmellington, the one highly visible remnant of coal mining in the upper Doon Valley.

The Pennyvenie site was subsequently reworked for

extraction of opencast coal, opening in 1987 and operated by Scottish Resources Group, the largest surface mining group in the UK. Scottish Coal is responsible for developing and managing the Group's surface mining interests, providing over 4 million tonnes of coal to the UK's major power generators in the 2011 financial year.

Left: An aerial view of Pennyvenie Colliery, showing the road skirting round the waste bing with the small wagonway running to the top to allow spoil to be tipped. Pennyvenie Nos. 2, 3 and 7 were operated by the Dalmellington Iron Company and from 1931 by Bairds and Dalmellington until nationalisation in 1948. It had an average workforce of 581 and the output was 124,000 tons per year. Pennyvenie No. 4 was sunk in 1911 was closed in 1961 whilst Pennyvenie No. 5 was also sunk in 1911 and was closed in 1953.
(Photo: Courtesy of EAC Doon Valley Museum)

Left: Pennyvenie Colliery and a rake of dirt hopper empties await being filled with spoil and taken to the dump at Laight near Waterside.
(Photo: Courtesy of EAC Doon Valley Museum)

Above: Pennyvenie Colliery towards the end of its life, closing in 1978. The small hutch line that ran up the bing has been lifted. The Kirk o' the Covenant can be seen (centre) as well as the 'Square woods' (top left) on Craigengillan Estate. The area is now covered in trees, nature having claimed back its own.
(Photo: Courtesy of EAC Doon Valley Museum)

Death in opencast mining

The opencast site at Pennyvenie employs around 130 workers, produces 750,000 tonnes of coal a year and is a 24-hour operation. Tragically, the price of winning coal is still high: on

26 February 2007 at 1 p.m. Brian French, a 48-year-old foreman fitter, and Colin Ferguson, a 37-year-old tyre fitter, were fatally injured with when a Terex TR100 dump truck collided with their Landrover on a working site at Pennyvenie. Both vehicles were the same colour and the driver of the huge Terex was making a manoeuvre and simply failed to see the Landrover, leading to this tragic industrial accident.

Pennyvenie Mine around the time of closure in 1978 with the colliery headgear and winding tower still in place. This was the last deep mine in Ayrshire's Doon Valley. Coal mining has existed in Scotland since the 12th century. The development of the steam engine by James Watt in the 18th century began to increase demand for coal. Railway development in the 19th century increased demand for coal further and mines therefore had to be dug deeper. Here you can see the small hutches used for loading coal and spoil underground.
(Photo: Courtesy of EAC Doon Valley Museum)

Tourism

Patna, Waterside and Dalmellington, on the upper reaches of the River Doon, so proud of their rich social and industrial past, now lack any local employment of significance. Most people travel to Ayr or further afield to find work. Attracting tourists has been helped with the creation of the Scottish Industrial Railway Centre, where some excellent industrial locomotives have been preserved.

They were originally at Minnivey and now they are headquartered at Waterside, where steam train specials are regularly run on Sundays during the summer months. One can only think that the Reverend G S Hendrie would have been rather proud of the volunteers who have worked tirelessly to preserve steam in the Doon Valley, drawing tourists from far and wide, meeting Hendrie's dream of visitors flocking to his beloved valley.

Unfortunately, the museum at Waterside, which had the aim of developing Europe's best example of a Victorian ironworks, closed in 2005 due to lack of funding. However, Doon Valley Museum at Cathcartston, Dalmellington, is a real gem and preserves a great deal of local heritage in its archives.

Employment

Developing tourism to enjoy the natural surroundings such as Loch Doon and Ness Glen must be high on the local agenda. However, attracting a large employer of local labour is undoubtedly the greatest need to help regenerate an area of historical significance and outstanding natural beauty. This is indeed a recurring theme and was well illustrated by the Dalmellington blacksmith-poet, Robert Hettrick, in 1823 when he penned fine words about his vision of prosperity for Dalmellington in his poem 'The Petition of the River Doon'. He saw Dalmellington as a busy manufacturing base where full employment would ensure prosperity for the town and its people.

Let party strife be set aside,
The public good your councils guide;
Let commerce round my windings ride,
Triumphant there,
Then will I be the flower and pride
Of a' this shire.

Dr E S Lee – Sweat of Miners

Perhaps the lure of the upper valley of the River Doon and its people is best summed up by the late Dr E S Lee, a General Practitioner in Dalmellington for over forty years. Born in Singapore in 1906, he studied medicine at Edinburgh and came to the village in 1933 following a short spell in Alloa.

At his retiral presentation in 1973 he said: 'If I could live my life again I would come to Dalmellington. This is predominantly a mining area and most of my patients over the years have been miners. I do not know of anyone who works harder than the mineworker. Although the price of coal is high to the consumer, the reward for producing coal will never be sufficient. I realised long ago that coal could not be won by machines alone, but only by the sweat of miners. And I remember with sadness the early deaths and chronic ill-health of some of your colleagues due to their work in the pits. Some of my most poignant memories are of having to knock on doors to inform local folk of the deaths of husbands and sons in mining accidents.'

Education and heritage

The author is someone who is proud of the education provided at Dalmellington High School, demolished, rebuilt and renamed Doon Academy. The words of a much-loved former English teacher, Arthur W Wilson, are therefore a fitting conclusion to this brief overview of aspects of life in the upper reaches of the River Doon. In three short verses he manages to capture the very essence of the history and heritage of the area in a way that is sure to strike a chord with former pupils. Regularly sung with vigour and pride at Dalmellington High School's weekly assembly.

The High School of Dalmellington
It stands beneath the hills,
Where rushing rivers mingle,
And the wind blows as it wills.
These hills hid ancient dwellings,
Crannogs were in the mere,
Then marching feet of Romans
'Neath the eagle wings of fear.

Our steadfast Covenanters
Put God before the King,
Upholding their religion
Whatever fate might bring.
Skilled were our village weavers,
Thoughtful and studious men,
Now stout courageous miners
Dare death beneath the Ben.

These were the folk before us,
Be proud of them, be proud,
These Scottish folk who bred us
We sing their praises loud.
With all of our endeavours
The future will abide,
May the sons of our sons remember
Dalmellington with pride.

Arthur W Wilson
January 1963
(Set to music by Stuart M Robertson)

Opposite: A class at Lethanhill School 1947/48. Where are they all now and how did life turn out for them?
Back row (l to r): Andrew Meldrum, Andrew Beggs, Jean Meldrum, Margaret McFarlane, Lilly Gilmour, John McEwan and John Kennedy.
Middle row: Billy Johnstone, Margaret Johnstone, Ella Knox, Marjory Fawcett, Elizabeth Dalziel, Helen Torbet and Bert Daly.
Front row: John McDermont, Francie Bryce, Billy Brown, Harry Ferguson and Hugh Gilmour.
(Photo: Courtesy of EAC Doon Valley Museum)

Dalmellington Primary School class of 1952.
Back row (l to r): Billy 'Buff' Johnstone, Jimmy Rowan, Eddie Farrell, John McBurnie, James Hose, Billy Currach, Robert Currach, Jock Reid, Norman Hughes, Neil Summerville (now in Lanarkshire) and Tom Clydesdale.
2nd back row: Netta Whalen, Joanne Black, Elizabeth Murray, Margaret Brown, Kit Rowan, Margaret Branagan, Jean Murphy, Mary Dempsey, Alice Johnstone, Margaret Coughtrie, Esther Keary and Dorothy Currie.
2nd front row: Euphemia Galloway, Esther Barclay, Eileen Stead, Janet Johnstone, Nan Coupland, Ann Wilson, Frances McCartney, Margaret Watt, Christine Calderwood, Cathy McCart, Marion McCreath and David Barclay.
Front row: Gilbert McBride, Quintin Stirrat, Jock Rowan, Billy O'Neil, Billy Lamb, John Bennet, Jim McLatchie, Archie Scobie, Jim Fitzsimmons, Jimmy 'Chimes' Rowan, Billy Murphy, Billy Saunders and Alex Aitken.

Bellsbank Primary School football team in 1963. Bellsbank had a very good team over a number of years when they regularly won the Doon Valley cup which was competed for against Dalmellington, Xaviers at Waterside, Patna and Dalrymple.
Back row (l to r): John P Kennedy, headmaster who was a benevolent dictator and the first headmaster of the school when it opened in 1957; Donald Reid (author), John Robertson, David Dempsey, Hugh Hose, Tom Gilbert and Robert Beattie (teacher).
Front row: Andy Givens, Donald Tyson, Joseph Stevenson, Andy Ferguson, Billy Currough, Robert Goudie and Tommy Martin
(Photo: Courtesy of Donald L Reid)

Chapter 2

Patna

O, sweet grows the lime and the orange,
And the apple on the pine;
But a' the charms o the Indies
Can never equal thine.
Will Ye Go To The Indies My Mary

Robert Burns

Patna stands on both banks of the River Doon, some 10 miles south-east of Ayr and 5 miles from Dalmellington on the A713. All the Doon Valley villages have a lot in common through their shared history of coal and ironstone.

Piggot's Directory of 1837 has a little information on Patna:

Patna is a small village, in the parish of Straiton, situated on the banks of the Doon, which abounds with trout. Lime and coal are obtained plentifully in this neighbourhood, and give employment to the villagers. Andrew Kerr is a publican; John Dick a tailor; Thomas Dick a shoemaker, John McConachie a mason, James McCoull the schoolmaster, Alexander and James Ramsey joiners and Cartwright in the village.

Patna has a population of around 3,500 (2004 figure) and is connected to the A713 Ayr–Dalmellington road by two bridges over the River Doon, the Old Bridge of 1805 and New Brig, built in 1960. From 1856 Patna had a thriving railway station on the Glasgow & South Western branch railway between Ayr and Dalmellington. The passenger service ended on 6 April 1964, although the line is still very busy, operating coal traffic from Minnivey Loading Point.

William Fullarton

Some historians have suggested that the name Patna is derived from the Gaelic, *Pait 'n Ath*, 'the water of the eminence', for the old village was built upon a steep hillside west of the River Doon with a boat connecting the village to the east. However, it is more likely and now generally accepted that the village received its name from its founder, William Fullarton of Skeldon (near Dalrymple), whose family had connections with the city of Patna which stands on the banks of the River Ganges. John Moore in his interesting publication, *Gently Flows the Doon* (1972), outlines the background to the naming of Patna.

Patna, the second surviving Doon Valley village, whose name conjures up visions of rice paddy fields, in fact owes its title to the great Indian city on the Ganges. It was founded in the early years of the 19th century by William Fullarton, whose family had a close connection with the Bihar State. Fullarton's uncle, William Fullarton, in 1745 was in the service of the East India Company as surgeon at Fort William, now Calcutta. After a mixed career as a soldier and surgeon, he returned eventually to Scotland in 1770 where he bought the estate of Goldring (later Rosemount), near Kilmarnock. He died in 1805 with no family. This William Fullarton had a brother, Major General John Fullarton, of Skeldon (near Dalrymple). General Fullarton was also in the service of the East India Company and died in India in 1804. He was succeeded by his second son, William, then aged 24.

Fullarton proved himself to be a kindly benefactor to Patna. He built the first house actually in the village to house the manager of his coal mines. This, with offices attached, was to become known to later generations as Patna House. He then had the sixteen houses of the former High Row built, each with a small byre attached to house two cows and he allowed them free grazing on Keir Hill. This helped the workers augment their wages as they were often laid off from mining in the summer. These were quickly followed by a further sixteen houses, known as the Low Row. Both rows were demolished in the 1920s. The houses were thatched and each householder had a small garden where it is said they often grew corn which was thrashed and ground locally.

Water for the village

One particularly useful service provided by Fullarton to the village was the provision of a pipeline, which was built from Craignessie Well at the foot of Patna Hill and brought water into the village. This was the only water supply in the village until 1871 when the decorative fountain at the top of Main Street was gifted to the village by J Archibald Walker of Camlarg, Dalmellington. Despite some very severe droughts over the years, this source of water was always available and dependable.

Patna Auld Brig

Fullarton was also responsible for erecting the schoolhouse. This building, originally thatched with heather, later became the Workmen's Institute. Fullarton is said to have been largely responsible for the construction of Patna Auld Bridge in 1805. The architect was Mr Gilbert McAdam, a relative of the inventive engineer who gave his name to the world-famous improved surfacing for roads.

The strength and longevity of this narrow structure, still in use today, is a lasting memorial to the craftsmen of those early days. Never designed to carry the high numbers of heavy vehicles of the twenty-first century, the fact that it has stood the test of time is testament to the margins of safety built into these early bridges. Indeed, this bridge was to serve Patna well for the next 155 years until the new bridge was built at the southern end of the village and officially opened on 25 March 1960. The auld brig is still the main entrance over the Doon at the northern end of the village.

Employment

William Fullarton was a remarkable man. He might best be described as a benevolent autocrat, but he did leave Patna with some welcome benefits. Fullarton Place in Patna commemorates this kindly benefactor who did so much for the village, including building a school, creating employment in his coal pits and limestone works, providing housing for workers, ensuring that the village had a clean water supply and, as just mentioned, being a catalyst for the building of what today is known as Patna Auld Brig. By any standard this was a highly commendable contribution to the social and industrial development of Patna and a lasting legacy for a local industrialist with a kindly heart.

The Co-operative was very strong in the Doon Valley. Patna Co-op celebrated its centenary in 1969. Billy Mitchell (1905–83) worked there for fifty years, rising to become manager.
(Photo: Courtesy of Mrs Giles Hutchison)

Lime kilns

In the late eighteenth century Patna was very sparsely populated, the chief occupation then being wool and cotton weaving by artisans working from home. The land was more suitable for grazing than cultivation, hence the precedence of the home-based weaving industry which was common throughout Ayrshire.

In addition to farming and weaving, Patna had a very profitable lime-producing industry, with kilns giving a good supply for both the building trade and agriculture. The Patna workers were housed in two rows, each of five houses, known as High and Low Carnshalloch. A small mill, rejoicing in the peculiar name of Drumna-Driddle, stood on the banks of the Doon opposite Jelliston and continued to function until 1820. The mill pond was later to give many years of service as a curling pond, but disappeared completely during building operations many years later.

Downieston Thread Mill

Downieston Thread Mill, situated south of the Old Bridge, was owned by Messrs Marshall and Reid and had its power supplied by a dam on the upstream side of the bridge. The water was conducted through the smaller of the bridge's two arches. The mill itself ceased production in 1850. On the lower side of the bridge a second dam provided the power for a corn mill. This closed down in 1852, but the buildings, known as Currie's Mill, remained. There was also a mill on the river at Polnessan, but it was of much earlier origin and little is known of it.

Like its near neighbours, Dunaskin and Dalmellington, Patna relied heavily on coal mining and remained a very small village until the inhabitants of Lethanhill and Waterside were rehoused there in the mid-1950s. The consequent building of local authority housing gave the village a boost which included a new school and improved local shopping facilities.

The Kirk in Patna

Around 1817 the Reverend J Paul of Straiton was conducting occasional evening services in Patna and by 1834 the villagers of Patna were delighted when Paul's successor, the Reverend R Paton, arranged for an evening service to be conducted in the village every third Sunday evening, providing continuity of opportunity for worship. A Parish Church with a hall was established in 1837; attendance was good and it is recorded that there were high levels of giving by parishioners.

However, it was not until 1849 that the congregation managed to secure a permanent minister for the village, the Reverend McFadzean. Over the years there have been many ministers serving the village, but suffice to say that following a linkage of Patna with Waterside and Lethanhill in 1971, a further linkage with Dalmellington was formalised in 2004 under the leadership of the Reverend Kenneth Yorke, then Minister of Dalmellington.

The school

In 1865 Patna is reported to have had one of the worst school buildings in Scotland. Patna Parochial School had one teacher and 134 pupils on the roll, although presumably they would not all have been present at one time, for the school only had one room. It was reported that the walls were damp and mouldy and the floor was of brick, so these were very poor conditions by any standard and definitely not conducive to learning.

The building later served as the village recreational institute and in the 1970s as an Orange Order Hall. A new school was built in Patna in 1960, initially as a secondary school, but shortly thereafter became and remains a primary school. In 2011–12 it was replaced by a brand-new building on the adjacent greenfield site, giving a further boost to educational opportunities for the primary-age children of the village.

Opposite top: Littlemill Primary School class of 1950–51.
Back row (l to r): Billy Gibson, Hugh Green, Robert Johnston, Harry Vass, Jim Ronald and Hugh McNeilly.
Second back row: Sandy Warnock, Joe Williamson, Rita Leslie, Jean Lindsay, Francis Courtney and William Leslie.
Second front row: Eunice Pollock, Ann Ferguson, Marjorie Whiteside, Mary Brown, Jean Thomson, Jean Carol, Jean Laidlaw and Jim Lorimer.
Front row: William Poole, George Lennon, Tom Brown, Ian Spiers, John Brown and Sam McFadzean.
(Courtesy of John Grant collection)

Opposite middle: 1927 photo of Lethanhill School as pupils transfer from the old school to the new village school, sitting high on the plateau above Patna and the River Doon. Many folk in the Doon Valley will be descended from this group.
Back row: (l to r) William Bryce, Adam Gillespie, Willie Bell, David Beggs, Robert McConnachie, John Ravie, Willie Ferguson, Jim Baillie, Bobby McDerment and Mr Rankine (teacher).
Second back row: Billy Tait, Kenny Surgeon, Bella McCormick, Agnes Gillespie, Lottie Taylor, Jeanie Grant, Muriel Boyle, Margaret Wylie, ? Bryce, David Watt and Frank Knox.
Second front row: Tom Bunyan (killed at Battle of El Alamein), Agnes Grant (sister of Jean), Mathew Boyle, Minnie Hainey, Betty Miller, Bella Sturgeon, Ella Peters, Jean McClymond, Lizzie Ferguson, Agnes Finlay and Tommy Hose.
Front row: Jackie Cunningham, Willie Ferris, Andy Gibson, Tom Haggart, Jim Park, James McFadzean, Tommy Knox, Tommy Spears, Anthony Thomson and Andrew Henderson.
(Courtesy of John Grant collection)

Opposite bottom: Patna Public School in 1960. Many of those in this photo would have been among the last pupils at Lethanhill School, which closed its doors in 1959.
Back row (l to r): teacher ?, ?, ?, A Kirkwood, J Stewart, J Pettigrew, A Currie, R Law, J Cran, D Brown, ? Ashley, B Robertson, Billy Boyle, J Goodwin and D Robertson.
Second back row: Gordon Robertson (teacher), A Ballantyne, J Graham, ? Whiteford, ?, ?, A Lindsay, M Lafferty, A Graham, E Stevenson, ? Clark, J Smith, J McDougall, J Fitzsimmons, J Bradford, J Logan, M Finlay, H Lymburn and Mr May (teacher).
3rd back row: ? Graham, C McDonald, A Kennedy, M Knox, M Gillespie, M Torbet, J McWilliams, L Graham, I Johnstone, E Ferguson, E Dinwoodie, M McCallum, A Knox, A McDerment and teacher ?
Second front row: S Lang, E Hamilton, M Tinman, E Thomson, M Murray, M Boyle, M Thomson, A Ballantyne, J Grant, J Kilpatrick, A Hainey, E Brown, J McGuigan and E Black.
Front row: G Graham, J Lynn, T McBride, ?, J Bryce, K Ferguson, ?, ?, G Peters, J Faulds, ?, and J Graham.

Houldsworth Colliery

Another boost to Patna came in 1900 with the sinking of Houldsworth Colliery, at a cost of £250,000 to the Dalmellington Iron Company, and a marked change came over the district. This provided employment for the men and their sons after them. It was hard and exacting work, but dependable, and in any case the valley folk were no strangers to hard graft.

From then on, the Colliery with its top-grade steam coal would play an important part in the life of Patna, providing continuity of employment for the next sixty-five years. Wages in those days were poor, but security of employment was important and many Patna men will proudly tell you that they 'wrought at the Houldsworth'. Sadly, it produced its last coal under the auspices of the NCB in 1965, but later reopened as a private mine for a number of years, employing a small number of men.

Houldsworth Colliery which sat high above Polnessan Row on the A713. This pit was sunk in 1900 and closed by the NCB in 1965. This worker is heading back down to the main road.
(Photo: Courtesy of EAC Doon Valley Museum)

Council houses

The first council houses in Patna were built at Jelliston in 1927, followed a year later by those in lower Main Street. By 1937 the nearby hamlet of Kerse was demolished and its population rehoused at the newly built and nearby Polnessan, whilst others went to live in Main Street, Patna, with some others dispersed to Dalrymple. Times were indeed changing.

Today local folk of necessity travel to Ayr or further afield to work. There is a small factory in the village adjacent to the New Bridge, BDF Healthcare, producing first aid products, which provides welcome employment for a few local people. This used to be a clothing factory, producing a variety of garments, but it closed in the mid-1990s. There is a Community Centre, a large Games Hall, Patna Church, a library, one public house and a licensed club in the village.

The Hill of home

Many of the older inhabitants of Patna formerly lived in Lethanhill and Burnfoothill (the Hill), they and their fathers before them having been ironstone and coal miners. With the gradual depopulation of the Hill villages, including Waterside, villagers came to Patna in the 1950s. However, a few surviving villagers and their descendants have strong emotional ties to what they still consider to be home on the Hill.

A service of remembrance following one of the early Hill reunions. This was led by the Reverend Ritchie of Symington. The Dunaskin Band was conducted by John Robertson. Everyone is within the remains of the old schoolhouse. Perhaps the reader can recognise someone.
(Courtesy of John Relly collection)

Indeed, it can be haunting, on a visit to the remains of the cottages, to discover that flowers, wreaths and cards have been left in the ruins of a former home or tied to the branch of a tree or carefully set beside the war memorial – which is all that now remains highly visible, as the ruins of the houses are engulfed in a small plantation of fifty-year-old spruce trees. However, the links with the past remain solid and people do remember their loved ones who lived a tough life on the Hill.

The following statistics relating to The 'Hill are gleaned from the Parish Register.

Last Birth	- Robert Holland at 70 Burnfoothill on 24.7.52.
Last Marriage	- David Campbell, 92 Burnfoothill to Rebecca Maxwell, c/o Downieston Farm, Patna.
Last Death	- Edgar Holland, aged 3 months, on 3.12.53. 70 Burnfoothill.
Last Adult Death	- Jane Conway, aged 81 years, on 29.10.52.

Principal Speakers at The 'Hill Re-unions

1965	William Murphy
1966	David Wylie
1967	Jas. Bryce (Cherry)
1968	William Sodden
1969	Robert McCall
1970	William Smith
1971	George Allen
1972	Andrew Sim
1973	Alex Bryce
1974	Betty Moore
1975	George Sturgeon
1976	Jessie Wilson
1977	Cancelled
1978	James McFadzean
1979	Hugh Ferguson
1980	Sandy Thomson
1981	William Love
1982	Jack Millar M.A.
1983	Tom Hainey
1984	Tom McQuillan
1985	Agnes Stevenson

Some statistical information relating to births, deaths and marriages and some of the speakers at the Hill reunions.
(Extracted from *The Hill: Its People and Its Pits* by T C McQuillan)

The future

What, then, is the future for Patna? It is likely that locals will have to continue travelling to Ayr and further afield for work, but sadly the local levels of unemployment are unacceptably high, giving little prospect of a bright future for new generations.

However, the Doon Valley area provides plentiful opportunities for recreational and sporting activities, including hillwalking, bowling, golf, fishing, brass banding, football, shooting, geology and natural history.

Cultural history and natural history

The cultural history of the valley is important too: poets such as Robert Hettrick of Dalmellington (1769–1849) and Matthew Anderson (1864–1948), known as the policeman-poet of Ayrshire, celebrate the area in their writing, recalling the Covenanters among other aspects of the region's history. The Dalmellington Band was formed in 1864 and the Dunaskin Doon Band in 1869, encouraging a love of brass band music in local men and women through the efforts of their talented musicians and supporters. And of course Benwhat, another of the lost villages, was also able to boast its very own brass band, formed in 1871.

There are Sites of Special Scientific Interest at Dalmellington Moss, Dunaskin Glen, Benbeoch, Bogton Loch, Ness Glen and Loch Doon. The future development of the industrial site at Dunaskin, linked to the important work of the volunteers at the Scottish Industrial Locomotive Centre, are all potential areas for development in the future.

All these elements are closely linked to the Cathcartston Visitor Centre, now known as Doon Valley Museum, at Dalmellington, where an interesting range of displays of the social and industrial history of the area covering subjects such as weaving, farming, mining, village life and brass banding are among those regularly held.

There are indeed opportunities and challenges lying ahead for the people of the Doon Valley, but with the UK still in recession (2012) and jobs difficult to find, one can only hope that better days lie ahead.

Nae treasures nor pleasures
Could make us happy lang;
The heart aye's the part aye
That makes us right or wrang.

Epistle to Davie, A Brother Poet
Robert Burns

Lethanhill Pipe Band in 1935. They were very successful in competition in demand for a range of events. They later moved to Patna.
(Courtesy of John Relly collection)

Patna Badminton Club was extremely popular, as evidenced by the large number of club members. They would take part in local Ayrshire leagues and it was always a good place for local folk to socialise. Readers will quickly identify many well-kent faces.
Back row (l to r): Tom Magill, Ivy Hutchison, Jim Grant, John Kelly, Jackie Campbell, William Muir, John Watt, Jim Fry and Tom Hawthorn.
Front row: Elsie McClymont, Elizabeth Robertson, Peggy Blain, Hazel Clement, Jane Clement, Margaret Dalziel, Elizabeth Blain, Mary Brown, Chrissy Thomson, Margaret Rowan and Bessie Stafford.

Mr Patna – Alexander ('Sanny') Aitken

Aft hae I rov'd by bonie Doon
To see the rose and woodbine twine,
And ilka bird sang o' its luve,
And fondly sae did I o' mine.

The Banks o' Doon
Robert Burns

Alexander 'Sanny' Aitken was arguably Patna's best-known character of the 20th century. A diminishing number of older villagers still fondly talk about him and his rather eccentric ways. He was a larger-than-life character of the old school. A railwayman all his days, he was the popular Station Master at Waterside on the Ayr–Dalmellington branch railway line in his beloved Doon Valley.

His love for and knowledge of Patna and district was extensive. Some of his personal recollections appeared in the columns of the *Ayr Advertiser* around 1962 through the efforts of the then Patna correspondent, Mr Jim Harvey, who also had a great knowledge and deep love for this part of the Doon Valley. A short tribute to Alexander Aitken appeared in the *Ayr Advertiser* of 8 April 1971 and what follows is party based partly on that and other sources.

Known to his friends as Sandy, Alexander Aitken had an amazing knowledge and a wonderful memory for events. Anyone visiting the village and wishing to learn more would be pointed in his direction and he was always delighted to share his knowledge of Auld Patna. This knowledge was based on information handed down from his own grandparents who told him stories about the very beginnings of the village bordering the famous River Doon.

A lover of the works of Robert Burns, it was fitting that his home, Castle Garden, built with his own hands by around 1931, was located near Patna cemetery on the banks of the River Doon, immortalised by Scotland's Bard. He would tell visitors that far back in history, a small castle or fort had stood on the top of the access road to his home, and that his home stood on the ground which had actually been the garden of the castle.

Known for his amazing wit, and with his tongue in his cheek, he was fond of acknowledging that he had been born in 'Buchanan Street', for this was the rather imposing title conferred upon Stewart's Close by Patna villagers, whose sense of fun was evidenced in the nickname given to people and places. Sandy was regarded as something of a local philosopher and was a strong advocate of education. In fact he relished all aspects of learning and was still attending further education classes ('Night School') in the days when he was married.

He had a fine singing voice and would enjoy singing at social events in the village. In fact he would often say that he was so good that he really should have trained to sing in opera, such was the quality of his fine tenor voice. He was a pioneer of the Labour movement in Doon Valley and took an active interest in politics to the very end.

Essentially Sandy was a man of the country with a passionate love for everything relating to Ayrshire's Doon Valley. He had an excellent fund of stories relating to worthies of the past generation and enjoyed recounting them to anyone who would listen. He also kept abreast of national and international affairs by reading newspapers and periodicals. He enjoyed engaging with others on topical issues. There is no doubt that he was a competent and popular conversationalist on most subjects.

The following intimation was read out at the first service in Patna Parish Church following the death of Sandy Aitken in April 1971 in his eighty-third year:

It is with regret, tempered with thankfulness at the quietness of his going, that we have to note the recent death of Mr Alexander Aitken of Castle Garden. His life was long and his interests in what it had to offer were many sided. For him life was indeed a many coloured thing. To those of us who knew him he was a fund of 'wise and witty sayings'. A genuine character of whom the world today is too poor.

Patna had lost a wonderful character of the old school and much-loved son who was fiercely proud of this little village on the banks o' Doon.

And there's a hand, my trusty fiere!
And gie's a hand o' thine!
And we'll take a right gude-willy waught,
For Auld Lang Syne.

Auld Lang Syne
Robert Burns

Patna's Knight – Professor Sir David Campbell

Thou'll break my heart, thou warbling bird,
That wantons thro' the flowering thorn!
Thou minds me o' departed joys,
Departed never to return.

The Banks o' Doon
Robert Burns

Patna's Knight, Sir David Campbell.
(Courtesy of EAC Doon Valley Museum)

A proud son of Patna rose to become a knight of the realm. Sir David Campbell, professor at Aberdeen University, was a contemporary and great friend of Alexander 'Sandy' Aitken and often called on him at Castle Garden on the banks of the River Doon, on his frequent visits to Patna.

Sir David was knighted in 1953 and received the honorary degree of LLD at the opening of Liverpool University's medical school by Queen Elizabeth, the Queen Mother, later becoming President of the General Medical Council. He was educated at Patna Public School, Ayr Academy and Glasgow University. He was always acutely aware of his roots by the River Doon in the village of Patna and made many return visits to the area.

Interestingly, Patna also has another son who received a knighthood. Sir Andrew Barclay (1824–93) made his special mark becoming Lord Mayor of Liverpool and endowed Lady Walker Ward, in the former Ayr County Hospital. So this small Ayrshire village, straddling the River Doon, can boast two knights of the realm!

Sir David Campbell was born at Patna on 6 May 1889 to Agnes Smith Campbell, a seamstress. He spent his formative years in the village, attending the local school and playing about the fields around the River Doon. He continued his education at Ayr Academy, going on to study medicine at Glasgow University and graduating in 1911 (BSc and MA Hons) and 1916 (MBChB Hons). Volunteering for the war effort, he served with distinction in the Royal Army Medical Corps from 1916 to 1919, being awarded the Military Cross in France in 1918 as an immediate decoration in the field. On demobilisation he returned to Glasgow as assistant to the renowned Professor Ralph Stockman. In 1921 he became Pollok Lecturer in Materia Medica and Pharmacology at Glasgow.

In 1924 he took his MD with honours with a thesis on rheumatoid arthritis, winning the coveted Bellahouston Gold Medal. Between 1925 and 1930 he was Rockefeller Medical Fellow at Johns Hopkins University in Baltimore, USA, and he also worked at the Western Infirmary in Glasgow. In 1928 he published *A Handbook of Therapeutics* which received high acclaim at that time. In 1930 he was appointed to the Regius Chair of Materia Medica at Aberdeen University and within two years was Dean of Faculty – and he held this post until his retirement in 1959. In 1936 Campbell joined the General Medical Council (GMC) as the representative of Aberdeen University and his skills and abilities were recognised by colleagues who elected him President of the GMC in 1949, a post which he held until 1961.

He was knighted in 1953 and received honorary degrees from the universities of Glasgow, Liverpool and Trinity College Dublin. He was a fellow of the Royal Society of Edinburgh, of the Royal College of Physicians of London and of the Royal College of Physicians and Surgeons of Glasgow.

In 1921 he married Margaret, daughter of Alexander Lyle, head teacher at Kerse near Grangemouth. The couple had no children and he died at his home in Aberdeen on 30 May 1978.

During his life and despite rising to the highest echelons in medicine and education and contributing significantly in both fields, he never forgot his roots in Patna where his mother raised him in difficult circumstances on her own. He made many return visits to his home village, regularly meeting and reminiscing with his great boyhood friend and renowned local character, Alexander 'Sandy' Aitken. Sandy pre-deceased Sir David by seven years in 1971 and after his old friend's passing, Patna's Knight never again visited his old village by the banks o' Doon, but he would doubtless keep the memories of early days close to his heart.

Ruin's wheel has driven o'er us;
Not a hope that dare attend,
The wide world is all before us,
But a world without a friend.

Strathallan's Lament
Robert Burns

A group of workers at Dalmellington Iron Company, Waterside with the date on the board 1896. No names are known, but doubtless many of their descendants will still be living in Ayrshire's Doon Valley. Clearly no one asked them to 'smile for the birdie'.
(Photo: EAC Doon Valley Museum)

A group of older folk meet at Waterside village war memorial before joining socially to enjoy the Waterside Reunion. The dominating ironstone bing shows how dramatic a scene it created until it was reduced in size from the early 1970s.

Chapter 3

The Dalmellington Iron Works

We labour soon, we labour late,
To feed the titled knave, man;
And a' the comfort we're to get
Is that ayont the grave, man.

The Tree of Liberty
Robert Burns

Mining begins

The Doon Valley owes its industrial development to the existence of prolific amounts of coal and ironstone. Coal had been mined for centuries in the valley, albeit in small amounts in drift mines where the coal was located near to the surface. This fact is well documented in the *Statistical Account* of 1793, where the Minister of Dalmellington, the Reverend Duncan McMyne reported that 'the parish is full of fine coal, and freestone, in almost every corner of it' and recorded that coal was transported 30 miles away into Galloway. 'There is also iron-stone to be found in the parish, and lead in some of the hills.'

Nearly fifty years later this was still the case, but deeper mining was now evident, as revealed in the *Statistical Account* of 1837, when the Parish Minister of Dalmellington, the Reverend Robert Houston wrote: 'The coal pits have been many, especially in low situations, where till lately the coal was worked at less than 3 fathoms from the surface.'

And it was from these beginnings that a small industrial revolution was to take the valley by storm. In the 1840s the entrepreneurial Houldsworth family, originally from Yorkshire, and with established ironworks in Coltness, Lanarkshire, formed the Dalmellington Iron Company. The following extract from the *Glasgow Herald* of 27 September 1848 highlights the anticipation of the arrival of the new industry.

The Dalmellington Iron Works, belonging to Messrs Houldsworth, Glasgow, were blown in for the first time on Monday week, and the first casting took place on Wednesday. The machinery was found to work smoothly and everything went off well. Ayrshire is nearly now girded round with ironworks.

Houldsworth influence

Henry Houldsworth was the founding father of the Dalmellington Iron Company at Dunaskin. He was seventy-four years of age when he began this project in the 1840s. His life illustrates well the tremendous energy and technological change of the 19th century which transformed the once pastoral southwest of Scotland, a land of quiet hills and valleys, into a booming industrial heart of Empire.

Waterside store was the HQ for all things supplied by the Dalmellington Iron Company. Three horse-drawn wagons in the early 1900s are about to set off to the neighbouring villages to replenish supplies and deliver orders. The sign on the centre wagon reads 'Dalmellington Iron Co. Ltd., Stores, Waterside'.
(Photo: Courtesy of EAC Doon Valley Museum)

Ironworks

After three years of hectic major construction operations at Waterside, by 1848 the results of this mini industrial revolution were evident to all. The first furnaces were in blast, belching out smoke and dust in this quiet unspoiled land of hills and valleys. New villages were hurriedly constructed to house the large workforce required to mine the coal and ironstone and to carry out all the operations at the ironworks, and by the end of the 1860s most were in place.

A group of Carters at Dalmellington Iron Works opened at Dunaskin in September 1848 by the Dalmellington Iron Company. This was probably taken in the late 1890s. On the site in 2012 the visitor will find the much-reduced remains of a typical mid-19th-century iron smelting works. The most notable surviving structure is the Italianate blowing-engine house with round-headed windows, dated 1847, which was later part of a brickworks. The single-storey ashlar locomotive repair workshops are still in use by the Ayrshire Railway Preservation Group. The slag hill, where tipping last occurred about 1921, much reduced by recent excavation, is still a landmark on the A713 Ayr–Dalmellington Road at Waterside.
(Photo: Courtesy of EAC Doon Valley Museum)

New villages

Whilst the industrial conditions were far from ideal, the local population were pleased that many jobs were created. Indeed there was a scarcity of local workers, and outsiders, keen to gain employment, flocked in from the Highlands of Scotland, Ireland, Lanarkshire and elsewhere and took up residence in the new villages, with the appealing names of Lethanhill, Benwhat, Corbie Craigs, Craigmark, Pennyvenie, Kerse, Tongue Row, Cairntable, Beoch and Waterside, also known as Dunaskin.

The influence of railways

The twin villages of Lethanhill and Burnfoothill were built between 1849 and the 1860s on the Knockkippen Plateau at 900 feet above sea level and 1 1/2 miles above Patna and the River Doon. The villages were a series of miners' rows built by the Dalmellington Iron Company close to the iron pits where the men worked converting iron ore extracted from surface workings into pig iron in open hearths.

The fast-moving industrial development meant that transport links were vital to ensure that the coal, ironstone and finished pig iron could be readily transported to the harbour at Ayr. This was accomplished in 1856 with the building of the Ayr–Dalmellington railway, by which time frenetic local activity resulted in a spider's web of railway lines running along the plateau above the Upper Doon Valley, the remnants of which can still be clearly seen and followed today. This was an amazing feat of industrial construction and many navvies must have been engaged in the extensive engineering operations which led to these many lines being laid along the 900-foot to 1000-foot contour high above the Valley of Doon.

Wage boom and social life

The 1870s can be regarded as a period of great prosperity for the Dalmellington Iron Company and its workforce. Industry was booming across Britain and the wages of local miners rose to an incredible £7 to £8 per week. In later years the miners and their families were to look back nostalgically on this period, which they referred to as 'the time o' the big money'.

It was around this period that many of the miners in these villages acquired the status symbol of that era – an American organ. The miners valued education for their children in the hope of guaranteeing them a better future. There was a well-organised social and recreational calendar of events which included football teams, quoits, athletics, choir, pipe band, Burns Club, brass band, bazaars, educational improvement classes, cantatas and concerts.

There was the annual sports event, a day never to be missed, with great athletes competing from near and far. Indeed, modern-day communities would have difficulty replicating the range and variety of social and recreational facilities available in the Doon

Valley's lost mining villages. All of this was not only self-created but self-supported. There were no grants available in those times to support a range of community activities.

Community spirit

The villages were new, but the workers were all of the same social background and were determined to make the best of the circumstances in which they found themselves. Indeed, most of them probably considered themselves fortunate to have a job, because losing it also held the prospect of losing a home, a real fear for any miner with a large family to support.

They were, nevertheless, proud people and the sense of community spirit was evident from the earliest days of these newly created mining communities, with neighbours being friendly and helpful to each other. There was a sort of shared sense and understanding of living life in difficult circumstances in relatively remote areas which helped everyone to pull together. This facet of life in the lost mining villages was always commented upon by former residents and was apparent right up until the final days of depopulation. When former villagers held reunions, this facet of life was always emphasised.

The spirit of 'Esprit de Corps' or the 'one for all' and 'all for one' spirit was strongly emphasised by Mr John Relly, principal speaker at the seventh annual Benquhat Re-union which took place on Saturday in Dalmellington Community Centre. Special reference was made to togetherness of the homely folks of Benquhat with happy smiles in evidence when he made reference to the 'Hill Line' and the many courtships and ultimate marriages between the Hill (Lethanhill) and Benquhat couples. He spoke of how a serious illness was the concern of the whole village and how physical help was provided and how on one occasion after a great snowstorm the villagers banded themselves together hurriedly, to clear away the snow and so allow an ambulance to quickly remove a very sick man to hospital.

Ayrshire Post, 13 March 1970

Changing times

The pendulum quickly swung back from the good days of high wages and by the 1880s wages were back to around 25 shillings per week. Times were again pretty grim for the miners and furnacemen in the Doon Valley, as they were often laid off for weeks at a time with no wages. To help the family survive these difficult times, they would sell off possessions. The second-hand shops in Ayr were reported to be full of American organs, sold off by struggling miners, putting food on the table being more important than making music.

There was overcapacity in the mining industry and English firms were doing much better than their counterparts in the Doon Valley, the remoteness of the local ironworks at Dunaskin being a distinct disadvantage for the once highly regarded Dalmellington iron ore. Times were changing and sadly not for the better.

Mining population

By 1911 the section of the Ayrshire population representing the mining industry numbered around 40,000 people. Of this number roughly 30,000 lived in miners' rows or villages owned by the local mining companies. The remaining 10,000 lived in towns and other villages. By 1913 the period of mining expansion had come to an end and no more rows of houses were built, whilst little or no maintenance was carried out on the existing housing stock.

End of iron production

Waterside, which consisted of some eighty-nine houses in 1851, grew around the original ironworks, which were built between 1846 and 1856. The Dalmellington Iron Works ceased production of pig iron in 1921, but the size of the dominant slag bing at Waterside, which has been reduced immeasurably since then for road bottoming, testifies to the huge amounts of iron which must have been produced at Waterside between 1848 and 1921, a period of only seventy-three years.

In the early 20th century, the industrial development of Britain was firmly based on steel making, another nail in the coffin of iron production. Moreover, with the ever increasing levels of imported iron ore from Spain, to replace the worked out Doon Valley iron ore, the end of iron production in the Valley of Doon was inevitable. Only the outbreak of the Great War gave it a stay of execution.

After the war the demand for iron and coal fell. Local production costs soared, wages began to fall and this was a period of increasing industrial strife. Dalmellington Iron Company miners took part in the three-week strike in October 1920. With the threat of another such strike looming in March 1921, the board of the Company took the decision to close the ironworks and move away from the Doon Valley. The famous Dunaskin furnaces were blown out, never again to produce the world-famous Dalmellington iron, and no further tipping of molten slag on the famous Waterside bing occurred after 1921.

Mr Robert McCall, a former headmaster at Dreghorn speaking at the 1969 Hill Reunion, remembered his boyhood days and touched on the impact of the iron production.

Many a time I walked and often ran from the Hill down to Waterside to catch the train. Down there in the valley was Jimmy's burn where we dooked (swam) and guddled. In the distance was the road up past High Keirs. Many a time I have walked that way to Straiton. In the middle distance was the enormous slag bing, dominating the valley, which used to glow and brighten the night sky in my boyhood days.

So 1921 was indeed a defining moment in the history of industrial Doon Valley, with the end of iron production, but old King Coal would still reign supreme until the last Doon Valley colliery at Pennyvenie closed in 1978. Strangely enough, within a few years of the end of deep mining, opencast mining came on stream in the Doon Valley, surface mining producing amounts of coal that underground miners could only dream of.

Bairds and Dalmellington

William Baird & Co. Ltd, coal and iron masters, had been founded in 1830 with their industrial base centred in Lanarkshire. They also had interests in Ayrshire related mainly to various coal and ironstone pits and the Muirkirk and Eglinton ironworks. However, as we have just seen, by the early 1920s the winds of change were blowing through industrial Scotland and there was a gradual downturn in mining and iron production caused primarily by a drop in demand for iron, closely linked to an inability to compete against cheaper foreign imports of ironstone. Unfortunately, the blackband ironstone seams in the Ayrshire and Lanarkshire coalfields became more difficult to work and consequently they were unable to produce ironstone in the quantities and at a price demanded by the market. This culminated in the closure of ironworks at Muirkirk, Dalmellington and Kilwinning in the 1920s and the coal owners then concentrated on coal production in the rich, if difficult to work, Ayrshire and Lanarkshire seams.

Bairds and Dalmellington followed on from Dalmellington Iron Company and in 1947 the NCB took over the site. This team was made up of staff who worked in the offices at Waterside. Many of them lived in the lost villages.
Back row: (l to r) James Roberts, John Ferguson, Frank McKie, Willie Dougan, John Relly and Louis Scott.
Front row: Tommy Rafferty, Ian Robb, Willie Burns, Billy Thomson and Campbell McMillan.
(John Relly collection)

The two principal companies involved in coal mining were William Baird & Company and their competitors, the Dalmellington Iron Company, the latter being in poor financial shape due to the Depression, whereas Bairds seem to have been more financially resilient. In 1931 the two companies amalgamated: the new company was rebranded as Bairds and Dalmellington and concentrated its efforts in coal production for the home market and diversified into brick making.

The new company, 75% owned by William Baird & Co. Ltd, controlled some 70% of the Ayrshire coalfields. In 1933 they employed around 7,244 miners in over twenty collieries in the county. This number included pits in the Doon Valley: Beoch,

150 miners; Bogton No. 1, 90 miners; Houldsworth, 260 miners; Pennyvenie No. 4, 160 miners; and Pennyvenie Nos. 2, 3 and 6, 440 miners.

By 1938, despite the years of depression, Bairds and Dalmellington's gross profit stood at 17.5% and this was not only sustained but rose to 20% during the war years and peaked at 27.5% in the year before the nationalisation of the coal industry.

The year 1947 was a key year for industry in Scotland, with the majority of coal mines being taken under government control under the auspices of the National Coal Board. At the time of the nationalisation of the coal mines in 1947, the Doon Valley pits taken into the national fold were: Beoch Nos. 3 and 4, 369 miners; Bogton, 96 miners; Chalmerston, 262 miners; Bowhill, 37 miners; Houldsworth, 248 miners; Pennyvenie No. 4, 216 miners; Pennyvenie Nos. 2, 3 and 7, 417 miners. But nationalisation sounded the death knell for many small mining companies, including Bairds and Dalmellington, which was finally wound up in 1953.

The NCB later used the ironworks site at Waterside for administrative purposes and coal-related storage and movement. The brickworks and kilns at Waterside finally closed in 1976. The Scottish mining story continued until the closure of the longest-serving colliery during the National Coal Board era in Ayrshire, a proud record which goes to Barony Colliery near Auchinleck, which maintained production from 1947 until it was closed as the last Ayrshire deep mine in 1989. However, the last deep mine in Scotland was Longannet in Fife, which closed in 2002, leaving only many opencast sites in the Scottish coalfields, and these will continue for many years to come.

Capturing the industrial past

Through the efforts of hard-working local volunteers led by Miss Anne Joss MBE of Dalmellington and District Conservation Trust, Dunaskin was given a new lease of life as a significant outdoor heritage museum in 1983. There had been many years of diligent preparatory work before the opening stage was even reached. Dunaskin was a visitor attraction for all the family, taking them on a historical journey through time looking at the industrial past in terms of iron production, coal mining, working steam engines and brick making. Indeed, the history of the Doon Valley is in many ways a microcosm of the history of Scotland, making this museum one of exceptional importance. The Dunaskin Experience allowed the visitor to explore the past as it was actually lived by Ayrshire people.

Museum site

An open-air, living museum set amidst beautiful rolling countryside, it followed the story of the people and places of the Doon Valley through the industrial revolution, two world wars and right up to modern times. The Mary Gallagher Experience was an audio-visual presentation which recreated Ayrshire life in the 19th and early 20th centuries.

Classed as a Scheduled Ancient Monument, the museum's 110-acre site had historic buildings and walks, including nearby Dunaskin Glen which is a designated Site of Special Scientific Interest. There was also a period cottage and industrial machinery as well as a restaurant and shop, all aimed at the making the visitor experience as pleasant and interesting as possible.

Sadly, the museum was forced to close in 2005 due to a lack of financial support and perhaps a lack of vision by those in authority who controlled the purse-strings, not realising the importance of this industrial site, not only at Ayrshire level, but as a national gem. In 2010 Ayrshire Railway Preservation Group moved their many industrial pugs from Minnivey, near Dalmellington, to Dunaskin. They have given the site a new lease of life, with even more steam trains available to tempt visitors to once again recall the days of steam railway and wonder at the magnificent heritage of ironmaking, coal mining and brick production.

We cam na here to view your warks
In hopes to be mair wise,
But only, lest we gang to Hell,
It may be nae surprise.
But when we tirl'd at your door
The porter dought na bear us:
Sae may, should we to Hell's yetts come,
Your billie Satan sair us.

At Carron Ironworks
Robert Burns

Chapter 4

The Hill

We twa hae run about the braes,
And pou'd the gowans fine
But we've wander'd monie a weary fit,
Sin auld lang syne.

We twa hae paidl'd in the burn
Frae morning sun till dine,
But seas between us braid hae roar'd
Sin auld lang syne

Auld Lang Syne
Robert Burns

I would warmly encourage readers to obtain a copy of a fascinating local book: *The Hill: Its People and Its Pits*, a detailed history of the village of Lethanhill/Burnfoothill by a former Hill resident, Tom Courtney McQuillan of Patna. He wrote from the heart with personal knowledge and experience because he was a Hilltonian. The following is simply a brief overview of aspects of life on the Hill which I trust will give a flavour of the past.

Desperate times

The closure of the ironworks at Dunaskin in 1921 meant really desperate times for some of the families of the Dalmellington Iron Company, although the company continued to operate the local pits in the area. Skilled furnacemen and labourers were left without jobs. Some chose to relocate, whilst others remained and sought work in the coal pits locally.

Hardship was to be the lot of many former workers and their families for years, not least for those living on the Hill, 900 feet above sea level on the Knockkippen Plateau, 11/2 miles above and to the east of Patna. They and the villagers of Benwhat, Corbie Craigs and Beoch were living in what today would be regarded as extreme isolation from the villagers located in the valley of the River Doon. The closure of the ironworks was part of a downward spiral and the financial collapse of 1929, which began in USA, inevitably spread across the globe and by 1930 the Dalmellington Iron Company was in a perilous financial position.

Bairds and Dalmellington formed

Fortunately, William Baird & Company came to the rescue of the coal industry in the Doon Valley. They were already the top coal company in eastern Ayrshire and had many interests in central Ayrshire and Lanarkshire. By October 1931 a new company, Bairds and Dalmellington Ltd, was successfully floated and took over control of DICo operations and stock including Houldsworth, Pennyvenie Nos. 2, 3, 4, 5 and 6; Beoch Nos. 2 and 3; Clawfin No. 2; Chalmerston Nos. 4, 5 and 6; Bogton and Sundrum No. 3, as well as eleven locomotives in the stock of the Dalmellington Iron Company.

They also further developed and modernised brick making on the Dunaskin site and this coincided with a rise in house building. However, with the government again taking control of coal production during the war, it was in 1947 that the National Coal Board took over operation of most pits. Private owners would no longer have the profit motive as their top priority at the expense of poor wages, working conditions and abysmal housing for workers and their families. With the backing of the treasury, the new organisation could modernise and develop the coal industry and improve safety and working conditions. It was said that men in the nationalised industry had never known it so good.

Inspired names

Residents of Lethanhill/Burnfoothill adopted the convenient name the Hill to collectively identify the two close communities. Burnfoothill, the smaller of the two, consisted of two miners' rows, known as Polnessan Row, whereas Lethanhill was much the larger with many miners' rows with imaginative names such as Stone Row, White Brick Row, Briggate Row, Whaup Row, Step Row, the Laigh Rows, Peewit Row and Diamond Row.

Lethanhill with villagers clearing the remnants of what has been a heavy fall of snow, whilst other villagers go about their business. By 1954 this mining village had been abandoned and was later demolished. (Photo: Courtesy of EAC Doon Valley Museum)

Houses on the Hill

Originally, the Hill consisted of only two short rows. One, designated the Peewit Row, consisted of six single-apartment brick houses with a bedroom-cum-kitchen, and a small scullery which jutted out at the back of the house. This row was situated on the brow of 'Lethan Hill' overlooking Drumgrange Farm.

The second was known as the Whaup Row, about 200 yards further up the moor and more central to the rest of the village which was to follow. This row consisted of twenty-four single-apartment brick houses, similar to those of the Peewit Row. These two original rows were named after the most common species of bird life which inhabited the wild lonely moor around them.

The rest of the Hill came under construction in the 1870s until the full complement of 256 houses had been built. The Step Row contained twenty single-apartment brick houses. The front of this row looked out at the village church and war memorial and onto the rows at Burnfoothill. The Old School Row contained twelve single-apartment brick houses and was adjacent to Whaup Row. Step Row and Old School Row were the last two rows to be evacuated in 1954.

The Store Row was a short row of six single-apartment brick houses reaching up behind the store buildings. This row was in line with Step Row and looked out north-west across the Firth of Clyde.

The Stone Row consisted of twenty two-apartment stone-built houses and the Briggate Row consisted of eighteen single-apartment brick-built houses. Both of the rows used a common pathway and faced down into the Doon Valley.

The White Brick Row contained twenty single-apartment houses. The Briggate sat adjacent to the White Brick Row, and the front of the White Brick Row looked out over the Drumgrange incline to Waterside and the hills of the south-west. The White Brick Row was also, like Step Row and Old School Row, among the last to be deserted in 1954.

Rail on the Hill

Strangely enough, the Dalmellington Iron Company's Hill railway system passed through the village. This was a branch of the Bowhill–Benwhat main line of the Hill rail network and originally came to Drumgrange No. 4 pit, which was located next to the Briggate Row and carried on through Lethanhill to the pits at Burnfoot No. 9 and Downieston No. 5. When Downieston closed in 1892 the line was cut back, leaving only a small siding, which originally served Drumgrange No. 2 and stopped by the village store. Up until at least the 1930s the village store received its supplies by rail from the Company's central depot at Waterside.

Burnfoothill rows

Meanwhile at Burnfoothill there were three rows of houses known to everyone in the district as 'Ponessan Row', which was more properly called Polnessan Row. These lay in one long straight row facing out over Patna and at their peak consisted of eighty inhabited houses. At the end of one of the rows, two houses had been converted for use as a Miners' Institute. The Institute had a small library or reading room with a variety of newspapers and periodicals, a billiards table and a variety of games including cards, dominoes and 'summer ice', which as the name implies, was a miniature indoor game based on curling.

Generally speaking, most of the Hill houses were of the same type as those of the other Dalmellington Iron Company mining villages in the Doon Valley. They also had outside dry toilets, usually in the form of a small wooden hut. The principal speaker at the 1969 Hill Reunion, Robert McCall, recalled visits to the toilet in the middle of the night.

When I look back at my life at the Hill I do not remember having lived in squalor. Perhaps I was too wee and just accepted it. I do remember the adventurous journey to the 'wee hoose' with a candle and a box of matches, and I can tell you that a box of matches was needed for the candle had the nasty habit of being blown out.

There was no running water, except in latter days when some individual houses had been connected privately by the tenant. The water was supplied either by a pump, of which there were generally one or two adjacent to each row, or by free running water from the hills which ran through 3-inch pipes to form a spout and villagers could collect water from this source.

Coal storage

Originally there were no separate coal houses, and the coal to feed the fire had to be kept in the scullery or below the bed in the kitchen. This bed was made of cast iron and was a permanent feature, being put in by the Company when the houses were built. Latterly, nearly all the houses obtained a small brick outhouse in which to keep their coal, thereby keeping the kitchen and scullery much cleaner.

Electricity arrives, 1933

In the kitchen there was a coal-fired 'Dover stove' for cooking and for heating the house. They were versatile and the women loved them, as they allowed them to cook and bake to a high standard. In the small scullery, all the tenants had, in later years at least, electric boilers for washing clothes, before which everything was washed by sheer physical effort in a large tub. Electricity only came to the Hill in 1933, although the power station had been built at Waterside, in the valley below, as early as 1918. Supplying additional living benefits to their tenants and workforce would seem not to have been high on the Dalmellington Iron Company's agenda, otherwise they would have connected the Hill and Benwhat with power after the First World War.

The rear of Lethanhill School about 1953. The small boy is David Young, aged three, with his mother Mrs Janet Young, and the girl is Janet Foden, who was visiting the Young family at the store house, Lethanhill. The sheep seem content in their company and simply roamed freely around the houses. Jack Young was the last manager of the Lethanhill store, then operated by John McDonald, the father of well-known Doon Valley man Matt McDonald, fondly remembered as the publican at the Palace Bar, Waterside until the early 1970s. (Photo: Courtesy of David Young)

School on the Hill

The old school at Lethanhill, closed in 1927, was made of brick and contained six classrooms. After the new school was built in 1926 and opened in 1927, the old school was then used as the village hall, and was well looked after until the village was abandoned in 1954.

The new school was a much bigger and more modern building than its predecessor and included a room for cooking lessons. This new building was located just north and west of the old school building and across the burn towards Burnfoothill.

In front of the school, just behind the war memorial, was the site of the Hill church. The church was surrounded by railings embedded in concrete. The church building was made of corrugated iron. Interestingly, the Lethanhill church name was kept going after 1954 when the village was deserted, as it merged with Waterside Church. Both of these were later merged with Patna Church, which in turn was subsequently merged with the Kirk o' the Covenant in Dalmellington.

Between 1948 and 1954 the people of the Hill were moved mainly to Patna in the centralisation scheme under the auspices of Ayr County Council. Lethanhill had once been able to boast the largest population in the Doon Valley. Surveys in 1881 showed it had a population of 1,690 compared with Waterside's 1,681 and Dalmellington's 1,437.

What's in a name?

The reality was that the accommodation on the Hill and other Dalmellington Iron Company villages was basic and the rooms small, with overcrowding an accepted part of the fabric of day-to-day life. Lethanhill also had a village store, smiddy, school and Kirk, a locomotive shed and a garage. Lethanhill and Burnfoothill were adjacent and divided only by the Hill road and Kirk Brae, and so it became common for them simply to be referred to as the Hill. To all intents and purposes they were indeed one community with the unsatisfactory situation of having two different names.

1851 Census

The 1851 Census records show that there was already a thriving small community on the Hill. There were eighty-nine houses at Dunaskin near the ironworks with a further ten at Lethanhill, adjacent to the top of the railway incline and close to several ironstone pits. The Company always endeavoured to house workers as close as possible to where they were working, believing that this would result in less absenteeism and more control over the workforce. It was, in short, a benevolent form of social control by the Company over the workers. The Company also had the ultimate form of sanction in that if a worker was dismissed, this would probably mean having to move from the Company house.

Hill reunion 1965

The late Willie Murphy, a former Lethanhill resident and retired schoolteacher who became rector at Fort William Academy, was guest speaker at the Hill reunion in 1965 when aged seventy. Amazingly, 500 former Hill residents attended this function, showing the very special affinity which the former residents had with their village, despite the shortcomings of the living conditions. Indeed, it is doubtful if, in the long history of the Hill community, so many of them had ever gathered under one roof. Willie, who had left Lethanhill some forty years before, movingly described some aspects of village life as he remembered them.

Front cover of the 6th Annual Hill Reunion on 29 August 1970.
(Photo: Courtesy of EAC Doon Valley Museum)
Inside programme of 6th Annual Hill Reunion held on 29 August 1970.
(Photo: Courtesy of EAC Doon Valley Museum)

My earliest recollection of the Hill was of the little Pug engine cruising slowly along the line which skirted the rows to celebrate the Relief of Mafeking. It must be difficult, almost impossible, for young folk today to capture a true image of the Hill as it was then. When the DICo started operations in the 1840s, Lethanhill was developed as a miners' camp, a supply depot for the labour force required to work the coal and ironstone. In retrospect it was also an isolation camp, almost literally cut off from any contact with the outside world. Certainly there was a road (up from Patna) but that road was kept locked and barred by the company's orders.

No outside trader dared trespass up the Hill as the DICo wanted to have no competition. The road was closed except for residents moving into or out of Lethanhill, funerals and urgent medical cases. The company's provision store provided the essentials for life and in some cases what the wife didn't pay against her debt book, the husband spent in the Beer Store, so that the next week his earnings had all been returned to the company. About 1908 this physical barrier to trade was removed by the local Member of Parliament, James Brown, and the company's monopoly was burst wide open.

This view of the Dalmellington Iron Company as a ruthless, uncaring and self-indulgent organisation aimed purely at procuring and maximising profits by controlling and directing workers over where they should purchase their food, clothing and other necessities may not have been an altogether accurate view.

In the interesting booklet, *The Rise and Fall of Mining Communities in Central Ayrshire in the 19th and 20th Centuries*, published by Ayrshire Archaeological and Natural History Society in 1999 (Ayrshire Monograph No. 22), Gavin Wark writes:

Certainly forcing workers to the company store was more prevalent in some places than others. Fortunately in Central Ayrshire the system was not as widespread but it did exist. Some coal companies were better than others. For example, the Dalmellington Iron Company (DICo) owned four company stores and the workers were free to use them only if they wanted to. This company also refused to give advances in wages, paid wages weekly and did not charge for poundage, thus proving to be fair in this respect. They were one of the major employers of men in Central Ayrshire when, for example, in 1871 they employed 2,000 men. Thus, the Truck system was not as widespread in Central Ayrshire as elsewhere.

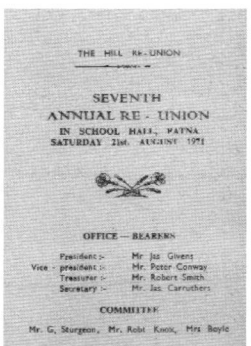 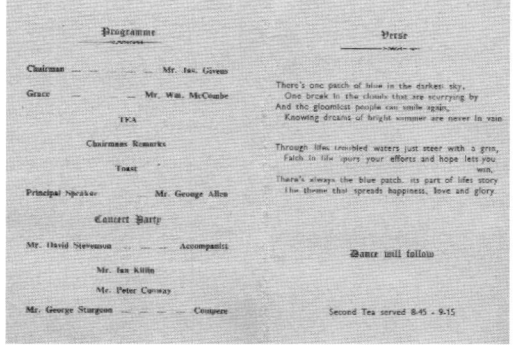

A memorial to Lethanhill, known simply as the Hill, by former villagers. This remains in place today, although opencast coal mining commenced in the area in 2011.
(Photo: Donald L Reid)

Conflicting views

It may well be that Mr Murphy was simply passing on erroneous information which had gained credibility as people reflected – perhaps wrongly – on times past. Employers such as the Dalmellington Iron Company were always likely to be seen in a negative light by workers, especially when living and working conditions were difficult and it would be reasonable to blame most unpopular things on the anonymous DICo 'bosses'.

Perhaps a more balanced view is given in the Wark account and there is strong evidence from personal recollections of villagers that travelling shops were allowed access to the Hill and other Doon Valley mining villages without restriction, certainly from the 1930s. However, myth is often more exciting than reality when reflecting on yesteryear.

Tough times

All the lost mining villages of Doon Valley had a fairly similar and very basic level of domestic provision when compared to what is taken for granted today. Many houses had an open hearth fire in the kitchen, and in the early years water was carried in buckets from the street standpipe. Water was heated on the hearth in large kettles. There was the standard outdoor dry toilet, hated by the women.

The families in the villages tended to be large, because there was no adequate form of birth control widely available. Overcrowding was acute, and big families were the rule rather than the exception. This was simply a way of life, with several children sharing the same bed. It was tolerated by the residents, who had no real alternative but to make the best of a poor lot.

Social adversity

All the residents shared the same plight, and that shared experience of social adversity made residents more accepting of bad living conditions because everyone else was in a similar position. Life for women, too, must have been extremely difficult, having to carry out all their domestic chores with none of the benefits that are taken for granted in the 21st-century home. This strength of community spirit was remarked upon by Gavin Wark in his book on the mining communities, mentioned above:

Despite the comment that the life of a miner above and below ground appeared to be rather cheerless, there is no doubt that the people of the mining rows shared a sense of community and togetherness, which was lacking in other non-mining towns and villages. This was perhaps due to the people sharing the same occupations, standard of housing, and similar circumstances.

The villagers on the Hill lived very close to nature and to the elements. Living at almost 1,000 feet above sea level, the weather was often challenging, and the heavy snows of winter and fairly constant wind and rain can be compared and contrasted with what former villagers tend to remember as boyhood days running around shoeless on the wild moors in the delightful and carefree days of summer.

Willie Murphy, at one time rector of Fort William Academy, recalled some of the vibrant characters and scenes of his happy days living at Lethanhill, which for him made the place very special:

I recall sitting in class as David Vallance, the village dominie, his eagle-eye flashing fire, told off Andy Bickerstaff for misbehaving; hearing the rhyming 'puff-puff' of the winding engine at the Drumhead incline and of the faraway Glasgow and Southwestern locomotive.

There was, too, the mute elegance of the village War Memorial bearing the names of the sixteen Hill boys who did not come home. And as I wandered among the scenes of early days I would murmur the two saddest words in the language: No more! No more! For this now was a place of ghosts and they come back and speak.

I have happy memories of Jimmy Forsyth, Malcolm Ross, 'Jegger' McCutcheon, Billy Boyd and 'Aunty Tilda'. And of course some of the well-known village names – Ballantyne, Moore, Gillespie, Park, McClymont, Bryce and Talman.

One of the most kenspeckle, picturesque, versatile characters ever raised on the Hill was Jock Park, who by his personal magnetism gave sunshine for shadow and laughter for tears.

Lethanhill's long rows of terraced houses were scattered along the 900-foot contour with little sign of thoughtful planning in design and layout. The drab barrack-like uniformity was designed more with the needs of the intersecting railway lines in mind than the needs of the local population. The sinking of ironstone pits, which were built on once exhausted, in the centre and edges of the village also highlighted how the products of the earth were of paramount importance, much more so than the needs of the miners and their families. Some saw the village as being simply forbidding and unattractive, although the spirit and fellowship of the people were always a strong point remarked upon by just about everyone who lived on the Hill.

Matthew Anderson, policeman-poet of the Ayrshire Constabulary, born at Truffhill, Waterside, in the valley below the Hill, knew and loved the Doon Valley and wrote the following lines in praise of the Hill.

All hail, ye noble hills,
Dear objects of my dreams,
And all you queer, wee, mossy drains
In which we fished when we were weans
And thought them splendid streams.

Wild, woodless Lethanhill,
Long years have slipt away
Since last across the heath I sped
And gazed upon this bold drumhead
Still standing here today.

Good-bye, bare Burnfoothill,
Home of a hardy race,
But I'll come back and see thy rills
And those great, rugged, Loch Doon hills
That stare thee in thy face.

Burnfoothill, Dalmellington
Matthew Anderson (1912)

Time to move

The late 1940s and early 1950s were generally a period of relocation of the population of the Doon Valley's lost mining villages. Some folk were delighted to leave to enjoy the new Ayr County Council houses with modern facilities in Patna, and others left their roots with great sadness. It was said that some folk from the Hill and Waterside moved very reluctantly to settle elsewhere, whilst the residents of Benwhat and Corbie Craigs moved to Dalmellington and the new housing estate at Bellsbank. Some of the older residents would naturally have reservations about leaving what for them was a dear home, steeped with special family memories, despite the basic conditions that existed in these mining communities.

Teach erring man to spurn the rage of gain;
Teach him that states of native strength possess'd,
Tho' very poor, may still be very blest.

The Deserted Village
Oliver Goldsmith

By 1955 everyone had moved away from the Hill and the houses lay forlorn and were soon demolished, removing part of the unique social history of the area. A few years later a small cairn was constructed by former residents near to the war memorial at the Hill with a proud farewell salutation emblazoned in white letters:

A memorial to Lethanhill, known simply as the Hill, by former villagers. This remains in place today, although opencast coal mining commenced in the area in 2011.
(Photo: Donald L Reid)

It is difficult to think of any other small community where 500 former residents would turn up at a single reunion ten years after their village had been abandoned and demolished. These were indeed caring people with a genuine love and passion for their old home, meeting to share many precious memories.

The year 1955, when everyone had left, was the end of an era that is still recalled with a happy smile by a dwindling number of former Hilltonians who remain grateful for their family life on the Hill. Strangely enough, although the villagers had left by 1955, the school remained open until 1959, with the children bussed up from the Doon Valley. The only house to remain occupied was that of the headmaster, Mr Donohoe, and his family, living a secluded life in the deserted village. For the Donohoes it must have been a rather strange experience, being the last villagers on the Hill (see Chapter 19).

Today, ongoing opencast mining around the Hill, which began in 2010, has changed the entire plateau at least for the time being. However, it will eventually be returned to more or less how it was once all the valuable coal is extracted. Only then will the ghosts of the past return to haunt what remains of Lethanhill, as evidenced by the cards, flowers and poignant messages remembering former villagers, lovingly laid near to ruins of former homes.

This once vibrant mining community, still fondly remembered by those few remaining Hilltonians and their families, is marked now only by the ruins of homes hidden in the plantation of trees, the Hill cairn and the war memorial. What would those who names appear on that lonely war memorial have made of it all?

Be it granted to me to behold you again in dying,
Hills of home! And to hear again the call;
Hear about the graves of the martyrs the peewees crying,
And hear no more at all.

The Whaups
Robert Louis Stevenson (1850-94)

Chapter 5

Benwhat and Corbie Craigs

Not but I hae a richer share
Than monie ithers;
But why should ae man better fare,
And a' men brithers?

Epistle to Dr Blacklock
Robert Burns

The reader is encouraged to seek out a fascinating little booklet entitled *Benwhat and Corbie Craigs: A Brief History* by Robert (Robin) Farrell. Published in 1983, it tells part of the story of the social history of Benwhat and Corbie Craigs. Sadly, Robin Farrell, who was a Benwhatonian, passed away in 2011.

Benwhat

Benwhat (the locally preferred spelling, rather than the Ordnance Survey's Benquhat) was probably the most exposed of Doon Valley's mining villages, lying on the 1,000-foot contour below Benwhat Hill (1,426 feet). From here you have a panoramic view of the Doon Valley and can see the majestic hills of grey Galloway and Goat Fell on Arran. Benwhat and its close neighbour Corbie Craigs, small villages on the high moorland above Waterside, were linked to the valley by the Corbie Craigs incline which, for the residents, became their shortest route down to Waterside. Corbie Craigs was probably the original Hill village or miners' row and consisted of only ten houses in a single row, built in 1847 to support the ironstone pits at Corbie Craigs. Remarkably, there were still people in residence in Corbies in the early 1950s.

It is interesting to note that in 1940, at a time when the country was short of a variety of raw materials because of the war, the Ministry of Supply in London carried out a survey of the area, and consideration was given to the reopening of shafts at Corbie Craigs to mine the estimated 29 million tons of ironstone reserves known to exist in the area.

Although Corbie Craigs may originally have been intended to be the centre of a large hillside mining community, its growth was stopped by the shift of interest to Lethanhill and Benwhat. The need to develop mines elsewhere on the high moorland led the Dalmellington Iron Company to build Benwhat, beginning in the early 1860s when a total of twenty houses were built in what became known as the Laigh Row. They were single apartments with a small jutting out scullery.

A school and a store were then built and two of the houses at the end of the Laigh Row were converted to provide a Miners' Institute where the men could socialise. The school at Benwhat had three classrooms, one of which had a glazed partition dividing the room into two. This facility allowed the room to be enlarged to cope with weddings and other social occasions in the village.

Benwhat store after the old school to its rear had been demolished. This photo was probably taken in the early 1940s. You can see some of the rows of houses and to the right high on Benwhat Hill can just be seen the war memorial, erected in 1921. Interestingly, the village brass band was formed in 1871.

The years between 1870 and 1874 proved to be a boom period for the Dalmellington Iron Company and a further 110 houses were built at Benwhat in four rows in one long line running towards Chalmerston Hill and 30 yards further up the hill from the original twenty houses of the Laigh Row. Between the two rows lay the gardens, most of which were of an excellent standard, producing potatoes and vegetables in abundance as well as flowers.

The first row of the extension was known as the Stone Row, constructed of stone from Dunaskin Quarry and not the regulation DICo brick from Waterside, like the other houses. This comprised twenty-eight houses of which most were single apartments with a scullery. There were three other rows constructed of Dunaskin brick and called the Middle Row (sometimes known as the Brick Row), which was directly opposite Benwhat's store. The Post Office Row contained a house with a post office facility at the beginning of the row. The final row was the Heath Row, so named presumably because it looked out onto the wild moorland below Benwhat and Benbranigan Hills.

Housing conditions

The houses at Benwhat were similar to others provided by the Dalmellington Iron Company. They were small and compact with little privacy. Some larger families were lucky to obtain two back-to-back houses and converted them into one house to make domestic conditions more tolerable. All the houses had low roofs and wooden floors in the bedrooms and kitchens. The floors of the entrance porches consisted of fireclay flagstones, manufactured, as was every other building material, in Dunaskin. The Company always endeavoured to be self-sufficient in providing building materials from their own local resources.

Originally there was no running water in the houses at Benwhat. The water came from street pumps, two provided in each row. However, there was a plentiful supply of gravitational water coming down from the springs on the hillside above the village. One spring, known as Campbell's Spout, still runs to this day and regular visitors, mainly older former residents and their families, walk along the remains of the rail beds from the Hill to Benwhat and drink the pure water before making the return journey to Patna, usually carrying bottles of the spring water for use at home. It is crystal-clear and thirst-quenching. Another water source was known as Squibbie's Well, a small pipe stuck into a moss hag banking below Benwhat Hill, through which water ran all the time.

All the toilets at Benwhat were of the outdoor dry type, apart from three which were indoor and originally intended for 'high heid yins'. Robert 'Bobby' Douglas, who lived there from 1944 until 1951, recalls that his family at No. 118 Benwhat in the Laigh Row had such a toilet, but they were considered to be fortunate. Electricity only arrived in the village in 1933 from the generating station built at Waterside in 1917–18, which was meant to power all facilities at the ill-fated School of Aerial Gunnery at Loch Doon (see Chapter 1).

The new school

The new village school was built in 1926 and Mrs Jeanie McCreath, whose memories are recorded elsewhere in this book (see Chapter 15), transferred from the old school to the new, together with other residents such as the late John Relly. The new school, still considered modern when it closed in 1952, was much bigger than the old one. It even had a fully equipped domestic science classroom. The school was busy, the teachers kindly and encouraging. The school is a reminder to visitors to the ghost village that real people inhabited this lonely, windswept moor and that they led a full and active life.

In 1951 when the village was on the edge of extinction with only eight families remaining, the school was described by Mrs Paterson, the village teacher, as being 'up-to-date in every way. It has a cookery room, gymnasium, woodcraft room and two fine staff rooms. If it only could be put on wheels and moved to Dalmellington what an advantage it would be.' However, it was unceremoniously demolished in 1953.

Playing field

On the Chalmerston side of the pre-1926 school is a large flat area of short grass, once well used as the village football pitch. This was a popular playground for the children of Benwhat and where its amateur team held its last formal match in 1951. The pitch was laid on the char hearth for Corbie Craigs No. 5 works. It was here that thin layers of ironstone and coal were spread out and slowly burned to get rid of the ironstone impurities, the purified ironstone being known as char. The remains of the school sit adjacent to the prominent ironstone bing of Corbie Craigs No. 4 pit.

Above: Benwhat School class of 1939 gather for a photograph around the time of the beginning of the Second World War. One can only imagine their hopes and aspirations mingled with fear growing up during a time of great uncertainty.
Back row (l to r): Tom Gardiner, Willie Filson, Andrew Armour, Sam Pyper, Richard Armour, Guy Deans and Andrew Galloway.
Second back row: Jeanie Thomson, Betty Bennett, Annie Stewart, Thora Bakkom, Moira Hill, Betty Gracie and Sadie McKinstry.
Second front row: Effie Douglas, Nellie Wilson, Ella Douglas, Anna McHattie (wearing a jersey which she had knitted herself. Anna is well known in Dalmellington and a tireless worker for the local Kirk) and Mary Coughtrie.
Front row: Andrew Wilson, Paul Relly, Adam McHattie, Sandy Robertson and Neil Hainey.
(Miss Anna McHattie collection)

Coal and ironstone mining

There were many ironstone pits on the 1,000-foot contour, but they were shallow and worked at different times: the lives of these pits were usually quite short because of problems with access to continuous seams and layers of ironstone being too thin to make working economic. The Benwhat coal miners worked mainly at Chalmerston, Pennyvenie, Bogton, Benbain and Beoch, although some also worked at Houldsworth, north of Patna. The Benwhat miners were hardy and thought nothing of walking 4 miles to work and back again at the end of a long, hard shift.

Above: Benwhat School class of 1949 when the village was quickly being depopulated with most moving to Dalmellington and the new housing scheme at Bellsbank.
Back row (7) l to r: Scott Hannah (Janitor), Mrs Campbell (cook), Andrene Campbell (daughter of Mrs Campbell, cook), Betty Brown (Corbie Craigs), Andrew Armour, Susan McLeish, Thomasina Hill.
Second back row (10): John Carruthers, Robert Douglas, John Kennedy, John McLean, John Johnstone, Billy McFadzean, David Rowan, Miss Paterson (teacher) and Mr Jeffrey (headmaster).
3rd back row: (10): Marion McCreath, Rebecca Ballantyne, John Buchanan, Flora McCulloch, Nancy Currie, Gertrude Auld, Jean Murphy, Susan Cairns, Mora Murphy and Robert Hearton.
Second front row (11): Elizabeth Wightman, Andrew Currie, Francis Kennedy, John Bennet, Tom Wightman, Alec Armour, Kathleen Moore, Billy Douglas, Gwen Millar, Jean McHattie and May Barbour.
Front row (8): Archie Galloway, Alec Ireland, ? Cairns, Bobby Galloway, Drew Galloway, Jim Murray, Jim Murphy and ? Cairns. The three Cairns pupils (one girl and two boys) were only briefly Benwhat residents and their first names are unknown.
(Photo: Robert Douglas collection)

Deserted village

The population of Benwhat in 1881 was 772, compared with Dalmellington (1,437), Waterside (1,681), Craigmark (383), Patna (603) and Lethanhill (1,690). In 1947 with the nationalisation of all coal mining after the war, the National Coal Board acquired all mining concerns, including ownership of the old Dalmellington Iron Company villages, which had operated since 1931 under the auspices of Bairds and Dalmellington.

It is impossible to escape from a certain feeling of sadness when confronted with the scene in 1951 of a dying village, then with only eight families remaining and three pupils still attending the school. By 1952 Benwhat was a ghost village and shortly thereafter, abandoned and forlorn, it was demolished and nature quickly hid the remains of the houses.

Meanwhile, over at Corbies in November 1951 there was only one young couple remaining, Mr and Mrs Joseph Thomson, whilst the other nine houses in the row were empty. This couple was just waiting to be allocated a house in the new Bellsbank Housing Scheme. So Corbies, too, was also about to lose its last residents. Times were indeed changing fast.

Kind herts were dwellin' there
An' bairnies fu' o' glee

Voices of the past
Visiting this deserted area today, it is difficult to find any substantial remains other than coal spoil heaps, the foundations of the rows of houses and part of the 'new' schoolhouse. However, the village war memorial is a permanent reminder that Benwhat was once a substantial village where its hardy men made the ultimate sacrifice in both world wars. Although opencast mining is still going on, the area is tranquil and invigorating and it is a good place to visit to get the very best views of the uplands of Galloway and a vista of Arran. In your imagination, if you listen carefully, you may just hear the voices of children playing football during a break at Benwhat School; see the women heading for their messages to the village store; hear others blethering as they put out a washing; listen to the magical sound of the village brass band playing a hymn tune prior to beginning their rehearsal in the school dining hall; and watch the miners contentedly walking from the rows ready for another hard shift at the nearby pits. Scenes like these, vanishing in the mists of time, are still fondly remembered in the hearts and minds of a diminishing band of former residents. Yes, Benwhat was a real community with talented, kindly folk who appreciated their gifts and gave much back in return.

Corbie Craigs

Corbie Craigs, a lonely deserted row of cottages, was constructed around 1850. Located high above a spur running off Dunaskin Glen, it overlooks the Rough Burn. It consisted of ten cottages and originally some of the workers operated the Corbies incline, which ran from the village down to Waterside and was used for bringing mining materials up and down. It was abandoned around 1952, but substantial ruins of the houses still remain, a tribute to folk who lived there.
(Photo: Donald L Reid)

Corbie Craigs sits precariously on the edge of Dunaskin Glen, some 875 feet above sea level, on the same slope as Benwhat, half a mile below. It is also close to Burnhead Farm, now in ruins. The row of houses was actually named after the steep-sided rocky glen which lay to its north and west, 'corbie' being the name for a large black crow, common in this area. These craigs are still very scenic with many waterfalls and their rocky outcrops constantly changing as the Burnhead burn from Benwhat Hill cuts its way through the hillside before becoming part of the Dunaskin Glen burn, eventually reaching Waterside and the River Doon.

Travelling up from Dalmellington, there is a small stone bridge over the Rough Burn and Corbie Craigs can be seen from there. Care should be taken on approaching the substantial ruins as the route passes over rough undulating ground. The Corbies, as it is better known locally, was built in 1847 by the Dalmellington Iron Company and it is perhaps somewhat of a misnomer to refer to it as a village, bearing in mind that it is only one row of ten small houses.

Robin Farrell in his book mentioned at the beginning of this chapter suggests that the row was originally established for the workers who maintained and operated the Corbie Craigs incline which runs from Corbies down to Waterside. This incline was used for bringing coal and ironstone to the furnaces at Waterside. In 1866, however, the Dalmellington Iron Company reorganised their railway network connecting their various pits on the Knockkippen Plateau and the Corbie Craigs incline was made redundant in favour of a more modern system – the Drumgrange incline – which ran from Lethanhill down to the north side of Waterside.

Villagers at Corbies had slightly better accommodation than their near neighbours at Benwhat, though they were closely linked in their isolation. The Corbies children attended Benwhat School and it was to this village that people would go for social and recreational activities. The only access to the Benwhat Road was by a small pathway, now overgrown. However, many of the folk from Corbies also regularly walked down the incline bordering Dunaskin Glen to Waterside, which of course had the Aladdin's cave, the central store of the Dalmellington Iron Company where just about anything could be purchased, such was the range and variety of its offerings.

It is likely that the Company intended to extend Corbies, but with the development of seams nearer to Benwhat and the Hill, it was decided not to proceed with further house building. It would be nice to think that one consideration was that Corbies was dangerously close to Dunaskin Glen with its steep rocky sides, not a suitable place for young children to be near. Interestingly, there were still folk living in this row of houses in the early 1950s.

What is certain is that without ironstone and coal mining Corbie Craigs and Benwhat (and the other lost mining villages of Doon Valley) would simply not have been built. There were at least six Corbie Craig pits in the immediate area of the row of houses, and three Drumgrange pits in operation between 1859 and 1919.

There were absolutely no amenities for the residents at Corbies and they had to travel to Benwhat to use the sparse facilities there or go to Dalmellington or Waterside. Cooking was carried out on an open range known as a Dover stove. Most houses also had a coal-fired boiler for heating water to wash. At its busiest, the row only housed about fifty inhabitants, but they did consider themselves completely independent from those living in Benwhat and Waterside.

Corbies folk

The ruins of Corbies are certainly the best preserved of any of the lost mining villages of Doon Valley, with the walls and framework still in remarkably good condition. This was considered by some to be the loneliest of the Dalmellington Iron Company villages, as well as the smallest. There are still several residents in Dalmellington today who will tell you proudly that they were raised at Corbies and not Benwhat. Well-known local folk who lived at Corbies over the years included Jimmy Brown, Pat McGuire, the Rileys, David Bradley, Willie McHendry, John 'Punt' Ferguson, John Hainey, Jimmy Lindsay, George McCart, Tommy Kirk and Jenny McGuire.

The 1861 Census shows that the following were living there: at house No. 1 Benjamin Dalziel, No. 2 John Campbell, No. 3 Janet Campbell and David Campbell (son), No. 4 John Kirk, No. 5 Thomas Gault, No. 6 John McGuire, No. 7 John Potter, No. 8 John Carmichael, No. 9 John Logan and No. 10 William Kirk. In the 1925 Census the changes were: No. 1 Adam McHattie, No. 3 Pat McGuire, No. 4 John McGrevy, No. 5 Fred Wilson, No. 6 James McKnight, No. 7 Peter McMurray, No. 8 Thomas Newall, No. 9 Henry Rice and No. 10 Alex Johnstone.

A visit to the substantial ruins of Corbies when the mist is rolling up from Dunaskin Glen does indeed create the aura of a ghost-like village. In the mind's eye the visitor may see the hardy miners heading off for a shift at Chalmerston; the women busy with household chores or chatting across the gardens; the children guddling for trout in the Rough Burns or searching out nests on the moorland. When the mist lifts they have all disappeared and all that remains are lonely ruins, marking a deserted village of happy memory to many.

But the visitor should remember that real, kindly folk lived here in this outpost of the Dalmellington Iron Company. The ruins retain their own secrets, but on a clear day the views of the Valley of Doon and Galloway from Corbies are simply spellbinding. A few of the residents in the Doon Valley are still very pleased to tell that their families were born and brought up in this proud little row of houses overlooking Dalmellington, known to all simply as the Corbies.

Guarded by many a grand old hill,
And many a diamond-sparkling rill,
Where River Doon, at her sweet will,
Flows gently on,
I see thee nestling calm and still,
Dalmellington.

Dalmellington
Matthew Anderson

Chapter 6

A typical scene of Craigmark which is now but a happy memory to the very oldest former residents. Most of the men from the village worked at Chalmerston and Pennyvenie as well as other pits in the area. Around 1924 the Dalmellington Iron Company began construction of modern rows of houses at Burnton and the residents of Craigmark over the next few years began to move to Burnton and Dalmellington. The road leading to Benwhat can be seen in the background.
(Photo: Courtesy of EAC Doon Valley Museum)

The ruins of the ten houses at Corbie Craigs, known locally as the Corbies. Behind can be seen Burnhead Farm, sadly now a ruin.
(Photo: Donald L Reid)

A lovely clear photo of 'Dear Auld Craigmark' so described by Billy Greig in his poem of this now lost mining village. The reader will be able to make out the outline of the road leading upwards to Benwhat on the plateau above. The first row was known as the Laigh (low) Row.
(Photo: Courtesy of EAC Doon Valley Museum)

Chapter 6

Auld Craigmark

I sing a song o' Auld Craigmark;
For Craigmark was oor hame.
Tho' times were hard, an' siller scarce,
We loved it jeest the same.

Dear Auld Craigmark
Billy Greig

The late Alex Johnstone of Dalmellington, a wonderful character and a member of the well-known Johnstone family of Craigmark and Dalmellington, produced in 1995 a short history of Craigmark, *Craigmark: 1800 to 1937*, which has proved a valuable source of information.

Named from a farm
This small village lay one mile due north of Dalmellington and within the parish of Dalmellington. The village took its name from the small farm of Craigmark, which in 1802 was occupied by George Gibson; in the 1841 Census the occupier was a shepherd, Mr Kennedy. The Census of 1851 reveals that the farm was then occupied by David Chalmers, his wife Mary and three children. This same David Chalmers was later reported as having the best garden in Craigmark.

Houses in the village
Apart from Corbie Craigs, which many would describe as a miners' row or clachan rather than a village, Craigmark was the smallest Dalmellington Iron Company village and reportedly the first to be completed. The village consisted of 100 single-end houses, mostly back-to-back (houses on each side of the row). The 1851 census records that of the 100 houses in Craigmark, 82 were occupied and 18 were empty, and at that time there were 459 residents in the village.

Craigmark consisted of six rows of houses. The Laigh Row was situated opposite Craigmark store, and these houses were back-to-back. The Single Rows consisted of three rows, some of which were back-to-back, and the Doublin Rows were two rows, with only one house at the end of each row being back-to-back.

Mining
Craigmark, like the other lost villages of Doon Valley, was created to house workers near to where pits were being sunk. In this case Sillyhole No. 1 pit was opened in 1845, with Nos. 4 and 5 opened in 1852, whilst No. 6 was opened in 1866. Meanwhile, in the same area there was further frantic work going on, with Minnivey No. 1 opened in 1848, whilst Nos. 2 and 3 were both opened in 1852. Craigmark No. 1 pit was driven in 1866, with Chalmerston Nos. 1, 2 and 3 opening around the same period.

In all, sixteen pits were opened between 1845 and 1866 in the Dalmellington end of the Doon Valley. These pits employed a large number of workers who had to be housed locally. Craigmark coal was of the very best quality and always in demand, as highlighted in the booklet, *Coal Mining in Scotland*, quoted by Alex Johnstone in his book:

Dalmellington Parish was full of fine coals. It was the cheapest and best in the west. Craigmark house coal held pride of place among British Coals until it was worked out in the 1950s.

The Company opened a provision store at Craigmark across the burn from the Laigh Row. The first store manager was Samuel Heron. Attached to the provision store was a beer store (or pub). Now called the Craigmark Inn, this building is still a pub/restaurant today. No doubt its walls could tell many stories!

Craigmark memories
Billy Greig, a wonderful character and lifelong member of Dalmellington Band where he played drums, is still fondly remembered by many folk in the Doon Valley. Writing many years ago, he recalled the Craigmark village store of his day with

affection and mentioned some of the friendly rivalry which existed.

Craigmark Store was a wonderland of merchandise, dealing in drapery, groceries and butcher meat – the lot! The back premises served as a public house. In those days the company (DICo) did not allow spirits to be sold, but the workers could buy beer and porter.

Above the store was the manager's house and at the end of the building was the company pay office where the workers would call to collect their weekly wages. Thursday was known as 'uplift day' when the women of Craigmark would go to the Provision Store and collect their weekly supply of goods, called messages. At the same time the men would enjoy a beer with fellow miners. There was a bit of friendly rivalry between the people of Craigmark and Dalmellington. The young folk used to shout this little jingle to try to upset us:

'Yonder lies Craigmark,
Wi' neither kirk nor steeple –
A water barrel at every door,
And damned impiddent people!'

Mind you, the good-hearted neighbourly Craigmark folks were not unduly upset by this slanderous jingle. Obviously it had originated in the rival township which, they claimed, was 'too big for a village and too small for a toon'. We used to say they were too big for their boots! I think they were just a wee bit jealous of our special little village, I suppose.

The houses at Craigmark were built of stone from Dunaskin Quarry and some may have been taken from the nearby Caldwells Glen at the side of the road leading to Benwhat. Like the other lost villages there were many large families. Craigmark houses consisted of one single room measuring 14 ft by 14 ft, with two built-in beds, a large open grate and the floors were of flat fireclay flagstones. Wash houses were provided with one for every half row and these were situated at the end or in the middle of the rows.

Local women had to come to an arrangement about days and times for using the wash house. Initially there were no toilet facilities provided, but these were later added along with outside coal houses and were built adjacent to the wash houses. Anyone requiring the toilet during the night had to walk outside irrespective of the weather, but this was seen as a big improvement on the prevailing situation which involved using bed pans or pails which were emptied each day in the nearby midden.

It can be said that this same situation was generally the norm in most of the lost mining villages of Doon Valley.

Craigmark Burntonians, the local junior team in Dalmellington, who originally played in a park at Burnton with many of the original players being from Craigmark. This was taken in 1949.
Back row (l to r): J Murphy, A McGinn, R Thomson, Alan Dick, H Logie, T Mathieson, J Gill, J Blain.
Front row: F McCourt, J Milby, J Rees, W Ferguson, W Stewart, T Leitch.
(Photo: Courtesy of EAC Doon Valley Museum)

Education

Education was seen as being important for the children of miners. The Dalmellington Iron Company provided a school, built midway between Sillyhole Farm and Craigmark near to where the road rises steeply towards Burnton. This building still exists today and over the years operated as a social club, but the building is currently not in use.

It is recorded that the first schoolmaster at Craigmark was a Mr Kidd. He was supported by only one other teacher and everyone was taught in composite classes. There were no toilets provided in the school, but a toilet block was located near to the adjacent burn with one compartment for the boys and the other for the girls. The school operated very successfully until 1926/27 when all the children had to go to Dalmellington School and that left the school building empty.

The Institute

The people of Craigmark and Dalmellington formed a committee and with the permission of the Dalmellington Iron Company turned the old school into a Workmen's Institute for recreational purposes. The 'wee end' had two billiards tables and the 'big end' had carpet bowls and table games. No gambling was allowed. The 'big end' was used for weddings and social functions, as had been the case when the school occupied the premises. All mine workers from Craigmark and Burnton in the local pits had twopence per week deducted from their pay to finance the upkeep of the Institute.

Planned house building was taking place in Dalmellington behind Broomknowe Houses between 1935 and 1938. All the Craigmark families had been rehoused in just over two years and the former village was demolished. The only building to survive was the Craigmark store, still in use today as a public house and restaurant, appropriately called 'Craigmark'. Prominently displayed in this building is a painting of the village by the talented Billy Greig.

Most of the villagers were rehoused in Dalmellington's Park Crescent and Hopes Avenue, whilst others went to Burnton, adjacent to Craigmark. The new streets were named after two diligent local councillors – George Park of Craigmark and James Hopes of Dalmellington.

The 1921 strike

During the famous miners' strikes of 1921 and 1926 the women of Craigmark ran a soup kitchen because families were really in difficult circumstances. The children always had priority when it came to supplying meals and in some ways working together in adversity helped to further bond an already close-knit community. One of the wash houses in the single rows would be washed and scrubbed out and all the food would be prepared there. The children were delighted to be fed and, weather permitting, would enjoy sitting out on the green with their soup and bread, whilst in the evening they would have tea with bread and jam. No one ever went hungry, but times were hard. It must have been very worrying for parents trying to feed families during these difficult strikes when no money was coming in. During the strikes, the men would be digging for coal from the many outcrops in the glen above Craigmark. Children were not allowed to go near these places because they were extremely dangerous, even for experienced miners. If any miner was unfit to dig for coal himself, the black gold mysteriously appeared in his coal bunker. No questions were asked, the coal just appeared.

A tragedy

During the 1921 strike, some girls aged thirteen and fourteen years ventured into Caldwells Glen and went into a tunnel left by the miners. The girls started digging out some coal, thinking they would be helping their parents. Meanwhile the whole embankment slipped and trapped two of the girls. Someone further up the glen, also digging for coal, saw the incident and alerted the Craigmark miners and everyone joined in digging with their bare hands until the two girls were recovered. Sadly, one of the girls, Mary Hastie, was dead. The other girl, from the Calderwood family, was shocked but otherwise uninjured. Alex Johnstone, just a wee boy at the time, recalled the event:

> *I wasn't quite six at the time, but I will never forget the sight of the men carrying the small body through the village to her house at No. 3 in Laigh Row. All her clothes, her face and her fair hair were matted with yellow clay.*
>
> *Some of these hardy miners were crying too, tears running down their blackened faces. This was a hard blow to this lovely family, greatly respected in the village. Money was very scarce during the strike and funerals cost money. Like many other children in the village Mary Hastie belonged to the Rechabites, so Mr Matthew Wilson who ran this organisation arranged all of the funeral.*
>
> *Matthew Wilson stayed at No. 19 and he was one of nature's gentlemen, a wonderful Christian man, greatly respected by everyone in Craigmark and the surrounding villages. If something had to be done, he would do it without any fuss.*
>
> *Families in such devastating circumstances were never*

alone in their grief, the whole village would be on hand to give every assistance. There were many tragic events when men were brought home from the pits badly injured. Unfortunately there were fatalities, too, the very nature of the work made these occasions all too frequent.

Village life

Life for the children of Craigmark was said to be very happy. They could play anywhere without fear and all a parent had to do was call them and they would eventually appear, word of the summons being spread by other youngsters. In the summer it was not unusual to see women out in the rows playing at skipping or peevers with the girls. The men would play football with the boys. It was the way of things then simply to join in, but that would seem rather strange today.

The men would be up at the Herd's House or on the quoiting green or playing pitch and toss at Doublin Corner. Children always had plenty to do and the word 'bored' had still to be invented. Games all had their season. Spring was the time for moor burning, and boys would come home at night smelling of grass reek. Summer time was for guddling for trout in the burn, swimming in the bigger pools and flying dragons (kites) or bird-nesting. This would be done in bare feet.

Autumn was always a time for playing marbles and even some of the men would take part, playing 'Big Ringie' at the Coal Houses at Doublin. Winter had all the games suitable for dark nights. The frost would see children playing at slides which ran from Hose's Corner to the bottom of the Laigh Row. Of course at that time television had not been heard of and the wireless (radio) was in its very early stages of development. Sanny Rankin, the Store Manager at Craigmark, had a crystal wireless set, but by the standards of today this would be of extremely poor quality. However, it did create great local interest and it was fascinating for boys to hear voices coming from the speaker. Suffice to say that life was never dull for the young folk at Craigmark.

Music

Music was something most miners loved, especially brass bands, a tradition in mining communities. In Craigmark the McLelland and Boyle families were brass players. John Boyle (senior) was for a time the conductor of Dunaskin Band. James Telfer was a brilliant violinist and his brother Robert 'Beefy' was a good cornet player, and for a time he was bandmaster of Dalmellington Band. He later emigrated to Australia with his family.

Billy Greig. A talented man as an artist and musician and possessed of a wonderful sense of humour, he will forever have a special place in the annals of auld Craigmark. He was born in Craigmark on 17 June 1903 and died on 26 November 1986 in Ballochmyle Hospital.

Billy Greig, a talented man and larger-than-life character, and Jimmy Torbet were drummers in Dalmellington Band. Many of Billy Greig's paintings of local scenes around Craigmark found their way to homes of former residents all over the world. Billy was also the local barber in the village and was good at just about everything he turned his hand to. A large painting of Auld Craigmark by Billy still hangs in the Craigmark store (Inn) to this day.

Hugh Johnstone MBE

Another Craigmark man, who subsequently made his special mark on the world of brass banding, was Hugh Johnstone MBE. Hugh is one of those wonderful characters who possess boundless energy, talent, skill and professionalism. He was born at 61 Craigmark and moved to Burnton when he was about six years of age.

As a teenager he joined the ranks of the Dalmellington Band and that became a commitment for life. Hugh conducted the band when they became Scottish Champions in 1969 and again in 1976. He worked in the coal mines for many years, later taking up an appointment as a teacher of brass to young people at Auchinleck Academy. A legendary character who has tutored many brass players who later made their mark in major brass bands and orchestras, his commitment to brass banding in Scotland is unlikely ever to be equalled, let alone surpassed.

Hugh Johnstone MBE whose extensive knowledge of the Doon Valley is a great benefit to those carrying out local research. He is indeed the giant original man of Dalmellington (via Craigmark!) and his contribution to the civic life of the community and especially to Dalmellington Band is immense. Many fine musicians, including famous Scottish composer James McMillan, have benefited from Hugh's guiding musical skills.
(Photo: Donald L Reid)

His commitment to the Dalmellington Band is admired by all who know him. He is still (2012) at the age of eighty-seven a tireless worker for the Scottish Amateur Band Association and his services to brass banding in Scotland resulted in him being awarded the MBE. Hugh recalls sad and happy times at Craigmark.

I was born at Craigmark on 1 April 1925, second youngest in a family of twelve. My early lasting memory is of my eldest sister Kate emigrating to the New World of Hamilton, Ontario, Canada in 1928. Everyone in the village turned out to see her leave. She travelled by cargo passenger ship from Glasgow to Montreal and then by train to Hamilton. Thirty-two days later a letter arrived at Craigmark to say that she had arrived safely. She married in Canada and had two children.

By 1931 hard times had come with the Depression and later that year my mother received a letter from Kate in which she said that if there was a bridge over the ocean she would walk every day with the children to get back to Craigmark. My parents managed to borrow some money from the Coal Company which would be repaid off my father's and older brother's wages and they managed to get Kate and husband Bob and the two children back home. Back here they were housed in the Beoch Rows and Bob got a job as a surfaceman at Beoch Colliery.

In 1932 Kate died in childbirth. Pleasant memories of Craigmark include summer days that seemed endless, with picnics up West Chalmerston Glen or to Dalcairney Lynn. In autumn we picked raspberries along the railway line bank at Minnivey farm and crab apples in the glen near Laigh Farm. As children we could spend a penny on a Friday in Rosie Telfer's wee shop where toffee apples were on sale all year round. In summer an added treat was Bob McTier coming round the rows with Bertellotti's ice cream cart pulled by a small pony from the café in Dalmellington Square.

In winter the frozen path in the gully between the Single and Doublin Rows provided an ideal venue for all sliding games. As boys it was wonderful to sit on our hunkers at Meechan's corner listening intently to Tam Hastie, who lived at No. 3 Craigmark, with his endless tales of village life and his worldwide travels. We would be in awe listening to stories of gold mining in South Africa and his adventures with Buffalo Bill Cody across the American Wild West. In reality, of course, it never happened, but as youngsters we were captivated by the convincing charm as Tam told us his tall stories.

In these days the women of the house were great knitters, and a birthday or Christmas present was simple, useful and welcomed, unlike the modern hysteria of consumerism. You would get a pair of socks or a jersey, practical and needful and very gratefully received, too.

A highlight every year was the Sunday School outing. The whole village turned out for it and it was usually held in a field in the surrounding area and on alternate years all the children of Dalmellington and Craigmark would go by train to Ayr to spend time at the Low Green. We were led by Dalmellington Silver Band and these excursions for young folk created an ever-lasting memento of enjoyment to young and old alike.

Sillyhole Smiddy

Halfway between Sillyhole Farm and Craigmark School was a blacksmith's shop, known as Sillyhole Smiddy. The origins of its location may be linked to the original pack road into Dalmellington which came over Kilmein Hill, past Burnhead Farm (now in ruins), down the Hare Craig, past Craigmark Farm and into Dalmellington. A blacksmith's shop would have been conveniently located here for travellers on this ancient route to Irvine.

Midwife

All the mining villages had their own midwife, who usually was not professionally qualified, but a trusted local woman of experience, having attended and supervised many births. In Craigmark this honour fell to Mrs Buchanan from No. 47 in the Single Rows. This old lady must have brought many children into the world and must have been very proud to see families grow over the years, knowing that she helped bring them into the world. By 1938 villagers had all moved to Dalmellington and Dear Auld Craigmark was demolished. All that remains today is the old store, now the Craigmark Inn, and the foundations of a few of the former rows.

The well-known Johnstone family of Dalmellington. This was the golden wedding of William and Mary Johnstone (centre front).
Back row (l to r): Addie Johnstone, Jimmy Johnstone, Janet Johnstone (Mrs McConnachie), and Alex Johnstone (formerly Councillor in Dalmellington).
Middle row: Quintin Johnstone (emigrated to Canada), John Johnstone, Andrew Johnstone and Hugh Johnstone (Dalmellington Band conductor awarded MBE for services to brass banding in Scotland).
Front row: William Johnstone (police officer in Manchester), Mrs Mary Johnstone, Mr William Johnstone and Mary Johnstone (Mrs Wilson).
(Photo: courtesy of Hugh Johnstone MBE)

Dear Auld Craigmark to you and me,
The sweetest spot on earth.
Remember now the sunny days –
Forget the strife and trouble.
As wistfully you stan' an' gaze,
On heaps o' dust and rubble.

                        Dear Auld Craigmark
                        Billy Greig

Chapter 7

Death Knell for Deep Mining

I remember well, those scars of blue,
That covered my Granddad's hands.
Hands that were gnarled and wrinkled,
The hands of a working man.
Many a man bears the scars,
From the work they had to do,
But only the working miner's hands,
Have the scars forever blue.

Scars
Ian Winstanley

A difficult and dangerous occupation

Coal mining is a dangerous occupation wherever it is carried out and no matter how stringent the safety rules. One only has to look back to 1950 when the country was holding its breath and praying fervently as 129 miners were trapped in the Knockshinnoch Mine at New Cumnock. Amazingly, 116 were rescued in dramatic fashion, whilst tragically 13 men lost their lives.

More than half a century later it is a commonly held view, especially in former mining communities, that Prime Minister Margaret Thatcher's Plan for Coal destroyed the industry across the nation. Jobs were lost and entire communities were rocked to their very foundations as coal mines closed and populations began to dwindle, close family ties being cut, as families moved away in search of work. However, what could not be so easily destroyed was that spirit of caring that marked out mining communities.

Deep mining in the UK was seen as being increasingly expensive when compared to cheaper imports from South Africa and Australia, where opencast operations won coal at a fraction of the cost. This, too, was later to be proved true in Cumnock and Doon Valley. With conflict between the National Union of Mineworkers and the Thatcher-led Tory government in 1984–85, the writing was on the wall for deep mining in Scotland and the UK. It was indeed the beginning of the end with pit closures rolling in quickly like the unstoppable tide.

Memorial to the miners of the Doon Valley located to the lower front of the war memorial. It was unveiled on Sunday 31 March 1996, which was the last day of Cumnock and Doon Valley District Council before it became East Ayrshire Council. Councillor Eric Ross, the Convenor of the Council, carried out his last official duty that day.
(Photo: Courtesy of EAC Doon Valley Museum)

The man operating the boring machine is Hugh Uriarte, the nearest man is Alex Millar, and the furthest away miner Jock Kennedy.
(Photo: Courtesy of EAC Doon Valley Museum)

One of the things that depressed many folk in the 1980s in Britain was that society seemed to be so divided. Because of the miners' strike and the Falklands War of 1982, people either really didn't like Thatcher at all, or they really loved her, marking her down as one of the truly great British prime ministers. She was something of an enigma – loved and hated in equal measure. Her legacy will certainly show her strengths and leadership skills, but mining communities across the UK will doubtless still have little time for her because of her role in the demise of deep mining in the UK.

The great strike has been over for more than a quarter of a century, but certain memories – as rock-hard as the coal itself – endure. In Ayrshire and other mining communities, a few of the men and their families who endured the hardships of a strike that lasted from 5 March 1984 for one difficult year, regrettably cannot bring themselves to forgive those who 'scabbed' – crossed the picket lines and continued to work. It should also be remembered that those who worked on had their own reasons for doing so and they were primarily linked to supporting their families and perhaps having the foresight to know that a prolonged strike would hasten pit closure. Indeed, they were proved right.

However, it was certainly true that the strikes in the mines in the 1984–85 period heralded the death knell for deep mining in the UK. The Ayrshire miners of Barony and Killoch were a proud and determined lot and with cast-iron support for the strike from family and friends, they were prepared for a long stoppage, perhaps hoping that it would end quickly in victory. But victory is not a word that can be used on either side of that momentous dispute.

These were difficult times with real financial consequences for many families. Inevitably there was conflict between the strikers and those who chose to work on – so-called scabs – and sadly the remnants of that schism still live on to this day in the Cumnock and Auchinleck communities.

From personal experience, I recall the typical scenes of conflict vividly. At that time I was a police inspector in charge of contingents of men who carried out policing operations at Barony Colliery, where large numbers of pickets endeavoured to stop non-striking miners and lorries loaded with coal entering and leaving the pit. It was a difficult period for strikers and working miners and their families, of that there can be no doubt.

Miners' remember

Here are a few of the views expressed at the time by miners involved, giving a brief insight into the impact on them and families of the strike.

> 'We need to keep fighting. Don't forget, we have gained more than we lost – friendship and pride.'
> 'I took my seven-year-old son to the doctor, who said he was suffering from anxiety. He was worried about me because I was on strike.'
> 'My attitude has changed. I thought I was a socialist all my life, but now I know what socialism really is. It's a whole way of life and we're living it now during this strike.'
> 'You're not allowed to stop the lorries. The police won't allow

peaceful picketing and that aggravates the men.'
'I lived through the '72 and '74 strikes, but it was a picnic compared to this strike.'
'We were fighting for our jobs, our children and our communities. It was a hard few months, but I'm proud of it.'

Pennyvenie closes

The following is an excerpt from the *Ayr Advertiser* of July 1978 highlighting the closure of the last pit in the Doon Valley, pre-dating the 1984 strike by six years. Whilst there were no coal pits operating in the Doon Valley at that time, many of the Doon Valley miners worked at Barony and Killoch.

Thursday, July 6th 1978 was an historic and in many ways a sad day for Dalmellington and the Doon Valley. It marked the end of an era with the closure of the last pit in the area, Pennyvenie Colliery. With the setting up of the Dalmellington Iron Company in the early 1840s coal has been produced commercially throughout the valley for upwards of 130 years.

The closure of Pennyvenie in July 1978 meant 450 job losses in an area already severely hit economically and socially by earlier pit closures. In 1960, thirteen years after nationalisation, some 2,500 men were employed in the industry throughout the Doon Valley. Nowadays (2012) there are none, except for a few who work on the Chalmerston and Benbain opencast sites, where huge machines have been substituted for manual labour.

Pit families

Pennyvenie was a colliery employing whole families over many years. Family names with long service include Calderwood, Dempsey, Kennedy, Paterson, Semple, Reid and Wallace. A proud tradition of deep mining in the Doon Valley had come to an end, but it has to be said that many miners were rather relieved that their own sons would no longer have to work in the small, dark, damp and dangerous bowels of the earth. Ironically, within a further twenty years there would be no deep mines left anywhere in Scotland. The closure programme had indeed been an unstoppable tide of change and the view of many is that strikes simply hastened the end.

At the pithead. The first chap is greasing a locomotive used to haul hutches underground. A large number of skills are required to ensure safe operation in any colliery.
(Photo: Courtesy of EAC Doon Valley Museum)

End of Ayrshire deep mining

Killoch was closed in 1986, only one year after the strike ended. Not far from the Doon Valley, the Barony Pit near Auchinleck had been originally sunk in 1907, enlarged by Bairds and Dalmellington in 1938, and further developed by the NCB after 1950, with a new shaft 2,052 feet deep sunk. It, too, suffered economic problems and was finally shut down in 1989, when it had the honour of being the last NCB pit in Ayrshire.

A further twist of irony is that today (2012) more coal is being extracted from the Doon Valley than there ever was in the days of deep mining. Opencast mining began in the Doon Valley a few years after the closure of Pennyvenie. A railhead was developed at Minnivey and two trainloads of coal were removed almost every day, to the sorting facility at Killoch. Rail coal movements to Minnivey ceased, perhaps temporarily, in 2011.

It was common to look up towards Benbeoch Craig from Dalmellington and see towering industrial haulage vehicles wending their way over the hill delivering coal to the Chalmerston loading point for removal by rail. The miners of the early 20th century would simply be staggered to see how coal is won in the second decade of the 21st century.

Surface mining methods produce view-changing mountains of earth, removing all the coal and eventually backfilling the area, returning the hillsides to their former natural glory. After each opencast site is complete it would be difficult to comprehend that large-scale mining had actually taken place – in many ways an ideal scenario and a tribute to modern surface mining methods.

With the end of deep mining in Ayrshire in 1989, no other miners would be killed or maimed in the old-style deep mining – all too often the price of winning coal. However, tragedies still occur in surface mining with fatalities still part of the cost of gaining coal.

Winds of change

Now, with its deep coal mines gone and opencast in terminal decline, a new model of power generation looms ominously upon the horizon of the Doon Valley, and the local community does not like it. The next few years will reveal if they have been successful in fighting off the winds of change, as industrial windfarms, which already scar much of Scotland's countryside, present a real threat to scenic Doon Valley. One can only hope that the people are successful, but can they stem the tide of change?

They brought him up the pit shaft,
And took him out of the cage.
His face was covered with coal dust,
They could not tell his age.

In fact, he was a young lad,
On his first day down the pit,

He did not hear the noises
Just before the pit prop split.

Down came the roof and crushed him,
Against the stone hard floor,
Squeezing out a young life,
That would run and laugh no more.

Who would tell his mother?
Who would tell his dad?
That the coal had claimed another
And this one just a lad.

The Lad
Ian Winstanley

Aboveleft: John Kennedy of Dalmellington was manager of Beoch Mine and Pennyvenie. His father, also John Kennedy, was under-manager at No. 2 Pennyvenie for thirty-four years. His brother, Ben, was also under-manager from 1954 to 1968, highlighting why Pennyvenie was known as 'the family colliery,' employing whole families over the years. This photo was taken in 1978 at the time of the closure of the pit.
(Photo: Courtesy of EAC Doon Valley Museum)

Above right: Bobby Jackson, blacksmith at Pennyvenie working away. The blacksmith produced a variety of metal accessories for use in the coal mines and they were very skilled in their trade.
(Photo: Courtesy of EAC Doon Valley Museum)

Chapter 8

Bygone Lethanhill

James McFadzean

*For a' that, an a' that,
Our toils obscure, an a' that,
The rank is but the guinea's stamp,
The man's the gowd for a' that*

A Man's a Man for A' That
Robert Burns

James McFadzean
(Photo: Donald L Reid)

Donald L Reid interviewed James McFadzean at his home in Rankinston in 2003. He kindly shared his memories of life at lonely Lethanhill where he was born and spent his formative years. He passed away in February 2007 aged ninety-three.

My family

I was born at 57 White Brick Row, Lethanhill on 27 January 1914. It was the year when the whole world seemed to go mad, with the outbreak of the Great War. My father, who was also called James, was a miner at Houldsworth Pit which had opened in 1900 and he worked there all his days. He died on 1 August 1941 during the Second World War.

My mother, Elizabeth Adams, had me baptised by the Minister of Waterside and Lethanhill church, the Reverend William Gracie, on 11 October 1914. I had four sisters, Lizzie, Agnes, Annie and Sadie. Lizzie and Agnes went into farm service when about fourteen years of age. Agnes went to Carnachon Farm, Patna and Lizzie went to Dormaston Farm, Trabboch. Perhaps not surprisingly, they both subsequently married men from the rural community.

Sister Annie had polio when young and was left with a bad leg, so she wore a caliper. She worked for quite a time in service to the Minister at Waterside, the Reverend Anderson. Sadie was the youngest and worked in Ayr for a baker and later worked at Seafield Hospital doing domestic work. The only one surviving today is Sadie. I was the second youngest in the family.

Lost villages

My mother originally belonged to Tongue Row. This was a row of houses on the (B730) road from Rankinston to Kerse, about half a mile from Kerse at the side of the road. Neither Kerse nor Tongue Row nor indeed nearby Cairntable survive, all long gone now, but they were lovely wee places when I was young and everyone was working. The old school with schoolmaster's house at Kerse, which the local children all attended, still stands, although it's really in a very sorry state. However, it's many years since it was operated as a school.

So, Tongue Row, Cairntable and Kerse are all really lost villages with a wonderful past because they were full of characters that faced life at the sharp end with great fortitude. None of these places had anything but very basic facilities that folk today take for granted. But I suppose it was just what they were used to and they wouldn't be any the wiser as there were no TVs in those days. All the folk around them were in the same position.

My family moved from the Hill in 1946 and my mother died a year later in Ayr. She was a great woman and looked after our family very well indeed at the Hill and I can tell you that things weren't easy for her, but she simply got on with doing the very best she could. We were lucky to have such a great lady. Even now as an old man, I remember her with great fondness.

Electricity arrives at the Hill

I can remember one great occasion living at the Hill. That was in 1927 when I was thirteen years of age. The Dalmellington Iron Company (DICo) put electricity into the houses. It was just great to have lamps in the street. I remember the men who put them in. There was John Robertson, another was 'Ooie' Thomson, who belonged to Waterside and the third was John Nixon.

This was a great thing for everyone because before that we had no street lights and the lights we had indoors were paraffin lamps which were smelly and bad on the eyes. The men put one lamp at each end of the rows and this became a gathering point for local folk at night.

Mind you, this put a shilling a week on the rent and that didn't please my parents. I remember the date well because it coincided with our move from the old school at Lethanhill to a new school which was built up nearer the war memorial.

Step Row, Lethanhill looking towards the ruins of the old school *circa* 1960.
(Photo: Courtesy of EAC Doon Valley Museum)

Living conditions at the Hill

Living conditions at the Hill in those earlier years, and I remember them clearly, were poor. No other word can describe it. Families had to go out into the street to fill pails from the street pumps and carry them home and then had to boil the water for washing using the coal boiler. Everyone was the same as there was no running water in any of the houses in those early years. The cooking was done on the range stove or over the open fire. It was amazing the wonderful food that mother could produce and her baking was memorable. I can smell the scones and girdle scones as we speak. Mmmhh! She was a real gem and I was so fortunate!

Company store

My mother had to get all our provisions from the DICo. When I was a boy all the provisions for the Hill were brought up the Drumgrange incline from Waterside, loaded onto the pugs (small steam engines) which took them to the Hill store and then on along the railway line to supply Benwhat store. That will seem strange to folk today, but that was just how things were done. The incline was a great system when you think about it. All in all an amazing feat of engineering.

Rail network on the Hill

At that time Benbranigan Pit was still working and many of the men from the Hill and Benwhat worked there. The railway on the Hill was crucial for getting supplies to folk as well as for moving the coal and ironstone. Later on vans came up to the Hill from other suppliers such as the Co-op in Patna.

As I recall the rail network on the Hill was lifted about 1929 although lower down the railway lines still ran to Houldsworth Pit where many of the men worked. The Drumgrange incline still operated for several years after that, probably finishing in the early 1930s.

I remember that Alex Beattie was one of the engine drivers and Jimmy Stevenson and John Campbell were fireman and guard in my schooldays. They also operated the incline which ran from the Hill down to the north side of Waterside.

Lethanhill School in 1956. The entire population of Lethanhill and Burnfoothill, known simply as 'the Hill', had been removed to Patna and Dalmellington by 1955, but strangely enough the school remained open and the pupils were bussed there until 1959. Little sign of the village remains today except the lonely war memorial, and trees cover the area where the rows formerly stood.
Back row:
Billy Bryden, Jim Guthrie, Billy Brown, M Auld, Margaret Mulholland, Madge Bain, Charlotte McClymont, Ann Robertson, ?, Margaret McDermont, May McHattie, J Givens, Agnes Knox, Elizabeth Laughlan, John McLeod, Alex Kirk and Francie Bryce.
Second back row: Andrew Brown, Irene Gillespie, Elizabeth Murray, Margaret Johnstone, Mary Muir, Jean Grant, Mamie McCormack, Rita Wylie, Christine Coughtrie, Margaret Ferguson, Margaret Gillespie, Jessie Wilson, Ann Graham, Marjorie Fawcett, Helen Mitchell, William Walker and W Campbell.
Second front row: John Dunn, William Bryce, Betty Orr, Betty McCubbin, B Brown, S Ballantyne, Jean Findlater, Ella Knox, Helen Boyle, Mary McDougall, Jessie McLeod, Nancy Brolley, Janice Bradford, Marion Bryden, A McDougall, Agnes Fyvie, Annie Ferguson, Jim Stevenson, James Whiteford and James Spiers.
Front row: Billy McDermont, Jim Milligan, Tom Chalmers, Ian Wallace, Alistair Muir, J Lafferty, Alex Anderson, A Patterson, Wallace Lapslay, Robert McDermont, Andrew Currie, John Findlay, J McQuillan, Alec McCulloch and Joe Tinman.
(Photo: Courtesy of EAC Doon Valley Museum)

Opposite right: Lethanhill School in 1904 with headmaster David Vallance wearing a bowler hat. The children may perhaps be involved in some sort of entertainment or dance routine. Unfortunately, the names of the pupils have not been recorded but their descendants will doubtless still be living in the Doon Valley.
(Photo: Courtesy of EAC Doon Valley Museum)

School on the Hill

One teacher at Lethanhill School I can remember was Miss Ward. She belonged to Orkney. She took lodgings at the Hill and was very much involved in the life of the community. In fact she married Tommy Allan. Tommy was the manager of Pennyvenie Pit in those days, but belonged to the Hill. There was also Miss Joanne Campbell. She belonged to Wick. She married Malcolm Ross, who was a Hill man who also trained and became a teacher. There was a Miss Doull. She came from up north too. I can mind them all fine.

Mining

When I started work in 1928 at Pennyvenie No. 4 my mother got me up in the morning and made the fire, boiled the kettle on the open fire and made my breakfast then made my piece (sandwiches) and saw me out to work. All the women on the Hill did this duty for their husbands and sons – it was just how things were done in those days. They knew that working down a pit was dangerous and demanding work and they wanted to make sure that every man was well prepared.

Down the incline

I would then walk across to the drumhead and down the Drumgrange incline to Waterside. There was a pug (steam locomotive) waiting there with five wagons which took the miners from the Hill, Patna and Waterside along the line to Pennyvenie. On arrival there was a small surface hutch (small wagon) mineral line which connected up Clawfin Nos. 1 and 2, Benbain and Beoch.

The men had to walk from No. 4 Pennyvenie to Clawfin. There was what they called 'an endless haulage' to Beoch. Hutches went one way and the full ones came the other way. Men could use the endless haulage to travel in between Pennyvenie and Beoch. They simply sat down in the empty hutches for the journey. That's how things were done in my days at the pit and there was no such thing as health and safety. By and large we managed fine and watched out for one another.

Happy man

In 1937 I got a job at Houldsworth, working down the mine. I was there for nine years. I then worked in Berbeth Mine at Coalhall for about five years and then when it closed I transferred to Littlemill Pit between Rankinston and Cairntable. I worked there until I retired in 1974. I would say I have been very fortunate in my long life and looking back I don't think I would have wanted to change much. I was very happy with my lot in life and if you can say that, I think you are saying quite a lot, especially as the world is so complex and, at times, very cruel for many folk.

Fare-thee-weel, thou first and fairest!
Fare-thee-weel, thou best and dearest!
Thine be ilka joy and treasure,
Peace, Enjoyment, Love and Pleasure!

Ae Fond Kiss
Robert Burns

Norman Eric Kirk, a descendant of a Lethanhill miner, made his indelible mark in New Zealand. John Kirk, his great-grandfather, came to Lethanhill in the earliest years of the Dalmellington Iron Company and worked in various ironstone mines. Then in 1868 he left his home at 58 White Brick Row, Lethanhill, and took his family to a new life in New Zealand, when his youngest son, George, was only six weeks old. Fifty-five years later George Kirk's grandson, Norman, was born on 6 January 1923 and went on to become 29th Prime Minister of New Zealand until his untimely death on 31 August 1974. He was the fourth Labour Prime Minister of New Zealand, but the first to be born in New Zealand. He was described as 'eloquent in speech, devastating in criticism, a humanitarian with wide horizons, a man of the people writ large'. Interestingly, Norman Kirk visited the Doon Valley in 1968 hoping to trace family connections. Tom White, Dalmellington District Clerk, was able to put him in touch with two members of the Kirk family, Mrs Mary Logan and her sister, Mrs Isabella Ballantyne.

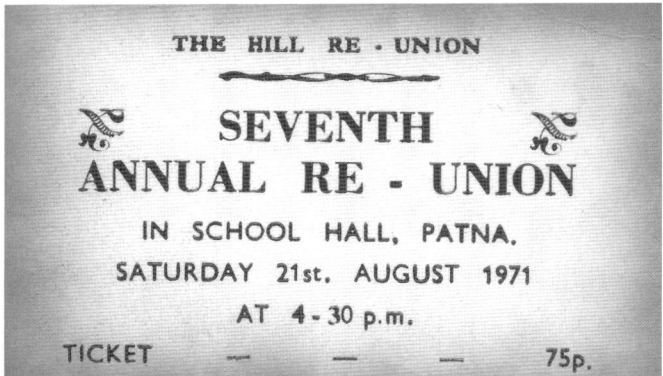

A ticket for the 7th Hill reunion on 21 August 1971.

Chapter 9

Benwhat – Random Reflections

James 'Jimsy' McPhail

These were the folk before us,
Be proud of them, be proud;
These Scottish folk who bred us
We sing their praises loud.

Arthur W Wilson (1963)

James 'Jimsy' McPhail, then in his eightieth year, was interviewed by Donald L Reid in 2003. Sadly, Jimsy died in 2011 after a short illness. He was raised in Benwhat in a family of ten, not by any means uncommon in the lost villages. He worked in the mines locally all his working life. A lifelong and very committed member of Dalmellington Band, he served more than sixty-eight years as a player and was a playing member of the band when they became champions of Scotland in 1969 and 1976.

All his life he was a staunch supporter of this wonderful band. Indeed, for many the band is synonymous with the village from which it takes its name. Jimsy was a popular man about Dalmellington and he would be rather pleased that his random thoughts, going back to 1929 when he attended Benwhat School, are a lasting legacy to be enjoyed by those who follow in his footsteps.

Remote Benwhat

I lived at Benwhat with my parents and their eight children in conditions which by standards of today were very, very poor, but I know that we were a happy lot, despite the hardship of living in such a remote place. With ten folk in a small house of two ends there was no privacy. In my family there was Chrissy, Robert, Catherine, John, Elizabeth, myself, Helen and Calum. My father was Malcolm and my mother Catherine.

Benwhat School *circa* 1910. There is a small boy in the group with crutches.
(Photo: Courtesy of EAC Doon Valley Museum)

School

I remember going to school at Benwhat as a wee boy. My teacher was Miss Kidd in the infants class in 1929. Francis Ferguson was the headmaster, a reasonable and popular man, who came from Dunaskin and travelled via Dalmellington up the hill to Benwhat every day in an old car.

Other well-known teachers at that time were Miss Mary Hill, who later stayed in Ayr Road, Dalmellington; Miss Florence Kerr, who later married Louis Scott, a well-respected man from Waterside; and Miss Munro, who lived in digs in Benwhat with Mrs Galloway. I remember that the school was used for dances, concerts and cantatas which were also called soirees. Weddings were also held in the new school, which opened in 1927, and in many ways it was the hub for special social occasions for the village.

No nonsense store

The store was operating at that time and Sanny Orr was in charge. I remember later that Harry Moore took over running the store. In fact I think his daughter is still living in Prestwick.

The store to the left with the old village school at Benwhat *circa* 1910. The old school was replaced with a new school to the north side of the village around 1930 and this school building was then demolished when the village was abandoned as folk moved to Burnton and Dalmellington.
(Photo: Courtesy of EAC Doon Valley Museum)

We used to queue up for the daily paper to take home, before going to school, but if we talked too loud and got up to nonsense, Harry would order us all outside. He stood no nonsense. The local men enjoyed going for a pint at the store, especially on a Saturday. They worked hard all week in the pits and were keen to enjoy a social drink at the store which opened from 11 a.m. until 3 p.m. and again from 5 p.m. until 9 p.m. in those days. At that time the beer was sixpence a pint and if you wanted to carry out a screw-top (bottle of beer) it was ninepence. No whisky was sold in the store.

Mother's domestic work

As I said, there were ten in my family and we lived in very cramped conditions, but many others were just like us. My mother had a difficult time and had to work very hard to look after us all. She was always on the go – cooking, cleaning, sewing or doing the washing up. The wash house was in the back porch with a built-in boiler to heat the water from a coal fire.

Once or twice a week the boiler fire was lit and a big washing was done by my mother. The houses at Benwhat were mainly one and two bedroom. There was no such thing as central heating, but there were open fires. Quite a few folk used what was called Beatrice Paraffin cookers in the porch to cook on.

Hungry lads

As boys we simply got on with life at Benwhat. We would enjoy running about the moors, playing football, and going to find birds' nests, and we often spent a full day pottering about Dunaskin Glen. I remember that at times we were starving, having been away all day and could hardly walk home, we were so hungry. Happy days, though.

Craigmark Burntonians season 1957–58. They play at Station Park which is at the rear of Dalmellington Community Centre.
Back row (l to r): A Wilson, Andy Hainey, J Whalen, Pat Malone (trainer), T Harper, D Johnston and R Whiteside.
Middle row: M Dalton, T Calderwood, M McLaughlan, M Gray and A Birch.
Front row: W Conell, B Smith and Tommy Blackwood.

Doon Harriers and Heatherbell

There was the Doon Harriers based in the village. All the older boys were members and everyone was proud of one famous runner, Robert Reid, who was a champion of Scotland. Adam McHattie was also a great harrier in these days.

We also had Benwhat Heatherbell and Rising Star, two amateur teams made up of local men, and between them they were very successful and won many trophies. There was one player, David Murray, who went from junior status to play for Aston Villa, not bad for someone coming from a remote hill village like Benwhat. The folk I recall involved with Rising Star were Jimmy Wilson (manager), Tommy Stewart, Hugh Murray, 'Riddy' Murray, Jimmy Stewart and 'Daidsy' Wilson.

A local harrier, Bobby Reid, with No. 40 vest is beaten by Peter Atwell of Beith Harriers as they race along the front of the rows at Benwhat. Reid, who worked in Dalmellington Co-op bakehouse, went on to be successful with Birchfield Harriers. Benwhat was a thriving small community with many activities for the residents, not least the village brass band formed in 1871.
(Photo: Courtesy of EAC Doon Valley Museum)

A group of what is believed to be Benwhat Harriers in the early 1900s.

Progress in life

David Relly, better known to us boys by his nickname 'Dykes', was a great Labour supporter and Rangers FC daft into the bargain. I recall him boasting of people born in Benwhat who did well in life. He was very proud that there was a doctor, headmaster, chief accountant and a minister born there. As I recall the minister was Robert Pollock and John Watson was the accountant. A village worthy (character) whom I remember as a boy was 'Sybus Galloway'. His job was to chap all the miners up (wake them up) in the morning to make sure they got to Chalmerston Mine on time for their shift starting.

The reading room

The Institute in Benwhat, better known as the reading room, was enjoyed by most folk and competitions were held every week. Newspapers and periodicals were available for anyone to read. There was a little shop in the Institute and it was under the control of Andrew Hannah, known locally by the nickname 'Snat'.

Billy Torbet followed on from Hannah and was caretaker for quite a while. One of the jobs that he had to do, which was quite sad, was going round houses and advising everyone when there was a death in the village and giving folk the times and details of the funeral. I remember that he had a bit of a temper and would shout and fling things if the boys misbehaved in the reading room. The membership of the reading room was one penny per week and that later rose to twopence, but it was worth it despite the hefty rise! There was a whist club held twice weekly and it was very popular, too.

Romance

Romance also blossomed at Benwhat and inevitably villagers married. Off the top of my head I think particularly of Jimmy Gordon who married Jeanie Bennet; Will Hodgson and Peggy Murray; Davy Torbet and Matsy McMahon; and Alan Dick and Janet Robertson. There were others, too.

Caring Co-op

At one time the Co-operative based in Dalmellington played a big part in the life of the people of Benwhat. They fed you, cled (clothed) and even buried you. A comprehensive service, you might say. Most of the folk used the Co-op and the service was first-class with vans calling regularly.

From 1929 they came to Benwhat with horse-drawn vans providing services such as the baker, butcher, milk and rolls, paraffin and briquettes, so the villagers were well provided for, although they were remote from the rest of the folk in the valley below and they were subject to the elements to a much greater degree – the weather in winter could be horrendous, the village sitting 1,000 feet above sea level.

Burns and Benwhat

The works of Robert Burns were popular in the village and with miners in general. Benwhat Burns Club was formed in 1940 during the war and affiliated to the Burns Federation in 1944. David Dunsmuir, a Benwhat man and Glasgow policeman, gave the first Immortal Memory and James Hill was the chairman that night. There are only two members of the club alive today (2003) – myself and Johnnie Gray (Jimsy McPhail subsequently passed on in 2011 and Johnnie Gray in 2012). Many good speakers came to Benwhat including John Pollock, a headmaster and his father before him; Major John Weir DSO OBE, Miss Ferguson and David Dunsmuir (junior). I still have possession of the Benwhat Burns Club certificate of membership of the Burns Federation.

Parker brothers killed in Great War

I clearly remember my Granny Hill, she lived at 66 Benwhat, telling me about two brothers she lost in the Great War. They were Jim and Tom Parker. In the 1939–45 war Benwhat lost John Robertson, Tom Bunyan and Bobby McMahon. All these men were known to me and popular in the village. Quite a few others served and thankfully came back, but it's sad to think of the lads from our little community who were killed. What can you say about men like those who never returned? Only that 'we will remember them'. They were our neighbours and friends.

Halloween

At Halloween I remember that a special cart came up from Dalmellington with all sorts of nuts and apples for the young folk to celebrate Halloween. This was great for the children. Mr John Robertson, somewhat balding on top, came up to sell his wares and was shouting about the good nuts on offer when one of the boys, 'Toy' Bennet, shouted back: 'Aye, they're monkey nuts, hazel nuts and baldy nuts too.' It was all fun and taken in good part.

Rechabites

The Rechabites is a biblical name used by Christian groups in my day keen to promote total abstinence from alcohol. They were organised as the Independent Order of Rechabites. Most of the young folk in Benwhat were members of the Rechabites and went to the regular meetings held in the school hall. You got a Bible lesson delivered by one of their members, we played games and then you got a drink of lemonade and a bun to eat. This was run in Benwhat at that time by Robert Bryan, Sunday School Superintendent and Kirk Elder at Dalmellington. He lived next door to us. He was a kindly and well-respected man.

Contrary canary

Alan Dick was another great character. He could talk all day about canary breeding and looking after budgies, which was his passion. He once sold a canary to a Mr Aitken, who told Alan that he wanted one that was a good whistler. A week later Mr Aitken arrived back at Benwhat and told Alan that the canary had a broken leg. 'Well,' replied Alan, 'you said you wanted a good whistler, not a step-dancer.' He was a real character.

Brass band

The village had a good brass band. In fact there were three brass bands within a few miles of one another. They were Benwhat Band (1871), Dalmellington Band (1864) and Waterside Band (1869). Mining areas had a strong brass band tradition. I'm proud to say that I have been a lifelong brass band enthusiast, still playing until a few years ago. Now, I am still fully involved in the committee of Dalmellington Band, formed in 1864, having been treasurer for many years.

Benwhat Band was formed in 1871 when the conductor was Jamie Armour, and the Armour family was always involved in the band thereafter. Benwhat Band was supported by locals in the village and the Currie family had five members who all played. Every year the band played at the memorial which was located on the brae face of nearby Benwhat Hill. Everyone was proud of this small village band. They practised twice a week in the school hall and I can still remember the music floating across the moorland.

Families in Benwhat

Like the other villages and small communities that no longer exist, the families tended to be large. In Benwhat we had McHattie, McEwan, McPhail, Galloway, Gordon, Thomson, Ferguson, Currie, Relly, Wilson and Dunsmuir, all with some wonderful characters who made village life special. The village midwife was Granny Wilson who lived in Stone Row. She delivered most of the babies and many folk who were born there will be grateful for her skill and self-taught expertise.

War planes

I remember that we often heard the planes going over during the war, probably in early 1941. At the time of the Clydebank Blitz there was a social evening being held in the school and we heard many German planes flying over late in the evening. We could hear them clearly but we were not aware of who was catching it. Poor souls! The wardens warned us all not to use torches or light matches. You could hear the blasts and see the sky lit up. Later on, a light bomb was recovered at Kilmein Hill between Benwhat and Lethanhill and it had probably been jettisoned by a German bomber returning home.

Winter of 1947

I think it was in 1947, the winter was incredibly bad and on one memorable occasion we were snowed in for about a week with heavy drifts which made the roads impassable. The vans couldn't get through from Dalmellington, so we had to walk down and carry supplies up by hand to Benwhat. That was just how things were done. The circumstances were difficult and we had to respond accordingly.

I remember that the first van to get through on the Friday was Malcolm Ross, a popular Dalmellington butcher for many years. His shop was located just off the Square at the Burnside and today William Paterson runs the shop. As Malcolm drove up into Benwhat he got a big cheer and everyone was out to greet him.

We don't seem to get such bad winters nowadays, but it was made all the worse because we were living on the high moors at 1,100 feet above sea level, so if the weather was bad in the valley below, we got it even worse. It was not uncommon for the snow to be up to the top of the back door and many a time we had to shovel our way out of the house to get to the coal shed.

Starting work

I left school in 1938/39 and started work at Chalmerston pithead just at the time war was declared. Robert Filson was the shift gaffer and Willie Miller the manager. I worked there until Christmas 1959 when Chalmerston closed. By that time Minnivey was operating and I started there in January 1960 after the New Year holidays. I eventually retired from the pits in 1981 and by that time I was working at Barony Colliery near Auchinleck as all the Dalmellington pits had closed by July 1978.

Leaving Benwhat

I remember that our family was among the first to leave Benwhat and that was a sad occasion indeed. We moved to 103 Park Crescent in 1943. We liked Benwhat and were reluctant to leave, because it was a great wee community and it was what we were used to all our days.

For all the lack of amenities, it had been my home all my life up till then, so it was a bit of a wrench to leave all that we knew and cared about, because it was a great wee community. In fact my brother John was so upset that he used to go back to Benwhat several times a week to the reading room to socialise with his auld pals. He found it hard to let go and settle in to the social life in Dalmellington. Benwhat had that sort of pull on you.

I suppose it would be around 1952 or slightly later before the last folk left Benwhat and I think John Thomson, who later became a well-known bookmaker in Dalmellington, would be one of the last to move. Even by 1947–48 folk were moving out steadily and demolition was ongoing in some of the vacant rows even at that time when folk were still in residence in others.

It was, I suppose, a case of happy enough to move to a new modern house, but sad to leave an old home and good neighbours and happy, even joyful, memories. I can say without any fear of contradiction that the McPhail family were all very proud to belong to Benwhat.

Why am I loth to leave this earthly scene?
Have I so found it full of pleasing charms?
Some drops of joy with draughts of ill between;
Some gleams of sunshine 'mid renewing storms?

                Stanzas On The Same Occasion
                          Robert Burns

Chapter 10

The tip of the bing at Beoch Mine, closed in 1968, shows that work on clearing the site was well under way. It was located on the north side of the Dalmellington–New Cumnock Road some 5 miles from Dalmellington. The sinking of Beoch No. 3 began in 1866 and the houses would have been erected some time thereafter. Beoch No. 4 was sunk in 1937 and closed in 1968. In 1948 No. 4 was producing 330 tons per day, 90,000 tons per annum with a workforce of 169 miners. Screening of coal took place at Pennyvenie and washing at Dunaskin.
(Photo: Courtesy of EAC Doon Valley Museum)

A cutting from the *Ayrshire Post* of 13 March 1970 when the Benwhat Reunion was held allowing former villagers to reminisce and remember a village they were all proud of and to recall special days of yesteryear.
(Photo: Courtesy of EAC Doon Valley Museum)

Chapter 10

Big-hearted Beoch

Andrew Knox Bone

Benbeoch Craig, grim, weird and wild,
That awed me when I was a child,
Where rocks on mighty rocks are piled,
The wonder of Dalmellington.

Dalmellington
Matthew Anderson

Known locally and affectionately in the Dalmellington of his day as 'Knoxy', the late Andrew Knox Bone was a proud miner at Beoch. He had a great interest in the social history of the Doon Valley and recorded his research in several manuscripts. The following consists of edited highlights of *Memories of Beoch*, written in the mid-1970s. Andrew Knox Bone died on 18 June 1984, aged seventy-seven, and is buried in Dalmellington Cemetery.

Family from Beoch

My grandparents (Bone) lived at North Beoch (off the B741) for some years in the 1890s. During that period my father was Superintendent of Beoch Sunday School. After the passing of his parents and sister, Mrs Findlay Lorimer, he left Beoch and went to live in Ayr. But his heart was always with the Beoch folk. In Ayr he got a job as an agent with the Refuge Assurance Company. He was subsequently transferred to the Dalmellington run and soon had a regular call to the Beoch to collect insurance money. On a Saturday in November 1901, he was just passing Beoch Mine when he was told that his uncle, James Wallace, had been killed in an accident in the mine.

Pennyvenie

In later years when we all lived at Pennyvenie – some three miles from Beoch on the B741 road – my father and my sister restarted Beoch Sunday School. My father seemed to have a nice way with the children. In fact, some of the scholars still remember him with reverence yet, even some who live as far away as London.

My father died in 1932. In the summer he would walk from Pennyvenie to Beoch, a distance of just over two miles. Some of the children who attended the Sunday School used to walk along the road from Beoch to meet him and my sister, and after Sunday School was over they would again escort them part of the way from Beoch to the Main Road which runs from Cumnock to Dalmellington as they walked back home.

Where do sinners go?

One Sunday he was asking the children some questions, one of which was: 'Where do sinners go?' Up shot the hand of a little boy, who said: 'Ma mither pits the big yins in the fire and the wee yins in the ashpan.' This caused great hilarity, especially among the older children who understood that he was mixing up the word sinners for cinders, the various ashes left on the fire after coal and wood is burned. My father must have had a great knack for working with children. He could see the funny side of things, too, which helped him in his work.

Soirees at Beoch

My father and sister were assisted at the Beoch Sunday School by Harry Halliday and Bob Reid. Bob was the father of Bobby Reid, the Scottish Cross Country Champion who ran with Benwhat Harriers before going on to better things with the famous Birchfield Harriers. The Reverend John A Kinloch (Minister of Lamloch Church, Dalmellington from 1933 to 1944) used to enjoy the social evenings at Beoch, especially the soirees, when the children started singing their favourite choruses. They were great singers and full of such enthusiasm.

Miss Walker of Camlarg

Miss Jean Walker of Camlarg House, Dalmellington, was a very generous and good friend to Beoch Sunday School. When it came near Christmas time Miss Walker would send word for my father to come across from Pennyvenie to Camlarg House. When he went over he was made very welcome and always came away with a very generous donation from her for the Sunday School.

Here is just one instance I have on record: the usual annual gift of a Christmas tree, cut down and delivered to Beoch by James Thompson or John Morgan, both estate workers at Camlarg. Along with this there was £2 in cash, six Bibles, six books, and a bag of sweets and an orange for every child at the Sunday School. And at that time in a little isolated place like Beoch, 5 miles from Dalmellington and over one mile from the main Dalmellington–Cumnock Road, there were fifty-nine children in the Sunday School. Miss Walker was a very generous donor. And it was the same procedure when it came round time for the Sunday School trip. A nice donation in cash was given to ensure that all the children were well fed.

Beoch children of 1926

Here are the names of the children, with ages in brackets, who attended Beoch Sunday School in 1926. This information is gleaned from records in the possession of my father.

David Shearer (10), Douglas Shearer (8), Robert Shearer (2), David Givens (12), Andrew Givens (9), John Givens (7), Mary Givens (3), Willie Givens (1), James McLelland (13), Peter Halbert (5), Thomas Halbert (3), Willie Halbert (2), Samuel Halbert (1), Mary McLarty (4), Samuel McLarty (3), Alese McLarty (1), Elizabeth Chalmers (12), David Chalmers (10), Rachel Chalmers (7), James Chalmers (5), Willie Chalmers (3), Isa Chalmers (1), Paul Chalmers (13), John Chalmers (11), Annie Chalmers (9), Jean Chalmers (7), Margaret Chalmers (5), Nell Chalmers (3), Nan Chalmers (?), Willie Reid (10), George Reid (7), Elizabeth Reid (5), Matthew Reid (3), James Reid (1), Margaret Rowan (13), Grace Rowan (11), George Rowan (9), John Rowan (6), Adam Rowan (3), Marion Halliday (13), James Halliday (8), Matthew Halliday (3), Henry Halliday (1), Willie Jackson (5), Stewart Jackson (3), Robert Jackson (1), Annie Gavin (7), James Gavin (6), Agnes Gavin (5), Margaret Gavin (3), Marion Gavin (1), Margaret Rodgers (15), Thomas Rodgers (13), John Gray (1), Jean Shedden and Willie Shedden.

Dalmellington High School class of 1959.
Back row (l to r): Mr William Irving (headmaster), Clifford Wilson, Billy Blane, George Dunn, Hugh McCreath, William Donnan, Ian McDowall, John Riggans, David Stewart, Billy Coughtrie, ? Reid and Billy Thomson.
Middle Row: Doris Jackson, Isobel Bryson, Ellen Logan, Jean Bell, Marlyn Rattray, Shona Limond, Anne Dempster, Carol Rae, Jean Wilson, Laura Rudland and Jennifer Anderson.
Front row: Joan Steele, Jean Grant, Janet Hutchison, Hannah Wallace, Eleanor Storrie, May Barclay, Jean Barbour, Ella Maxwell and Lillian Hewitson.

Kind and generous folk

Readers will appreciate that the children of entire families were members of the Sunday School and parents saw to it that their children did attend. My father had to give up teaching the Sunday School in 1928. And the good folks of the Beoch, to show their appreciation, gifted him a 'Dennistoun' gold pocket watch, and they gave my mother a silver-mounted umbrella. They were kind and generous people and this was wonderful when you consider that they were very poor themselves. After this my father continued to serve in the Lamloch Church Sunday School in Dalmellington until his death in 1932 which came after a short illness.

Beoch hospitality

The Beoch folk were always famous for their hospitality and friendliness. They used to have some grand nights, especially at

Dalmellington Primary School *circa* 1958.
Back row (l to r): Douglas Baird, John Campbell, John McFarlane, Ernest Millichip, Wilson Tyson, and Billy Coughtrie.
2nd Back Row: Billy Orr, Ronald Niven, David Wilson, John Blackwood, Brian Brown, Willie McMillan, Tom Gault, Andrew Carruthers, Andrew Torbet, and Andrew Barclay.
2nd Front Row: Jimmy Brands, Joan Steele, Martha Torbet, Nan Hodgeson, Ellen Logan, Mary Wilson, Margaret Donnachie, Jean Bell, Joan Hose, Elizabeth Stevenson and Hugh McCreath.
Front Row: Eleanor Storrie, Betty Whalen, Linda Parker, Jean Barbour, Mary O'Neil, Maureen McMinn, Mary McMillan, Ellen Coughtrie, Carol Rae and Margaret Brown.
Two boys at front: John Boyle and David Scobie.

the ferm (farm) dances. James Paulin used to play the fiddle at these dances. Nancy Smith and Rab Smith played the piano, and fiddle too. Auld Willie Riggins, a real worthy, used to teach the young ones how to dance and took them through each routine. Willie was a fine old man, one whom I highly respected. Tragedy struck in his family twice with two of his sons, Walter and John, both killed in mining accidents. And yet he still had a wonderfully positive outlook, always wishing to be helpful to others.

The schoolmistresses and teachers that come to mind from Beoch, where there was a small school, were Miss Eaglesham, Mistress, and she was a sort of mother to the whole community. Then there was Miss Nicholson, Mrs Keillor, Miss Irwin, Miss Dickson and Mrs Park, who served at different times at Beoch School.

Walking to church

I used to hear my father tell the story of old John Smith, farmer at Beoch Farm, which was very near to the Beoch row. He was a keen Free Churchman, and each Sunday morning he would leave for the church in Dalmellington wearing his working boots, and his fine boots would be slung over his shoulder.

When he came to what was called the Collier Row, later Camlarg Cottages, just past Pennyvenie, he would call in at old Mrs Currie's house, change into his fine boots and continue his journey to the church in Dalmellington. On his return from the service of worship, he would call again and have a meal with Mrs Currie, change into his old boots and continue walking all the way back to Beoch Farm.

Beoch had its share of pigeon fanciers, too, and names such as Chalmers, Curragh and Findlay come to mind. It also had its share of keen fishermen and those who were prominent included Rowan, Black and Holland to mention but a few.

Beoch families

The folk of Beoch who were household names in my time included Chalmers, Curragh, Carruthers, Paulin, Riggans, Wilson, Findlay, Anderson, Jess, Black, Rowan, Gavin, Halliday, Rodgers, Givens, Reid, Shedden, Hallers, McLarty, not forgetting the Smiths of Beoch Farm. If I hear mention of any of these names, it brings back happy memories of Beoch.

My wife and I kept friendly with the Rodgers family. Mary (Mrs Duncan) lived at Skerrington, Cumnock. Grace (Mrs McCallum) lived in Ayr. Margaret (Mrs Paton) lived in Bexley Heath, Kent and she died in 1962. Tom Rodgers lived in Broadstairs, Kent. This just shows how folk from the Beoch moved to a variety of different places, but every one of them held a special place in their heart for that small isolated community.

My wife, son Edward and his wife and myself have been down to Margaret's on holidays. On one of our visits Margaret got on to talk about the happy days at Beoch and Pennyvenie. Margaret was a frequent visitor to our house in Pennyvenie and she was just like one of the family. Margaret veered the conversation round to the Sunday School at Beoch.

Soon we were wandering way down memory's lane,
For there we were engrossed 'twas very plain.
With a proud, and somewhat sentimental rule,
We talked of nought, but Beoch Sunday School.
Of how the classroom always rang,
With the choruses, the children sang.
Or the soirees, when they used to say,
Their pieces are always bright, and gay,
And of the trips they used to have,
And run the races for a laugh,
And oft my father's views were sought,
For he was the Superintendent of the lot.

Those privileged to live at Beoch will, I am certain, retain very happy memories of this lonely place on the wild lonely moors towered over by Benbeoch Craig because it was very special. It was home.

Craigmark, Benquhat and Burnfoothill,
All give my heart a glorious thrill,
While memories cloud my eyes until
I scarce can see Dalmellington.

Hills over hills like waves arise
Beneath these health-inspiring skies.
God bless this earthly paradise –
My own, my dear Dalmellington.

Dalmellington
Matthew Anderson

An aerial view of Beoch Colliery which was located about 1 mile west of the Dalmellington–Cumnock Road (B741) some 5 miles from Dalmellington. There were many small mines in this area, but Beoch No. 4 was operated by Bairds and Dalmellington and was sunk in 1937. Peak output was in 1948 with 330 tons a day and there were 169 employees. It closed in 1968 when most of the workforce were transferred to Pennyvenie.
(Photo: Courtesy of EAC Doon Valley Museum)

The Benwhat war memorial, which sits sentinel on the front of Benwhat Hill, affording wonderful views across the Doon Valley.
(Photo: Donald L Reid)

Robert Douglas, born at Benwhat where he spent his formative years, visits the refurbished war memorial prior to the re-dedication service on 12 June 2011. As a boy Robert recalls that several of the rows were already being demolished as they used to play in them when the workers went home. The opencast site at nearby Lethanhill can be seen and the Clyde coast and Arran are in the background on the right, highlighting the wonderful views from Benwhat Hill.
(Photo: Donald L Reid)

Voices & Images of Ayrshire

A panoramic view of Cairntable by former resident and keen artist, Tom Smith of Drongan, who has fond memories of this little community located on the B730 Kerse to Drongan Road, abandoned in 1963. A memorial cairn now marks the location of the former village.
(Drawing: courtesy of Tom Smith)

A 1984 drawing by Tom Smith of his beloved Cairntable, one of the lost mining villages of the area.
(Drawing: Courtesy of Tom Smith)

Billy Greig, who was born and raised in Craigmark, situated in the valley below Benwhat, painted this picture of Benwhat as it was in the early 1900s. The village store can be seen on the right and the old school building (white) is on the extreme right. The new school, built about 1930, was located to the left of this painting close to the nearest row. Billy was a keen member of the Dalmellington Band and wrote pieces of local poetry.
(Photo: Donald L Reid)

Benwhat folk walk to Marquee, where a memorial service was held to rededicate the village war memorial on June 12 2011.
(Photo: Donald L Reid)

Robert 'Robin' Farrell (centre), a Benwhatonian, who attended the service of re-dedication, died a few months later. Known fondly simply as Robin in the Doon Valley, he wrote a small book about Benwhat which is very popular.
(Photo: Donald L Reid)

More of the guests who attended the re-dedication of Benwhat war memorial on a fine day in June 2011. Dalmellington Junior Band provided the musical accompaniment and the service was led by Deaconess Muriel Wilson of Dalmellington Parish Church.
(Photo: Donald L Reid)

More Benwhat folk and their families gather in the marquee prior to the service of re-dedication on 12 June 2011 and it was this event that became the catalyst for this book.
(Photo: Donald L Reid)

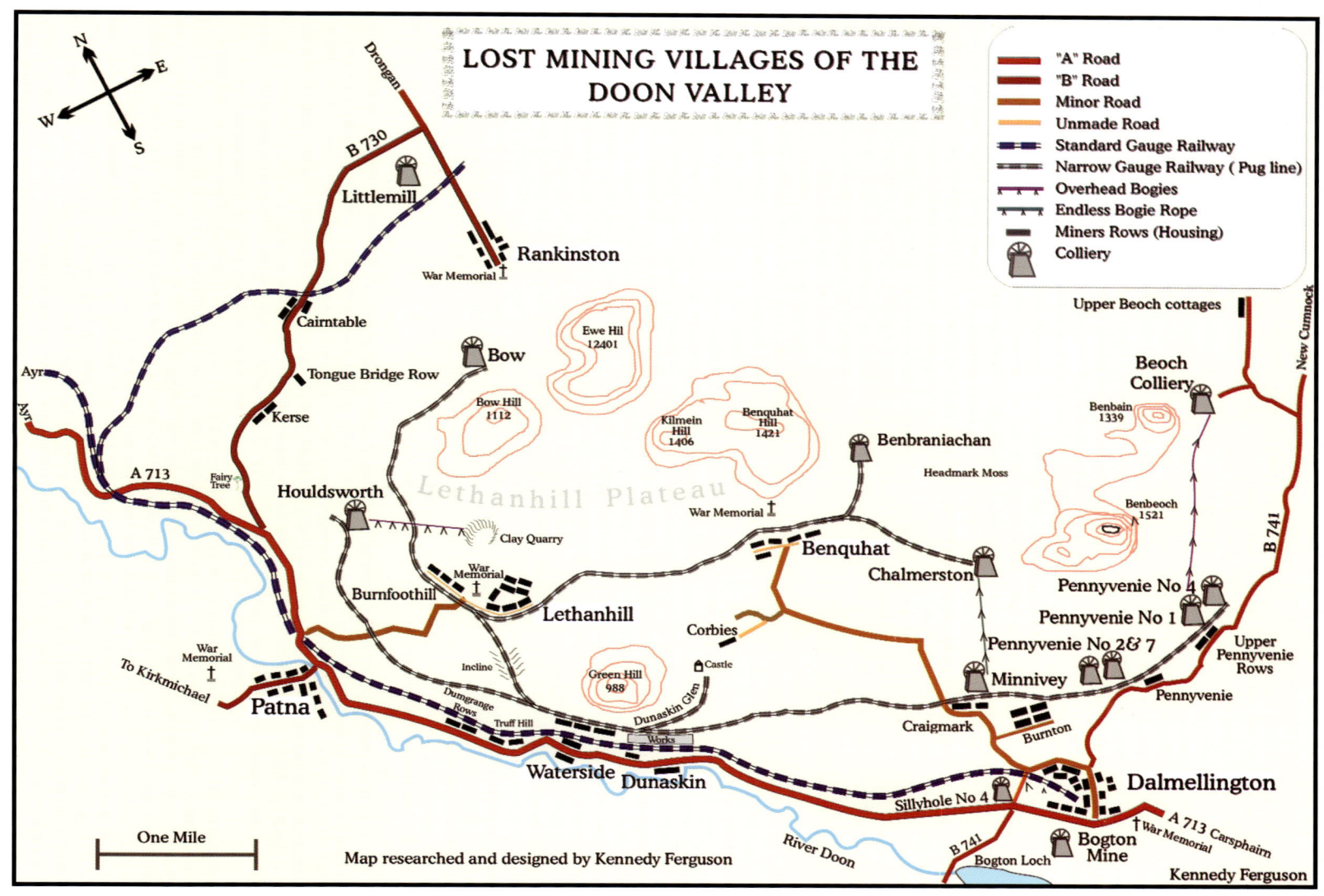

A map, specially prepared for this publication, showing the location of the lost mining villages of Doon Valley by Kennedy (Kenny) Ferguson of Dalmellington, who was raised at Lethanhill.
(Courtesy of Kennedy Ferguson)

Voices & Images of Ayrshire

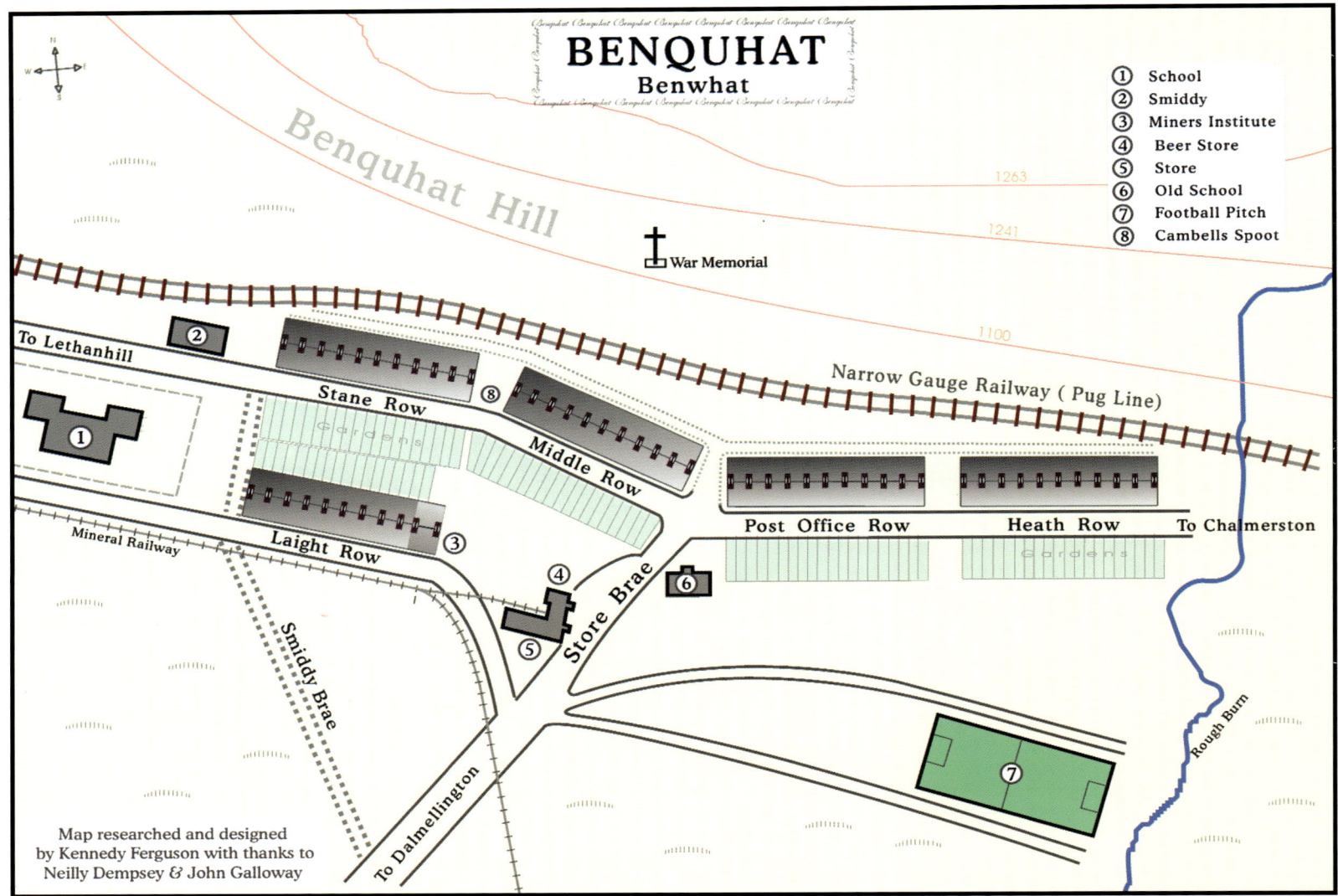

A detailed map of Benwhat, sometimes spelled Benquhat, from the pen of Kennedy Ferguson, which will prove invaluable to anyone wishing to learn more about the village.
(Courtesy of Kennedy Ferguson)

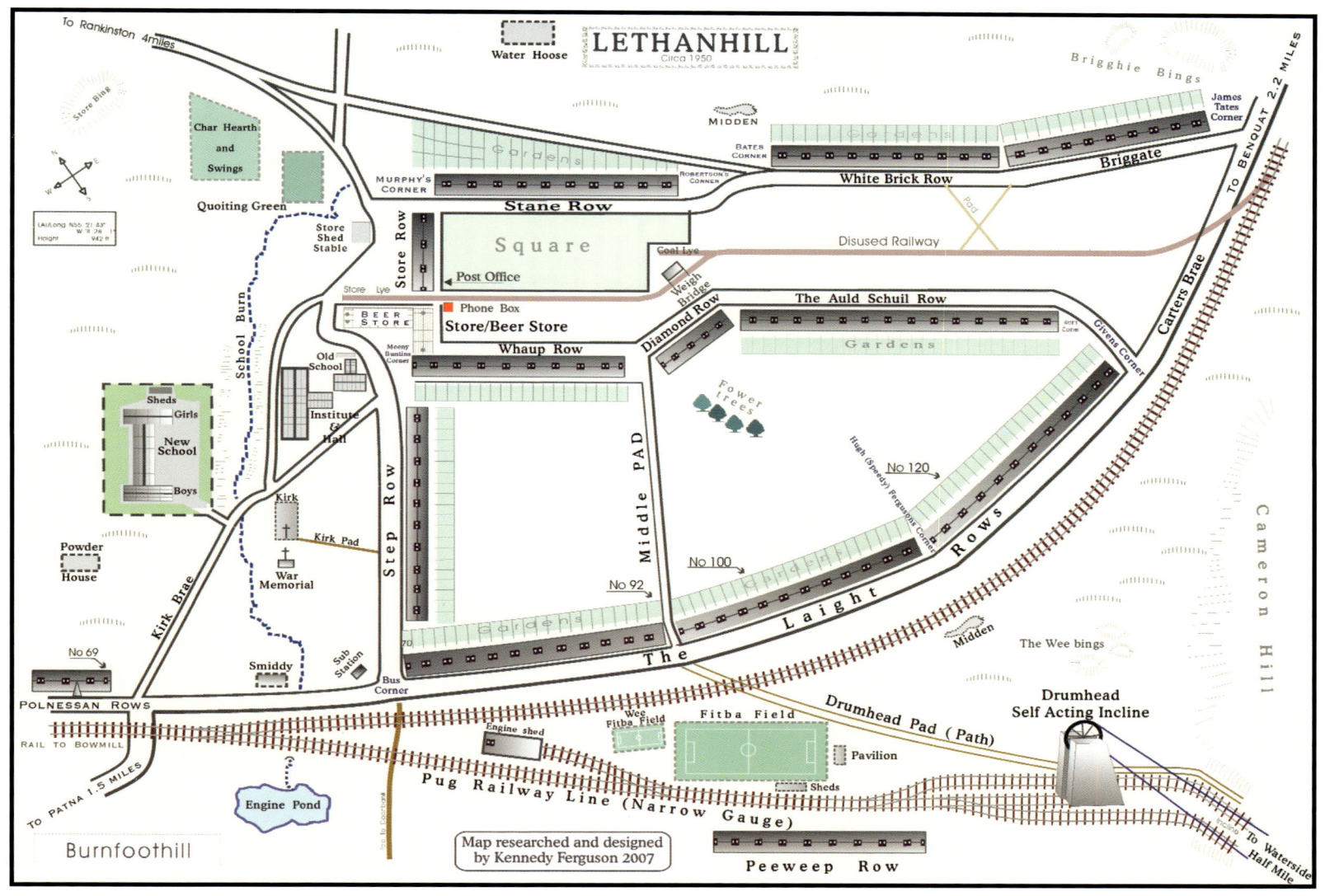

A plan of Lethanhill as recalled by former resident Kennedy Ferguson, now of Dalmellington.
(Plan of Lethanhill: Courtesy of Kennedy Ferguson)

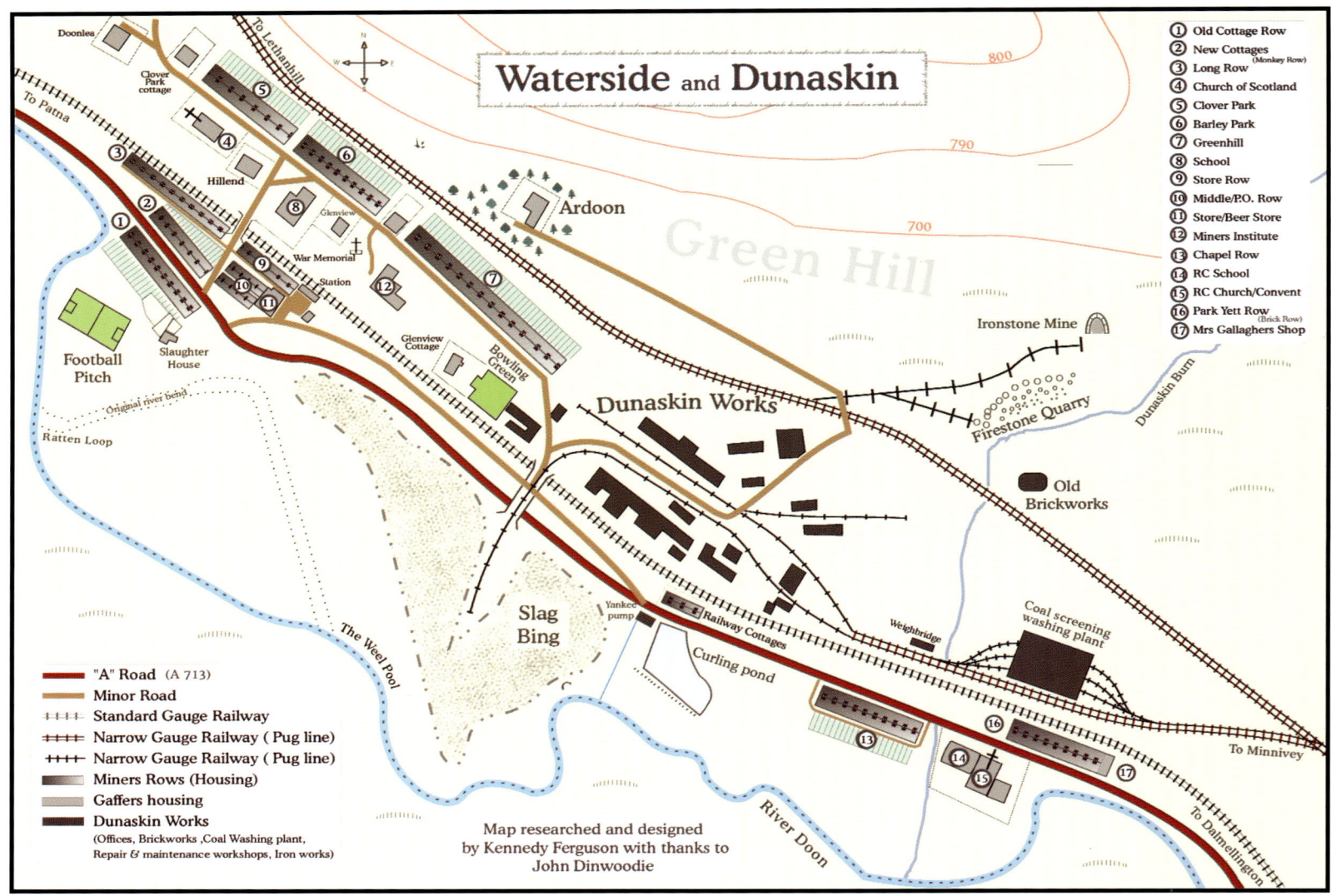

An excellent map of Waterside, carefully prepared by Kennedy Ferguson of Dalmellington.
(Map by Kennedy Ferguson)

Mamie Ireland (centre) is a kenspeckle figure in Dalmellington. A talented lady with great energy, she has raised funds for many good causes over the years, including taking part in Doon Valley Raft Race. She has even parachuted from an aeroplane. She is currently one of the volunteers at the Kirk Shop in Dalmellington Square. On the right is Betty Miller, née Shaw, and the couple on the right are Neillie and Molly Dempsey of Burnton.
(Photo: Donald L Reid)

Deaconess Muriel Wilson with Florence Scobie, née McCulloch, who was born in Benwhat and attended the re-dedication service marking the refurbishment of the war memorial located on Benwhat Hill. It was a very moving service.
(Photo: Donald L Reid)

Two sets of twins that we know of, the Galloway girls and the Filson lads, were born in Benwhat. It was timely to photograph them at the re-dedication ceremony of the war memorial on 12 June 2011. Sadly, Tommy Filson died in February 2012, but his story had been recorded earlier.
Back: The Galloway twins – Effie (left) and Jean.
Front: Tommy Filson and Andy Filson.
(Photo: Donald L Reid)

The steps leading into Benwhat School with the war memorial seen on Benwhat Hill in the background.
(Photo: Donald L Reid)

Sighthill Cottages, Pennyvenie are in a sorry state when photographed on 1 November 2011. A short time later they were demolished.
(Photo: Donald L Reid)

Bellsbank Primary School classes 6 and 7 who enjoyed working with Barrmill Jolly Beggars members on a local history project. It is hoped that they will remember their Doon Valley mining heritage.
(Photo: Donald L Reid)

The old codgers of 33rd Ayrshire Dalmellington Scout Group enjoy meeting to remember those happy days at camp and the friendship of Scouting. All of them still proudly give back to their old Scout Group, passing on their knowledge, time and talents to the up and coming scouts.
(l to r): Craig Dempsey, John Paterson, Peter Findlay, Michael Carruthers, Jode McArdle, David Brown, Ian Riggins, Brian Bingham, Ross McCulloch, Joe Robertson and Gerry Harkins. Front: Barry White and Scouting legend Frank McHugh, who holds the top Scouting Award in the UK and has been a dedicated leader of the 33rd Ayrshire for over fifty years.

The happy trio of Tom 'Tam' McKnight, Margaret and David Rarity. Tam is very passionate about Waterside and is an almost daily visitor to Dunaskin Glen where he enjoys seeing the flora and fauna of the area. Margaret and David Rarity are Tam's next-door neighbours and they are good friends of Donald L Reid, all three encouraging him in his quest to record more of the local history of the Doon Valley.
(Photo: Donald L Reid)

Chapter 11

Beoch – A Caring Community
Tom Reid

The tender thrill, the pitying tear,
The generous purpose, nobly dear,
The gentle look that rage disarms –
These are all immortal charms.

My Peggy's Charms
Robert Burns

Beoch rows, also known as North Beoch, was built to accommodate miners working at nearby Beoch Mine. The sinking of Beoch No. 3 began in 1866 and the houses would have been erected some time thereafter. Beoch No. 4 was sunk in 1937 and closed in 1968. In 1948 No. 4 was producing 330 tons per day, 90,000 tons per annum with a workforce of 169 miners. Screening of coal took place at Pennyvenie and washing at Dunaskin. This posed photo shows the villagers; most of the children are barefoot, which was commonplace in the summer. There was also a village school which took children from ages five to fourteen, but those who were brighter had to attend Dalmellington Higher Grade school. The village was serviced by Dalmellington Co-op vans. There are water butts outside each house and the horse and cart was the only transport in the 1890s until after the Great War. Beoch rows were abandoned around 1938 when most residents had moved to Dalmellington.
(Photo: Courtesy of EAC Doon Valley Museum)

Tom Reid was eighty-four years of age in 2004 when this interview was carried out. He was the eldest son of Tommy and Catherine Reid who in later years lived in Gateside Street, Dalmellington. The other family members were John (Jock), Jimmy, Bill, Margaret, Donald and Cathy. Tom was born in Tarbolton in 1920. When he was about nine years of age the family moved near to Dailly to what was a row of very basic miners' cottages known simply as the Rumily, no longer in existence. His father, Tommy, worked in Blairquhan Colliery at this time.

Again in pursuit of work, the family moved from Dailly to Beoch, located on the Dalmellington–Cumnock Road (B741), some 5 miles from Dalmellington. After working for a few years at the Beoch Mine after his schooling, Tom married Clarice in 1948 and moved to Barnsley. His only daughter, Moira, is married and lives in Goole with her husband, Mike, and children, Kerstin and Keely. Tom spent the major part of his working life at Barnsley Main Colliery until it closed in 1966. Thereafter he worked at ICI Chemicals in Huddersfield, retiring in 1983. Tom was very artistic and enjoyed painting and drawing, and he often thought back to happy family days at Beoch – a great wee place.

Fortunately, Tom had many vivid memories of his years at Beoch and many of these are highlighted in the following extract from the interview. He painted a wonderful picture of the way life was at Beoch in the 1930s. Tom passed away on 14 February 2008.

Arriving at Beoch

I would be about ten years of age when I came to live at Beoch in 1930. I remember sitting on the back of the lorry with the furniture piled high behind us. My mother and father were in the front with the driver. My mother had my youngest brother, Wee Don, on her lap. I remember that it was a lovely day. What I remember most was coming over the road from Straiton, with long steep hills and the lorry struggling to win the hills.

When we got to the top of the Beoch brae, turning off the Dalmellington–Cumnock Road, I could see the solitary row of houses with the red-top slate roof of the school just beyond down in the valley. I remember that all the lums (chimneys) were reeking, the smoke curling high into the air. The lorry then trundled down the ash-surfaced road, past the coal bing, where men were tipping muck and rubble from the mine, and into Beoch which would be my home for the next eight years. It was just one row of houses with a two-storey building at either end of the row with external wooden steps leading to the top storey.

Moving in

My father, Tommy Reid, got the key to our house from the factor and he removed the wooden shutter from the windows. The neighbours turned out to watch us move in. The men were very neighbourly and offered to help us unload: 'Can we gie ye a haun, Sir?' they asked my father. And soon we were established with the beds set up, a good fire going, kindly neighbours offering broth and bread. 'The wee ones must be starving', was the invitation to a welcome meal, which we gladly accepted. Folk in those days seemed to be genuinely caring and interested in each other.

Blackleading the fireplace

With the place swept out, and a great fire burning and the kettle on the swee, the oil lamp lit and the beds set in their alcoves, we retired snug and happy to sleep on our first night at Beoch, of happy memory. Next day we were scrubbing the floors, putting the valances and the screening curtains around the inset beds and blackleading the fireplace and the ovens, set at both sides of the fire. We all mucked in to help.

Settling in

My father, Tommy, naturally started work immediately at Beoch Mine, because in those days if you didn't work there was no money coming in. He was a skilled machine man, used to all the different types of coal-cutting machines. His work entailed being on nightshift. We settled well at Beoch, getting to know everyone within a few days. The place just felt right for us and we were happy from the outset.

Camlarg was erected in the late 1700s as the main house of Camlarg Estate. The house was purchased from Sir James Cunninghame of Milncraig by William Logan, son of James Logan of Castle Cumnock, supposed to have been the younger son of Logan of that Ilk. He married Agnes McAdam, daughter of the Laird of Craigengillan and they had three sons. William Logan (younger) sold Camlarg about the year 1780 to John McAdam of Craigengillan. Camlarg was the HQ of the Royal Flying Corps, then based at Bogton Loch and Loch Doon. Camlarg House was demolished after the Second World War as it had been affected by subsidence cause by earlier mining operations, and was demolished around 1947.
(Photo: Courtesy of EAC Doon Valley Museum)

Beoch School

The schoolhouse was quite a modern building of grey painted wood, with a reddish slate tiled roof. It was located about 200 yards from the houses. The teachers of my day, Mrs Park and Miss Taylor, both had their own quarters attached to the school. They came by taxi to Beoch and lived at the schoolhouse till late on Friday then went home for the weekend. Mrs Park, the headmistress, was married to a local man. Her son, George, was about my age and in my class. She had two older daughters, at college, who spent all their free time with her. They were lively sociable girls who greatly added to the social life of the village and were great friends to my mother and others.

Mrs Park took three classes in one classroom (composite classes) while Miss Taylor also took three classes in the other classroom. Mrs Park taught those who were about nine to fourteen years whilst Miss Taylor taught the younger children. Looking back, they really worked wonders with us. It was hands-on education and contact at all time with the parents. I really enjoyed school at Beoch so much and learned a lot.

Local benefactors

In those days many local dignitaries and charitable trusts donated prizes and awarded bursaries to all the local schools. I wish I could remember all their names, but one or two I do recall. Miss Walker of Camlarg House was a benefactor of Beoch School. She gave an annual prize to the best scholar in all grades and toys for every child at Christmas.

The greatest prize was the Gavin Memorial Prize. It was a black japanned watch of real quality. This was gifted each year to the top pupil at Beoch and inscribed to the Dux Medallist of the year. Mr Gavin was connected to Craigengillan Estate at Dalmellington. I wish I could thank the families of these benefactors for the great pleasure their gifts and bequests gave us all, for we really had nothing and these gifts were special to everyone at Beoch.

Summer at Beoch

In the summer holidays we lads and lassies would roam many a mile around Beoch. We would go down to the River Nith where we guddled for trout and bathed in the deeper pools. The Nith begins its journey to the sea on the Solway coast just a mile from our picnic spot. Further downstream was the Pochery, which flowed steeply down from Maneight to join the Nith.

This was a favourite picnic spot for everyone. On nice weekends, and there seemed to be many of these in my boyhood days, families walked over the hill from Beoch and past McLarty's cottage to picnic at the Nith. We were often joined here by folk from the Cumnock area who had travelled to this favourite spot on bicycles and motor bikes. Life just seemed so much simpler in those carefree days.

Sojourn to Benbeoch Craig

We would go out in the morning and not return till dusk. Our parents never worried where we were because they knew we were safe from harm other than bruises and bumps. Being hungry on these occasions never worried us. We had only to call at the local farmhouses and the farmer's wife would bring out buckets of buttermilk and piles of scones and cheese and oatcakes. We also made regular sojourns to Benbeoch, simply called the Craig. We would climb up to the cave where, it was said, Paterson and Peden took refuge during the persecution of the Covenanters during what was known as the 'killing times' in the 1680s.

Beoch Farm in February 2005.
(Photo: Donald L Reid)

Our water supply

There was a spring of clear water on the Craig below the scree of huge boulders, many bigger than houses. In those days this spring supplied Craigview and Pennyvenie with their drinking water. The Beoch was also supplied by a spring just off the Cumnock Road, 100 yards below the Beoch brae.

Besides fishing and guddling for trout, there was an abundance of rabbits. These were a seasonal addition to our diet along with wild birds' eggs in spring. The ones which were commonly eaten and looked forward to immensely by the folk at Beoch were peewits, stankeys (water hens), grouse and whaup (curlew), and occasionally wild duck.

Sports

When we were not roaming the countryside, there was always some sporting activity going on and we played football just about every night. These games involved both men and boys, the men joining in after coming home from the pit. The girls and women enjoyed skipping and beds (peevers) and many young people today may find this rather strange.

A favourite with everyone was rounders. The whole population turned out for this, including the older folk, grandmothers and grandfathers. There was real community spirit and a willingness by everyone to have good fun and take part. There was always something to do, but it was self-made.

Vans calling

Another aspect of the social life in this remote village was the van men calling with their various wares to sell. Every day, except Sunday, there would be two, three or more van men calling at Beoch. They didn't just come to pay us a passing call. They came for an hour or two. Some in fact came for the whole day. They were all friends. Practically every family had a favoured friend among the van men.

Friday evening was exceptionally busy. This was settling-up day for the grocers, butchers, greengrocers, drapers and bakers, who plied their trade almost always on credit, because money was scarce and the women were always waiting on the weekly pay packet to settle bills. Thinking back, these must have been worrying times for our parents trying to make ends meet, but they must have hidden it well.

On one occasion my father was unable to work for almost a year because he hurt his hand down the mine and had blood poisoning which left him with limited movement. On hard times such as these the traders allowed families to run up bills which families could only partially repay until the breadwinner was fit for work. There seemed to be a genuine compassion towards one another in these times and perhaps it was because it was a very small community and everyone knew the business of the other.

Doctor Lee calls

Bobby Currie was a grocer who owned Craigbank store, New Cumnock. He was a staunch friend to our family, as was Willie Slonimski, who had a small general store in New Cumnock. To these people we owed more than money. Every week, or more often when we needed him, the doctor paid a regular visit. It was essential on the day of the doctor's visit that my mother, Catherine, made a full pot of broth.

Dr Lee was a small lean young man of Chinese extraction. He was a man of good humour and very popular with all his patients. Years later when we had all moved far away, and when I came home to visit the family in Dalmellington, Dr Lee would make his way to visit us and reminisce about the old days at Beoch. He was a lovely man and a doctor of the old school. Many folk of my generation will realise what a special man we had as our doctor and friend.

We also had other people who gave of their time to us at Beoch, which we greatly appreciated. Mr Eddie Bone walked every Sunday from Pennyvenie, almost four miles each way, to hold a Sunday School meeting. And later on, when old Eddie died, this duty was taken on by Dan Wallace, and Dan's son-in-law, John Brown, also from Low Pennyvenie.

The Reverend Ninian Wright

Another man who was very popular, especially with the lads at Beoch, was the Reverend Ninian Wright, at that time Minister at the Kirk o' the Covenant in Dalmellington. He formed a branch of the Scouts at Beoch which we really enjoyed. Scouting was very popular in those days. He spent a great deal of his time on us, besides running the main troop of Scouts in Dalmellington and attending to his many church duties. He had quite a famous brother who was the 'Radio Doctor' for the BBC for many years. Ninian Wright was an impressive, kindly man, who is fondly remembered.

Bus service arrives

The advent of the bus service from New Cumnock to Dalmellington in 1932 was welcomed by the Beoch people. Although it was only one every two hours, it made a tremendous difference to the social life of folk at Beoch. Suddenly we had reasonably easy access to the amenities of Dalmellington such as the picture houses (we had two of them), the pubs and the shops, owned by Italians – the Bertellotti Brothers and Andersons – both providing supplies of all sorts.

Saturday in Dalmellington

'Callie' Anderson then opened the Merrick Café and Merrick Hall in High Main Street, Dalmellington. This proved to be very popular on Saturday nights with people flocking in from all over the Doon Valley and Cumnock to dance the night away. Many men from New Cumnock were working at the Beoch Mine and the Blackwater which had only recently been opened. Because of this, the late buses back to Beoch and Cumnock were always jam-packed.

Many of the men were inevitably slightly drunk and in good humour. It is hard for me to describe the happy atmosphere on these late buses, but suffice to say that when I think about it I always smile. There was laughing, singing and some shouting. It had to be experienced.

At the top of the Beoch brae we disembarked, walking down the brae in groups, still laughing and singing; those slightly the worse of drink tailing off to relieve themselves. It was an estimated 1.3 miles from the bus stop down to the village and if it was raining you were totally soaked.

Hunter's Sports

A big occasion for us every year, and indeed all the other pit villages for miles around, was Hunter's Sports, held in Dalmellington. This was a semi-professional event with quite big sums of money to be won. In fact in the five-a-side football competition, teams from Rangers and Celtic and other professional sides took part. But invariably, the winner of this event was a team consisting of the Scobie brothers and friends, who hailed from Craigmark and Burnton. They were virtually unbeatable, even in their late thirties.

There were also bicycle races, foot races at every distance, as well as weightlifting and highland dancing to entertain the large number of spectators who turned out for this major event. We were especially interested in the tug-of-war as the Beoch Mine team invariably won it. Pipe bands and the Dalmellington Silver Band added greatly to the atmosphere of what was always a very special day.

Wull (William) Hunter, the sponsor of the sports, was a great benefactor to many people in the Dalmellington area. He had been injured in a mining accident at Pennyvenie and with his compensation money he started a bookmaker's business in Dalmellington. Betting was against the law in those days, but many folk enjoyed a bet, especially on the horses, so Wull Hunter prospered.

When we moved to Dalmellington I got to know Wull very well and I believe he was one of the most honest and decent men I ever knew. He occasionally got into hot water with the local police because of the betting laws, but he was a great man for the village and very well thought of by everyone.

Snow

Coming originally from Tarbolton and later Dailly, then moving to Beoch in 1930, we were quite unprepared for the heavy snowfall which we encountered at Beoch. One winter morning we woke up to complete darkness in the back room. When my father opened the back door there was a white solid wall of snow. There had been a blizzard blowing all night and the wind had brought drifts which completely blocked the backside of all the houses, except the larger ones at either end of the row.

Sledging

Every house at Beoch had a sledge. We inherited one which had been left in the coal house by the previous occupants. And over the years we built others, some good and some bad. The good ones invariably had runners of spring steel. The main sources of these were the long suspension springs from perambulators (prams). These were greatly sought after and prized.

The Givens family were experts at building good sledges. They had one long sledge which could take six people and this was very popular with the grown-ups, who also enjoyed sledging, sometimes more so than the children. We had several ready-made sledge runs. The nearby Spring Hill was the most popular, with the run starting some 400 yards above the village, down a gradient of about 1 in 5 using a track, now grassed over, which had been used originally to transport coal tubs down to what we called the 'old line'.

This was an old track which went as far as Dalricket Mill, with a bridge over the River Nith of which only the stone supports remain. At Dalricket Mill attempts had been made to bring locomotives through to the Beoch from the Cumnock direction. Rails had been laid for a considerable distance, but abandoned probably for economic reasons. However, we had great fun, young and old, tobogganing down these slopes.

Foraging for coal

Another very practical use for the sledges was transporting coal. Although concessionary coal was available, it cost 10 shillings (50p) per ton. And for the families who had only one breadwinner, having a ton of coal to pay for was something they could ill afford. And, of course, for those families who had a breadwinner ill or injured and unable to work, it meant having to forage for coal on the bings (coal spoil heaps). In the winter the sledges were ideal for transporting coal from the bings.

There would always be four or five people on the bing in the evenings, when the tipping of spoil had finished. On the better days in the spring, summer and autumn, for transporting the sacks full of coal and dross, we had old bicycles. These were constructed from old bicycle frames and wheels found in the dump at the back of what was known to us as the Stable brae. The stables were, of course, long gone.

Low Pennyvenie probably in the 1940s when all the houses would have been occupied by local miners and their families. In the background is the Big Mine. None of this exists today, all the houses in High and Low Pennyvenie, a scattered community, having been demolished from the 1960s onwards with none remaining by 2006.

Families at Beoch

When my family first arrived at Beoch in 1930, there were some nineteen families in residence. Most of their names I can recall, but some were comparative newcomers like us. Some of the older families had moved out to more modern houses mainly at Craigview and Pennyvenie, on the main bus route and closer to Dalmellington.

These families had spent all their lives at the Beoch. And all the menfolk still worked in the Beoch Mine. Families such as Chalmers, I think there were five families of them, two of whom still lived at Beoch at that time. Others I can recall were Findlay, Curragh, Black, Riggans and Jess. Eddie Jess, though much older than I, was a great friend of mine. He was a qualified masseur, having studied for this in the evenings after work. From Eddie Jess I picked up his great appreciation of music. The great tenor of the day was Enrico Caruso. As we worked together he would hum or sing the arias from the operas and other orchestral works of great composers. There were many men with wonderful talents at Beoch.

Gramophone music

Every family at Beoch had a gramophone. Now, you have to understand that Beoch had no electricity, so these were powered by clockwork mechanism. You had to wind the motor up by means of a handle. Popular songs of the day were mainly from the music halls, Irish songs and of course Scottish songs. A great favourite was Arthur Tracy and among the popular songs I still remember were 'Alice Blue Gown', 'Oh I Wonder, Yes I Wonder', 'Silver Threads Among the Gold' and 'I'm Only a Strolling Vagabond'.

And of course there were the wonderful waltz songs sung by the great Richard Tauber. Jack Buchanan was also very popular, with songs such as 'Goodnight Vienna'. Another great favourite was Frank Crumit with 'Abdul Abulbul Amir' and 'Granny's Armchair'. In these days people sang in the home, in the shops and at work. It was wonderful and so natural. Folk in those days seemed to be happier and less self-conscious.

Radios

Radios at that time were few and far between. My father, Tommy Reid, had been a radio enthusiast from the early days. He bought a radio kit advertised in the *Radio Times* magazine. It was a Mullard make with two valves with a black metal case. It could be constructed without the use of solder. There was one instruction on the manual which read: 'Do not omit the spacers.' It puzzled us. What does omit mean? It was a word we had never encountered before. We often laughed about it later. Luckily we hadn't omitted them. The kit cost £2 10s. And in due course almost everyone eventually had one, because it allowed us access to the world news, although the quality was very poor.

Pocket money

Soon I would be working and earning money. My father had promised I would get half-a-crown (2s. 6d.) pocket money when I started working. Up to this I earned 3d. a week from Mrs Stewart for fetching her butter from Maneight Farm, about 1½ miles over the hills from Beoch. I also got 3d. a week from Andy Rodgers for feeding his ducks.

More families at Beoch

Among the families at Beoch during our later years there were McArthur, O'Neil, Stewart, Rodgers, Givens, Gavin, Carruthers, Halbert, Reid (our family), Paxton, Halliday, Rowan, Chalmers (James), Chalmers (William) and Clark. Then shortly afterwards, came families of McCabe, Prasher and Standring. A family who could also be included was McLarty, who lived just over the hill in the Shepherd's house near the Nith. Their children attended Beoch School, as did other children from nearby farms. Amazingly, these families had between them some seventy offspring. There would also be lodgers, usually relatives, living with many of the families, as was common in those days. When you include the parents there would be around 140 people living in twenty houses at Beoch. Our family, at a later date at Beoch, had my uncles Archie and Johnnie Lees to live with us when my grandfather Lees died. They lived with my mother and father for the rest of their lives and moved with the family to Gateside Street, Dalmellington in 1938.

School to Beoch Mine

I left school in 1934 at the beginning of the summer holiday and started work at Beoch Mine almost straight away. My best friends, Jim Halliday (who later was lost at sea in 1940 when the ship he was on, HMS *Esk*, went down with all hands), Colin McArthur (who pulled me out of the River Doon when I fell in up Ness Glen, when I was drowning), Peter Halbert and others of my age, were all working at what we called 'the platform'. This was so named because the coal tubs coming up from the mine came onto a flat section. The tubs, in fours, had a device called a 'smallman clip' which fastened on to the haulage rope. These clips had to be changed from the front of the tubs and put on the rear, because at the end of the platform the haulage ropeway started dropping down again on its way to Pennyvenie No. 4 (known locally as the Big Mine), where it went into wagons.

Tipping at the bing

At the platform there was also the blacksmith's shop, and a hut where we had our 'snap' (something to eat). Another job we had was disengaging the tubs of pit waste, stones, rocks and other debris, which had to be tipped on the bing which ran straight out on to a steep hillside. At that time it went out about 600 yards and had a height at its end of over 100 feet.

It was great working in the summer, earning money and building up our stamina, because the work was hard. The clips were tedious and tiring at first, but this was greatly alleviated by our contact with our fellow workers. In breaks we would help the men who tipped the muck tubs, and help the blacksmiths by pumping the bellows or doing general work about the shop. The roadman, a cheerful chap, muscular and strong, was called Joe Rollo. He had been in the USA, as had the blacksmith, Willie Dempsey. We loved listening to their tales of the Depression in America where, for a time, they had been hobos (tramps).

Wages

Though as young workers we were earning, it wasn't a great deal. My wage was one shilling and eleven pence halfpenny per day. For six days I took home ten shillings and ninepence including stoppages (deductions from wages). Working on the platform in the winter was vastly different. The platform was so exposed to the elements. During periods of heavy frost the haulage cable, a one-inch steel rope, had to be kept moving, so the tubs had to be run off or held unclipped.

Big fires were kept burning to keep the clips warm and frost free. The empty tubs, sent up along the line from Pennyvenie, had to be held at the platform and the wheels locked or snubbed with iron or wood lockers. On one particular morning my father came in off nightshift. A gale was blowing, with ice-laden rain driven almost horizontally. He said to my mother: 'Don't get Tam up this morning. It's not fit for man or beast out there!' I was awake listening in my warm bed, thinking about the poor devils who had to go out.

Up for work

But at 8 o'clock there was a thumping at the door and at the front window. My mother opened the door. It was 'Knoxy' Bone, the pit gaffer, and he said to Mother: 'What's up wae Tam? Get him out now.' And, of course, I had to go. Some other lads from further afield had failed to turn up. They lived as far apart as Waterside and Craigmark. Their mothers no doubt had the same idea as mine had. And all for one and eleven and a halfpenny! That particular morning it was all hands on deck. The blacksmith and his striker, David Gemmell, had been co-opted with Joe Rollo to keep the tubs going. The coal had to be moved at all costs.

Down the mine

We had just over a year of working on the platform when a new set of lads left school. They came not only from Beoch, but from as far away as Patna, Waterside, Dalmellington and Craigmark. And so it was our turn to go down the mine. We got half a crown a day underground. Big money! Incidentally, the wages of the adult surface worker at this time were six shillings and threepence a day.

On my first day down the Beoch Mine I was quite apprehensive. Although I had played around the pits for years and I had walked quite a distance into the mine at Clawfin, at least as far as natural light would allow, I had never been down a mine. So, my first day down the mine was interesting. I went with men I knew well, down through the two steel doors into the back airway. It took at least two of us to open the door and go through into the return airway. When we were all in and the door had clanged shut behind us, we had to open a second door and go through this.

Roaring fan

There was a roaring noise from the great fan which blows air into the roadways. Looking up at the giant fan through the protective mesh grill, one could see daylight through the massive blades sucking air from all parts of the mine. The sound was really deafening. There was a strong draught of hot air on our faces. We had to walk bent over. My feet were in a ditch created by water running into the mine. On my right side were 6-inch-diameter pipes taking pump water from the lower part of the mine to the surface for disposal.

This was the end of an era in Doon Valley deep mining. The last NCB-operated coal mine in Ayrshire's Doon Valley at Pennyvenie closed on 6 July 1978. Here some of the last stalwarts are seen with pit manager, Mr John Kennedy (hands clasped).
Back row (16) (l to r): Davie Galloway, Matt Reid, Jim McCracken, Neil McKnight, Nikolay Melnitschuk, Jim Auld, Tom Robertson (under-manager), Tom Meechan, Drew Napier, John Kennedy (manager), Tom Archibald, Willie Calder, John Dempsey, Willie Calderwood, Neil Dempsey and Jimmy Stewart.
Kneeling left to right: Jim Gemmell, Jack Thomson and Billy McClelland.
(Photo: Courtesy of EAC Doon Valley Museum cuttings file)

The mine bottom

I was glad when we got to the mine bottom because I could stand up again under 8-foot arch girders. There was a great hustle and bustle at the mine bottom. The main haulage from the underground workings was at right angles to the haulage taking the coal tubs out to the surface and bringing the empties back. Because of this all the tubs had to be slewed on a large metal plate before being clipped on to the main haulage. The same applied to the empties coming in. I was set on assisting this operation. After a year at this as well as other jobs on transporting closer to the coal faces, I eventually got a job with a collier as one of his two 'drawers' or trammers. This involved filling tubs and fetching them to haulage pick-up points.

Talented miners

In the mines it was surprising just how many well-cultured and knowledgeable people you worked with. One such was Jock McKenzie. He travelled every day from Waterside to work. He was an accomplished artist and sculptor. He was able to sculpt the most beautiful figures in anthracite. Besides this, he made musical instruments such as violins and banjos as a hobby.

I also met mathematicians like old Duncan Gray from New Cumnock, who taught me the basics permutations. Football pools were very popular then. Others who worked with me in the mine were members of brass bands and pipe bands and very skilled in these pursuits. There were many very kindly and talented men in the mines.

Co-op dividend

With being in work, my friends and I would go to Bertellotti's café in Dalmellington on a Saturday night and blow half-a-crown. Well not all! We saved a bit for the pit holidays at Glasgow Fair time. Holidays were not paid in those days. They were just days off. People depended on the Co-op dividends. Of course, families bought just about everything from the Co-op, so if you had a big family, you got a large dividend at the end of the quarter. This was a godsend for most folk in the Doon Valley at holiday times.

Cycle touring

A good touring bike cost £4 19s 6d. and getting this gave us great freedom. At weekends we toured far and wide. A Sunday run would be to places like Dumfries, Castle Douglas, Barrhill or Girvan. We would go cycle touring during the summer holidays. We would be laden with tents, primus stoves, kettles, pans and blankets as well as spare clothing. We went to Rothesay one year and camped on Canada Hill overlooking Rothesay bay.

Another year we went to Maryport in Cumbria when it rained all week and we had to sleep in a farmer's barn. We usually saved about 30 shillings for the holidays, which was quite sufficient. In fact one year we went to Portobello and I had enough left to buy a few presents for the family. My cycling pals on holiday were Jim Halliday, Colin McArthur and Peter Halbert.

When we went down the Nith or roaming elsewhere near Beoch, practically all the lads of the village went with us. Danny Standring, younger than we were, was a 'slowcoach' and we always had to wait for him to catch up. But we had wonderful times and looking back we were so happy and fortunate being so close to nature.

Home Guard

Years later, during the war, there were a great number of troops around Dalmellington, engaged in exercises prior to invading North Africa. I was in the Home Guard involved in some of the exercises. We were pursuing some soldiers concealed at the side of the road. One of them shouted to us. It was Dan Standring. He came to the house later to reminisce about the happy days he and his family had spent in the Beoch. Betty, his sister, came after the war from her home in Canada to see us. Other old neighbours also came to visit us when we moved to Gateside Street in Dalmellington. That was the sort of friendships that developed at Beoch.

Leaving Beoch in 1938

When we got to know that we would have to leave the Beoch, this was in 1938, we were all unhappy. I was eighteen years of age and very much a working man by then. We had been such a close-knit little community, in the real sense of the word. Caring and sharing in a very genuine and non-judgemental way. We were to move to much better houses in Dalmellington with hot water laid on and a flushing toilet. We had none of these at

Beoch. However, had we been given the choice we would have remained where we were. Well anyway that's how I felt at the time, but I suppose it was inevitable that it had to end.

9 February 2005 with the former school toilet block at Beoch. Now, even this building cannot be seen as it is entirely surrounded by spruce trees.
(Photo: Donald L Reid)

Looking back

But we would return to the Beoch again and again many years later to reminisce and remember those days, when we hadn't much in terms of possessions, but so much in terms of real friendship and freedom to roam. Years later I'd take my mother and father down to where the houses used to be at Beoch. All that remained were the foundations and the old school toilet block where the farmer at Beoch later used to store materials. All the stones and bricks had gone, but vivid memories of the past remained with us. And we would wander up and down roughly measuring and saying: 'This is where our house must have been. Mrs Chalmers lived up there', and so on.

Precious memories

Wonderful memories came flooding back of special folk and happy boyhood days. My mother would say touchingly: 'I loved this place', and I would notice a tear in her eye. She would no doubt be thinking of the year when my father was unable to work and the family of seven (and later nine when uncles Archie and Johnnie came to live with us at Beoch) all had to survive on 26 shillings a week.

My mother helped to earn more by taking in washing. There were several of the larger families at Beoch who were glad of my mother taking in washing to help them in that way. She would get between 5 shillings and 10 shillings a week. It was 10 shillings for a big washing and half of that for a smaller one. And there was no condescension in this. It was simply 'neebor' helping 'neebor'. Despite these hard times my mother really did love her years at Beoch, because all her family were around her and family was everything to her.

A happy place

I don't think the Beoch was unique in being a happy place to live in, despite the lack of basic amenities. But everyone there was in exactly the same boat and perhaps that was one reason for us being happy – content with our lot – with what was, in retrospect, a very basic existence by today's standards. But everyone was on the same level.

From what I hear from other people who lived in similar small mining villages in the Doon Valley at that time, they all look back to happy memories of growing up. We had what doesn't exist today – and that was a freedom to roam without restriction – in perfect safety. We had a trust in our fellow man and a simple lifestyle which younger folk of today couldn't even begin to understand. The villagers were hardy, down-to-earth folk with great compassion and practical kindness. I am very proud to say that I was one of the folk privileged to live at Beoch and work at Beoch Mine.

Farewell my friends true and leal,
Where'er we stay or restless roam
True-born hearts shall ever feel
We'll always call Beoch home.

Chapter 12

Reflections on Beoch

James L Reid

When shall I see that honor'd land,
That winding stream I love so dear?
Must wayward Fortune's adverse hand
For ever – ever keep me here?

The Banks of Nith
Robert Burns

James L Reid born in Tarbolton and raised there and at the Rumily, Daily and then at Beoch before coming to Dalmellington around 1937. Some of his memories are recorded in Reflections of Beoch

James L Reid spent forty-two years of his life working in the coal mines of Ayrshire, including Beoch, Pennyvenie and finally Killoch, rising to become an oversman and deputy manager. He was married for fifty-four years to Mary Hose and they had a daughter, Anne, and sons, Donald, Jim and Hugh; grandchildren Fraser, Mark, Samantha, Elaine, Christie and Shannon; and great-grandchildren, Charlie, Taylor, Owen, Emmy and Amber.

Jimmy was an elder at the Kirk o' the Covenant (now Dalmellington Parish Church) serving as treasurer under three different ministers, beginning with the Reverend John Morton. He was also treasurer of Dalmellington Bowling Club for many years. A keen trout and salmon fisherman, he really enjoyed fly fishing which he saw as a great escape from working in the coal mines. At the time of this interview (2012) Jimmy was aged eighty-eight and living in Dalmellington Care Centre.

Looking back

Looking back on life and seeing what progress has been made in your family, work and social life can be an enriching experience. As we all travel through life there is a tendency to become so embroiled in the day-to-day business of living that we sometimes fail to appreciate the value of taking time to reflect on the many and varied experiences which have led us to where we are today and hopefully to see what is really important about life.

In my own boyhood days at Beoch, there was only a wireless (radio) to learn about what was happening elsewhere in the world. Reading in the evening was difficult because the only light we had was from a smelly paraffin lamp.

Entertainment and play were self-made. And yet as I think back I did have a very happy time in this remote community situated just over a mile from the B741 Dalmellington to New Cumnock Road. I marvel at how life has changed so much from the 1930s until today.

In writing this short note of my memories, I can honestly say I have thoroughly enjoyed the journey down the road of my boyhood days and seeing again in my mind's eye the folk who made my own days of youth so interesting. I hope those who shared similar experiences in close-knit communities like the Beoch will enjoy these brief reflections.

Where I was born

I was born the third son of Thomas and Catherine Reid (née Lees) in James Street, Tarbolton on 12 October 1923. It was a row of old dilapidated houses known locally as 'Snail Row'. When I was about five years of age we moved to Westport, Tarbolton. My father worked at nearby Tofts Pit at that time.

Moving to Daily

I started my schooling at Tarbolton and attended primary school for about one year before our family moved to a small village near Dailly and close to the Maxwell Colliery. This small community was known as the Rumily and although we lived very near to Maxwell Colliery, my father actually worked as a borer at Killochan Pit about 3 miles away.

Following the long and bitter miners' strike of 1926 most collieries in Ayrshire were on two, three or four days of work per week, hence the reason why there was much movement of miners around Ayrshire in order to get the most beneficial conditions to support their families, so it was the practice for mining families to move about for the best jobs. While we lived at the Rumily I attended Wallacetoun School for about one year. This school, now closed, was approximately 2 miles from our house, which meant that at the tender age of six or seven years I had to walk 4 miles each day.

North Beoch

Some time during the early 1930s we flitted (moved house) to a remote village called North Beoch or simply Beoch. The reason for the move was because my father was more or less guaranteed a full week's work at Beoch Mine, which was situated less than a mile from the rows where the miners and their families lived. The community consisted of twenty houses and was situated some 4 miles north-east of Dalmellington on the B741 road and some 2 miles westwards off this road along a rough track. The village consisted of a double-storey block with an open stairway at either end of the row with sixteen single-storey houses between.

My family

When we came to Beoch our family consisted of my father Thomas, my mother Catherine, older brothers Tom and John, myself, Willie, and Donald was the baby. During our years at Beoch my sisters Margaret and Catherine were born. My mother's brother, Uncle Donald Lees, came to live with us because there was no work for him at Tarbolton and he stayed with us and worked at Beoch Mine. Uncle Donald as a young man in his twenties sustained a football injury to his leg which turned poisonous and he died. After that Uncle John and Uncle Archie, also of Tarbolton, got work at Beoch Mine and came to live with us. In fact they spent the rest of their lives with the family, moving to Dalmellington with us around 1938.

Our house

The houses at Beoch were all room-and-kitchen with two set-in beds in the kitchen and two beds in the room. Jutting out at the front of each single-storey house was the scullery which had a cold water tap and sink. Our furniture consisted of a dresser, a table, four chairs in the kitchen, two chests of drawers and two chairs in the room. There was also a cupboard in the scullery.

The lighting in the house was by paraffin lamp and also by the use of candles. There was no electricity. There was a large open fireplace with a side oven. Over the fire there was what was termed a swee, which could be swung in over the fire for baking purposes or boiling the kettle. The swee had a number of chain links which could be used to raise or lower cooking pots over the fire as required. At the front of the fire there was always a fender and wooden footstool. The fender was made of steel and was always gleaming bright due to liberal application of Brasso rubbed in with emery paper.

A dirt road ran the full length of the row in front of the sculleries and on the opposite side of the road there were coal houses plus two blocks of four wash houses. The women of the Beoch took turns at using the wash houses and it was normal practice to ensure that the large boiler was always full of hot water to provide washing facilities for the miners returning from work at the nearby mine.

Beoch School in 1935. It seems strange that a small row of miners' houses in a remote area warranted a school of its own. However, it also served the farming community in the district. Beoch was abandoned in 1937–38.
(Photo: John Reid)
(additional information on page 201)

The midden

Needless to say, the sanitary arrangements were extremely primitive. There were three large middens measuring approximately 12 by 6 by 3 feet into which all forms of rubbish were dumped. In those days (the 1930s) we usually had a considerable period of warm summer weather, so you can just imagine how convenient three middens were in providing a perfect breeding ground for all sorts of bugs.

It was little wonder that one year we had an epidemic of scarlet fever and diphtheria which affected every family to some degree. Periodically, Jimmy Bell came with a horse and cart to empty the middens and the contents were taken away and spread on fields around Pennyvenie.

Snowed in

Although we normally had good summers, we also had severe winter weather with considerable falls of snow which nearly always resulted in heavy drifting. I can remember a number of winters when Beoch was cut off by deep drifts and no form of transport could get through. Villagers had to trudge through the heavy drits to Dalmellington and carry essential foodstuffs back and that was a long and tortuous walk, even in good conditions, but must have been grim in such poor weather.

In the 1930s, Beoch Mine employed a good number of men from the New Cumnock area and it was not unusual for these men to be marooned at the pithead until the road was cleared by manual labour and a bus got through to take them home. The villagers, although they did not have an excess of bread, cheese and other basic foods, always managed to supply food to the stranded men.

Beoch village school

The village school at Beoch had two classrooms with three or four grades in each room. These would be called composite classes today. There were two teachers at the school in my time. Mrs Park took the older pupils and Miss Taylor taught the younger children. The standard of teaching was very good because I don't know anyone from Beoch School who did not receive a good grounding in the three Rs, unlike today's education system where we have a large number of pupils leaving school unable to adequately read, write or count.

I spent a very happy three or four years at Beoch School, where I found the three Rs easy to comprehend. I would dearly have liked to remain at Beoch School, but Mrs Park decided my education would be more complete if I went to the Higher Grade School in Dalmellington. In hindsight I don't think either Mrs Park or my parents thought about the difficulties of getting me from Beoch to Dalmellington in order to be there when the bell was rung at 9 a.m.

Getting to Dalmellington

In those days there was no such thing as transport provided for pupils, regardless of the distance from school. I had to walk the 2 miles from the village up to the main road and get the first bus into Dalmellington at 9.40 a.m., arriving in class about 10.00 a.m., thus missing one hour of teaching each day. I had to borrow notes from another boy and write them up at home by the light of a paraffin lamp, and sometimes they were long. This very unsatisfactory arrangement, which was in place for my first year at Dalmellington, had, I believe, a very detrimental effect on my education.

All these shops in High Main Street were occupied by various departments of Dalmellington Co-operative Society, which was established in 1879. By 1951 the society employed seventy-one people and had a membership of 1,455 with an annual turnover of £144,000. This photograph is from *circa* 1920 and the man holding the horse is Tom Bryden of Burnton Farm. From its earliest days until after the Second World War, the Co-op had several horses and carts for delivering groceries and butcher meat.
(Photo: Courtesy of EAC Doon Valley Museum)

After that the Education Authority, in their generous wisdom, provided me with a bicycle in order to get me to school in time to start at 9 a.m. In some of the very bad weather days, I managed to get a lift to Dalmellington from Jimmy Currie, the Co-op van driver, who delivered milk and rolls to Beoch about 8 a.m. He was very kind, because the Co-op policy was strictly that no one should be given lifts.

When I look back at my schooldays I feel certain that if I had been able to have had higher education at Beoch instead of all the difficulties involved in getting to Dalmellington, I would have achieved greater educational qualifications.

I was always happy at Beoch School, where I had all my friends and all the joyful out-of-school adventures, whereas the time spent in cycling to and from Dalmellington plus writing up notes when I was unable to get there on time, proved a real headache and I was never quite happy with that arrangement. Nowadays young folk simply wouldn't understand that a young person would be expected to cycle more than 5 miles each way, in all weather conditions, to attend school. However, that was the way things were and you simply had to get on with it.

Happy boyhood days

Although the Beoch was pretty isolated and had little or no modern facilities, I look back on my boyhood days spent there as some of the happiest days of my life. In the summer time, the boys went in search of all kinds of birds' eggs, including peesies' (lapwings'), which were plentiful and delicious to eat. We also found whaups (curlew), snipe, golden plover, partridge and a whole host of smaller birds – mavis, blackbird, wren, skylark, chaffinch and sand martin.

Swimming and guddling

We used to swim in the River Nith which was about 2 miles away over the hill. We had no bathing costumes or towels and we used to race each other back home to Beoch. The Nith and Beoch burns both had runs of salmon and sea trout in the autumn, in those days. I used to catch large sea trout by guddling in the burns. This involved lying on a stone, placing your hands around the large stones in the water, and catching the trout in your bare hands. All the boys enjoyed doing this in my day and you could come away with several good-sized fish that were cooked and greatly enjoyed that same night by all the family.

Sledging

In the winter we had home-made sledges. The runners were made with old pram springs which were conveniently shaped, nicely curved upwards at each end. The drill was to pull the sledge with someone sitting on it until the runners were nice and shining, and then take the sledge to the top of a nearby fairly steep gradient. In our case this was an abandoned railway track bed and there we had a miniature Cresta run. Everyone including the adults enjoyed sledging when the weather was right.

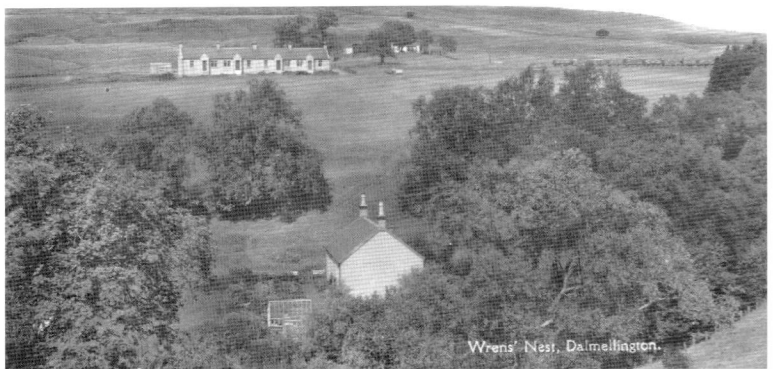

The Wrens looking towards a row of cottages at Pennyvenie called Sighthill. These houses were generally occupied by higher ranking members of the workforce at Pennyvenie Colliery such as managers. You can see the rake of coal wagons and the Pennyvenie Farm behind Sighthill. The farm was demolished to make way for opencast working and re-established on the opposite side of the B741.
(Photo: Courtesy of EAC Doon Valley Museum)

Beoch characters

The Beoch had a number of characters among its residents. There was Lewis McArthur (senior), Jimmy Rowan, Sam Paxton, Tom (Tam) Standring and Andy Rogers. All had their own peculiar idiosyncrasies. Lewis McArthur bore a good resemblance to W C Fields, a film star of that period, and for some reason, which I never understood, he used to get very hot under the collar when some mischief-makers called out 'cuckoo' when he passed.

Jimmy Rowan was a big man, over 6 foot, very fond of a drink, but was said to be afraid of being alone in the dark. Sam Paxton was a small man with very little to say, particularly in the presence of his wife. Tam Standring, although very obviously not flush with cash, liked a tanner double on the horses and a game at cards. Tam seemed to be forever on the cadge. If it was not a cup of sugar, dry tea or a loaf, he would find some other item to borrow from neighbours. Andy Rogers' wife and family left him. I don't know the reason, and thereafter he became more or less a recluse.

Demise of Beoch Row

The villagers of Beoch were all rehoused in council houses in Dalmellington in 1937. My family were allocated a four-apartment house at 3 Gateside Street. What a transformation from our previous home. We now had electric light, hot water tap and flushing indoor toilets. Needless to say, we were all delighted, but there was still a degree of sadness at leaving a place where we could wander freely and had many good friends.

My mother in particular was very sad to leave Beoch, despite having such a good house in Dalmellington. I think Beoch Row was demolished probably around 1938 and all that remained was the old school outdoor toilets which the local farmer later used as a storehouse. Today the area where the row was is covered in spruce trees and the only identifiable area is the old toilet block, marking where Beoch row stood.

Beginning work

I left school at Dalmellington in 1938. I was unemployed for a short time, then for a few months worked as an apprentice cobbler with John Kissell, who had a footwear repair plus cycle shop in Croft Street. This was later to become part of Gibson's garage, now also closed. My first wage was 10 shillings (50p) a week. I didn't enjoy this work and managed to get a job at the pithead at Benbain. I was working there when the Second World War began and I progressed from the surface to working underground with my father.

Pit accident

I remember one incident at the pit, when I was about eighteen years of age. I was working in the pit with my father, Phil Dunn and Hugh McCreath. At that particular time we were working down the pit and the only light we had was the carbide lamps. Five holes had been drilled in the seam, using a hand machine – rickety – and gelignite and strum detonators had been inserted in the bore holes. The strum was ignited in each hole in turn and this had to be done fairly quickly in order to allow time to seek shelter before the first shot exploded.

We counted one, two, three, four, explosions, but there was no fifth. After waiting a considerable time and assuming that the fifth strum had not been lit, we all ventured back into the workplace. Hugh McCreath had just bent down when the shot exploded, sending a shower of coal particles and dust into his face and eyes. As far as I can remember, Hugh lost the sight in one eye and his face was left badly marked for the rest of his days. Following that I worked on my own through nearly all the various categories of conventional mining.

The last shift finish up at Minnivey Colliery in December 1975 and another colliery closes in Ayrshire's Doon Valley. The present mine began production in 1958, and of the 280 miners, 148 were transferred to nearby Pennyvenie, whilst 64 were being retrained for salvage purposes and a further 64 accepted early retirement. The newspaper commented: 'As coalmining in South Ayrshire gradually becomes a dying industry, so the area becomes more depressed.'
(l to r): William Filson (union rep), James Auld, William McMahon, David McGill and John McPhail.
(Courtesy of *Ayr Advertiser*, 4 December 1975)

Mining education

When I was twenty-seven years of age and had been married for four years, I rather belatedly decided that there was not a great future in working my guts out for a living at the coal face. So I started attending night classes in Glasgow. I worked hard and got a colliery deputy and shotfirer's certificate and after further study at the Royal College of Science and Technology in Glasgow, gained a Colliery Under-Manager's certificate.

I was shotfirer, deputy and finally oversman for about sixteen years at Beoch Colliery, then ten years as dayshift oversman in Pennyvenie, and my final three years in the coal industry were spent as oversman, covering three different shifts at Killoch Colliery. I was very happy to retire from Killoch in August 1981 and have enjoyed many pleasant years since then. But I can say with much understanding and honesty, and I believe any miner would agree, that forty-two years in the coal mines of Ayrshire was more than enough for any man.

> *Hard-handed stalwarts of labour,*
> *Nurtured to grin and to bear,*
> *Seldom a thought of the danger*
> *That haunts every corner down there,*
> *Praying to Christ it was shift change*
> *But not in the language of prayer.*

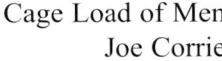

Cage Load of Men
Joe Corrie

Benbeoch Craig stands sentinel over the Dalmellington–Cumnock road (B741), although the opencast mining has changed the landscape. It was here that the Dalmellington Covenanters would hide to escape persecution. Conventicles were also held in this area.
(Photo: Courtesy of EAC Doon Valley Museum)

Benbeoch Memories

Entitled 'Benbeoch Memories', this poem highlights the association of the men of Dalmellington with what became known as the Killing Times in the 1680s, when villagers held conventicles in the hills around Benbeoch Craig. This dramatic hill, with its rocky formations giving it all the hallmarks of a miniature Giant's Causeway, stands sentinel close by the village of Dalmellington. It can be seen at its most dramatic on the Dalmellington–Cumnock Road just east of Pennyvenie. The poem is signed 'Milreoch', but the name of the author is unknown. It was penned some time before 1929 and is reprinted in the paper entitled 'Extracts from Wodrow's Manuscript Reprint Relating to the Covenanters who fell in Dalmellington Parish 1666–1686', prepared in 1929 by Hugh Gibson.

> *Listen:*
> *I hear the call of the moorland bird,*
> *Warning the men, who have faith in the word,*
> *That the troopers are coming to trample roughshod,*
> *The homes of the rebels who trust in their God.*
>
> *Listen:*
> *It is calling, calling, calling today,*
> *Like a voice departed, or far, far away,*
> *But no troopers trample the meadow or moss,*
> *To harry the home of a Notson, or Sloss.*
>
> *Listen:*
> *I hear the Psalm of the Covenant swell,*
> *From the back of Benbain, to the 'Lone Free Well',*
> *Afflicted, afflicted; but shall we prevail?*
> *Now may Israel say, 'The Lord shall not fail.'*
>
> *Listen:*
> *In the rocks of Benbeoch it echoes aloud,*
> *And the sons of the Parish, stand upward and proud,*
> *As they think of the strength that comforted the strong,*
> *How mighty the sword; how great was the song. Listen.*

Chapter 13

Cairntable Capers

Tom Smith

And fare thee weel, my only luve!
And fare thee weel, a while!
And I will come again, my luve,
Tho' it were ten thousand mile!

My Luve is Like a Red, Red Rose
Robert Burns

Tom Smith was born and raised at Cairntable. He enjoys painting and has several sketches of the Cairntable area.

Tom Smith, a retired miner with an artistic skill as a painter, now lives in Drongan. He was interviewed in March 2012 about his memories of life at Cairntable, another of the lost villages. Cairntable, on the B730 Polnessan to Rankinston road, consisted of two rows – forty-eight houses in all – built a few years before the 1914–18 war. The houses were erected for the miners who worked in 'Barr's' mines and at the old pits near Rankinston.

All the villagers over the years knew each other well. 'Auld' Andrew Lindsay was a miners' representative at the colliery and ran the Sunday School. Elspie Knox's shop at the 'Wee Row' and Bob Deans' at the top of the village served the community well. When children would shout 'shop' as they entered, Bob would say: 'You're making some noise, son – can you no' shout without raisin' your voice?'

With the passage of time only a few will remember Jean Watters, who was always present when there was an illness or trouble in the village. She could prescribe a cure for just about anything from a cold to corns.

Other well-known villagers were Jimmy Colvin, who looked after the village hall; David Wilson, a kind and genuine man, who was headmaster of Kerse School; Geordie Irvine, whom everyone admired for his contented nature. Cairntable as a village is no more. The last tenant had moved out by July 1963 and it was demolished shortly thereafter.

My family

I was born at 4 Cairntable on 13 August 1938. I was the fifth youngest in a family of ten. From the oldest to the youngest, my sisters and brothers were Robert, Andrew, Isa, Margaret, George, myself, Mina, John, Marion and Elizabeth. We lived with our parents, Robert and Charlotte. My sister Margaret stayed in Trabboch with her Gran McDonald. My father was born nearby in Tongue Row, a small clachan located just above Cairntable. My mother died at the age of forty-five shortly after we moved to Drongan in 1951.

A drawing by Tom Smith of Killoch Colliery Pithead. Killoch was sunk 1953, coal production began in 1960 and it closed in 1987. (Courtesy of Tom Smith)

Kindly mother

Mother was a kind-hearted body and if there were ever any rows in the house, they were caused by my father as my mother had a lovely nature. She worked very hard to look after my father and my brothers and sisters and her life revolved around the home. She was always cheery and mixed among the other folk in Cairntable. They all went on regular walks along the railway line as I suppose there wasn't really an awful lot else to do in such a small community. Cairntable lies about 2 miles from Polnessan and Rankinston on the B730 road.

My father worked first of all in Littlemill No. 3 and then when No. 5 was opened up he worked there. The pit was located about half a mile from the rows. The miners walked along the railway to get to the pit. He worked as a miner all his days.

Cairntable village, erected in 1914, was located on the B730 some 2 miles east of its junction with the A713. It is still remembered with affection by former villagers. The last family departed in 1963 and the houses were all later demolished. Jimmy Dunn with his distinctive beard and hat, a former villager born there in 1931, arranged for the erection of a memorial stone now marking where another of the lost mining villages of Ayrshire once stood. He is joined by former villagers at the inauguration of the memorial stone in 2007.
(Photo: courtesy of Jimmy Dunn)

Our wee village

Cairntable was a small mining village which consisted of forty-eight houses in two rows. There was a row with twenty and then a gap and another twenty houses above that, and across the road there were another eight houses. The forty houses consisted of one room and kitchen and a small scullery. The row of eight houses, we called it the Wee Row, had two rooms and a kitchen.

Although there was electric lighting in the house, there was none in the street. However, when I was young the County Council installed three street lights to cover the entire village. The first was located at the bottom of the rows near the railway bridge. The second was near to No. 21 at what we called the Middle Corner. The third was situated at the small shop at the top of the village.

Earliest memories

My earliest memories of Cairntable were that we ran about with a gir'n' cleek (gird and cleek – a metal hoop and stick) and my mother used to say jocularly to me: 'Are you going to school this morning on the bus or on your gir'?' She had a smashing sense of humour. As you can imagine, living in a small house with mother, father and eight children was quite crowded.

There was no indoor toilet, but there was a flushing toilet in an outhouse which was shared with the next-door neighbours. In our case we had John and Sadie Colvin and they only had one son. So, it wasn't all big families, but small families were in the minority.

When I think about it now, it must have been very hard for my father and mother, what with such a big family and with poor wages in the pit. My mother never worked, but her time was taken up to the full in looking after us all.

Living conditions

There was what you call inset beds. The house was what we called a room and kitchen. The kitchen was also the living room. In the kitchen there were two inset beds and in the other room there was one inset bed. We also had a bed settee and I remember that it was myself, Robert and Andrew who slept in that at night. My mother and father slept in the inset bed in the kitchen. The girls, Marion, Mina, Elizabeth and Isa, slept in the living room. It was quite chaotic.

At the back of the rows there were five outhouses with four toilets in each. Each toilet was shared by two families. Mind you, and anyone who lived there will tell you this, they were kept spotless. You simply couldn't leave a mess for someone else to clean. That wasn't acceptable and everyone knew it.

The coal preparation plant at Littlemill Colliery. Many men from lost mining villages such as Cairntable worked at Littlemill. On 19 December 1938, before nine o'clock, three miners were killed and five were injured as the result of an underground explosion. The names of the dead were John Leslie sen. (55), 6 Littlemill Place, Rankinston; James Graham (45), Kerse Terrace, Rankinston; and William Brown (28), Kerse Terrace, Rankinston. The names of the injured were John Leslie jun. (24), son of John Leslie, 6 Littlemill Place; William Ferguson (23), son-in-law of John Leslie, Burnfoothill; Joseph Kirkland (28), Kerse Terrace; Rankinston; Robert Kerr (18), Kerse Terrace; Robert Howatson (25), Station Row, Rankinston. (*Scotsman*, 10 December 1938)

> The death-roll was raised to four by the death in Ayr County Hospital on Saturday, of Robert Howatson (25), Station Row, Rankinston. About 16 men were working at a face in the Ashentree main coal section when there was a terrific explosion which threw them in all directions, overturning hutches and wrecking gear in the vicinity. An appeal for volunteers drew most of the male population of Rankinston and the neighbouring hamlet of Cairntable to the pithead (*Scotsman*, 12 December 1938).

(Photo: Courtesy Scottish Mining Museum)

Radio entertainment

My grandmother also lived in Cairntable with us. She was a great knitter and I remember that she loved sitting in front of the fire knitting away furiously and listening to the radio. The programme she liked best was called *The Man in Black*. There was also Dick Barton and later on the whole family enjoyed the McFlannels, and of course Jimmy Shand and his country band was a real toe-tapper. Later on my grandmother moved to Rankinston to live with my Uncle Andrew and Aunt Mary and this gave us a little more room in our house. There was no television in those days unless you were very rich, and no one had a TV that I was aware of in Cairntable.

Railway halt

There was a railway halt next to the village. This line ran from Holehouse Junction on the Ayr–Dalmellington line and it ran right up to the main Kilmarnock–Dumfries line. As boys we would walk along the line down to Kerse Loch and enjoy swimming and bird nesting. There were always lots of plovers' eggs to be found, but funnily enough you hardly see a plover today.

Bathing at Kerse Loch

I also remember that in those days the summer weather seemed to be brilliant. Folk today will find this strange, but there were no baths (showers) at Littlemill Pit. My father and the other miners would often come home from the pit in the summer, perhaps off early shift, and get some soap and walk along the railway line to Kerse Loch and go in for a swim and a wash, because they were covered in coal dust from working down the pit. The circumstances in which we lived were just accepted by us, but today's generation would find it outrageous, but that was simply the way things were. There were absolutely no luxuries to speak of.

Old Smithstone Farm and what was known many years ago as the Old Fairy Tree at Kerse. This tree blew down in a gale many years ago. There are now two houses at Kerse in addition to Old Smithstone Farm. The area once had its own Kerse brass band.
(Courtesy of Tom Smith)

Home cinema memories

My father was a man who in many ways was ahead of his time. He had a cine-projector and some nights he would invite neighbours into the house. He loved his photography. He would set up a big white sheet and the house was bursting at the seams with folk crowded in as he showed a film to the delight of everyone.

The kids would even be trying to peer in the window to see the film. He was also interested in short-wave radio and he would repair radios for local folk. In fact I still have a reel of his cine film which I had put on video and copied for the family. This is now a great record of our early days at Cairntable. I never tire of looking at this magical video and seeing my parents and brothers and sisters as they were in 1946 as youngsters.

It is especially poignant now that Mum, Dad, George, Andrew and Margaret have all passed away and it seems strange watching them in their younger days as happy-go-lucky kids. The fact that my father had the foresight to make these movies is a wonderful gift to us today and it does bring great joy tinged with sadness. The video is a great record of some aspects of life at Cairntable and helps us to enjoy a journey down memory lane.

I remember when my father bought a sound projector and a big screen. He hired films every week and showed them round the village halls in the district with Dick Nisbet of our village. Dick had a car and took my father to the halls and these were a great attraction for local young folk. He started in Cairntable and then showed these films in Tarbolton, Drongan, Rankinston, Lethanhill and Patna in the 1940s. They went down a bomb.

Gala day

There was annual gala day at Kerse Whinny. This was the hill above Kerse School. Every year this went on and there would be sports and stalls and competitions and everyone from Cairntable, Kerse and elsewhere would be there. It was always eagerly awaited by us and was really a big day for us living in a small village.

Games

Games we played were common such as kick the can, hide and seek, football and running about with our gir's. Sliding down the railway embankment on old hessian tattie bags was common in the summer. Bogies, made by my father, were also great fun and on the video taken by him is footage of me going down the hill into the village lying face down on my bogie. A bogie was a wooden frame with four wheels which could be steered and it was great fun for a daredevil youngster.

There was also a playground at the back of the rows with four swings and a roundabout which we played on most days. We would go on walks up Ashentree Glen which was located near to the farm by the same name. We would often go up and spend the day there. We'd make a fire and roast tatties, which were always delicious. I remember that we would catch minnows in the burn and have a competition to see who could catch the most.

Picnics at Kerse

We were often in bare feet as the summers seemed to be so good and the tar would often stick to the soles of our feet. Our parents also took us on picnics along to Kerse Loch and we had great fun playing games. Again my father captured these special moments on film and it's grand to look back at them today. As well as filming our family, he also filmed many of our neighbours. Of course, many of them have also passed on, but the memory of these days is all the more special probably because they are no longer with us.

Village shop

There was a small wooden shop at the top end of the village. In my time it was run by Bob Deans and his wife. This was where the villagers shopped, although the likes of Patna Co-op had a mobile shop which called in. At Deans' shop you could buy bread, cheese and lard. I don't recall my mother going to Ayr for her shopping, but she would go on the bus to Patna Co-op.

The buses serving Kerse were single-deckers because of the railway bridge at the edge of the village and later on I remember seeing the first double-decker bus, which was quite something for a wee boy. In these days there was very little traffic passing through Cairntable.

Steam loco stranded

I remember about 1947 when it was a very severe winter. A steam engine came along and got stuck in one of the railway cuttings near the rows. I remember all the men in the village and

Littlemill Pit going onto the line to help dig out the train. Because of the snow the men had to walk from Cairntable to Patna to get bread to feed their families. So, although the summers seemed to be very good the winters were often dreadful.

Pals of yesteryear

My pals of early days in the rows were John Grant (now of Ayr); Dan Easton, now of Dalrymple; Harry McTimpany, who became a policeman and lives in Ayr; David McCulloch, who died a few years ago; Robert Paterson of Dalrymple; Tom Campbell, his sister Irene Campbell; Janette Callaghan and Maureen McKie. All these folk and their families and many others besides, lived in Cairntable when I was growing up.

Above left: Kerse School with the happy class of *circa* 1948.
Back row: (l to r) John Dunn, Bert Wallace, Peter Callaghan, Billy Hewitson, Dan Easton and David Wallace.
Second back row: Hugh Robertson, John Grant (lives in Ayr and contributed photo), Janet McWhirter, Catherine Robertson, Peggy Paterson, John Hewitson and Sydney Seaton.
(Photo: Courtesy of EAC Doon Valley Museum)

Above right: Kerse School *circa* 1948.
Back row (l to r): J Nisbet, Henry Ferris, John Smith, ?, and John Ferguson.
Middle row: Teacher Helen Dykes, Robert Paterson, Betty Wallace, Callaghan and Jim Colvin.
Front row: Janet Dalziel, Wallace, ?, Wylie, Margaret McTimpany and Irene Campbell.
(John Grant collection)

Kerse School

We all attended the school at Kerse and went up the hill to school on the SMT bus. The teachers I remember were Miss Hynds, Mr Johnstone and the headmaster was David Wilson. He lived in the headmaster's house next door to the school. Later on he moved to Hollybush School. I remember going to Ayr with the school to see the film *Scott of the Antarctic* in the Gaumont Cinema in High Street. It was great as a boy to see that. We also took part in cross-country running at school.

Leaving Cairntable

My family left the village in 1951 to move to Drongan when I was aged thirteen. I remember being quite sad at having to leave Cairntable, because that was all I had ever known. The house we moved to was at 69 Glencraig Street. At the same time other folk moved in to Drongan from such places as Drumsmudden, Trabboch and Skairs, but most came from Cairntable.

They were starting to run Cairntable down with a view to demolition, because the sewerage system was apparently a major problem. Some of the folk from Cairntable also moved to Dalrymple, some to Patna and some to Polnessan. The village remained intact until the early 1960s with a steadily diminishing population and it was eventually emptied completely about 1963 and then demolished. Cairntable, a place of very happy memory, was a lovely little community.

The village was rased in 1963
Now nothing's left today.
If you ever travel on that road,
Don't look for such a place,
For mother nature has returned,
Now it's gone without a trace.

Cairntable
Tom Smith

Chapter 14

Tough Times at Corbie Craigs

Bill Bakkom

Then catch the moments as they fly,
And use them as ye ought, man!
Believe me, Happiness is shy,
And come not ay when sought, man!

Here's A Bottle
Robert Burns

Bill Bakkom as a wee boy in 1946. He was brought up in a wooden hut located adjacent to Corbie Craig rows. His memories of life there are illuminating and heart-breaking.
(Photo: Bill Bakkom collection)

Bill Bakkom was born in 1934. He has lived for many years at 3528 Hedalen, Norway. However, his formative years from 1935 until 1946 were spent at Corbie Craigs. Affectionately known as the Corbies, it sits high above Waterside on the 900-foot contour. It was a row of ten miners' houses located precariously on the edge of Dunaskin Glen.

Today the visitor will find that there are still substantial ruins at Corbies, with two trees standing guard over this lonely and deserted clachan. Bill suffered genuine hardship as a youngster and his glimpse of life is revealing and humbling. His son, Leif Erik, has visited Corbies several times over the years to 'touch base' with his family roots. This interview by Donald L Reid is a very moving account of a difficult life for a young lad and the chapter title, Tough Times at Corbie Craigs, is very appropriate.

A grateful, warm adieu;
I with a much indebted tear
Shall still remember you!

The Farewell
Robert Burns

Born Canada
I was born in Fort Frances, Ontario, Canada on 29 June 1934. My father was Gilbert Gudbram Bakkom, who was Norwegian. My mother was Robina McKenzie Reid and she was born in Maybole in 1894. Her father, William Reid, was the only chemist in Maybole at that time. Her mother, Margaret McKenzie or Reid came from the Orkney Islands.

My family
My mother married my father in 1920 in Canada. He had been in the Canadian army stationed at Kilkerran near Maybole where they met. She went to Canada to marry him. I had five sisters, the oldest was Margaret, then Olga, Thora, Lillian and Amelia. I was the youngest. My mother and father separated in 1935. He drank a lot and didn't treat her very well and I think that was why she cried so much. So, my mother came back from Canada with my sister Thora and me, to live in the Doon Valley.

Hut at the Corbies
Folk will find this intriguing and perhaps even difficult to believe, but mother had a basic garden hut built by the local joiner in Dalmellington and it was sited and erected about 50 yards from the row of ten houses at Corbie Craigs. That's how I came to be there and that was home to my mother, my sister Thora and me for the next eleven years. I suppose you could say that we were living in real poverty.

Meeting my family
My sister Thora, who was about seven years of age, came with my mother from Canada, but the rest of the girls, Margaret, Olga, Lillian and Amelia, remained with my father and they were looked after by a Mrs McLeod. In 1956 I met my sisters Margaret, Lillian, Olga and Amelia for the very first time in Canada.

As you can probably imagine, it was a very moving occasion and there were lots of tears. I think they found it unbelievable that mother, Thora and I had been living in a garden hut on a high hillside above Dalmellington for so many years, because it was indeed tough times at Corbie Craigs. Meeting my sisters was a happy time, but sad because of all the years that were lost to us as a family. I met my father the following year in Fort Frances.

Early memories

One of my earliest memories of Corbie Craigs was starting school at Benwhat in 1939. Benwhat was about 1 mile from Corbies along a rough road. My cousins Neil, Hugh, Willie and Mary Hainey also went to Benwhat School, as well as my sister Thora, who was seven years older than me. I hated school from the start and remember crying and not wanting to go.

As this was the start of the war we were all issued with gas masks which were in a little cardboard box with a string so we could carry it on our shoulders. As I recall I wasn't very popular at school, probably because I was different from everyone else, living in a hut at Corbies.

School at Benwhat

My fellow pupils were poor, but my family was even worse off in every possible way because we lived in a garden hut. I remember that I was regularly picked on by other boys at school and I was desperately unhappy.

We used slates with wood frames at that time for our writing. One good thing, however, was that I got meals at school and to be honest without them I think I would have starved to death. Unlike me, my sister Thora loved school. She was very bright and popular. She won the best school prizes every year. She died in America of cancer some years ago, but throughout her life she had fond memories of Corbies and school at Benwhat, despite living in a wooden hut.

Silent films

Meals in our hut at Corbies tended to be tea, bread, treacle or fried oatmeal. Happier times at school included going to the gym to watch silent Charlie Chaplin films and of course enjoying school lunch. I also loved when we got out of school to collect bags of sphagnum moss or work in the school gardens.

Head lice and injury

I remember that there was a lot of head lice at school and my mother always over-reacted. She would wash my hair with paraffin and use a fine comb for the lice. Perhaps that's why today in my seventies I have so much hair! One time I got my annual pair of tackety boots. I had a hole in my socks and I got an infection in my foot which was really bad. Had it not been for the wonderful Dr Lee in Dalmellington I might have lost my foot.

Winter

I had to walk from Corbies to Benwhat every day, which was fine and healthy and enjoyable. Being located so high up on the hills, the weather could be very harsh. In fact I can remember that the winters were very severe and on many occasions I was unable to go to school because the roads were covered with heavy drifting snow to a deep level.

Cooking and baking in the hut

My mother cooked all our meals in the hut. We had oatmeal, onions and lard which she cooked for dinner. We had a cup of tea without sugar because it was rationed during the war. She sometimes made treacle scones, which was a great treat. At Christmas it was a clootie dumpling, which was wonderful for us and she would put farthings in it and it was great to find one as you enjoyed eating the dumpling. Simple things were precious when you didn't have a lot, and in our case that was an understatement.

We were very poor indeed. The folk in the rows at Corbie Craigs were also poor, but the difference was they lived in proper stone-built houses. They had cold running water, but no electric light and like us had to use a paraffin lamp, but they did have indoor toilets. In our wooden hut we had absolutely no facilities.

Coal

There was a coal stove which my mother used to cook everything on. There was no lighting except that provided by a paraffin lamp. We often had no coal and I had to try to find wood or go looking for coal in the outcrops in the glen, but this could be a dangerous, risky business because the banking was steep and unstable and a rock fall was always a possibility. But, it had to be done and as a wee boy I always felt a responsibility for my mother and sister.

I also went down to Waterside with my mother on a regular basis to try and find some twigs to fire the stove. I remember that the nuns from Waterside used to visit my mother a lot. I was scared of them, but I think they appreciated our precarious situation.

Prejudice
Strange to think we lived in the only wooden hut on the plateau and because I wasn't Scottish I was treated quite badly by the other young folk in the district. I was often knocked about by other youngsters. During the war we could hear the air-raid sirens going off at Dalmellington and Waterside. From our hill location we could see the German planes flying towards Clydebank. We had identity cards which we had to carry and my mother had ration cards which she gave to the shopkeeper to buy her entitlement of scarce food.

Collecting peat and water
I remember Mr Bell, farmer at nearby Burnhead Farm, located just behind Corbie Craigs. He used to cut peat and I would get some to burn on the stove in our hut. He appreciated that we didn't have much and he probably took pity on us. We had no toilet in the hut where we lived. We only had a toilet pail which was used in the hut, especially during the night and was emptied well away from our hut in the morning.

I also had to collect pails with drinking water and my mother would put a cloth over the pail to keep the water clean. The hut consisted of one small room – it was just a small garden hut. My mother and Thora slept in the top of the bed and I slept in the bottom. Mind you, some of the families had ten folk living in a room and kitchen at Corbies, so our situation was by no means unique.

When it was windy, and it was often like that, the whole hut would rattle and shake and in winter when the snow was bad and being driven by the winds, it would actually come through the joints in the hut. Mind you, with the stove on, it was actually quite cosy.

I remember that as a boy I was always hungry. I never had a Christmas present as such, other than an apple or orange. My mother didn't work and she depended on the state to keep us going. We simply accepted our lot, but we were very poor indeed and I often wished I could have done more for Mum and Thora.

Coin find
When I was about eight years of age, I found a lot of coins below a large stone on the ruined walls near to the Rough Burn below Corbies. A man came along and I showed him the coins. He gave me sixpence and took them. Later on I wondered if they had perhaps been valuable Roman coins, but I'll never know. However, I'm sure that the plateau area will have been rich in antiquities still to be discovered.

Family feelings
Looking back, the summers seemed to be much better, but the winters were very bad and the hut was draughty. My mother used to cry every day because she had left her other daughters in Canada. She must have had a broken heart. I missed the fact that I didn't have a father and that hurt me quite a bit. I grew up quite unhappy at times and life seemed to have dealt us a very unhappy hand. Part of my sadness, I suppose, was for my mother, and my sisters who were living in Canada, and I think they would have been feeling the same, being separated from us.

My great pal was Robert McCart, who lived at Corbie Craigs. I sometimes played with William Hainey, who was my cousin. I also played with Jimmy McGowan. We used to run about the hills and roads with a gir'n' cleek. The burn below the Corbies was also a popular place to play. We used to go looking for birds' eggs and we'd spend hours down the Dunaskin Glen.

Moving away
I left Corbie Craigs at the age of twelve in 1946 to go to live at Maidens in a house. I was pleased to be leaving our old hut. It was so claustrophobic to live in and as I got older I found it more and more difficult to put up with it. There was simply no privacy whatsoever. Can you imagine any children of today living as a family in a garden hut on a high hill in the middle of nowhere?

Visits to Corbies
I've returned to Corbie Craigs on several occasions over the

years and find it very moving and nostalgic. On reflection I am glad that I lived there and have no lasting regrets now, even though there were some very unhappy times. I believe it gave me a greater understanding of life and people. I survived with very little, but I believe that I appreciated better that small things in life are important and sometimes you simply have to get on with things and make the best of the situation in which you find yourself. There are always folk worse off than you.

Bill Bakkom on a visit to Corbie Craigs with Donald L Reid in 2004, a place which still holds dear memories for him, although times were very tough.
(Photo: Donald L Reid)

Greatest regret

I suppose the greatest regret was being separated from my sisters in Canada and there is still a hurt in me that we were brought up separately in different countries. These are the things that unfortunately happen when there is a breakdown in the family unit. I always felt very sorry for my mother because she was constantly grieving for her girls who were in Canada.

As a wee boy I always wished I could have done something to help her, but it was like a death in the family and she was simply heartbroken for her daughters, probably always wondering how they were and what they were doing. I went to live in Canada in 1956 and travelled by boat from Southampton to Quebec.

Mother's visit to Canada

In 1958 I was delighted to be able to bring my mother across to Canada and she stayed for about two months and saw her daughters and her husband. It was a great joy for her being reunited with the girls and there was a real sparkle in her eye that I'd never seen before. However, my mother and father wouldn't talk to each other and there was still great bitterness in that relationship. My mother returned to Scotland and lived in Maybole where she died in 1972. I don't think she ever quite got over losing her daughters, and you can understand that.

I travelled greatly over the years. I went from Canada to Norway and now at the age of seventy-eight I still sometimes think about returning to live in Ayrshire, but I certainly won't be living at Corbies in a hut! One thing, however, is certain: Corbie Craigs – the place of my early years – will doubtless draw me back to glimpse again my days of youth and to quietly remember and shed a tear of sadness and joy.

The past was bad, and the future hid,
its good or ill untried, O.
But the present hour was in my pow'r,
and so I would enjoy it, O.

My Father Was a Farmer
Robert Burns

Chapter 15

Benwhat – My Hame
Jeannie Mowat or McCreath

I'l act with prudence as far as I'm able,
But if success I must never find,
Then come, Misfortune, I bid thee welcome –
I'll meet thee with an undaunted mind!

Fickle Fortune
Robert Burns

Mrs Jean McCreath, née Mowat, of Benwhat who fondly recalled many years living at Benwhat. She was born on 29 May 1920 and died on 12 January 2009 aged eighty-eight.
(Photo: Courtesy of Alice Wallace)

With a good memory of the past, 'Auntie' Jeannie McCreath, who was born in the village of Patna on 29 May 1920, was a weel-kent and much-loved lady. Donald L Reid is indebted to Alice Wallace, a good friend of 'Auntie Jeannie', for her kind assistance in this 2007 interview. Mrs McCreath passed away on 12 January 2009 at the age of eighty-eight, but will be fondly remembered by everyone, to whom she will always be 'Auntie Jeannie'.

Benwhat years
Memories outlined in this reflection of the past cover the period when I lived in Benwhat, from 1926 to 1951. It was a special wee place and we were all proud of it. I suppose with the passage of time as we all get older and tend to look back on our formative years, places like Benwhat become even more precious. It was located high up on the hills above Dalmellington on a flat plateau with hills to the rear and great views out across the Doon Valley to the Galloway Hills and Loch Doon.

Mind you, the weather could be pretty atrocious because of the open location. But it was a friendly and welcoming wee place. I often think back to those special days and the folk of that era, because I am among the last that actually grew up in Benwhat. We didn't have much compared to nowadays, but everyone was in exactly the same situation and perhaps that made it not so bad. I suppose the young folk of today would be appalled at the living conditions with no proper toilets or baths, but we just accepted that was how things were in those days.

Flitting and Mother's passing
I was born on 29 May 1920 in Patna. I remember flitting to Benwhat when I was five years old. The flitting was by horse and cart and I was perched precariously on top of the furniture as the horse made light work of the track which ran from Burnfoothill along the hill (former railway) line to Benwhat. My family had lived in Patna in the old building near the Doon Brig that was later a shop and most recently was Armour's Funeral Parlour.

My family consisted of my mother and father, brother George who was born when we stayed at Brigend in Patna, and wee sister Mary, who sadly died when she was only eleven months old. More sorrow was to visit our family when my mother died at the age of forty-two when I was just nine years of age. From that time on I had to grow up very quickly as I then took on the role of keeping house for my father. I suppose having to do housework every day after mother's passing really did spoil my childhood years, at least a little.

Earliest memories
Among my earliest and happiest memories was my mother coming to school at 11 a.m. with cocoa and toast and she always wore a shawl around her shoulders. The reason for this was that it could be very cold up on the high moors above the Doon Valley and a shawl kept you very warm.

When my sister Mary was born I remember that she wore a plaid with the wee one (child) tucked inside to keep warm. A plaid was a tartan blanket worn across the back with the baby tucked in at one side. Every woman would use a plaid in these days and in fact it was common right up into the 1960s. The plaid allowed the woman to have one hand free to do chores such as stirring pots as the meal was being prepared.

Father's passing

Further sadness came to my family with the passing of my father. He had been a well-respected man in Benwhat. But he was unable to work due to ill health. His joints were all swollen and very painful with arthritis. He was librarian of the village reading room and secretary of the Soldiers' Comfort Fund. However, he had a long life and died aged eighty-three.

On the move

Our family lived in four different houses at Benwhat – Nos. 1, 27, 31 and 105 – at different times over the years. There were usually some empty houses in the village, so if you fancied a move to a better house, you made application and it was normally granted. There were single and double houses in the rows which had been built to house the miners and their families near where they worked. With no wages coming in because father didn't work, I had to go down to the DSS of those days. This was known locally as 'the Parish' and to avoid the stigma attached to this, I chuckled and told children with me that I was going down to see the doctor.

Family income

The family's income was £1 12s. 6d. from the Parish and 7s. 6d. half-benefit from the Miners' Union, making it £2 for the week. Out of this I had to pay 3s. 6d. rent each week, which included electricity. Bob Burgess from Waterside used to come up to Benwhat on a motor bike with sidecar to collect rent from the villagers, but I was resourceful and worked on ways of making a little more money by doing odd jobs, which helped our family a lot.

Earning extra money

For example, when Nurse Gilmour or Nurse Harvey, the district nurses, came up to deliver home births, I used to help by boiling water and laying everything out for them and cleaning up after the delivery. I took the bedcovers and towels home for washing. This had to be followed up for two weeks because at that time the new mother took to bed for at least ten days, a system which young mothers of today would find strange indeed. For these two weeks of hard work I earned 10 shillings.

To get some extra coal for the living-room fire I would help neighbours by carrying in their load of coal, and for doing this I was given four pails of coals. So, as you can imagine, life was not easy.

I remember Sally Reid (Gray) and myself carrying buckets of coal up the incline from Waterside, which was no easy task. I also helped locals with housework, not just for the money, but because I enjoyed socialising. The welfare of friends and neighbours in Benwhat was important as it was a very close-knit community. The villagers were a hardy and independent lot. They had their own way of thinking and dealing with things with strong determination. They had their own culture which was quite remarkable.

Schooldays

I started and completed my schooling at Benwhat, beginning at age five in 1925 and leaving when aged fourteen in 1934. In 1926 the new school was built in Benwhat. I can remember all the pupils walking from the old school to the new school carrying their books. There were classes in the school for all the children, so there were brothers and sisters of different ages sharing the same class and teacher.

In later years Benwhat School was used only as a primary school and when children were eleven years old they went down to the Higher Grade School at Dalmellington. When the headmaster came up to the village in his car, the children had to stop playing and acknowledge him. The boys had to salute and the girls had to bow. I recall some great teachers.

Miss Hose taught infants. Miss Young, Miss Davidson, Miss Kerr, Miss Paterson and Miss Hill I remember well. The headmaster was Mr Frank Ferguson and later a Mr Jeffries, the last headmaster in the village. As well as covering all subjects at school, they taught recreation and gym. During the 1926 strike the old school building was used as a soup kitchen. The school janitor was Scott Hannah and the cook was Mrs Campbell.

Benwhat School Cookery Class in 1930/31. Each girl neatly dressed.
(l to r): Hugh M Ferguson, headmaster, Mary McKnight, Margaret Murphy, Jean Hay, Georgina Dick and Mary Ferguson.
Front row: Peggy Murray, Agnes Tinman, Chrissie Relly, Mary Hodgson and teacher unknown.
(Courtesy of John Relly collection)

Benwhat School team 1931/32 with John Relly, captain, showing off the team mascot.
Back row: (l to r) Hugh Gourlay, Tom Tinman, Eddie Dick, David McEwan.
Middle row: Tom Todgson, Bill Gage and Sandy McFadzean.
Front row: James Relly, Tom Fraser, John Relly (captain with team mascot), David Wightman and Neil Dempsey.
(Courtesy of John Relly collection)

Benwhat School woodwork class in 1930/31. Each boy holding a woodworking tool.
Back row: (l to r) James Adams, Alex Robertson, Hunter Torbet, Mr Hugh Ferguson MA, headmaster, John McKnight and John McKnight.
Front row: Vincent White, John Relly, John Wilson, Ritchie Campbell and Sandy McFadzean.
(Courtesy of John Relly collection)

My family

I married Allan McCreath when I was aged twenty in 1940. We were well suited as we both had an easy-going nature and enjoyed a good laugh. Our marriage was very happy and we had three children: Marion, George (also known as Pordy) and John. At present there are five generations in the family – Jeannie, Marion, John, Hugh and Lee. I have twenty-seven grandchildren and great-grandchildren and two great-great-grandchildren.

In 1951 after twenty-six years living very happily in Benwhat, Allan, I and the children moved to Bellsbank when I was aged thirty-one. We were allocated a house in Bradon Avenue and I still live there to this day. (Mrs McCreath passed away in 2009.)

Neighbourliness

I believe that living in Benwhat gave me the ability to cope with difficult times assisted by good friends and neighbours.

Everyone living in the village had very little and depended on the wage coming in each week, and that just kept us at a basic level with very little to spare. We were all at the same level with no one better off than the other.

In fact if someone was having visitors they could go to a neighbour and borrow rugs for the floor, crockery and cutlery. That's the way it was. Folk would always rally round to help. I suppose young folk today, trying to understand how we lived, would be aghast at this, but that was the reality of living life with not very much. We did share, and yes we did really care.

If the doctor or ambulance came up to Benwhat, folk would wander up to the row wherever it was to enquire who was ill, what was wrong, in the hope that it wasn't too serious, and genuinely offer help. They would hover about to see if they were needed or how they could help. Life was difficult but everyone was in the same position, with most folk having enough to meet basic needs, but not having any luxuries. The villagers shared tough times and good times and lasting friendships resulted. Aye, these friendships carried on long after we all left Benwhat for Bellsbank.

Looking back

Life revolved around work, eating and sleeping, rather like today, but life was harder then with little opportunity for luxuries such as holidays or modern conveniences in the home. Folk were, however, resilient and created their own entertainment in the village institute or school hall. They were generally concerned and looked out for each other and most of the houses were kept clean and tidy. I was friendly with Sadie Douglas, Ethel Thomson and others of that era and we still enjoy talking about happy times at auld Benwhat.

Women's work

The women didn't have it easy. They had to go outside to the water pump in the street to fill pails of water, whether it was for drinking, cooking, cleaning or washing. White enamel pails were used for the drinking and cooking water and zinc pails for anything else. In the house there was a basin used for washing your body. You stripped off your top and gave yourself a good wash as far as possible, and then you stripped off your bottom half and did the same.

Hugh Relly (left) and John 'Jock' Relly visit Benwhat and have a seat in the ruins of the village school on 31 May 1954, as they recall special memories of their auld village.
(Courtesy of John Relly collection)

Toilet time

There was a zinc pail for use as a toilet, so you had to hurry to use it just in case someone came in. You see, there were no indoor toilets in Benwhat. Some villagers had built a small outside hut for use as a toilet, but the toilet pail had still to be emptied outside well away from the houses. Holes were dug in which this could be deposited and this was just accepted as a part of daily life. When visitors came and asked where they did the toilet, they would be told: 'From here to Rankinston. Pick a spot.'

Visiting sheep

House doors were left unlocked along the rows. Often folk would leave the door off the latch and it was quite common for a sheep to wander in looking for a tattie (potato). One day I remember leaving my dishes sitting on a card table and a sheep came in, knocked it over and broke all the dishes. This was quite a big loss, because they weren't easily replaced, especially during the war years as you just couldn't get replacements.

Benwhat Comforts Fund (Ladies' Committee) 1939–1945 war. The ladies are pictured outside Benwhat School after one of their meetings where they made plans to raise funds to support the men serving in the forces during the 1939–1945 war. Many of those in the photograph have relatives still living in the Doon Valley.
(l to r): Mrs Margaret Campbell, Mrs Agnes Gourlay, Mrs Phamie Douglas, Mrs Annie Campbell, Mrs Sarah Filson, Mrs Scott Hannah and Mrs Alex McHattie.
(Miss Anna McHattie collection)

Reading room

The reading room, also called the Institute, was two houses knocked together at the end of a row of houses. This was used by villagers for reading books, magazines and newspapers. The men also played cards there and they gambled for small amounts of money.

Winters living at Benwhat

The winters were often hard, with snowfall and drifting making life difficult. I remember the snow drifting to roof level at the back of the rows. The men went out the front door, then round the back to dig a way through to the water pumps. Unemployed men were paid 1 shilling per hour to dig a clear path down the road to Dalmellington rail track where the miners got a pug which took them to the pit. Some went to Beoch and others to Pennyvenie.

If the unemployed refused to go out and clear the snow, they were refused their benefit money. There is a photograph showing heavy snow at Benwhat, which meant that the men were unable to get to the pits and that qualified the miners for a Bevan shift – they were paid for the shift.

Drying clothes

The miners had to walk to their work or to the toll road for a lift on railway wagons in all weathers. Their working clothes were often soaked and they had to be dried, ready for the next shift, and that was a real chore for the women because there was no central heating in those days. All we had was a coal fire in a draughty and damp room-and-kitchen. Young folk today wouldn't even begin to understand what it was like, being so used to central heating and modern facilities.

So, the working clothes would be draped on the winterdykes around the fire. Working trousers were made of moleskins, so they took a long time to dry. They were difficult to wash and patch. Dalmellington Iron Company, later Bairds and Dalmellington, owned the pits and the miners' houses. The pits were mined for ironstone in the early days, but later it was mainly for coal. There were also contractors and sub-contractors at the pits. Some of the children collected the wages on a Friday from Archie Kennedy and took them straight to their mothers.

Mother's passing

I mentioned earlier that my mother had died when I was just nine years of age, so I had to learn to cope with housework very quickly. Mrs Florence Thomson was a great help to me and encouraged me greatly. She was always a welcome visitor to our home. I quickly learned how to make soup and I could always go and see Florence to discuss problems.

The Thomson family consisted of Tom and Florence and they had eight children, namely, Nancy (Mrs McCulloch), Ethel (Mrs John Buchanan), Alex (married Cathy Coburn), Jack (married Jean McVey), Jean (Mrs Andrew Gilmour), Helen (Mrs Robert Knox), Flora (Mrs Robin Heaney) and Ena (Mrs David Aitchison). The strong family friendship continues to this day with me, now eighty-six years of age, and surviving members of the Thomson family.

Meet for tea

After moving from Benwhat to Bellsbank, I would meet with Nancy, Ethel, Jean, Cathy and Lizzie Yates for a blether and tea every Wednesday. Each took their turn to host the others and this still continues after fifty years, which must be something of a record. That was the sort of pull Benwhat had on us all.

Wash days

When washing blankets you had to be sure of a good day, because they were needed on the bed again at night, because there were no spares. Everyone was the same. We only had the basics and no more. The washtub was filled and we had to trample the blankets with our feet. This was actually quite enjoyable and after rinsing and wringing them through the big wooden mangle, it took two of us to shake them out.

Some women didn't even have a mangle, so they had to squeeze and wring them by hand, which wasn't easy. The drying greens were up the back of the rows and the clothes would be hung out to dry. This was quite a heavy job and we had all the other household chores to do as well, but it was nice to have the lovely fresh blankets on the bed at night.

Cooking

The open coal fire was used for cooking and the kettle was always on for something. There was also a Dover stove in the kitchen and a primus stove. Most of the women were quite good at making a guess at the heat and time required when baking. Pancakes and tattie scones were made every week and toast was made at the fire which was simply lovely.

Stone floors

The floors of the houses were stone-flagged, but were easily swept out then scrubbed. Carpets were homemade rag rugs. Stookie was used to clean the floor and front doorstep and it was called a rubbing stone. This came from broken ornaments, often in the form of popular items such as Umbrella Twins and Whistling Boy.

Electricity arrives

The same items were used to fill empty polish tins (peevers) by wee girls when playing at beds. Ash from the fire was good for cleaning the fireplace. Electricity came to Benwhat in 1933 from Waterside Power Station, which was previously built to power the ill-fated Loch Doon School of Aerial Gunnery during the First World War.

However, all that the tenants of Benwhat had was a light socket hanging from the ceiling to give them light. There were no sockets on the walls to plug anything in, simply the one from the ceiling to give light. Mind you, we didn't have electrical items to plug in anyway in those days.

When some women eventually got electric irons, they fitted them in the light socket to do their ironing, but if too many used them at the same time, the power went off. There was a Mrs McFadzean electrocuted when connecting her iron to the socket. Before the days of electricity the villagers used carbide or paraffin lamps.

Sports

Wull Hunter the bookmaker was a big man who organised and sponsored a sports day once a year. This was held alternately at Benwhat and Dalmellington. This was a great event for the whole community and the whole town turned out for it. It was the highlight of the year. The Benwhat Silver Band played at it when it was held in Dalmellington and everyone marched down behind them from Benwhat.

At the field there was a table set up showing all the event details and the prizes were displayed. A stage was set up for the highland dancers and Jimmy (Squeakie) Telford played the fiddle for them. Adam McHattie was a good runner in the Benwhat

Harriers and he generally won all of the men's races. And Jim Hose mostly won the high jump. Robert Reid was also a really good runner for the Harriers and he often went to Edinburgh to enter a Scottish Championship race and later became a famous runner with Birchfield Harriers. There were some wonderful people who belonged to Benwhat.

I remember when I ran in the races I had to borrow sandshoes from Tom Thomson and it was worthwhile. I remember winning a yellow teapot and a stand. There was usually a fancy dress parade at Hunter's Sports, which Beenie Torbet and Lizzy Kirk helped to organise. In later years, Anna Kirk (Willie Macintosh's wife) and Helen McPhail helped to organise it. The kids loved taking part in fancy dress.

sometimes begin fighting with one another. The men did not interfere and stayed clear as they were probably too scared to get involved. But sometimes things got out of control and there was a free-for-all at the finish. Benwhat did have its moments, you know!

My brother George Mowat was the secretary of the Doon Harriers. They were really good and they entered events competing against other harriers from all over Ayrshire and often with great success.

Benwhat was a very sporting and socially active community. Benwhat Heatherbell was an excellent amateur football team in the early 1900s just before the Great War. Descendants of those in the photo still live in the Doon Valley.
Back row (l to r): Neil Dempsey, Dan Parker, John 'Baillie' Armour, McGee, Pat Murray, George Long, Thomas Hodgson, John Hodgson, J 'Skip' Bryan and E Miller.
Front row: T Yates, 'Sand Dancer' Murray, Duff Hannah, J Murray, Kennedy and Charles Fisher. Thomas Hodgson and E Miller were both killed in the Great War.
(Courtesy of John Relly collection)

Benwhat Football and Sports Committee *circa* 1920s. Remote villages like Benwhat were very self-sufficient and organised for sports and athletics. This high moorland village had excellent football teams and harriers and could even boast a fine brass band. Grandchildren of many of those in this photograph still live in the Doon Valley. Like so many others of that era, this photograph was taken by William Winning, photographer in Waterside.
Back row (l to r): J Adam, J Givens, Joe Dougan, Scott Hannah, Simpson Allan, Joe McKinstry, Alex McHattie (Waterside) and John Filson.
Front row: W Torbet, R Hill, D McBride, George Cook, Alex McHattie, John Allan, J B Galloway, Hugh Murray and ?
(John Relly collection)

Memorable folk

Robert Bryan was a really nice, good-living man, who walked down to Dalmellington Church every Sunday. He was a hard-working pit man, just like the rest. But he was so kind and pleasant-natured. He ran a Sunday School class for the weans of Benwhat. I used to look at him, because he was such an

Fight at football

The Heatherbell football team played at Benwhat and whenever there was a home game, Beenie Torbet and Lizzy Kirk would inspirational man, and in my childlike way I would think he was just like God.

Georgina Watson was a Sunday School teacher and she only taught the girls. She was very pretty and was also nice-natured. At Christmas she gave all the girls a small gift. They all received the same, a lovely wee handkerchief folded inside a Christmas card. I thought she was like an angel. The hanky was far too good for me to use.

Sunday School trip

The Sunday School trip was another big event in our lives. Benwhat Silver Band led the way with all the children, mums and dads, grannies and family friends all following behind. We walked down the incline to Waterside to get the train to Ayr and then walked to the Low Green. We had the same walk back on the return journey but it was always worth it.

At Benwhat store, there was a wee area sectioned off and used by fly drinkers. It was called the Borehole. It was just a wee corner with a wooden seat. I acquired this wooden seat in later years and got Joe Wilson to use the wood to make me two lamps. One was a standard and the other a matching table lamp. I used them when I moved to Bellsbank and I still have them to this day. They remind me of Benwhat and I simply treasure them.

The war years and food

In Benwhat most people were healthy. They certainly had good fresh air, clean water and good basic food. The views across the valley on good clear days were simply stunning. During and just after the war years, food was rationed and there was a limited amount per person. Our staple diet was porridge, and home-made soup made with whatever vegetable we could find, and using a bone or a stock cube. Boiling beef was also used for stock and then the meat from that was used for dinner or supper. Nothing was wasted. Tatties and mince was also a staple food.

Poaching for rabbits or fish gave a welcome meal, too. Some folks also kept hens which supplied them and others with eggs, and some villagers had vegetables planted in their gardens, which had to be fenced off due to the sheep wandering about freely. Most of the women were good at baking scones and shortbread, clootie dumplings and pancakes or girdle scones.

Mr Alex (Sanny) McHattie, one of a prominent family in Benwhat, thoroughly enjoyed working in his garden which he maintained with great love, though it was located 1,000 feet above sea level and subject to some terrible weather conditions. There were many excellent gardens in the lost mining villages and much of their produce was for the family table.
(Photo: Courtesy of EAC Doon Valley Museum)

There was a swee at the open fire which the girdle sat on for making things like girdle scones. The orange juice which you got free from the clinic if you had a baby was mixed with dry milk to make lemon curd.

Santa calls

Georgina Dick, when working in the post office, used to run a Christmas club. Someone had ordered a sewing kit for their little girl and was then unable to pay for it. I, being a wee girl at that time, had asked Santa for a sewing set. My mother managed to acquire one at the post office. I remember getting it on Christmas day; I was simply overwhelmed because I believed in Santa at that time.

Wonderful neighbours

Isa McBride had a big family of her own, but she was a good and generous neighbour. When Sadie Douglas, next door, had a baby, Isa came round to see her. She brought round a cup of tea and a slice of bread and butter. All nicely set on a tray and covered with a nice wee tray cloth. Sadie was so grateful and said that her piece and butter was a real treat. Money can't buy the wonderful feeling when getting something like this, when you had very little. These wee things meant a lot to these people when times were hard.

Benwhatonians

Alan Dick used to breed and sell canaries. His son, Alan, married Janet Robertson. Alan became well known as a very good goalkeeper with Craigmark Burntonians. Some of the women were really good knitters. Bella McKinstry was one of the very best.

Jim Armour was the founder member of the Benwhat Silver Band. He was the father of well-known Benwhat folk Andy, Richard, Jim, Alec and Mary. Ravie Torbet, brother of Beenie, used to say the water from Campbell's Spoot (well) tasted better when it was in whisky. The water was rooted down from the hills by a pipe that fed Campbell's Spoot and this was lovely fresh water which everyone wanted to drink. In later days, after the demise of the village, when folk went back to visit, there was always a request from someone to fill a bottle of water for them.

The Relly family taken at the back of their house in Benwhat between the two wars. The family lived at Benwhat for thirty years before moving to Park Crescent, Dalmellington.
Back row (l to r): Jessie Relly (mother), Susan, Mary, Christine and Hugh Relly (father).
Front row: James, Hughie and John.
(Courtesy of John Relly collection)

Mobile merchants' visit

I remember that Jimmy Hair and Jimmy Hopkins were fruit merchants who came to Benwhat with their lorries to sell their produce. The first time as a wee girl I can remember having an apple and an orange was when I pinched them from Jimmy Hopkins' cart. In later years I remember being at a wedding with Jimmy Hopkins' son and I told him what I had done and I bought him a drink. When I think back to these times I still fondly remember Jimmy, who provided a great service to our community in Benwhat and in later years did the same for the people of Bellsbank, where I moved.

The Relly family lived at No. 66 and had six children; two are still living today, albeit they are well into their eighties. John and his wife Ina (Ferguson) were from Waterside and now live at the Braemar Residential Home, Ayr. They have one son, Murray, who actually owns and runs the Residential Home.

Entertainment

There were several annual events held in Benwhat and these were eagerly awaited and well attended. These included social evenings and the Eastern Star dance every year. Tom Hodgson played accordion and Hugh Gourlay played the drums and they were a popular local band in the Doon Valley. I remember I used to have holes in the soles of my shoes so I had to be careful that nobody could see these when I was dancing. Francie News was another well-known man who played accordion and Tommy Carruthers played drums. There was also Hugh Ferguson from the Hill (Lethanhill), another good musician.

Basket whists were popular. One woman would supply sandwiches and cakes for her four guests so that at the end of the card games everyone could have a nice tea. This would raise funds for whatever the purpose would be.

Going to the pictures

A wee treat, especially for the women, was going to the pictures (cinema) in Dalmellington. On Monday nights during wartime they would either walk down or get the bus. There was always a free matinee at New Year and you were given an orange as a treat by the cinema owner.

Cantata

A cantata was a concert or play. The folks of Benwhat were quite imaginative when it came to entertainment and many an enjoyable night was had listening to villagers entertain in style. The Filson twins, Tommy and Andy, were good singers and always keen to help out, especially for any charity event. Jim Armour was a very good organiser and planning plays was his forte and, of course, he was also the bandmaster. He had a nice manner and achieved much success because of this.

I remember when Jean and George Sturgeon were in a play called *Wee Curly*. I was also in it and with Ethel Buchanan (Thomson) we ended it by singing 'After the Ball Was Over'. In *The Creggie* Mattie Ivers was the head of the family, and Freddie Galloway was in *The Face at the Window*. So, a lot of men as well as the women got involved in the life of the community in terms of entertainment and it was always good fun and well supported by villagers.

Boat race in the sheugh

The boat race often took place on a Sunday and caused much noise and hilarity. The men each had their own boats which were modified matchboxes. The race started at a wee tunnel at the end of the Laigh Row. The sheugh (drain) ran through and down beside the row and the men and boys ran alongside their boats to keep track of their progress. They of course had bets on as to who would win and it also gave the villagers a bit of entertainment watching the menfolk running alongside the sheugh.

Sunday jaunt

When the miners would be enjoying a beer in the village store on a Saturday night, they often planned a wee day away for their family. When they returned home they would announce that they were going on a jaunt on Sunday, usually to places such as Ballantrae, Maidens, Croy Shore or Sandyhills. They had already booked a bus and would have organised enough names to fill it.

When they reached their destination there was usually a tattie field nearby and they would collect some Ayrshire tatties and these were boiled in sea water, already salted, using an old pan or a square biscuit tin on a primus stove. And when they were ready they were simply delicious with a blob of margarine over them. Sometimes, too, they would collect whelks from the beach and bring them home.

Granny's tartan legs

When the weather was good in summer, the women would wander round the rows, sit with a neighbour on the front step and enjoy a good blether. When indoors at night it was nice to sit on the footstool at the fire and make toast, using a toasting fork. Sometimes it would break off and fall into the fire. Some of the elderly women had 'Granny's tartan legs'. This was mottled marks on the skin due to them sitting too long in the heat of the fire.

At New Year the Benwhat Band would play march tunes and parade round the rows using carbide lamps to light the way, bringing in the new year. Many of the band members would be a wee bit tipsy, but it was all good fun. All the men and women would come out of their houses and they usually had a bottle of something, often port or sherry. Every door was open.

Clothes

Maybe on Mother's Day or on birthdays the women would get something new to wear. It was usually a new pinny (apron) or slippers. These were greatly appreciated. A woman always wore a pinny. Sometimes especially the older women wore the wrapover style, known as the Dutch overall. But even when they were dressed, for instance at Christmas, they at least wore a 'daidle', a wee front apron. Clothes were handed down or passed on, so if it fitted you, well you simply wore it.

During war years, even clothes were rationed, so you just wore what you had. After having a baby, a woman's treat was either new slippers or a pinny. If you were lucky enough to have something nice to wear, that was just fine. But you had little chance of having matching things to set it off. I fondly remember my first swimsuit. It was a knitted green one bought at Girvan.

Working clothes for the men at the pit were just their own clothes, shirts and old suits. But they had moleskin trousers. Men, women and children had really very little and the women had to make do and mend and make sure things were washed and dried as they were needed.

Some things were frowned upon as villagers mostly had high moral standards. If a woman stayed with a man and was not married to him she was called a concubine and she was looked down on by others. Also in those days if a family had a handicapped child, he or she was generally kept indoors, almost hidden away. That's just the way things were then.

Random memories

Many people had dogs and cats but the dogs were just put out for a walk. You didn't take them, and naturally they went looking for easy pickings. One dog, owned by the Bunyan family, nabbed a salmon from the van of Iain Marr the fishmonger. This was really a financial disaster for the fish seller. Another fish seller was 'Scous' Dunlop who came up to Benwhat with a van selling herring. This was very tasty when coated with porridge oats and fried.

Bus service

The first bus service to Benwhat was a charabanc, owned by Mr Gibson, the grandfather of Sandy Gibson, well-known former garage owner in Dalmellington. But the first real bus service was provided by Percy Hill, with a service running to Lethanhill and Rankinston. That enabled local folk, none of whom had a car, to make contact with the outside world without first having to walk down the road to Craigmark and Dalmellington or walk down the incline to Waterside.

Ringlets

Wee girls with long hair wore it in ringlets, the style then. To get this look they got their cloots in at night. Long strips of material, usually ripped from an old sheet, were entwined with the hair and tied up at bedtime, so in the morning the hair was in ringlets, which was very stylish.

Children could play outside safely. They had the freedom and joy of running all over the moors. They had a carefree and safe place to enjoy themselves. They had no fear of perverts, in fact, villagers had never heard of that word. It was unknown. The children respected their elders and all married woman were given the title of Mrs.

The mares (moorburn)

Even today I love the smell of burning grass – mares or moorburn. The smell reminds me of Benwhat and brings happy memories of when I was young. It meant to me that another spring was on the horizon. I happily remember being a right wee rascal and quite daring for a laugh. With my pals I played at kick the door on our way down the rows, both as a child and adult. We were a wee bit boisterous even as adults!

Games

There was a pond in Benwhat known as the Mosie which froze over in winter and this was used for curling or sliding by the children of the village. Both boys and girls played at bools (marbles) with their glass jawries, the coloured ones and gongies, which were white. Mothers would take a jawrie bool and keep it inside the kettle to keep limescale from forming. All the children played hide and seek and kick the can. We really did have the time of our lives.

Girls played with skipping ropes and peevers (beds). If you really were lucky you might get a broken bit of marble from the butcher, or we used a polish tin filled with mud as our peever. Boys would search out birds' nests and have a collection of eggs. When they found eggs they wanted, they were carefully carried home and the yolk removed by putting two small holes in the eggshell and blowing the yolk out. The eggs were then kept in a box of straw and identified to a particular type of bird.

The boys would go guddling for fish in the burn. This is where you stand still and put your hand under rocks, tickle the fish's belly before grabbing it and pulling it out of the water.

Granny Currie

Old Meg Currie, also known simply as Granny Currie, used to get me and my pals, when we were just girls, roped in to help make rag rugs. This way old Meg had more and nicer ones than most other villagers because she had a lot of help from the village weans. The back or base of the rug was made of sugar sacks, or even flour sacks. The top patterned area was made from old woollen jumpers and cardigans.

Any old knitted garments in those days were unpicked, ripped out and the wool was used again to knit something else, but if the garments were really past it, they were recycled for rag rugs. Old Meg had some of the girls cutting the jumpers into strips and some of them had to use a hook or even a wooden clothes peg with a nick cut into it to pull the fabric through the sacking. They were usually worked into a nice pattern, matching the colours.

Sometimes we even designed something special such as a dog or cat, which was very clever indeed. We worked at this all year to get special rewards at Halloween with a party. Meg would make us dumplings and these were shared between us with some homemade toffee which she pulled and stretched into stalks. It was all worth it and great to see something you had made yourself.

The young folk of Benwhat (circa 1939), like many other towns and villages, had a branch of the Independent Order of Rechabites. The sole aim of the Rechabites was to preach the message of total abstinence. On this occasion the young folk of Benwhat had received a test and afterwards gathered for a photograph.
Back row: (l to r) Drew McHattie, John Douglas, Sandy McHattie, Tommy Filson, Adam McHattie (Dalmellington), John Galloway, Margaret Campbell, A Mullen, Willie Lindsay and Andrew Filson.
Middle row: Marion Campbell, Betty McDicken, Mr James Hopes, Jessie Andrews, Mr Robert Bryan, Betty Templeton, visiting member of Independent Order of Rechabites and May Stevenson.
Front row: Adam McHattie (Patna), Jean Weir, Marion Lindsay, Ann McHattie, Beth Hill and Adam McHattie (Bellsbank).
(Miss Anna McHattie collection)

Religion

Religion brought no problems in Benwhat, at least not that I was aware of. There were meetings held in an empty house by the Brethren for the children, who really enjoyed the meetings, singing 'My cup's full and running over' and 'The wise man built his house upon the rock' and doing all the actions. We were all given a cookie and a cup of tea and I remember at one time we were all given a Bible.

I remember Margaret McGuire, who was a Catholic girl, attending Benwhat School. She waited outside in the corridor until the morning prayer was over and then she came in. Each Sunday the minister from Dalmellington came up to Benwhat School to hold an evening service. George Connell and Robert Bryan were elders.

The store

The song 'I Owe My Soul to the Company Store' certainly rings true with old folk of Benwhat. The Dalmellington Iron Company and later Bairds and Dalmellington owned the pits where the men worked and the houses the mining families lived in. They also owned the store where we got all our supplies. So the Company gave the men their jobs, houses and wages, and then got the wages back off them as the people needed to buy supplies to live.

There was a railway line running along the front of the Laigh Row (Low Row) to Lethanhill, which was used to bring supplies up from Waterside to Benwhat store. Sanny Orr was the store manager and he was the grandfather of Sheena Orr (Armour). In later years there were vans that came up from Dalmellington to Benwhat, mainly the Co-op. This brought a wider selection of goods and the villagers had the choice of what they could buy.

The Co-op took over most things as they could offer services such as the butcher, baker, grocer, drapery and shoe shops and their vans came up the hill providing these services. Even although most things were rationed, it worked quite well. Joan Connell came round the houses to get the message list so your order could be made up and ready for you to collect. During the war years when food was rationed the allowance was 2 oz butter per head per week. Sugar, tea, everything, corned beef was rationed. You were allowed one egg each per week. There was even a van came up from Ayr to Benwhat, operated by Lipton the Grocer, who supplied goods and collected money on a Friday.

Words we used

Some guid auld Scots words are still used in oor ain twang, honestly spoken, because we are proud of our roots. We daunert doon hame or roon the raws at nicht. Someone might say: 'Come in bye, ye're aye welcome.' If it was really cold we were 'foonert richt tae the bane'. If more space was needed in the front room I'd say: 'Shift the claeshorse and sit doon roon the fire.' If the table was problematic someone might say: 'This auld caird table's a bit shoogly.'

Benwhat to Bellsbank

The friendship and community spirit continued from Benwhat to Bellsbank when people were rehoused there in the early 1950s. The allocation of houses was based on the date on marriage certificates, so most of the older people moved there first.

The hut from Benwhat was moved and reconstructed in Bellsbank at the top of Ness Glen Road close to where the present-day shops are. This hut was well utilised for a number of social events. Wee Mary Ferguson sold sweeties in the shop at the front of the hut. The remainder was used for various purposes for the weekdays. It was a reading room, a hairdresser's salon for ladies operated by Anna Clark, barber's for men operated by Cudder Murphy, and the locals played carpet bools and billiards, bingo was held on several nights, and the Sunday School was also held there.

I left Benwhat when I was thirty-one, and had lived there from the age of five, going through all the stages of life until I was a married woman with three children. The housing conditions were by today's standards rather grim. It was a nice feeling leaving, knowing that we were going to a new-built house in Bellsbank. We threw all the stuff we didn't need into the midden and among them were old carbide lamps which today are collector's pieces. But of course when one door closes another opens.

Benwhat was slowly being depopulated and we were happy to leave, but our memories of our time in there grows ever brighter with each passing year. The memories will never fade, because it was our home: all we ever knew and we counted our blessings.

Benwhat today

All that remains now of Benwhat is the war memorial overlooking the former village from its hill command; the herd's house at Burnhead Farm which sadly is also now a ruin; some foundations of the school remain and those who search will identify the foundations of the rows where their former homes were situated. That can be very humbling and brings back so many happy and some sad memories of the past.

When returning for a nostalgic visit, former residents will search for the house where they lived and very often will select a brick from their former home to take back as a memorial – a wee keepsake. There are many of these DICo bricks used in gardens in Bellsbank and Dalmellington today and they are proudly pointed out to friends and relations. It keeps us in touch with our past.

Philosophy of life

Benwhat folk want to keep something visible to remind them of happy times in their special little village high above the valley of Doon. I think I was lucky to have been born there and experienced a special life with all its challenges. I often think these words by Anne Frank (1929–45) are important to remember: 'Think of all the beauty still left around you and be happy.' Now, to me that's not a bad philosophy to follow! How I really enjoy thinking back to good old Benwhat and its outstanding scenery and lovely folk. Those happy, special days can never return, but my auld hame will be forever in my heart.

Ae fond kiss, and then we sever;
Ae fareweel, alas, forever!
Deep in heart-wrung tears I'll pledge thee,
Warring sighs and groans I'll wage thee!

Aye Fond Kiss
Robert Burns

Benwhat as it was in the mid-1930s. The village store is on the right and the rows of houses in the centre whilst to the far left can be seen the new school built in the early 1930s to replace the old school located behind the village store. When the village was abandoned one teacher said she wished that the new school could have been lifted and moved to Dalmellington!
(Photo: Courtesy of EAC Doon Valley Museum)

Chapter 16

Boyhood Memories of Waterside

John Dinwoodie

Thus ev'ry kind their pleasure find,
The savage and the tender;
Some social join, and leagues combine,
Some solitary wander.

Song Composed in August
Robert Burns

The old Dunaskin brickworks were located at the foot of Dunaskin Glen, taken in 1905. Fourth from the left in the back row is David Colquhoun. He later worked on the new site at Dunaskin which began production around 1926. His young son David was killed during the Second World War. The men are holding brick moulds and some of them seem to be very young.
(Photo: Courtesy of EAC Doon Valley Museum)

John Dinwoodie was interviewed in March 2012 about his memories of growing up in Waterside. John was chair of Dunaskin Veterans' Group and they worked closely with Donald L Reid in 2002 in producing the very successful local interest book entitled *Doon Valley Memories*.

Lethanhill to Waterside

Long shall I remember those perfect early summer mornings when I was a child at Waterside. I am going back well over seventy years. Mum and Dad brought our family from Lethanhill to 1 Greenhill Row. My father was a foreman at Dunaskin Brickworks and our new house was a stone's throw from the brickworks. What a change that must have been for Dad, not having to walk up and down the incline from Lethanhill in all sorts of weather.

I have been blessed with a good memory and I was just coming five years of age when I arrived at 1 Greenhill. I remember coming down from the Hill in the back of a removal truck as if it were yesterday. I was sitting on my uncle's knee looking out the back door of the truck, watching the road disappearing into the distance. I shall never forget that early experience.

The first thing my elder sister Emma and I did was to explore the house, such as it was. But to us it was something new. Emma opened the back door and opened another outside door. Here was a toilet pan with a tank and a chain hanging from it. Emma pulled the chain and there was a noisy rush of water. I ran in panic into the house, scared of this new noisy toilet, as the one we had in Lethanhill was very quiet as they were known as dry toilets or privies.

Industrial noise

It was spring when we came to Waterside and I was a wee bit scared of all the unusual noises around the place. These noises seemed to wake us up in the morning, such as steam engines or pugs as they were referred to, shunting up on the bank line at the back of our house. There were pugs running up and down the pig iron line in front of the house. The main industry when I arrived at Waterside was coal, hence the non-stop racket of these pugs.

Another noise strange to my young ears was the crushing plant on the slag hill, which was also very near to us. This consisted of a heavy-duty crusher that reduced the slag into different sizes and it was then taken away by rail, the main customer being the LMS railway as this was used as ballast for the railway lines.

Still another noise which I recall was the non-stop running of the pan mills at the brickworks. They ran twenty-four hours a day. We also had the power station running twenty-four hours a day. I was dropped in at the deep end with all this noise as I had come from the Hill where all I ever heard was the bleating of sheep and the song of the skylark.

However, I had to get used to my new surroundings and my schooldays were about to begin. I started school after the summer and I remember my cousin Richard Denholm taking me there. This was the first time I had left the immediate vicinity of the house since leaving Lethanhill.

Schooldays

Now I was launched into life's great adventure – my schooldays. My first teacher at school was Miss Florence Kerr, who later married Louis Scott. Louis was always looked on as a pinnacle of authority in Waterside. Flo, my teacher, was a nice person and I was friendly with her until she moved to England, where she died a few years ago in her eighties.

Waterside School, which is now the RC school, was where I met my first pals. With new-found friends I began exploring the village which I now call my beloved Waterside. My first wee pal I sat beside at school was a lovely boy called Neil Coughtrie. One morning Neil never arrived at school and his absence turned into weeks. Later Miss Kerr told the class that poor wee Neil had died. I was upset for a little while, but when you are aged five you tend to get over things quite quickly. I was soon finding new friends.

A few pals I would like to mention for old times' sake are Andrew Roney, John Campbell, Billy Robertson, Eddie Uriarte, Jim Grant and John Kirkwood. It's strange how your first pals have an everlasting place in your memory. Now that I had made friends, I knew I belonged to Waterside.

Wartime at Waterside

Our next great event was the outbreak of the Second World War. I was only six and did not realise the seriousness of the war. There was great goings-on in the village, such as Jimmy McMillan going round the place instructing all tenants on how to black out their windows and skylights. This work had to be carried out straight away and I can still see my Mum and Dad painting the cream blinds black. Looking back, wee Jimmy must have been an air-raid warden.

Every house in the village was blacked out within forty-eight hours as the country was in a state of emergency. The village policeman, Tam Harvey, used to come round the village during the blackout times checking all the windows. Occasionally he would knock on Mum's window to report that a chink of light could be seen and she had to adjust the window until the constable was satisfied. This time of emergency was a great thing for children as there was always something going on relating to the war effort.

Local Defence Volunteers

Another chapter I will always remember was the forming of the Local Defence Volunteers. Alex Boyle, foreman plate layer, was appointed Commanding Officer of the Waterside contingent of the LDV. Alex saw service in the First World War and had served in India, too. Alex became Captain Boyle and in later years every time I watched *Dad's Army* on TV I always thought of Alex at Waterside all these years ago. When Alex had mustered his troops from the village, perhaps fifty or sixty men, he started to train them with brush shafts which took the place of rifles.

I can see them as if it were yesterday. Later on they were issued with rifles and uniforms and became known as the Home Guard. The MOD built Nissen huts in Alex's garden and these contained all the supplies and gear required for the volunteers. One thing that never failed to amuse the villagers was when Alex was working with some of his troops during the day and they called him Alex or Ackie, but on the parade ground it was 'Yes Sir', 'No Sir' or 'Sorry Sir'. This was the respect he commanded and got. Every village in the British Isles had their own Home Guard. Any man in the Waterside contingent who had fought in the First World War got a rank. But in Waterside there was only one Commanding Officer and that was the one and only Captain Boyle.

Jim Larmer, a workmate of mine and a good friend, often told me about the war years, as he was a good bit older than me. We worked together in the engineer's shop at Waterside and at break times he would tell me about the war years. I loved listening to his tales of yesteryear. Apart from what he told me I would ask him questions, thus learning more about what happened at Waterside in the war years. I also asked my parents about their young days. Dad was born in Waterside and Mum in Lethanhill.

Jim Larmer told me an amusing incident about the Home Guard. He was ten minutes late going on parade at the school. Captain Boyle demanded to know why he was late. Captain Boyle then sarcastically referred to his gleaming cap badge, which he said had dazzled him. In effect this was a little bit of sarcasm because his badge required to be cleaned.

Gas masks and promotion

Everyone in the village had to go to the village hall to be issued with a gas mask. A number of evacuees arrived at Waterside from Glasgow by train. The adults had to take them in and it was decided if there were two children from the same family, they would be kept together and lodge with one Waterside family rather than separate them. We couldn't take in any children as my mother had five of her own to look after. I often wonder if any of them still remember the good people of Waterside who took them in during the war years.

My friend Iain Halbert was also in the Home Guard. He decided to form his own unit. He lived a few doors from Captain Boyle and this gave him access to extra equipment. As children, you could join Iain's platoon irrespective of age. He had a group of about sixteen and I was one of them. Iain watched the Home Guard go through their paces and he copied what they did.

Iain's HQ was in the wash house at No. 30 Greenhill. Iain told me that I would be promoted to Lance Corporal if I would jump off a 12-foot-high wall. I was keen to get promoted and I never flinched as I jumped off the wall. I was aged about nine at that time. However, the CO honoured his promise and I stood to attention and my stripe was pinned on. Iain is now dead and gone but I have happy memories of him and his group of children who were the young home guard of the village.

Visiting Lethanhill

My mother never really accepted Waterside as her home. Until the day she died her heart was always in Lethanhill (the Hill), which was her home. So, during the war years she used to visit her dad who still lived in Lethanhill.

I used to do the messages for my mother and would go out in the morning early to get the bread and rolls from the Co-op store which had its own bakehouse in the village. I enjoyed being down early and would wait until old John Thomson brought the produce from the bakehouse to the store on the big bread boards. They were always nice and warm and my reward was being allowed to eat a hot scone on the road home.

When Mum visited Grandfather at the Hill, it was quite eerie. We left Waterside at 7 p.m. in complete darkness and would pass Barley Park, Clover Park and cross the Houldsworth line (railway) to the foot of the steep (Drumgrange) incline and then walk up to the drumhead and across to the rows. It was quite eerie in the dark. I can hear her shouting: 'Are you in, faither?' He would reply, 'Come in Jean, it's nice to see you.' When we eventually got back home, Dad and the rest of the family had gone to bed.

I can still see my grandfather holding the aerial in his hand trying to get a signal on the old Ecko wireless (radio), trying to get news of the war. It was an old valve-operated affair and if it started crackling Dad would put a piece of paper under the valves. There was no television or transistor radios in these days.

Those weekly visits to the Hill kept going till the end of the war. It wasn't always dark and it was quite pleasant in the summer evenings. My mother kept up these visits until 1950 when Granddad died. She went back once after he died and she was very upset. After that I often asked if she wanted to go back and visit the Hill, but she always declined. It was too painful for her as she had so many special memories of her old family home.

Boyhood exploits

As boys we were on the go from day till night. Eddie Uriarte was my boyhood hero, who showed me how to guddle for trout in the burn. Our fishing group consisted of Eddie, 'Buckie' Robertson and myself. This was the experienced squad and we knew the entrance under each stone and many a good trout we caught. Our day began meeting in the morning. We took along a frying pan and a few slices of bread. We entered the Dunaskin Burn at the west side of the Quarry Brig. We would then make our way up past the old brickworks into Dunaskin Glen. This was always a good place to guddle for fish.

We always seemed to be on the water when the Houldsworth pug (steam engine) was going up through the Quarry Brig, barking at full throttle, pulling a rake of wagons. The driver would be Tam Shaw or Kenny Bryden or his brother Buckley Bryden or big Wull Clark. They never failed to sound the whistle when they saw us. All Waterside men themselves, they had probably fished and guddled in the same burn when they, too, were boys. Every time I see the film *The Railway Children*, it reminds me of my carefree days at Waterside because locomotives, or pugs as they were referred to, were part and parcel of daily life. Everyone knew each other in the village.

We would light a fire and with a little lard in the pan cook the fish we had caught. It tasted great, a lovely aroma, a real feast just ideal for three hungry young boys. After lunch we would be back guddling for more trout. We worked our way up to the old clay pit where there were some very good pools. We now had maybe ten trout which we shared among us. We then walked home via the power station and gave the men a hand to fill the fuel hoppers with gum, which is a mixture of dross and slurry. There were no health and safety considerations in those days.

Our reward for giving this help was a free haircut when we required one from Archie Allison. Mind you, I don't suppose youngsters of today would be too impressed, as Archie was very basic with his haircuts, but it suited us and kept our parents happy.

Our next port of call was the brickworks where we would play with the bogies. We would get into a bogie and push each other up and down the line. This depended on the kiln burner being in a good mood. If he wasn't he would chase us, leaving us in no doubt that our backsides would be sore if we didn't move. When I arrived back I would see the smile on my mother's face as I handed her my catch. She would cook it later on that evening.

Dunaskin Doon Band was formed on 4 March 1869. It was formed as a works band at a time when the iron furnaces at Dalmellington Iron Works, Waterside, were in full production. The band has played at many venues over the years, including corporate events in Aberdeen, weddings in Troon, galas in Strathaven, concerts in Ayr Gaiety Theatre and contests in the Wembley Arena. The band repertoire ranges from classical to modern, opera to pop and from marches to the musicals.
Back row (12): (l to r) Tom Bruce, Jimmy Graham (visiting conductor), Tom McGill, Ian Bruce, William Seaton, Janice Rae, William Cochrane, William Dunbar, Blane McKnight, William Anderson, William Bell and Jim Guthrie.
Middle Row seated (10) (l to r): Donald Tyson, John Tyson, Douglas McQuater, John Louden, John Rae, Angus Cochrane, Marion Cuthbert, William Young, Stan (Tommy) Cuthbert and Jim Tyson.
Front row (5): David Young, Andrew Taylor, Jennifer Tyson, Andrew McIndoe and David Murray.
(Photo: Courtesy of Dunaskin Doon Band)

Dauner to the Red Burn

Next morning we would meet as usual to discuss what we would do that day. It would perhaps a dauner to the Red Burn over towards the Dalmellington–Straiton road. This was a fair walk, but we took it in our stride. First of all we would walk down to the store to see if Peter Magreichan had any ham nets. These were the nets which covered the hams and made excellent fishing nets. With these in our possession and some scrambled egg and potatoes in our bags would be off on our exploration.

There were no stones in the Red Burn so we had to flush the

fish from under the banking and into our nets. On the road over we would find a piece of wire which we threaded through the net to keep it open. It was pretty basic but quite useful.

Our route took us over Kiers bridge to Low Kiers and onwards to High Kiers. Johnnie McDowall was the farmer at High Kiers and he always had a friendly word with us as we passed through, because he knew that we were harmless and just enjoying the countryside. Turning left at the dairy took us past the ruins of a house known locally as Granny Blain's. No one knew why it got that name. Further on we came to the Red Burn and we were then nearer Dalmellington than Waterside.

Reaching the burn the first thing we did was to have a swim in one of the big pools. All the children from Waterside learned to swim in the Chapel Burn under the railway bridge. Interestingly, in the Chapel Burn you occasionally got the benefit of warm water being released from the condensers at the power station. The warm water would flow into the burn and it was nice and warm when it reached the pool at the Chapel Bridge. After trying to catch fish we would make a fire and boil potatoes which we thoroughly enjoyed as we were always hungry. We then walked back, which seemed longer than on the road up. We always parted with those famous words, 'See you in the morning.' Sometimes when I drive slowly past Waterside I look over to Kiers and think of those happy childhood days.

Harvesting

The war was still raging, but it had really very little impact on us as boys apart from the shortage of various foodstuffs. At the end of the summer holidays we then had to prepare to get back to school. We used to gather hazelnuts at Brogan's Glen. During the autumn the trees were laden and we would gather large numbers of them, which kept us going in nuts for a long time. We also gathered chestnuts at Ardoon, which was the manager's large mansion house sitting on the edge of Greenhill. The large tree beside the house, which is still there today, produced the best chestnuts. In the autumn everyone in the village went to gather brambles and our mothers would make pots of jelly. This was a necessity as jam was difficult to get during the war years. The only foodstuffs not rationed were potatoes and vegetables, which was because everyone in the country was encouraged to grow their own.

Dad always grew a large bed of onions, which he dried and they kept Mum going all winter. I loved working with Dad in his garden and in the spring he would order a cart of manure from Johnnie Hutchieson of Cutler Farm. When it arrived I had to barrow the manure to the garden. I loved doing this as I felt I was being a great help and the government had a scheme on the go to encourage folk to grow their own vegetables under the title 'Dig for Victory'.

Winter arrives

Autumn soon gave way to winter but we were able to keep ourselves busy. Winters seemed to be more severe then than now. There were also heavy frosts. We would go to the tarry (tarpit), which was a pond covered in tar with about 16 inches of water. This would freeze over and we would enjoy playing on the ice. This was located near to the wagon shop and in the 1960s it was filled in by the NCB to make a large coal stock yard, so there have been many changes over the years.

We could play at the tarry for hours, as it was always well lit with the new floodlights shining brightly at the coal washing plant. This hard frost could go on for weeks and it was cold in the houses as there was no such thing as central heating. When we went home frozen, Mum would make us chips and scrambled egg. The egg was powdered and came from America, but you would eat anything in those days. Flinging out food was simply unknown as there were such shortages.

Village organisations

As a youngster I attended the Life Boys. Kenny Bryden and Nessie Baxter were the leaders. We met twice weekly in the old village hall which stood near to Clover Park Cottage. It was an old army billet that had come from the School of Aerial Gunnery at Loch Doon during the First World War. The children also attended Sunday School in this old hall. We were forced to go by our parents but we really enjoyed it. Our Sunday School teacher was Maggie Smith, who gave us text cards to learn Bible verses for the following Sunday. I wish I had kept those mementos of my childhood days. The advantage of being in those organisations was that at Christmas you qualified for treats and parties and in the summer you would attend the Sunday School trips. Trips were difficult during the war as it was hard to get trains or buses. Because of this Mr George Kirkwood, manager, who lived at Ardoon, gave permission to use a field at Waterside for the trips. He and his wife would come out to lend a hand, as their own three boys were also members of the Sunday School. The eldest, John, was a great pal of mine until the Kirkwood family moved to Edinburgh when the coal industry was nationalised in 1947. I kept in touch for a couple of years until we were called up to do National Service.

Lethanhill men on a bus trip. In the centre a man is offering another a cigarette from his case. Those in kilts are likely to have been members of the Lethanhill Pipe Band.
(Photo: Courtesy of Doon Valley Museum)

I remember

I remember regularly having to go along the backs of the rows at Greenhills to clear away the snow after a blizzard. We then chapped the door and would be given a threepenny piece, which was just great for us boys. We were never in the house on winter nights. Another great thing to do if it was a wild night was to go along to the kilnhead (the Staffordshire – a chamber kiln named after the county where it was first developed). With the warm air rising up from the burned chambers, this kept us nice and warm.

We knew the three kiln burners, Jimmy Logan, Wull Innes and Wull McAllden. We would all sit round the kiln vents getting hot, then we would run down to the kiln top, jumping over piles of dross that were put down in advance of firing. The kiln burner watched us as we hurled over the dross and as sure as anything one of us would hit the top of the pile and this was followed by a loud roar from the kiln burner, who would shout, 'Get to hell out off there!' My dad was the boss of the brickworks and I didn't want him to know that we had been getting up to mischief. Wull Innes tended to be the one who chased us. Little did I know then that in later years I would end up as brickworks manager at Waterside and would laugh at the tricks I got up to as a boy.

Women at work

Another thing we used to do was help the women who were working at the brickworks during the war. They had to do this as it was classed as vital war work and released men to go to the army. The other work women would do was at the stamp works in Ayr, join the Land Army or sign up for military service. At least the women at Waterside could go home at night after working hard all day.

The first job the girls got was in the wood yard. Trucks brought the wood in and the driver threw it all in a heap. This wood was actually pit props and the girls would stack it in an orderly fashion. We (boys) knew so much about the job we could instruct the girls on how to do it.

I also went round the village twice a week with Willie Hose to empty the buckets. There wasn't much rubbish as packaging was minimal due to the shortage of paper. Most of the rubbish was tin cans and ashes from the coal fires. Willie would give me a couple of shillings and would let me drive the horse up to the dump.

This was located at the bottom of the works brae and across from where the railway cottages were. The horse's name was Dick and they had two other horses called Topper and Tam. The stables are still standing yet across from the New Cottages, but they have been derelict from the late 1950s. Really, there was never a dull moment in Waterside when I was a boy and I loved to keep myself busy.

The jackdaw boys

My young brother 'Buddy' and I were known in Waterside as the jackdaw boys. This was because each year a jackdaw nested on the roof of our house. They also nested in large numbers on the slag bing and in the pipes in the large retaining wall on the Waterside site. Every year we found a nest and would take one of the larger birds from the nest to our home and rear it until it was completely tame. After a few weeks of hand-feeding, the young jackdaw would be completely tame and would stand on my shoulder or head. They would never fly away although they could have, had they chosen to.

My mother was always getting on to us about keeping them because they would fly into other folk's houses and steal food and other items. This sometimes didn't go down too well with some neighbours. We used to put a coloured band on the leg of the jackdaws so we could distinguish between them. We got up in the morning and they were always waiting to be fed. The birds stayed with us all winter but left during the mating season.

I was in Ayr a while ago and met a former PT teacher from Dalmellington School. I told him my name and he responded by asking me if I was one of the jackdaw boys. I told him I was and he asked me about my brother Buddy, whom he clearly remembered. I had to tell him that Buddy had died nine years ago and he was quite vexed to hear that. For the record, the teacher was Mr Alex Scott and he was then in his eighties, but passed on a few years later. So Buddy and I must have been quite famous in the Doon Valley all those years ago.

Helping with the post

I recall when Mrs McCutcheon applied to become postmistress in the village. She was quite pleased when she was successful because she was able to operate the post office from her home, which was a real blessing because her son Jim was always in very poor health and was generally housebound. I got a little job with Mrs McCutcheon. I took the mail down to Waterside railway station every evening to be put on the Ayr train. For doing this I received 6 shillings a week. I also delivered telegrams at the weekend and for this I received a penny per mile.

Mrs McCutcheon had a small mile meter fixed to my bike. Most of the telegrams were for folk living in Lethanhill and would be in connection with deaths or forthcoming weddings. Sometimes the recipient would give me a tanner (sixpence) and I never told the boss about the tip or this would have been deducted from my wages. Mrs McCutcheon's son, Jim, died of tuberculosis (TB) about three years later. This was a terrible killer in those days.

Army convoy

Another interesting event which comes to mind was the army convoy that went through Waterside. The convoy travelled nose to tail continuously for what seemed to me as a boy to be at least the better part of a day, with only five minutes' stop about every half hour to allow people to cross the road. This was known as a mobile column and it was an impressive thing to see passing through the Doon Valley.

There was this endless stream of military vehicles as I sat mesmerised on the bridge at the slag hill. I never knew where it was going or where it all came from and the operation was never publicised due to military secrecy, but as boys we were fascinated by the whole operation. There were tanks, Bren gun carriers, heavy guns on tow, trucks heavily laden with troops, and dispatch riders moving alongside the convoy making sure that progress was not blocked for any reason. Some of the troops flung out some iron ration biscuits and it is little wonder that they were so called as they were full of vitamins.

I remember that one night Captain Boyle came round the doors asking if any of the families could provide a meal for soldiers who would be coming to Waterside. The very next morning about a dozen large tanks came up the works brae and parked in front of Greenhill Row. Most of the folk were out their houses and invited the soldiers in for a meal. My mother had three of the soldiers in for about half an hour and I was fair proud to play on the tank parked outside my door. In fact in my mind's eye, I thought I was a tank commander.

Rationing

Rationing was a terrible time, especially for the women, who had to make do with scanty supplies to feed families. There were seven folk to be fed in our house. Every shop my mother went to had a queue. Word would get round the village that the store was getting lemonade, but by the time you got down there was a long queue of villagers. The shopkeeper, Hugh Borland, would be shouting, 'Two bottles per family only now.'

Kerfuffle

Another day word got round that there were oranges in the Co-op in Patna. As sure as sunshine, I was up at the crack of dawn at 6.30 a.m. and down to the shop in Patna to buy a dozen oranges for mother. But even then there was a big queue down to about the Manse. Then down strode Jimmy Sadler, the Co-op foreman, and he promptly stopped halfway down the queue and put his arm across and in a voice of authority announced loudly that from that point back they might as well go home.

Workers at DICo store, Waterside in the early 1900s. This store supplied just about every need anyone in the community could wish for.
L to r: Willie Smith, Hugh Borland, Nancy Kerr, Peter McGeachan, Margaret McMillan, Bob Dunn, John Thomson, Tom Campbell, Billy Thomson (boy).
(Photo: Courtesy of EAC Doon Valley Museum)

Unfortunately for Jimmy, he stopped at a woman who was known to have more than a wee bit of a temper. All hell broke loose and fighting began and Jimmy had to flee for his life. When I got home with my dozen oranges my mum told me reports were coming in on the radio that a big battle had started at a place called Tobruk in North Africa. However, I was able to tell her that was nothing compared to the battle at Patna Co-op. My mother thought that was hilarious and so did I, because I witnessed it.

I must finish my thoughts on rationing with a lovely little story. I was always in Mrs Uriarte's house and one day when I went in she gave me a small piece of banana skin. Her son John was in the Navy out in the Far East and he sent his mum a letter and contained in the envelope was a little piece of banana skin.

The war was by this time in its fourth year and Mrs Uriarte told me to take it home and let my mother smell it as you couldn't get foreign fruit for love or money. All the folk near us in Waterside came to see this piece of banana skin and smell it and savour its aroma. I have told my own children and grandchildren this story and they think I was having them on. In fact during the war it was a great thing to get a raw turnip or a carrot to eat.

Cheesy smile

One day Mum said she had no cheese and she was very partial to it, but the weekly rations were almost exhausted and Mum asked if I would nip down to the store and have a word with Peter Magrechan, who was the grocer, and to make sure there was none of the bosses about. So down I went and had a quiet word with Peter who looked over his specs to make sure there was no one about. He disappeared through the back shop, and came back with a nice piece of cheese which he slipped to me. He bade me farewell, saying, 'Fade away and come back the morn.' Peter always said that to all his customers.

However, up I went to my mother with her wee bit of cheese. It was worth all the bother to see the delight on her face. Next week Mum got her Co-op book and here was a turnip marked down as sixpence. This was old Peter covering his tracks, putting the cheese through as turnip, as vegetables were not rationed. A lot of this went on during the war. If anyone was friendly with a butcher, grocer or farmer, they always got that wee bit extra. Dad, and his friends too, always got extra for the table. Sunday dinner in our house was often rabbit as my granddad was a gamekeeper for Bairds and Dalmellington. He handed a pair of rabbits in now and again.

Prisoners of war

Word went round Waterside that there were prisoners of war working at the slag hill, so it was parade to the bing by the villagers to see them. I thought we were going to see strange, evil men, but they were just like any other ordinary working folk. The only difference was that prisoners of war had a large round patch on the back of their tunic.

These men were loading lumps of slag onto trucks with their hands. Guards were patrolling up and down the rows of trucks, keeping an eye on the prisoners. They had rifles on their shoulders. We went over every morning to watch them working. My young sister Jean thought this was terrible, men being forced to work. Jean would be nine or ten years of age and felt sorry for them and asked Dad for two cigarettes.

When the guards weren't looking, she slipped the cigs to one of the prisoners. She did this quite often. In fact, she told one of the guards to give the prisoner a hand to load the slag. The guard just ignored Jean. Imagine if I had owned a camcorder in those bygone days. The film would now be priceless.

Clydebank bombing

Old Mr Winning, who was the blacksmith foreman, lived next door to us in Greenhill Row. He came knocking on the front door one night very late when we were all sleeping. I woke up and heard the terrible droning noise. Mr Winning came in and told us to come out to the door to hear the German bombers going over the village. Mum was crying and I was upset for her. It was pitch dark and we had to keep the lights out. There must have been hundreds of aircraft as the ground was vibrating with the noise. Once they had passed by, Dad took me up onto the bank line and kept looking north-westwards, and we soon saw the flashing in the sky. It went on for a long time.

Next morning we found out that it was the people of Clydebank who were bombed. This went on for a few nights, and many poor souls lost their lives. This was the reason for the evacuees being here. At least they were safe from the bombing. If any bomber going over Waterside saw a light, they might have dropped their bombs on us, so that was the good thing about the blackout.

'Happy' Young's loyalty

Dad told us a humorous story about his nightshift foreman. 'Happy' Young had been very angry about the bombing of Clydebank. Dunaskin Brickworks were producing 40,000 bricks every single day. They never sold a brick so there were several million bricks stacked around the works. It was like a maze of passageways. The procedure was that when workers at the power station received the purple warning of possible enemy aircraft, they dropped the breaker switch, which cut the power in the brickworks. One of the workers was sent down to make sure there was no dross burning on top of the wee kiln, as it had no roof. Happy was raging about production being disrupted and he demanded to know what was going on. He said to the man, 'To hell with the Germans. Production must go on.' This was 'Happy's' response to Hitler. These bricks were all used for the government after the war, building new houses at Patna, Bellsbank, Ayr and many other districts.

End of the war

I will never forget the day the war ended. I was thirteen and full of life. We helped everyone to put up their flags. Union Jacks on every roof and every chimney in Waterside. It was some spectacle. A chap called 'Spurkey' Burns climbed the flag mast and hung a large Union Jack. All the blackout blinds were taken down and there was a large bonfire to build.

The only assistance we got from Bairds and Dalmellington was old wood, sleepers, tar barrels – as much as we could carry. There must have been about fifteen boys working building the fire in the wee football field in front of Greenhill Row. Some boys made an effigy of Hitler and we stuck him on top of the bonfire. It was a great night when the fire was lit. It was set on fire about 10 p.m. when it was just getting dark, as it was in the month of May. The whole village was there to see it and everyone was in a happy mood.

There was also a dance band there called Bryden, Brannigan and Carruthers. This consisted of accordion, saxophone and drums. It was a great night for everyone and there was such relief that the war was over and better days would hopefully lie ahead. The whole village came out in force to take part in the festivities. The fire died down and we all eventually went home tired but very happy. We realised that the war was over and we had the satisfaction of taking part in what was a national celebration.

The Institute

No Waterside man today could talk about old memories without mentioning the Workmen's Institute. This was the village games hall and is now a private dwelling owned by an English family. Sadly and annoyingly, the village war memorial is now located within the grounds of this house and problems have been experienced with gaining access to the memorial. This saddens me greatly, as two of my uncles' names are recorded on Waterside memorial.

The Institute consisted of a reading room, small games room, and a large hall with three billiards tables. The first table as you entered was known as the McAdam table and was the newest. Apparently it was presented to the village by Mrs McAdam of Craigengillan Estate in Dalmellington. There was a small side room which had a table version of curling. We soon learned to play billiards and snooker. We spent every night of the week in the Institute with our pals and it was a great place to socialise.

Bobby Moore was the live-in caretaker of the hall. A good-living man, but a real diehard and disciplinarian, Bobby would adhere to the Ten Commandments and had about a further twenty of his own. Thou shall not do this, thou shall not do that! When he was working with generations of young boys, his patience must have been sorely tried. Bobby drew a straight line and expected all the young lads never to stray off it. So every night there was always some of us in bother with Bobby. If you argued with him he gave you one other chance, but if you re-offended you were out the door until the next night. By a Thursday night, with no money left, we would all sit round the blazing coal fire in one of the rooms. It's nice to think back to the cold winter nights chatting about our hopes and visions for the future. They were good days then with no malice in our minds.

Fire and fireworks

As I said earlier, we all sat round the fire in the Institute, even in the summer time when there was no fire lit. One night there would be about seven of us when in walked my cousin David Denham. He had a rocket in his hand. Fireworks were very powerful in these days. With no malice intended, David sat the rocket in the empty fire for safety reasons. We all started to discuss how to light it and how high it would go.

John Campbell, a true prankster, was sitting with a cigarette in his hand and touched the fuse, which ignited the rocket. It went up the chimney with a deafening noise and a large pile of soot came rumbling down the lum, landing on the hearth, flying all over the hall.

Within five seconds Bobby came charging into the room, shouting. Bobby had been sitting at his dinner when the rocket had been launched, and his wife Jean had heard the commotion. Picture the scene. Bobby came rushing in and we were all sitting like Kentucky Minstrels covered in soot. We were put out and later banned from the Institute for three months.

Mum's quotations

I have mentioned my mother quite a lot in my memories of boyhood days. She had many quotations which she regularly used which I can instantly recall. She used to say, 'Get up little children, the morning is bright, the birds are all waiting to welcome the light.'

Another one was when we came in from school to start the summer holidays. Every year she would say: 'Now lessons are over and the books put away. We are off to the hills for a scamper and play, but hark there is someone who ought to come too, it's our little doggy so faithful and true.'

In later years if I came in to see Mum when I was coming home from work, Dad would say to me, 'Jock, you are awfa dirty.' But Mum would respond by saying:

It's not the honest brown dirt, my lad,
That makes a man unclean
It's what he has in him, not what he has on him
That will forever make him a gentleman.

My favourite one was if anyone was in need of help, she always said:

Life is but a mighty river rolling from day to day
Men are vessels launched upon, some are torn and cast away,
So come along each one another, making life a pleasant dream
And help a worn and weary brother who is fighting hard against the stream.

Hector

Hector was a dog who wandered freely all over the village and was known to everyone. I suppose you could call him a community dog, because he wasn't owned by any one person.

However, he was well looked after and stayed in a different house every night and was well fed. When we came off the Dalmellington school bus, Hector was always sitting at the railway cottages waiting for us. He ran about with the boys all night.

One night we were looking for Hector, but he was nowhere to be found. Then word arrived that Hector was up at Lethanhill. He went to meet a bitch and this happened about twice a year as he would disappear for about a week. How did he get to Lethanhill? Believe it or not, Hector would get on the bus for Patna. He then got off at the Old Brig and waited for the Lethanhill bus and got off at the Hill. All the drivers and conductors knew Hector.

I suppose he would leave some offspring at Lethanhill as a memento of his visit. Hector must have died, because when I left school and started work I never saw him again. However, many old residents will have fond memories of this remarkable community dog.

First job
With my happy boyhood days over, I started my first job in July 1947 at Dunaskin Brickworks. With me practically being reared to brick making, I naturally followed in the footsteps of my father, who was the manager. My first job was as a loft boy. I had done this job many a time during my schooldays. You had to make sure that the feed tube to the machine was always full. This was an easy job in dry weather, but when it rained the clay came into the works wet. When it was wet it had difficulty going through the panmills which lowered the volume of ground clay coming from the loft. This meant more work for me on wet days.

After a few weeks in the loft, dad put me with a machine man to be taught to operate the brick machine. Within a short time I became a qualified mixer. When the machine was running well I had to clean the machine using dusters so that I wasn't standing idly about, which tended to annoy my father. Over the next few years I was taught the maintenance of the machinery, including learning all the engineering side of the brickworks. After Dad retired I became manager of the works.

Fling it in the Doon
Everything that was unwanted in Waterside at that time was flung in the River Doon. Old wringers, bikes, prams, beds – in fact anything not wanted – was tossed into the bonny Doon. The word environment was never used in those days. It was simple to dump stuff in the river. I think this went back to the times when there was no organised cleansing service, so it was a case of out of sight, out of mind.

One morning my young brother Buddy and I were going down to Patna on our bikes. We got the length of the Doon Bridge at Keirs, when we were stopped by Tam, the village polis. He asked us where we were going. Buddy said Patna. Tam said that he definitely wasn't going to Patna on such a wrecked bicycle and Tam told him that he had two choices. Walk home with the bike or chuck it in the River Doon. Buddy thought for a few seconds and then flung his bike into the river. Sometimes when I pass that bridge at Waterside I wonder if Buddy's bike is still in that deep pool.

Hunting treasure
I remember one of the boys found a set of grappling hooks consisting of three big hooks all welded together with a ring for a rope to be tied to. We got a rope somewhere and a gang of us headed for the river. We decided to clean the river from the works dam to what we called Devil's Island. We flung in the hooks and pulled them slowly across the river. When the hooks caught on something it was all hands on the rope and we all hauled until our treasure surfaced.

It would likely be a cast iron bed-end or some other junk. This was left near the riverbank, and unknown to us some Good Samaritan came along and chucked the lot back in. I don't suppose we were caring, as we were maybe looking for real treasure in the first place, as boys might do. We were probably boys dreaming of a magical world we didn't know or understand.

There was real treasure in the Doon – the famous River Doon pearls. Wallace Allen, the jeweller in Ayr, bought all the River Doon pearls. In fact, my wife Beth has a Doon pearl on a ring I bought her for our pearl wedding anniversary. Jimmy Hutcheon, of my age group, was a great pearl fisherman in the Doon and there have been several since then. Nowadays fishing for pearls is strictly forbidden.

Today

I am now happily retired and live in Bellsbank with my wife and my daughter Julie. All my other family members are grown up and live locally or abroad. I have many happy memories of Waterside and the great years when the Dunaskin Veterans' Group was active in the heritage museum. We had some great fun. Someone once said we were a bit like the characters from the TV series *Last of the Summer Wine*. But we were all keen to do what we can to ensure that the history of the area is kept alive for future generations. I have enjoyed recounting some aspects of my memories and I hope it gives you as much pleasure reading them.

And fare thee weel, my only luve!
And fare thee weel, a while!
And I will come again, my love,
Tho it were ten thousand mile!

My Luve is Like a Red, Red Rose
Robert Burns

Hill reunion guests gather before the event in Patna Community Centre in 1978. These reunions began in 1965 and ran for thirty-one years. The last speaker was Brian Donohoe MP in 1996, who was the son of the village headmaster of Lethanhill School until 1959.
Back row (l to r): John Gilmour, James 'Cherry' Bryce, Bobby Knox, William Stewart, Bertie Smith, Hugh Ferguson, Tommy Hose and George Sturgeon.
Front row: Peter Conway, Annie McFadzean, James McFadzean, Mrs Bella McCormick and Jim Carruthers.
(Courtesy of John Relly collection)

Chapter 17

Tales from Black Rock Glen
Jim McNae

Give me simple laboring folk,
Who love their work,
Whose virtue is song
To cheer God along.

Conscience
Henry David Thoreau

Retired police officer Jim McNae, now living in Ayr, served as village policeman in Dalmellington for many years. He was raised at Glenmuick Farm, near to Loch Muck. Here he journeys down memory lane and recalls some dark tales from the past.

The Black Rocks
The A713 Ayr to Castle Douglas road, or, to be more precise, the stretch from Dalmellington to the county boundary at Loch Muck, is far better known to Dalmellington folk as 'the road up through the Black Rocks when you're going up the country'. As roads go, it's not an old road. Tradition tells that the Roman legions made and marched along their own road that kept to the high ground about half a mile west of the present road. The next road would be the one that passes through Craigengillan Estate and up the Gaw Glen, over the Eriff Hill to meet the present road at the county boundary.

Glen Muick Farm
There would always be a track of sorts going through the glen, but it would be no more than a 'pownie pad' (bridle path). About two hundred years ago it was upgraded to take horse and cart! As a boy, living on Glenmuick Farm, I walked, ran, sometimes 'walked a pole, ran a pole' on that road. I've cycled it and travelled it by car, bus and lorry, in hail, rain, sleet and snow – and occasionally in sunshine. Cycling down the glen towards Dalmellington, the wind was mostly on your face, but going up the glen, especially in the early hours, the wind was always on your face.

Glen Muick Farm which lies at the top of the Black Rock Glen 2 miles south of Dalmellington on the A713 Dalmellington–Carsphairn Road. For many years it was occupied by the McNae family.
(Photo: Donald L Reid)

Tales handed down
My family came to stay at Glenmuick Farm in 1917. My grandfather, Jimmy McNae, and my father, Adam, told me the history and tales of the glen and those are what I will try and pass on to the readers here.

The journey starts at the meeting of the roads at Lendal

Cottage, the last house at the south end of Dalmellington: this was the local roadman's cottage and was occupied by Jimmy Henderson for many years. Travelling south, on each side of the road was the town's common grazing land. I think this land was owned by Craigengillan Estate, but a number of houses in Dalmellington had grazing rights for their milk cows. It's possible that the rights are still in the title deeds of these houses.

Jim McNae, a retired police officer who was raised at Glenmuick Farm, attended the rededication service of the Benwhat War Memorial (Photo: Donald L Reid)

The common was also used by shepherds and drovers taking sheep and cattle from the high hills of Galloway. They stayed there with their animals overnight before driving them on the old drove road up by Craigmark and Benwhat, through the nick at Kilmein Hill, down to Rankinston and on to the Ayrshire plains.

Herds' work
Later, with the coming of the railway in 1856, Dalmellington became the railhead for sheep being taken to the livestock markets at Ayr and Lanark. Robert McTaggart, still the shepherd at Beoch, Loch Doon, can recall how he and his father drove the Beoch sheep to the common, then waited with them until they had settled down after dark. They were back again before dawn to take the sheep to the loading pens at Dalmellington railway station. Robert helped to load sheep on to the last livestock train to leave Dalmellington in September 1963 – the last of the many thousands that were transported from Dalmellington railway station.

Some of the older residents will remember the wee cottage that sat on the east (left) side of the road, about quarter of a mile from Dalmellington. This was the old tollhouse. The last resident was Mrs Roxburgh; all that remains now is a clump of nettles.

The Kirn Pool
A little further on and you arrive at the Kirn Brig where the road passes over the Muck Burn. How the bridge got its name, I don't know – possibly from the more famous Kirn Pool in the burn on the topside of the bridge. Kirn is the Scots name for a churn, although I've also heard it used for a deep, rumbling pool in a burn.

The Kirn Pool was the 'dooker' where the youngsters of Dalmellington learned to swim in the days long before heated, indoor swimming baths. The Kirn doesn't look much now, but in those days, at the start of the summer, local boys built a dam across the burn at the bottom end of the pool.

This dam was constructed of stones and sods and was 2 or 3 feet high, making the pool 10 or 12 feet deep. I've seen upwards of thirty swimmers at the Kirn Pool at one time. Some brave lads used to dive from the 'sod' into the pool, a height of 10 feet. Dr Campbell, the local GP, stitched the scalp of many a boy who misjudged his diving capabilities. Aye, these were special times and remind me of daft boyhood days.

Road impassable
Travelling on up the A713, you come to a right-hand bend in the road where the Muck Burn laps the side of the road. Nothing remarkable there, other than that fifty years ago, on a wild, stormy night, the burn washed away the road. It was impassable for about a week, so no vehicles could travel south into Galloway. Nothing could travel north either, which was far more important to a ten-year-old boy who couldn't get to school. Aye, happy days indeed for me!

As the journey continues, the road runs straight now, and at the end of the straight stretch on the left can be found a carriers' well. It used to be maintained by the local roadmen: it was about 3 feet square, 1½ feet deep, with wooden sides and cold, clear water. It was overgrown the last time I saw it, but the water was still flowing.

Auld Mossdale

On up to Mossdale Farm, occupied at one time by a Mr Walker. Few people knew his name: he was better known as 'Auld Mossdale' and was quite a worthy in his time. The shepherd at Mossdale Farm was Willie Heaney. Willie was a small man, but exceptionally fit. He was Irish and came over from Limavady with his two brothers in the early 20th century. They worked in the pits in Fife before coming to Dalmellington to work, not in the local mines, but on the land. When Willie retired he lived in Bellsbank with his daughter, a Mrs O'Neil.

Older residents will remember Willie as a fervent and vocal supporter of Craigmark Burntonians football team. He urged on his team with shouts of 'All together boys, but one at a time', with a voice that had been trained to perfection as a shepherd. He could be heard all over the town.

Plane crash

From the farm, the road crosses the Mossdale Burn; two dams on the burn were the source of Dalmellington's water supply for many years. The Loch Doon road heads off to the right and disappears into the forest. A car park at the junction was the site of Mossdale Cottage. A family named Sheddan stayed there, followed by Andy Lambie and his wife. When they moved to Bellsbank the cottage was demolished.

The glen narrows here and just beyond a milestone you can see, on the left, a slight scar on the hillside. This was where a four-engine RAF bomber crashed during the Second World War. Some of the aircrew escaped by parachute, one fortunate man landing on the roof of Dalmellington School. Sadly, there were some fatalities.

Stone chapper

Matha Murdoch's quarry is a short distance further on. Matha Murdoch was the stone chapper, responsible for keeping that part of the road in a good state of repair. Next is the 'grey twins', a large boulder that split in half thousands of years ago when it rolled down the steep face of Mossdale Craig. Then you reach the dyke-end, the march between Mossdale and Glenmuick Farm: this is just before the 'Z' bends that take you into the deep, dark defile between the Heights of Craigwaughton on one side and the Craig of the Shore on the other. Two days after the blizzard of 1963 I walked up the glen and, between the two bends, there was a snowdrift the face of which was easily 40 feet high.

Whisky Well

On the apex of the second bend is the Whisky Well, another carriers' well. How it got its name is lost in the mists of time. One popular story is that one of the famous Carsphairn cairters (carriers – transporters of goods), a worthy called 'Baillie' Hunter, quenched his thirst there after imbibing in the hostelries of Dalmellington. The Hunter family from Carsphairn were well-known carriers or 'cairters' who travelled by horse and cart between Carsphairn and Dalmellington, carrying goods both ways but mainly picking up stores for Carsphairn at Dalmellington railway station. This happened Monday to Friday, every week of the year, blizzards permitting – hardy men.

A dramatic scene showing a railway accident at Waterside near to Cutler sidings on 25 April 1929. The locomotive (pug) No. 10 with a rake of coals left the line. Inevitably, three men and a dog (left) turn up too see what was happening! They were (l to r): James Kerr, John Kerr who was himself a former engine driver and Thomas Rowan, formerly the traffic foreman.

Tragic accident

The next bend is McClung's Corner, named after the unfortunate roadman who was setting cat's eyes in the road when a vehicle came round the corner and killed him. Mr McClung stayed in Kerse Cottage, near Polnessan. He was the grandfather of Vera Parker from Dalmellington who was Miss Scotland back in the 1960s. The road continues across the Sixpenny Brig that carries it over the Craig Burn: where the brig's name comes from I know not.

Jameson's Turn

The glen widens out now and the next corner is Jameson's Turn. This corner got its name from a farmer, Jameson, from Holm of Daltalochan, Carsphairn. One night Jameson set out on the 10-mile trip to Dalmellington by horse and trap. His parting words were, 'Hell or Dalmellington in half an hour.' He never reached Dalmellington. The following morning his pony and trap were found standing in the burn at the turn; months later his body was found in the River Doon. A 3-foot-high granite boulder, known as Jameson Stane, stands on the far bank of the burn.

Hangman's Brig

Before road alterations got rid of it, a couple of hundred yards further on you reached the 'Z' bend comprising the Hangman's Brig and Paddy's Loup. The brig got its name from the Hangman's Tree which grew on a nearby rock face. Legend has it that some time around the middle of the 19th century a family of gypsies was camped in the wee grassy holm just up from the bridge. This was a regular camping site for gypsies, who stayed a few days then moved on. The horses were allowed to graze free during the day, but were hobbled at night. One morning the shepherd from Glenmuick farm rose to find the gypsies gone and one of their horses hanged from a tree. I can remember the tree, a rowan; it must have taken some effort to pull the horse up the steep face of the precipice. There was no doubt the horse had been hanged intentionally. If they had wanted it dead, why not shoot it or slit its throat? Was it part of some dark secret rite? We'll never know.

As a young boy, I can remember gypsies with their horse-drawn caravans camping there. One time my father told them the tale of the Hangman's Tree; in the morning they were gone and never returned. Coincidence? I don't know.

Killing Times

You are now within sight of Glenmuick Farm where I was born and raised. A house has stood on this spot for hundreds of years. Covenanter conventicles were held here during the 'Killing Times' of the late 17th century.

Schooldays

My father walked the four miles to school in Dalmellington every day from the time he was five years old until he was thirteen, when the Education Authority supplied him with a taxi for his final year. I also travelled by school-car to school. It was a great excuse if you were late: 'Please sir, the school-car was late.' I was untouchable – no latecomer's punishment for me – or so I thought. One day I came ambling in after time to be confronted by the large figure of the late Bill Shankland, the formidable science and maths teacher.

I was lined up with the rest of the latecomers. 'Why were you late?' he roared. Confidence ebbing away fast, I gave my usual excuse. 'That's no excuse', replied the big man, 'Your father walked and was never late. Get your hand out.' One of the belt and it was a cracker. My hand was sore and my confidence badly dented, but I learned a lot that morning, just as Bill Shankland knew I would. A great man and a great teacher was 'Big Bull' Shankland.

Glenmuick of happy memory

I can still see Glenmuick as it was, sitting at the top of the winding path, clumps of daffodils covering the brae. The path was enclosed on one side by a drystane dyke, while Glenmuick Lynn spouted out from the rowan trees on the other. Many a tourist stopped to take photographs of the picturesque scene. The road goes through a cutting now, so you don't get as good a view, the winding path is no more, and the curse of the conifers has cut the flow of the water over the lynn.

The glen opens out now onto the moorland. And what a view – a whole panorama spreads out. Over the top of the purple heather moor and Loch Muck you can see the Merrick and the high hills of Galloway, a landscape so different from the one you've just travelled through. Down across the wee bridge over the Polnaskie Burn (burn of the fairies) and you're into bonny Galloway.

It really is fascinating that Black Rock Glen has three and a half miles of road with its own history and legends of joy and sorrow, happiness and sadness. Next time you travel that road I hope you remember there's more to it than tarmac and rubber.

For thee is laughing nature gay;
For thee she pours the vernal day;
For me in vain is nature dressed,
While joy's a stranger to my breast!

Revision for Clarinda
Robert Burns

The locally named split-rock in Black Rock Glen near Dalmellington. (Photo: Donald L Reid)

Chapter 18

The Doon Valley in Retrospect – The 1930s

Anne Joss

This is the place. Stand still, my steed,
Let me review the scene,
And summon from the shadowy Past
The forms that once have been.

The Past and Present here unite
Beneath Time's flowing tide,
Like footprints hidden by a brook,
But seen on either side.

A Gleam of Sunshine
H W Longfellow

Miss Anne Joss, ninety, who loves the Doon Valley and has worked tirelessly over the years to preserve much of its history and heritage. (Photo: Donald L Reid)

Miss Anne Joss MBE, a very well-respected lady from Dalmellington who has been active in the community all her life, played a prominent role in establishing the open-air museum at Dunaskin. She was deeply disappointed when it closed in 2005. Here she shares some of her precious memories of the Doon Valley of the 1930s.

Dalmellington by train

In mid-April 1930 I did wonder what kind of place I was going to as, with my mother and father, I rattled up to Dalmellington in the little one-coach train popularly called the puffer. I had heard of Dalmellington before, when I landed in Heathfield Fever Hospital with diphtheria and met, in the ward, an older girl from Dalmellington who was very religious and told us all that if we did not kneel down to say our prayers we would go to Hell. That was difficult, because, for some weeks, we were kept lying on our backs with no hope of performing the kneeling exercise. Thus it was that I had my childish reservations about this new place, over which the clouds of damnation seemed to hang. I had no way of knowing how the place would hold me for the rest of my life.

A policeman's lot

We moved into the upper flat of the old Dalmellington Police Station on 1 May 1930. As police sergeant, my father had a wide district, taking in Patna, Waterside, the hill villages – Benquhat (as it was then spelled) or Benwhat, Burnfoothill/Lethanhill (the Hill) – Rankinston and the small rows such as Tongue Row (usually Raw). The country district was widespread, from Loch Doon to the Kirkcudbright border, with farms and shepherds' cottages, all with their own emergencies from time to time. This was long before the days of the police car. Travel about the district was by train, bicycle and on foot. In good weather, a visit to Benwhat could be combined with one to Rankinston via the ancient pack road round the side of Kilmein Hill.

Dalmellington had three policemen – the sergeant, an experienced constable and a young trainee constable who had a room provided for him in the police station. There were also constables at Waterside, Patna and Rankinston.

Drownings

We arrived because of the early death of the previous sergeant from pneumonia, a killer in those days, which it seems he contracted following a lengthy search for a body in the River Doon. It was a period when several drownings took place in the river, perhaps because it was a time of great hardship for many, and depression perhaps set in for many people who were finding life extremely difficult.

Constable John Milne was famous for his eerie skill at finding bodies in the water. Fortunately, he came to no harm. One later drowning which has left its own memorial took place from the bridge over the Doon on the Craigengillan Estate. Postman McCutcheon (they walked or cycled then!) was in the habit of taking a rest on the bridge. He was seen by a passer-by but was reported missing when he did not return home. A search took place and he was found in the river – by John Milne. A sad mystery, but from then on the bridge has been called the postman's brig.

Shops and businesses of yesteryear

Dalmellington was a small town. Apart from some houses built for mining officials, little change had taken place for many years. As today, the town was well supplied with shops. In the Main Street were Murray's drapery with tailoring services, Isabel Clark's drapery and haberdashery, Jimmy Rankine's grocery and Lizzie Gibson's drapery. Soon there was Bell's bakery. Opposite were the post office and Cron's ironmongery and, before long, Blunt the hairdresser (the beginning of ladies' hairstyling, with the fearsome permanent wave machine), and the Bank.

In the Square there was Scott and Simpson's grocery, where Nice Days is now, Pollock's newsagent, a bakery which was soon to become McCallum's, and Murdoch's and Ross's butchers' shops. The Co-operative shops climbed up the right side of High Main Street, more commonly referred to as the Store Brae, and dealt in all types of merchandise. There were two tailors, two dressmakers, a barber and a blacksmith in the village.

Few cars were on the roads in these days. Dr Howat and his assistant, Mr Addison (who lived at Dunolly), and the Eglinton and Black Bull Hotels had cars and it was still fun to watch the train racing a car along the Moss (the long straight out of Dalmellington on A713 to Ayr). Jock Richardson, who drove the Eglinton Hotel car, still told stories about the horse-driving days when hotel guests were taken to fish at Loch Doon in the hotel horse and trap and the farmers were brought home from market by horse. No need to worry about drink driving! The horses knew the way home.

NUM branch meeting with local manager at Minnivey Colliery, Dalmellington circa 1964.
L to r: J Thomson, deputy manager; Sam Graham, NUM; J Miller, under-manager; J McArthur, manager; David Connell, clerk; John Easton, electrician; H Murphy, NUM and Adam Johnstone, safety and training officer.
(Photo: Courtesy of EAC Doon Valley Museum)

The Depression

To understand much of what follows, it is necessary to see events in the light of the history of the time. The 1930s saw Britain entering the period of the Great Depression, a worldwide event, following a period of poor economic achievement in the 1920s – the price, both in manpower and to the economy, of the First World War. The government of the time, in an attempt to provide employment for the unemployed and to solve the problem of poor housing in many areas, started what came to be called council house building.

In the Doon Valley there were two effects of this. The increased demand for bricks prompted Bairds and Dalmellington, the firm that had taken over Dunaskin from the Dalmellington Iron Company, to expand brick making there and so provide some jobs, and Ayr County Council began house building to rehouse people from the hill villages. By 1930, Castle Croft had been built and a beginning was made to the crescent part of Bellsbank Crescent. Later in the 1930s, a beginning was made to the Hopes Avenue and Park Crescent houses but this was halted at the outbreak of war in 1939.

The General Strike and its aftermath

The period was also the aftermath of the 1926 General Strike. It had been led by the miners and they held out for longer than other industries. Much damage was done to the pits of the time by flooding and subsidence and many miners did not find jobs when the strike ended. Those who did return to work earned less than they had before the strike started, and some mining companies were near to bankruptcy. Many industries were stagnant because of the Depression, so the demand for coal was low.

I was made well aware of how fortunate I was to have a father who had a regular wage. One day in Ross the butcher's shop, I saw the mother of a large family buying a small piece of steak. I later remarked to my mother that such a small piece of meat could not possibly feed all that family. She explained that the father was doing hard work and needed meat. The mother and children would have gravy and bread or potato. In that desperate period for many, with one million unemployed, one third of the working population, the entirely new principle of government action to relieve the extremes of poverty was born.

The Employment Exchange opened in the Main Street, Dalmellington, in the mid-1930s. It was well known that unemployed men were driven to it by their wives who were desperate to feed their families, but those queuing outside the Exchange door hung their heads as others passed by. They simply wanted to be able to work to feed their families and their personal pride was badly dented by having to accept handouts. This scene was repeated over all industrial areas and trades, and indeed around the industrialised world. People were dying in the streets of New York, following the Wall Street (American Stock Exchange) crash which ruined industries worldwide.

Many who had emigrated found themselves no better off abroad than those who stayed here. Billy McInnes, who went to join some of his family in the USA, told how he was lucky enough to ask the local butcher for a job. The butcher thought he was a good lad and, though he could not afford to pay him with trade so poor, said that, if he worked for him, he would get the off-cuts and scraps at the end of each day. That meat, together with some bread bought with the few cents earned by his brothers, made the difference between life and death.

The flower show

While most of the people in Dalmellington and district were miners, tradesmen and officials, there was a small community of railwaymen who, with their families, played a full part in the local activities. They were keen gardeners, as could be seen from the lovely Dalmellington Station garden which greeted travellers, and keen supporters of the village flower show. There was special competition in the big onion class and it was quite common to have a complaint by one neighbour that the other had been stealing his best onions before the show, quickly followed by the other neighbour complaining that the first was stealing his. Reason prevailed and there were no convictions.

Education

The school played a big part in the lives of the children. In primary school, the classes were large – forty or fifty children, but teaching was good and the school had a good reputation. Of course, the belt was used but few teachers ruled only by the belt. Play was an important part of the school day. At intervals, according to the season, skipping ropes, marbles, beds all had their times. Of course there was football for the boys and girls were very skilful at ball games against a wall.

In some places, singing games were played. Rounders was popular, but frowned upon because of danger to the windows. The janitor kept a wary eye on what was going on at intervals. Very often, he also had the job of bringing in the one or two who thought they might 'plunk' the school for a day – a very important and respected man, Mr McBurnie.

Secondary school education for all had just begun. There was a feeling about the new qualifying exam for entry to the secondary language section, but some readily opted for the more practical advanced division where woodwork, metalwork, cookery and sewing were taught.

A few of the pupils passed on to Ayr Academy from the three-year secondary and did well there. Many boys took advantage of the evening classes to advance in mining and in their trades, some going to the Glasgow Tech (now part of Strathclyde University) to do the manager's course. With the practical training in the workshops at Dunaskin and out at the mines, young tradesmen could take their skills round the world, which many did. The Dunaskin certificate in engineering was respected worldwide, covering as it did a variety of skills.

A new era was opening up for girls, too. Shorthand and typing were being used in business and the opening of Short's and Fisher's commercial schools in Ayr provided training for girls in office work. Dalmellington girls quickly gave themselves a good reputation around Ayr. For boys and girls, there was the competition to get into the Co-operative as an employee in shop or office. Some girls went away to train as nurses and teachers and some to domestic service.

Health and welfare

The problems of the time were reflected in school. Death was a reality to young and old alike. Deadly infectious diseases – diphtheria, scarlet fever, measles, whooping cough – all took their toll in their own seasons. Parents were encouraged to have their children protected with the new diphtheria vaccine, and each spring we had our throats swabbed to identify carriers of the disease. The unfortunate ones, not feeling ill, had to spend long weeks in hospital until they were cleared.

The all-season killer was, of course, tuberculosis. Fiercely infectious, it had a fertile breeding ground in the large families living in crowded, often insanitary conditions, in spite of the efforts of mothers to keep a clean home. As with the other infectious diseases, whole hospitals – the sanatoria – were given over to the care of sufferers. But, in the hard times of the 1930s far too many, both children and adults, did not have the strength to survive the disease and the fresh-air treatment to which they were subjected in all weathers.

Above: Lethanhill School circa 1930. Spot the two boys in the front row without boots or socks. In bygone times it was common for schoolchildren to run around without footwear in the summer months. Lethanhill was located on the Hill to the east of Patna. Many Dalmellington folk will remember Rab Coughtrie (front row 1st left) who for many years was a hard worker for Dalmellington Community Centre.
Back row (l to r): D McLean (teacher), R Thomson, J Bryden, J Gillespie, J Taylor, J Lansborough.
Second back row: Kirk, Peggie Ballantyne, Jean McLelland, ?, Sarah Sturgeon, Cissie McLelland, Mina Bryce, Annie Ravie, Sarah Conn.
Second front row: Ruby Grant, Margaret Thomson, Margaret Carruthers, May Neil, Effie Thomson, Marion Thomson, Maggie McClymont, Cissie Peters, Charlotte McTimpany, Nan Ferguson.
Front row: Robert Coughtrie, Joe Callon, Sam Beattie, John Boyle, Lally Finlay, Frank Knox and J Gillespie.

Left: Class of circa 1956 at Bellsbank Primary School, Dalmellington.
Back row (l to r): Dickie Bryan, Billy Ballantyne, Wilson O'Neil, John Baird, John McCreath, Hugh Kerr, Tom Baird, Ian Waugh, John Barbour, David Whiteman and Douglas McKie.
Middle row: John Chalmers, Danny ?, David McConnell, ?, Janice McCracken, Irene Coughtrie, Andrew Givens, Andrew Murphy, Billy Meechan and Jim Buchanan.
Front row: Jean McCurdie, May Neill, Nan ?, Barbara McCurdie, Anne Reid, Doreen Payne, Margaret McArthur, Christine Salmon, Ethel Murphy, Ann Sadler and Ruth McDickens.

The Second World War was to be over before we had the excitement of Streptomycin being specially brought from America and some people cured of TB. We had entered the antibiotic age. By the time I became a teacher, the rather complicated inoculation against TB was being carried out in schools, and protection against polio, another deadly and crippling disease of childhood, simply called infantile paralysis in my childhood, was overcome by inoculation.

There is an echo from the past today, because there was opposition to inoculation from some, but with the awareness of the terrible consequences of the disease, the greater good of the greater number prevailed. With school nurses, doctors and dentists, the school was indeed a battleground against disease. The beginning of school dinners during the war, when rationing was strict, was a good investment in the health of children. Later, the effect of the provision of school milk surprised many of us, for that little bottle of milk made such a difference to many children. It was not always hunger that caused competition for extras!

Dr Howat and an assistant provided the medical services in Dalmellington and district. Dr Peacock was well known for some years. Later, Dr Campbell took over the practice. The miners had their own insurance and were 'on the panel'. This was essential because of the dangerous conditions in the pits, with injuries ranging from minor to fatal. For others, a regular bill for a visit was a guinea (£1 and one shilling or £1.10 in modern money). This was a lot when a fairly common wage was £3 a week, but, quietly, the doctors had a sliding scale and some patients paid little or nothing according to need.

Dispensing was done by the doctor until Mr Fyfe set up his chemist's shop. In those days there were few ready-made pills and potions, so the chemist made up the medicines. Usually it was a bottle of medicine, sufficiently foul-tasting to be a deterrent to all but those who really had something wrong with them.

Lorna Dempsey, Glenhead, Dalmellington, founded her own charity, Butterfly Events, in aid of Cancer Research UK in 2007. She voluntarily organises fundraising events and has won many awards for her charity work. Lorna has raised almost £200,000, a quite amazing achievement.
(Photo: Lorna Dempsey collection)

The district nurse attended nearly all except the most difficult births, who were sent to hospital. There were many deaths in childbirth. After marriage, many women were seldom without a child at the breast or one about to be born. In hard times, many women were weakened as they sacrificed themselves for their husband and families. Tombstones of the time illustrate the toll of young life – mothers, babies and children – infant and just a year or so old.

But the birth rate was high and the Kirk o' the Covenant had the highest number of baptisms in the Presbytery of Ayr! The Dalmellington and Patna nurses co-operated and each had to double her workload to give the other a day off. There were no statutory hours in those days. The local midwife had almost disappeared, but granny, with plenty of personal experience, often served very well helping at births.

Loch Doon Dam and Castle

A sensation was caused in the 1930s when word got around that the water level of Loch Doon was to be raised as part of a great new hydro-electric power scheme. Loch Doon Castle would disappear under the water and the Tinker's Loup would be blasted away in the making of new lochs south of Carsphairn. Thanks to Mr Stewart, a keen amateur archaeologist who had been the grocer before Scott and Simpson took over the shop in the Square, with the support of Alex Glass, the District Officer, the banker, the doctor, the minister and the county councillor, the Ministry of Works (Ancient Monuments Division) was persuaded to move the castle from the island to the west bank of the loch.

The part it was possible to move stands secure, but officialdom moves slowly and there was no time for a full excavation. The big engineering project employed few local people – McAlpine came with his large force of migrant Irish workers. Work was hard and conditions harsh and they were little seen about Dalmellington except on Fridays, when some rushed down to reach the post office before closing time to send money to their wives in Ireland.

Saturday evening was different, when they escaped their hardships for a while to have an hour or two in the local pubs. A strategy was worked out. As they went into the pubs the policeman on duty collected a taxi fare from each man. At closing time, Mr Maguire's taxis were drawn up ready to take them back to Loch Doon. None were left lying about the streets and nobody was drowned in the river as he made his unsteady way back to what certainly could not be called home. The whole scheme was completed in 1936 and was an engineering wonder of the time, and it is still regarded as one of the most extensive hydro-electric schemes.

In 1950 the dam at Loch Doon was allowed to rise above safety level, the safety valves came into operation with force, and the water blasted away the trees on the opposite bank of the Ness Glen, destroyed the path, flooded the Moss Road on the A713 north of Dalmellington and raged on, flooding the low part of Patna and the Skeldon Mills and washing away fish-breeding tanks at Dalrymple. Lessons were learned!

Flooding

There was, of course, the Dalmellington flood in 1934 (following an earlier one in the 1920s) when the Muck Burn flooded the low part of the town, causing much damage to houses and property. This resulted in the taking away of the two bridges, the old humpbacked one which had been a great gathering place for the men, and the iron brig, built later to cope with bigger traffic passing through in the 1914–18 war. This made the Square a feature of Dalmellington. One good example of nature triumphing over technology was the carrying away by the flood of the first public telephone booth, newly erected just opposite what is now Paterson's butcher shop. It came floating down the Main Street.

Tramps and tinkers

Much that was commonplace at the time has now gone. There were the regular visits of well-known tramps turning up at the police station door looking for shelter on a cold night. The farmers were wary of allowing them into their haysheds because of the danger of fire, so their Woodbines (cheap cigarettes) or their clay pipes, and especially their matches, would be kept for their return, and, fortified by a piece (sandwich), they would set off to one of the farms to find food and shelter in exchange for a wee bit of work. They had their own round and resented strange tramps on their patch!

The coal in this area did not have a high gas content, but one of the pits in earlier times had coal with a high gas content so there were coke ovens there – a magnet for tramps in cold weather. They were strictly banned from them, but on many a cold night one of the policemen would take a turn out there to check that they were in no danger of being burned.

In summer, the tinkers came and went, for limited periods, to the Dalmellington common. They caused little trouble and most were well-known, respectable families. The women went round with their packs, but the traditional crafts of the men – pot mending and knife sharpening – had almost disappeared. I just remember both crafts being offered and my mother having a leaking pot mended. Rags and bones were collected. The modern world was rapidly ending the important role that the metal-working tinkers (or tinklers as they were called from their craft) had to offer to the housewife and farmer.

The seven Brothers of Lethanhill joined Lodge The Bonnie Doon Patna No. 565 in 1942, the first time so many from one family had joined at the same time. They were pictured in ritual Masonic wear at Dunaskin Glen shortly after the initiation ceremony.
(l to r): Joseph (Happy) Ferguson, Samuel (Sam) Ferguson, William (Wull) Ferguson, Hugh Ferguson, David Ferguson, Thomas (Tam) Ferguson and James (Jimmy) Ferguson.

The Kirk

Even though the government did not seem to take the danger of war seriously, as Hitler became more and more aggressive, there was some re-armament, which helped heavy industry, including coal, to pick up again. In spite of the hard times, there had been achievement. The parish church, the Kirk o' the Covenant, and the church hall had been modernised, thanks to the drive and leadership of the Reverend Ninian Wright, and provided the accommodation for most recreational activities.

The church was the centre of much of the social life of the town and the renovated hall was a pleasant place for most activities. Dances and concerts took place there, organised by the church and others. Work with children was mostly within the Kirk. Lamloch Church, the Christian Brethren and the Kirk o' the Covenant all had well-attended Sunday Schools. Some children even managed to attend two or three Sunday Schools, which of course meant three trips and three parties!

There were plays and pantomimes to rehearse for, and the performances drew the community together, as parents and friends came along to admire their children. The great events were the Sunday School trips, especially when, in alternate years, they went away to Ayr, Girvan or Troon, accompanied by the quite famous Dalmellington Band. No wonder the traffic stopped when our wonderful village band marched from the railway station followed by more than three hundred people.

Social life

Mechanisation had not arrived to any extent. The milkmen from Pennyarthur, Dalcairnie and Auchenroy still delivered milk, eggs and butter from their horse-drawn traps, although the dairies had to make changes to combat the TB scourge – tuberculin testing of cattle and milk and, eventually, pasteurisation. A limited bus service that Percy Hill had started was very beneficial, but the train was the main way of travel – the sixpenny Saturday excursion taking young people to the Bobby Jones in Ayr in that heyday of ballroom dancing.

People were being moved from Benwhat to the new houses in Dalmellington, with very mixed feelings. A new house with more accommodation, running hot and cold water and a bathroom was great, but the loss of a strong community was a sadness to many. All had their own social activities, their bands, football clubs and harriers. Some bandsmen and harriers were spotted at competitions and moved away to work for large firms to play for the firm's band or run for the firm's athletics club.

Bookies and sport

There was little serious crime. Gambling was against the law, but small card schools were sometimes discovered in quiet corners or among old pit bings. The bookie took his bets up back alleys and sometimes, when reported by a member of the public, would be arrested and fined, but few people were against Will Hunter. He was a good local benefactor and Hunter's Sports, held each year on the football field, attracted runners from outwith the valley as well as the local runners, and there was good fun for all.

This could be termed the last footballers. This team, with Mr George Donohoe and Mr Matt McLelland, would likely be the last official Lethanhill School team. The school closed later in 1959 with these footballers continuing their education at Patna. Who do you recognise and what memories does this photo evoke?
Back row: George Donohoe (head teacher), Richard Law, Billy 'Bunts' Hunter, David Brown, Andy Paterson (goalkeeper), George 'Punt' Ferguson, Willie Young, John McDonald and Matt McLelland (teacher).
Front row: Tom Tusler, Boyd Plenderleith, Tommy Campbell, Tom 'Max' Murray, Billy 'Buck' Robertson, Alex 'Shy' Kirkwood, David Fossett and ?
(Photo: Ann MacLean)

Pub closing hours were strictly supervised. A man drunk enough to be brought into the cells was very often quickly pursued by his wife, who had managed to raise a small sum of money to bail him out so that he could go out to work the next day. Earning the wage was most important. Safety at work was quite another issue! Patna remained a very small village. Its rapid expansion was to await the ending of the war when the Hill and Waterside were rehoused there.

New era
Wartime was to see the beginning of new-found prosperity for the coal industry – one that, it seemed, would be never-ending – quite a new chapter in the story of our ancient Burgh of Barony.

The world is moved not only by the mighty shoves of the heroes, but also by the aggregate of the tiny pushes of each honest worker.

Helen Keller

Chapter 19

Ann MacLean, better known in her Lethanhill days by her maiden name, Donohoe, recalls growing up on the hill.

The Donohoe family at Lethanhill schoolhouse circa 1958. Mr Donohoe was decidedly unhappy at his family remaining in deserted Lethanhill, the remainder of the village having been deserted in 1954 whilst the school remained open until 1959, the children bussed to the Hill. Brian Donohoe was later to become MP for Central Ayrshire. (l to r): Brian Donohoe (9), Catherine Donohoe, John Donohoe (4), George Donohoe, headmaster of Lethanhill School, Ann Donohoe (14), and George Donohoe (12). It was a strange experience for them living in the only inhabited house on the Hill. Strangely enough, this house still survives and is occupied today, still on its own.
(Photo: Ann McLean collection)

Chapter 19

Childhood Memories of Lethanhill

Ann MacLean

Amidst thy desert walks the lapwing flies,
And tires their echoes with unvaried cries.
Sunk are thy bowers, in shapeless ruin all,
And the long grass o'ertops the mouldering wall.

The Deserted Village
Oliver Goldsmith

Ann Donohoe arrived in Lethanhill, aged seven, when the village was in terminal decline. When she finally left, aged fifteen, it was a deserted village, the whole population having been rehoused in the Doon Valley, mainly in Patna. Ann married Donald MacLean in Irvine in 1966. They have two sons, Niall and Colin. Niall and Lorraine live in Paisley and have two children, Cara and Ruth, while Colin and his wife Narin have settled in Germany with daughter Emma. Donald and Ann have lived very happily in Kilmaurs for many years. She worked as a secretary in Ayrshire Metal Products, Irvine, for some ten years and thereafter became a full-time housewife and mother.

She is involved in voluntary work and is an elder, choir member, and past convener of the Guild, in what is now New Laigh Kirk, Kilmarnock. She is thoroughly enjoying retired life with her husband Donald. Her second youngest brother is Brian Donohoe, MP for Ayrshire Central, whose formative years were also spent at Lethanhill.

All the Donohoe family are very proud of their association with Lethanhill. They still enjoy taking a journey down memory lane to visit their former home, now a private dwelling and the only house remaining near Lethanhill. They also visit the lonely village war memorial as well as the remains of the ghost village on the high moors above the River Doon, lost amid a small forest of sitka spruce.

Headmaster at Lethanhill

George and Catherine Donohoe moved to Lethanhill from Kilmaurs in October 1951 with their three children. I was the eldest, aged seven, and my brothers George and Brian were five and three respectively. Dad, who was the new headmaster of the Lethanhill Junior Secondary School, had travelled from Kilmaurs (a journey involving three different buses) for some considerable time before the schoolhouse at Lethanhill was ready for the family to live in.

Lethanhill School was located high above Patna in the village of that name. Strangely enough, although the village was abandoned around 1954, the school remained open until 1959 with pupils bussed up from Patna and district. In 1959 they transferred to Patna Junior Secondary School and Dalmellington High School.
(Photo: Courtesy of EAC Doon Valley Museum)

Lethanhill School staff circa 1951.
Back row: Margaret McLellan and Jimmy Paterson.
Front: William Faucett (Janitor), Sadie McIndo, formerly of Smithston Farm who was the domestic science teacher; George Donohoe, headmaster. At that time, in addition to those in the photo, there was a Miss Faulder (infant mistress) and several other teachers.
(Photo: Ann MacLean collection)

Shortly before leaving Kilmaurs, Dad learned to drive and became the proud owner of a second-hand Hillman saloon. Although the houses at Lethanhill had electricity installed in 1926, our newly decorated schoolhouse was without electric power. Lighting was by Calor gas, and the kitchen was kept cosy by a Rayburn stove, from which Mum produced mouth-watering meals and superb baking.

Domestic bliss

Washing was done by hand with the help of an Acme wringer. To iron clothes, she used a heavy Calor gas iron, with gas jets round the inside of the base, always having to be especially careful when ironing garments with fringing or frills, in case the gas jets singed them. There was of course no television set, but we enjoyed listening to the battery-powered radio.

Our water supply came from a hillside storage tank to which lime was added from time to time to purify it. After such treatment the water looked like fizzy lemonade. On fortunately rare occasions, small frogs would emerge from the taps.

During the summer, if there had been a dry spell of weather, we could be completely without water. This normally happened during the school holidays, when thankfully we were able to use the school's storage supply, sometimes going into the cookery room to have a good wash in the large deep sinks.

Playground songs

On my first day at Lethanhill School the other pupils were very friendly and welcoming. The teacher for my class, which was a composite class of Primary 3 and 4, was Miss Parker. At playtime the girls formed a large circle, singing such songs as 'The big ship sails through the Illy Ally-O', 'Water water wallflower', 'I sent a letter to my love' and 'In and out the dusty bluebells'. When the weather was fine we would draw beds on the playground and play with peevers or use skipping ropes – one of the many songs we used to sing was 'Oh there she goes, Oh there she goes, Peery heels and pointed toes, look at her feet, she thinks she's neat, black stockings and dirty feet'.

At other times we would bring a couple of tennis or small rubber balls and bounce them off the wall, singing 'Plainy, clappy, rolly, backy' etc. The boys played with marbles, peashooters and conkers, but were always happiest kicking a ball about. We often played rounders, tig or hide and seek.

Moorland memories

The moor was an exciting extension of the playground. At weekends and holidays there was always plenty to do to fill our time. We played with metal fenders turned up at the front, using them like sledges to slide down the grassy slopes. Playing in the burn was great fun. We had races in the burn using empty tin cans, we looked for frog spawn, or tried to build a dam. In the spring we used to help the shepherd set the moors on fire, the lovely smell of burning grass filling the air. There was always a breeze blowing on the Hill, ideal for flying kites. Making a kite was a serious business, needing brown paper, canes and paste, with old newspaper and string for the tail. Some flew better than others, soaring to great heights before diving to the ground, startling any sheep that may have been grazing nearby.

Some distance behind the school was a disused quarry where there were still some tracks with bogies lying around. In the quarry, which was at least 1,000 feet above sea level, we found fossils of shells, showing us that the sea had at one time covered the area. We must have walked for miles, going by foot to visit friends down in Patna, or to the sweetie shop on Saturdays to spend some of our pocket money.

I can remember after a winter shopping trip to Ayr with my mum, getting off the bus at the foot of the hill at Downieston Farm. I was about ten at the time, it was very dark, and I must confess that I was just a little scared walking up the road to Lethanhill, and hearing strange sounds, my imagination running riot.

Coronation 1953

A date in history which I will always remember with great pride and affection was the Coronation of Queen Elizabeth. To commemorate the Coronation on 3 June 1953 the pupils of my age were presented with a long flat metal box which had a picture of the Queen on the lid. The box was filled with Cadbury's chocolates and was to be used as a pencil case afterwards. Some of the younger children were presented with Coronation mugs, and the older girls were given brooches in the shape of a crown with red, white and blue stones. There was a special Coronation Gala day in Patna with Queen Lily Gilmour and attendants. The schoolchildren were asked to come in fancy dress. Mum was kept busy before the big day making our outfits.

The outside of the schoolhouse was decorated in red, white and blue, as was the car. We received a prize of £1, which was quite something at that time. One of my brothers still has the note, which is twice the size of today's notes. In August of that year (1953) my youngest brother, John, was born at Lethanhill. I can remember proudly pushing him in his pram past some derelict houses so that a friend who was still in the village could see him.

The process of re-housing all the people of Lethanhill and Burnfoothill took seven years. The first families were allocated houses in Patna at the end of 1947 and by summer 1954 the last person had moved, and the once busy rows were completely deserted and forlorn. It was really quite sad, especially for our family, who were the only family to remain on the Hill.

Burnfoot Primrose Football Team in the 1920s. This was the local team based at Burnfoothill which was a Dalmellington Iron Company village on the hill above Patna.
Back row: George Bowie, Adie Park, Tanny Anderson, Hugh Givens, Dummy ?, Buller Dalziel, Pimpy Moffat, and J Graham
Front row: Sam Gillespie, D Logan, S Riddicks, Ruchie Leslie, J McDowall, 'Elkie' Clark and Tommy Kirk. The young boy holding the shield is George Sturgeon who later worked as a miner and was a member of the Mine Rescue Brigade. His son, George, still lives in Dalmellington. The small villages in the Doon Valley such as Burnfoothill/Lethanhill, Waterside, Craigmark and Benwhat all had active amateur football teams.

Old and new schools

When Dad had come to Lethanhill as headmaster, the younger primary pupils were taught in the 'Old School', which had been built in 1912 and had three classrooms. Older primary children along with secondary pupils were taught in the 'New School', which when opened around 1927 was one of the most modern and well-equipped schools in the county of Ayrshire at that time. However, within a year or two of him being appointed headmaster most families had moved to Patna. The influx of primary-age children was more than Patna School could cope with, so it was arranged that nine to eleven-year-old pupils would be taken by bus from Patna and taught in the 'Old School' at Lethanhill. They were regularly visited by Mr Baird, headmaster of Patna Primary, whose oft-repeated mantra to his pupils was 'Speed, Accuracy, Neatness!' This arrangement continued until a larger school was built at Patna. For this reason, around 120 secondary pupils were also being bussed back up the hill from Patna to the 'New School' building.

Deserted village

Although the miners' rows at Lethanhill lay in ruins, the sound of young people's voices and much laughter echoed round the deserted village during the school term, which was quite strange when you think of it now. At other times the bleating of sheep and the cry of peewits and skylarks in the summer skies were the only sounds to be heard.

Last residents

I have a photograph of the Donohoe family taken early in 1958 at Lethanhill which I treasure. This, as well as the one of the schoolhouse and the other of the two schools, was shown on Cliff Michelmore's television programme *Tonight*. Our parents had been asked to go to the BBC studios in Glasgow to be interviewed for the programme. This had come about because of an article in the national press. Dad had refused to sign the missive of let for the schoolhouse, as he wished to move to more satisfactory housing in Ayr.

However, the 'powers that be' decided that he must 'stay put' in Lethanhill, although we were the only residents living on the high moorland, with a deserted and ruined village as our nearby neighbour. The new secondary school at Patna wasn't going to be completed for another year or two, and until then the Education Committee were not prepared to relieve him of his obligation to live in the schoolhouse.

In the summer of 1959 we moved to Irvine. Dad had been appointed headmaster of Loudon Montgomery Primary School, a post he filled until his retirement. We lived in the Lethanhill schoolhouse for eight years. As a youngster that seemed like a lifetime. However, we have many happy memories of the Hill and of friends we made during our stay. We have all taken our families back to see where we grew up and, in brother John's case, where he was born. It is remarkably humbling to think back on happy days on the Hill.

But now the sounds of population fail,
No cheerful murmurs fluctuate in the gale,
No busy steps the grass-grown footway tread,
For all the bloomy flush of life is fled.

The Deserted Village
Oliver Goldsmith

The lonely war memorial at Lethanhill and Burnfoothill which bears the name of those who made the ultimate sacrifice. The following fell in the Great War (1914–18): Pte John Blain, Pte William Ferguson, Pte Robert Finlay, Pte Hugh Hynds, Pte Ivy Lafferty, Pte Thomas Lafferty, Pte David McClelland, Pte Robert McClymont, Pte John McCormick, Pte Robert Miller, Pte Robert Muir, Sgt Charles Nugent, Pte Dennis Nugent, Pte Samuel Pyper, Sgt James McG Talman, Pte William Talman. Those who fell in the Second World War (1939–45): Cpl William J Finlay, Pte James Gilmore, Tpr Alex Stevenson.
(Photo: Donald L Reid)

Chapter 20

A Lethanhill Lad
Hugh Hainey

Away from the roar and the rattle,
The dust and the din of the town,
Where to live is to brawl and to battle,
Till the strong treads the weak man down!
Away to the bonnie green hills
Where the sunshine sleeps on the brae,
And the heart of the greenwood thrills
To the hymn of the bird on the spray.

A Song of the Country
John Stuart Blackie

Hugh Hainey was interviewed at the age of ninety-one on 10 March 2012. This sprightly nonagenarian remembers Lethanhill with affection, but several tragic events also occurred during the years when his family lived there. Hugh now lives in Alloway with his wife Sarah and enjoys gardening. He is a member of Lodge St Thomas (Kilwinning) Dalmellington, and on 21 March 2012 received a special certificate marking seventy years of membership of the Lodge from Archibald Chalmers, Provincial Grand Master Mason of Ayrshire. Here Hugh looks back to mixed memories of days on the Hill.

Born at Lethanhill

I was born on 18 February 1921 at 136 Lethanhill, Dunaskin. This was the year of the general strike and times were very difficult for everyone in that era. My mother was Ann Kersal Scott, a housewife, and my father was Hugh Hainey. Father worked at the furnaces at Dunaskin. Like everyone else in Lethanhill, he would simply walk down the Drumgrange incline to go to work at Waterside each day. His family was of Irish descent and came to work at the Dalmellington Iron Company ironworks at Dunaskin, as did many other folk from different parts of Scotland and Ireland at that time. One of the by-products of the operations at Dunaskin was ammonia and he was a general labourer in the ammonia works.

Above right: Hugh Hainey, in 2012 a nonagenarian living in Alloway, was born and raised at 236 Lethanhill and has fond memories of boyhood days and some that were very sad and poignant. He recalled that the winters were often harsh on the Hill and here he is seen clearing snow from the pathway into his home. The building in the background is the outside dry closet toilet. In weather such as this a visit during the night was avoided at all costs. Hugh was a miner for many years in the Doon Valley.
(Photo: Courtesy of Hugh Hainey)

Above: Hugh Hainey, still smiling in 2012, recalled some happy and sad days living at Lethanhill.
(Photo: Donald L Reid)

Hainey family

I was the youngest of nine, having three brothers and five sisters. From the oldest to the youngest they were: Margaret; John, who was killed in a gas accident at Chalmerston Mine in July 1942; Mary, who never married; Scott; Anne, who always complained at our father putting an 'e' at the end of her name when her mother's name had none; Elizabeth, who married Peter Murray who worked with Willie Ireland, the joiner in Dalmellington; Williamina, known simply as Minnie; James (Jim); and myself, the youngest in the family.

When war broke out in 1939 Jim was called up to the army and served with the Royal Scots Fusiliers. He was with the British Expeditionary Force in France until he was taken off at Cherbourg after Dunkirk fell into German hands. He was missing for some time as he made his way from the tragic scenes of Dunkirk to Cherbourg. He re-entered the conflict after D-Day and fought through to meeting the Russians at Magdeburg. He later had a painter's business in Stranraer, and died aged eighty-nine in 2007. He was a larger-than-life character and perhaps that's what helped him get through the war largely unscathed.

Lethanhill church and school taken from what was known as the crossroads. The village was abandoned in 1954 except for the school and the headmaster's house. The school remained open until 1959, with children bussed there and back each day.
(Photo: Scott J Rarity collection)

Double wedding on the Hill

During the time when Jim was missing in France, as he made his way from Dunkirk to Cherbourg, two of my sisters were married in a double ceremony at Lethanhill Church, which obviously Jim missed. Margaret married Alex Wilson, a butcher in Hawick, and Anne married Dan Wallace, a miner. Sadly, Dan Wallace was killed in Pennyvenie by a rockfall in the early 1960s. His widow, my sister Anne, actually lived until the age of ninety-eight in Dreghorn. Isn't it strange how life can be so cruel to some folk?

Family tragedy

My father died in March 1938 and my mother, who was born in Hawick, went to the Miners' Home in Troon for a well-deserved wee holiday. Because of this my sister Elizabeth and her husband, Peter Murray, came to stay with us at Lethanhill while mother was at the Troon Miners' Home.

Peter and Scott were travelling from Lethanhill to Dalmellington to their work each day on a motor bike. One day at the bend at Jelliston, Patna, they collided with a brick lorry coming from Dunaskin and both were killed. It was a great shock to the whole family, and not least to my mother, who was also finding it hard to cope.

She died in March 1943, never quite getting over the loss of her son and son-in-law, especially as it came so quickly after the passing of my father. It was my birthday and I will never forget what happened. I came home from work and my mother said she had a surprise for me. It was a banana. We never saw fruit during the war years. As she was giving me the banana, she said she had a terrible headache. Within a short time she collapsed and she died ten days later without regaining consciousness.

It was a sort of tragic period of life for the family and it did teach me a lesson. Our time on earth is made up of all types of experiences, good and bad, and I think you simply need to accept both with good grace. The reality is that no one goes through life without pain and suffering, but that was a very difficult period for the entire family to come to terms with.

Home and railway

Our house at Lethanhill had only two rooms: a living room and one bedroom. There were two built-in beds in the living room. The toilet we had was a brick-built dry closet located in the back garden. The Lethanhill that I remember of my youth was rows of houses and everyone knew everyone else. It was a close-knit community. The road was made of stone chips, like an old farm cart track.

The railway was still working right beside the village until I was ten years old, with the pugs being an everyday feature of village life. The railway ran from Lethanhill, across to Benwhat, and further on to the Benbranigan Mine. The railway came to a stop in the centre of the village, running alongside the Stone Row and stopping near to the Store Row. I can remember the engine, with Alex Beattie as driver and Jock Campbell as fireman and Jim Stevenson, all well-known and popular Lethanhill men. There were always three men with each of the pugs in those days and they worked very hard indeed.

The incline

I remember that these same men also operated the Drumgrange incline, which ran down to the north side of Waterside. Alex Beattie operated the drum with Jock Campbell attaching wagons at the top of the incline and Jim Stevenson at the bottom. I remember them taking the boiler from Benbranigan Pit and taking it down the incline. Rails and all the other items recovered from Benbranigan were also put down the incline and taken away by train for disposal.

As a wee boy I once went to Benwhat on the railway with Alex Beattie driving the pug. There was one carriage which was used to take the men to and from their work in the coal mines. A group of Lethanhill boys and adults went on the train to see a football game at Benwhat between the local rivals, Burnfoothill Primrose and Benwhat Heatherbell. That was the only time I went on the engine on the Hill. I do know that before my time there used to be two engines on the Hill. One was used to run to the Bowhill pits out towards Rankinston and the other worked between the Hill and Benwhat.

School

I attended Lethanhill School. It was what we termed the old school at that time. In 1926, the year of the famous miners' strike, I can remember going to the soup kitchen in the school where we got soup and bread, because with the miners not working, there was no money to buy food or anything else for that matter.

My father suffered from bronchitis and had asthma and I think it was a result of working with ammonia at Dunaskin. I was seventeen when he died. I started school aged five and my teachers over the years were Mrs Miller, Miss Thomson, Miss Campbell and after that the class was taken by Miss Agnes Hill. Her sister, Miss Mary Hill, taught at Benwhat School.

There were thirty-two pupils in our class and as I recall there were nine classes in the old school, and they took children from age five to fourteen, so it was a busy wee school. The headmaster in my time was D B McLean and before him it was David Vallance. In fact I think the schoolhouse, which is still there today, was built for D B McLean. He was followed by a Mr J McAuley.

In those days there were no school dinners and no milk at break times. Everyone went home at lunchtime, grabbed a snack and got back to school as quickly as possible, usually eating a piece on the way, so we could play football before the bell summoned everyone back to our desks. A new school was built around 1927 and the old school was left and used as the village hall. Lethanhill School provided a top-class education in those days and I was mainly at the new school. I enjoyed science and it stood me well for the rest of my life, working as an electrical engineer.

Friends of early years

My close pals were Willie Gillespie, who later became a mine manager, and Jack Miller, who became a Church of Scotland minister and spent some time preaching in Cumnock. Sadly, both are now dead. Other boys I played with are all dead now, because I'm ninety-one, so most have predeceased me. Among the girls was Margaret Sim. I remember her because she later went for a time to Sierra Leone, where she was a nurse. She's dead now, too. That's the problem when you get to my age, most of your contemporaries are gone, but my memories of them remain fresh.

Names of the raws (rows)

In my time there were 202 houses in Lethanhill. The names of different rows included the three Laigh (low) Rows; the Step Row, so named because it ran up towards the school and was going uphill and had stepped gables; the Whaup Row was at right angles to the Step Row, and on the level with it was the Diamond Row and the Old School Row. And coming back into line with the Step Row you came across the village store. In my day Johnnie Miller was the manager and the store was operated initially by the Dalmellington Iron Company and after 1931 by Bairds and Dalmellington. It was a general grocery store with a pub attached and was a focal point for villagers.

Social life of the Hill folk

You had the church and the brethren for services on a Sunday and these were well attended by the young folk. They organised the annual trip, so you had to attend regularly or you didn't get to the trip. The trips would go by bus to Ayr shore and we enjoyed games on the Low Green; Alloway, Dunure and Maidens were also popular. You got to what to us seemed faraway places, because you have to remember that we were really very isolated, sitting at over 900 feet above sea level at Lethanhill, looking down on the valley of the River Doon.

Our village was able to boast a pipe band, a flute band and a male voice choir. The Women's Guild was active and popular. The janitor of the school was a well-known Scots comedian, Jock Park, and he organised the cantatas. He could fill the hall for a week without any problem and he was a wonderful storyteller and joke teller. Then we had the West Highland Players, who visited and held plays in the old school, turned into a hall for such entertainments.

Football was the staple game for the boys or we simply wandered about the countryside. There was a quoiting green for the men to play and gamble on who was going to win by getting the horse-shoe around the metal pin.

I was a Boy Scout, and our local troop also met at the Hill. The Scout Master was Billy Small. I think he was a Waterside man originally, later living in Dalmellington, but a great Scout man all his days. Such folk like Billy Small gave really outstanding service to these small communities and we were so lucky to have men with their commitment and talent.

Marriage

I married Sarah Peters in 1946 on Christmas day. Christmas was a normal working day at that time. Scotland didn't recognise Christmas as a holiday, but did have a holiday on New Year's day. Sarah had come to the Hill from Dalmellington and started school in the infant class and we met at school and I suppose our romance was sparked from those early meetings.

My wife later taught primary classes at Ochiltree and Ayr. We celebrated our 65th wedding anniversary on 25 December 2011. We are very proud of our son, Alastair, and daughter, Sheila, and grandchildren, Kirsten and Scott.

Snowed in

In 1947 I well remember there was the most horrendous snowfall which crippled the Doon Valley and brought everything to a standstill. I remember that a chap McMillan, whose brother was a doctor in Cumnock, was trapped in his car outside Patna. A search was organised and he was found dead there in the snowdrift.

It was a really severe period of heavy snow and nothing could move. We all had just to remain indoors until it gradually got better and men with shovels – snow ploughs weren't available in those days – were able to clear the roads, allowing supplies in.

Vans on the Hill

Tommy Paterson, the baker, used to come round the village with his van, selling his baking. Driving up the Step Row, which was quite steep, Tommy discovered that his brakes wouldn't hold him, so he used to ask me to go round with him, and when he stopped, I jumped out and put a brick in at the back wheel to stop the van running back. I was only about twelve at that time. Later on he would give me a shot at driving the van, which was really great for a young lad.

Jimmy Hare from Patna came round with a vegetable van and the Co-op would come round with the horse-drawn grocery van, and the Co-op bakery was also delivered by horse and cart. I recall they had two horses at the Patna Co-op when I was a boy. The drivers would take orders and later in the week they would come back with the orders and deliver them. It seems to me that in those days there was a far better service because everyone came to your door.

You didn't have to go to Tesco or Asda like we do today, ploughing round never-ending rows to get your messages. Very few folk had cars in those days, so the service from the Co-op and elsewhere was really first-class. When you think about it, the big companies of today couldn't provide such a personalised service where the delivery man was on first-name terms with every one of his customers and probably knew all the family, too.

Hill road opening

I remember my mother telling me about the Hill road opening in 1923. The children were taken down and walked up the road. Before the era of horse and cart service and later motorised vans, everything came up to the Hill via the Drumgrange incline. This was a self-acting ropeway that ran from the edge of Lethanhill and down a steep rail line to the north end of Waterside below. It was used to bring everything to the village before 1923 and for some time thereafter, too.

Moorland royals

I fondly remember great Sport Days at the Hill. The organising committee had the crowning of the Queen ceremony. On one occasion Andrew McBride and Lottie Grant were 'the Moorland King and Queen'. There was a nice piece in the *Ayrshire Post* around 1938 about this event, encouraging folk to come to Patna and walk up to the Hill or get Percy Hill's bus which ran regular services to Lethanhill. Percy was a great character, known to everyone. He had an advert for the event which read: 'Percy Hill's Busy Buses, brings Burnfoothill Bumper Business'. All great alliteration, don't you think!

I was the bugle boy in the Lethanhill Scouts and was quite good at this instrument. At the crowning ceremony, when the pageboys put the paper bugles to their mouths, I was in the background and had to play the bugle call, which was just wonderful and gave everyone in the audience a great laugh.

Willie Gillespie had what must have been the first car on the hill. But it was a ramshackle. This was used for the procession round the village, showing the royal party to everyone. It really was a great occasion for everyone.

Lifting the police

I remember when I was sixteen and driving the baker's van up to Lethanhill, Constable Campbell Stevenson, the village policeman in Patna, flagged me down on the Hill Road. I thought I was in serious trouble for driving without a licence, but he simply asked if we were going up the hill and he said that's fine, you can give me a lift, and he came into the van and we dropped him off in the village. That was how things were then – relaxed and sensible.

Great gardens

There were some wonderful gardens and keen gardeners on the Hill, despite it sitting nearly 1,000 feet above sea level on the high moorland. I remember Robert Filson of Benwhat gave me some chrysanthemums that had won prizes at a flower show. The folk on the Hill were very proud and enjoyed life to the full, of that there is no doubt.

I used to run in the Benwhat Harriers with Robert Reid. He waddled like a duck, but could he run! You'd run round and round and he'd lap you in no time. He was a baker in Dalmellington Co-op, but left the area to run with the famous Birchfield Harriers and everyone was very proud of his achievements.

However, it is important to remember that nostalgia can get folk carried away. I was really quite happy to leave the Hill in 1945. With the passing of my brother Scott and my brother-in-law Peter, and my mum, and the death of my brother John in the pit, it held some very sad memories. The physical living conditions were also very poor compared to what most folk expect as standard today.

Leaving the Hill

I left the Hill in 1945, at just about the end of the war. My wife's family had left the Hill in 1943 and moved to Doonbank, Patna. A lot of families were beginning to leave the Hill around that time. It was after the war that Ayr County Council began a major programme of building houses to enable folk from the Hill, Benwhat, Corbie Craigs and other small mining communities to be rehoused with modern facilities, hitherto unknown to the families of these remote communities.

Although it was a nice, friendly community, when you look back from our modern facilities of today, the conditions in Lethanhill were quite basic. However, everybody knew each other and we were all really at the same sort of level, which was poor, because nobody had very much and most folk lived from week to week with no great savings for a rainy day.

Nowadays where we live in Alloway we don't know many folk and they don't know us. That situation is totally different from the Hill, where there was a real sense of community spirit and a willingness to be neighbourly and supportive. I certainly miss that sort of relationship the most. It was a real hallmark of the Hill people.

Coal mines and TB

From the ages of fourteen to sixteen years I worked at the surface at Bogton and Chalmerston and then I began my apprenticeship as an electrician. I was sixteen in the February and started at Pennyvenie Nos. 2 and 3 in the July. When my time was out I was aged twenty-one.

I took TB and spent nine months in Glenafton Sanatorium. It was almost a self-contained community. They had a bowling green, pitch and putt and community hall. I was also asked to maintain some of the equipment. When I got out and told folk I had been there, they would take three steps back. Folk thought they would catch TB or some other terrible disease. There was a skeleton staff of nurses, but I think there would be 200 folk living there. I think Glenafton was on the go until penicillin came into its own.

When the war ended they started sending folk abroad to get them cured of TB. The medical world thought that TB was hereditary because in the past whole families had been wiped out by it. Once they discovered it wasn't hereditary and simply an infectious disease, they started shutting down the sanatoriums.

When I came out of Glenafton I went back to Pennyvenie to see about my job. Alex Stewart was the manager and he said I could start again. I don't think the fellows working beside me were too happy because of the prejudices against the disease, but I settled in quickly. I had also been attending classes at Ayr Academy to further my skills.

A lot of the tradesmen were a wee bit selfish and kept information to themselves. However, I worked away and between my fourth and fifth year, the electrician at Chalmerston Mine took ill, and the manager invited me to take over as the head electrician at Chalmerston. I explained that I'd lost nine months due to illness. He went out of the office and came back a wee while later with a letter confirming that I had served my full apprenticeship, so that was me off to Chalmerston. Apart from the apprentices, I was actually the youngest miner there.

Mining accident

One day one of the enginemen took ill and I had to stand in for him to bring the men up from the mine bottom in the cage. When I brought them up I met my brother John, who was an oversman at Chalmerston. He told me there was gas in the mine and he said that he had to go back down to clear the gas. I told him to be careful. Anyway, away he went with another deputy, Willie Galloway, and by the time I got home to the Hill I got word that there had been an accident at Chalmerston. My brother John and Willie Galloway were brought out. Tragically John was dead, but Willie Galloway fortunately survived.

I also worked at the Big Mine (Pennyvenie No. 4). The agent, Alex Stewart, asked me to carry out an inventory of all the equipment in the mine in 1945 and it turns out this was in preparation for nationalisation that occurred in 1948.

Scottish aviation

In 1945 I left the pits and went to work for Scottish Aviation Ltd (SAL) at Prestwick as an electrician working on aircraft wiring. Later on I worked for the British Thomson Houston Company (BTH). They were a manufacturing company who equipped power stations. All the equipment and sub-stations in Ayrshire were BTH equipment.

Afterwards I worked with the South of Scotland Electricity Board (SSEB) and I married Sarah and moved to one of the wee prefabs in Patna. I retired in 1984, having been executive engineer with SSEB. I've lived in Alloway since 1992.

In my spare time I took up ornithology and went on various trips with my wife, visiting good places for bird watching. We also had a couple of holidays in Australia and one in Canada. We also went to Russia, so we've had a great retirement, something none of the old-timers in Lethanhill could ever have dreamed of.

Happy and sad

Lethanhill for me is a place where I spent my happy boyhood days, but it was also a place where our family experienced very sad events that I remember vividly. However, it was my happy home for many years and no one goes through life with constant sunshine without dark clouds overshadowing happiness. Accepting happiness and sadness with good grace is, I believe, the secret, but I am proud to say that I was from the Hill.

Yet they wha fa' in Fortune's strife,
Their fate we shouldna censure;
For still, th' important end of life
They equally may answer.

Epistle to a Young Friend
Robert Burns

Left top: Polnessan Row, Burnfoothill was a long row of cottages housing miners and their families. Gradually depopulated after 1945, it was deserted in 1954.
(Photo: Courtesy of Scott J Rarity Collection)

Left middle: A happy duo. Jack Young, who was the last manager of Lethanhill store with Jack Hunter, who was the immediate past manager. This would be taken about 1948.
(Courtesy of David Young collection)

Left bottom: William and Maggie McClelland in their well-stocked garden at 54 Burnfoothill around 1944.
(Photo: David Young collection)

Below: Pupils from P7 at Lethanhill School in 1933. There were no school dinners or milk provided to the children in those days. They simply ran home to the nearby rows and back as quickly as they could to play games.
Back row (l to r): Charles Boyce, Andrew Gilmour, Angus Fergus, James Wyllie, David Picken and ?
Second back row: Rita Knox, Betty Bowie, Agnes Bunyan, Jessie Bowie, Nora McClung, Grace Peters, Agnes Sim and Lizzie Tat.
Second front row: Mina Bryce, ?, Marion Thomson, Lily Taylor, Bessie Smith, Sadie McFadzean and Maggie McTimpany.
Front row: John Callow, Willie Gillespie, John Hainey, Jackie Graham, Charles Hose, Willie Graham and Hugh Ferguson.
(Photo: Courtesy of Hugh Hainey)

Right: Fanny McClelland with three young children sitting enjoying the sun in front of 54 Burnfoothill in the early 1940s.
(Photo: David Young collection)

Far Right: Jean McClelland (left) served in the Wrens until 1946 and is joined by her sister, Jean McArthur in the garden at 54 Burnfoothill.
(Photo: David Young collection)

Below: A social gathering in Lethanhill village hall in the late 1940s. Perhaps an older reader can identify some of the Hill folk in this interesting photo. What comes through clearly in looking at all the lost mining villages is that they had an enjoyable social life.
(Photo: David Young collection)

Chapter 21

Cairntable Poacher Turned Gamekeeper
Jimmy Dunn

I'm truly sorry man's dominion
Has broken nature's social union,
An' justifies that ill opinion,
Which makes thee startle
At me, thy poor, earth-born companion,
An' fellow mortal!

To a Mouse
Robert Burns

Jimmy Dunn is a down-to-earth character of the old school and very proud of his association with Cairntable. He was responsible for arranging the memorial stone to be erected at the site of Cairntable, abandoned in 1963. He was interviewed by Donald L Reid in April 2012.

Parents and family
I was born at 26 Cairntable on 29 June 1931. The village memorial stone at Cairntable is located outside what was my front door. My father was James McCready Dunn, who was born in Drumclair, County of Slamannan on 6 April 1890, and my mother was Jane Stewart Baillie, born on 3 November 1897. She was always known as Jeannie and she was raised at No. 6 Lethanhill. I have a sister, Ella, who travelled for Patna Co-op taking orders from villagers and they were delivered later by van. Afterwards she was head of laundry at Ballochmyle Hospital. She then joined the police in England and remained there for about fourteen years, before leaving and working in Marks & Spencer. She is still alive today, aged eighty-four, living in Maybole. My younger brother, John, lives in Maybole and spent most of his working life as a plumber.

Walking
My earliest memories of Cairntable was when I was about four years of age. My father was a great walker and he didn't believe in using the bus. On a Saturday we would walk from Cairntable to Lochside, Ayr to visit my Aunt Aggie (Agnes). We also walked back and I would be 100 yards behind him and would be greeting (crying) and he would say: 'Lift your feet and they'll fall themsel'!' Some Saturdays we would also go to Crosshill to visit my Aunt Susan and we walked there, too. Father walked everywhere and plodded regularly to Dalmellington to see my Uncle Johnnie. We also went bramble picking in the autumn and we would have a big 14 lb basket and it took hours and hours to get it filled.

Jimmy Dunn, who now lives in Ayr, but has happy memories of living at Cairntable.
(Photo: Donald L Reid)
The memorial stone erected at Cairntable by Jimmy Dunn.
(Photo: Donald L Reid)

Awheel
I did a lot of cycling in my younger days. I was a member of the Dalmellington Wheelers and we met regularly. I also cycled with the Ayr Argonauts and the Ayr Roads boys. Every Thursday I would cycle with the great David Bell – fondly remembered by many under his pen name, the Highwayman, from his wonderful

descriptive articles in the *Ayrshire Post*. And a nicer man you could never meet. He was a great encourager of young cyclists. I took up road racing on my bike in 1953. During the first season I took part in twenty-one road races, winning eighteen, losing two and retiring in the other because of a puncture.

My first racing bike was a Dayton Roadmaster, which was a ton weight. However, my second bike was a Rotrax and I got this machine from Hughy Main of Ayr, who had paid £90 just for the frame. He could see that I was going to be a good cyclist and he gave me the frame and it was a great bike for me.

Cycling events

I remember going to the Ibrox Sports in Glasgow in 1954 and taking part in the half-mile and I won out the park. I won by a mile and when I went through the line there was no one near me. The next race was the mile and because I won the first race I was put in as the back-marker. The place was crowded, thousands attended this event, and I also won the mile that day. The prize was a Westminster chime electric clock for winning the half-mile and a table lamp for the mile. It was a great day for me and I was really chuffed. After the race a lot of cyclists were asking me to join the Glasgow Wheelers, but it was too far away from Cairntable.

Another place I raced was at Kirkconnell Professional Sports. That meant that I had to go under another name to protect my amateur status. There were about twenty bookies at this sports event and they had some of the finest athletes in the country taking part. I remember that Barney Yulle, who was a Yank (American), was a world sprinter. Tim McPate of Patna was a great sprinter in those days and a lot of folk were backing Tim to beat the Yank. However, although McPate was given 11 yards in the 100 yards, the American passed him like a flash, so fast he almost gave McPate the cold with his speed.

I took part in the famous Cumnock Rally organised by the Cyclists' Touring Club and beat Jim Love of the Doon Valley, who at that time was Scottish Champion. The other top men in that race were E V Mitchell and his brother Peter Mitchell, but I managed to show them all home that day, breaking the record in the process.

I continued competitive cycling until I was about twenty-three. I took part in the Marymass 25-mile race, which was an invitation event. It was a race where the last man in each round dropped off and there were twenty-five of the best cyclists in Britain taking part. I hadn't been on the bike for about six months, when Stuart Hay of Cairntable and Burnside came out and picked me up and took me to Irvine. I got through to the final and there were only two of us in contention. We were neck and neck and the other chap kept bumping me, but at the line I beat him by a tyre length. I got a beautiful cup and £10 for winning that race. I donated the cup to the best Norwich Canary at Ayr Cage Bird Society.

Plantation Row, Cairntable on the B730 road looking downhill and north to the bridge of the railway that ran from Mauchline to Holehouse Junction where it joined the branch line from Ayr to Dalmellington. Water butts are outside each house and it seems that villagers have been asked to pose for the photographer. This small community existed from 1914 and the last villagers left in 1963. A memorial stone now marks the location of this 'lost village'.
(Photo: EAC Doon Valley Museum)

Day cycle tours

On a Sunday the Ayr Roads Club met at the Auld Brig and it was about 10 miles to cover just to get there. Then we'd cycle to Strathaven and there would be twenty on the run. I hadn't a piece (sandwich) on that first run and nobody offered me a bite. They were a bit of a clannish lot at that time. However, on the way back I got the speed up gradually until I dropped them all and headed back to Cairntable.

Mining

I started working at the Bowhill Pit near Cairntable when I was thirteen and a half years of age. I got a six-month exemption to leave school early because my father had silicosis and couldn't work and someone in the family had to work in the pit or you were put out of the house and another family were put in. These were tough times. This pit was located on the hill right above Tongue Row, a small double row of houses less than half a mile from Cairntable. The houses were stone-built.

Cairntable was a small village on the B730 Kerse to Drongan Road. Former villager Helen Smith Waring, née Davidson, (born 1904) left Scotland in 1927 to go to Kearny, New Jersey, USA with her father, Andrew Davidson, whose 1883 Kyle poorhouse (Ayr) birth certificate name was Andrew Aitken, father unknown. The rest of her family (mother and siblings) came to the USA about two years later. Mrs Waring's son Fred remembers that she made Cairntable sound almost like a Utopia rather than a miners' row. Throughout her years in USA Mrs Waring always spoke fondly and proudly of Cairntable. The village was deserted in 1963 and demolished shortly afterwards. A cairn is all that now remains to show where this small mining community was located.
(Photo: Courtesy of Fred Waring, Ramsey, New Jersey, USA)

The Bowhill Mine produced anthracite coal only. There was a row of buildings consisting of the manager's office, the first aid room, the machinery room. There were no baths and you went home with the clothes you worked in. The coal went in six hutches at a time from Bowhill to a washing facility, cried the Monkey, at Rankinston. The coal was then loaded onto wagons and taken by rail to Ayr.

When Bowhill Mine closed around 1946 I then transferred to the Drake Mine at Littlemill Colliery, which opened in 1860 and closed in 1974. It was located midway between Bowhill and Cairntable. I worked down the pit and was also a wire rope splicer. There would be over 300 men at Littlemill in those days. It was a busy place.

Horse sense

There were some characters at Cairntable. One was Sam McFadzean, who was a great yodeller and he could often be heard, happy as Larry, yodelling away. Another character was Woods Smith. During the Derby he was talking about this horse called Peter Flower. I gave him £2 and he assured me it was guaranteed to win. Wee Cowder lifted the lines (betting slips) for Wull Hunter, the Dalmellington bookie.

As it turned out, the horse wasn't even in the first three and Woods had put three weeks' wages on the horse. As you can imagine, he was in a right pickle, not least with his wife. Sam McFadzean met him at the Cairntable Brig and he was lamenting to McFadzean about not having any money. McFadzean gave him £1. He apparently doubled up on all the races that day and ended up with £500. Woods gave me £10 from his winnings as he was a very kindly individual.

There was also Jimmy Pool, who had a dog, a lurcher called Patsie, which he used to catch rabbits and hares. Old Flo McPike had a grey whippet called Flossie. I used to go down to the burn and I would whistle and Mrs McPike would let her out, and she was absolutely excellent at catching rabbits and bringing them back, dropping them at my feet.

Boxing

There was also Bob Gibson of No. 1 Cairntable. He was a former show boxer and had a face like a pound of mince, with getting biffed on the face so often. Bob encouraged me to learn boxing and gave me a bit of tuition. He had a double-barrel 4/10 shotgun and I was keen to get that. At the end Bob sold it to me and that was the beginning of a great poaching career for me as I developed a great love of nature and the great outdoors, spending some time as a gamekeeper.

Thin ice and hare chasing

I had a great time and supplied Cairntable folk with rabbits, hares, pigeon and ducks from the nearby Kerse Loch. A story I was told, which happened before I was born, was that in the 1926 strike, some of the local men were working on extracting coal from the old pit bings at Cairntable. The local farmer from Kerspark Farm would come across the frozen Kerse Loch to buy the coal from the miners. On one occasion on the way back to the farm, the ice gave way and the horse and cart went through the ice. When I was boy and swimming on the loch, you could see part of the cart wheels and it's still there to this day at the bottom of the loch.

Whenever the snow was 2 feet in height in the fields around Cairntable you could catch hares. Because of the high drifts, we would chase after the hares and actually catch them with our hands. Hares can jump anything up to 8 feet in the air and end up yards away. My pals and I would find the hole in the snow where the hare landed and dive in and it would sometimes get away and we would chase it again and again until it tired out, lay down and started to cry and you can simply pick them up. The best field for hares was the field where Broomhill Fishery is today. Everybody in Cairntable enjoyed hare soup and the tasty meat.

In the swim

I went swimming one day in the month of March at Kerse Loch. I swam out to the middle and went to come back in to what was called the Coo-Creep, which was the lassies' dooking hole. It got to the situation where my arms wouldn't work and I went under. I was down in the silt and came back up and got a gasp of air but I was so weak and thought I was done for. Auld Bert Smith came in front of me like a vision and said to me: 'Ah telt you to do the Dogs Paddle if ever in difficulty.' I kept going until my knees hit the bottom. I was lying frozen until I recovered, but I was nearly gone that day.

At the pictures

Auld Bert Smith, a local miner, used to show films, the silent movies, at Cairntable, and this was a real treat for the entire village. He would show about two hours of film and charged a few coppers to cover his costs. He had a big white sheet up against a coal house and everyone was out, including the adults, to watch them. That was the entertainment in the late 1930s. He went all over, showing them at Rankinston, Drongan, Patna and the Hill (Lethanhill). (See Chapter 13.)

Shops and tramps

There were two shops in the rows at Cairntable. One was operated by Bob Deans and he sold groceries, whilst the other shop, owned by Elspeth Knox, sold sweeties. Each of them lived in the rows where their shops were located. In those days a lot of tramps came up through Cairntable. My mother always gave them a scone and a plate of soup. They went from our house up to Deans' shop and he would give them a roll of tobacco and maybe a piece and cheese. Mrs Deans would cut the cheese and a rat about the size of your hand would drop down from the rafters onto the cheese and steal a piece. Some of the things that happened in those days, you wouldn't believe.

Although Bob and Helen Deans ran the shop, their other income was from selling eggs. They had about 500 hens out the back door and they were scattered all over the place where he had hen houses. Bob did work in the pit at one time, because he worked with my father at one of the Littlemill pits. My father dug the coal while Bob loaded it onto the hutches.

Breast is best

I remember going on the train to Ayr with my mother when I was a wee boy and all the women who were breast-feeding would be in the one carriage and as a young lad I would be told to keep looking out the window while the women were feeding their weans.

Snow

I remember one year of the big snow. I was at the school and there was a huge amount of snow and everything was at a standstill. The army was out helping to clear the snow from the roads. All the houses at Cairntable were covered and it was even coming through the holes in the doors and inside the houses, such was the ferocity of the wind. We were off the school for what seemed like weeks. My father walked to Patna through the drifts and brought supplies back, but it was a tough time for everyone at Cairntable.

Taken at the rear of 8 Cairntable in 1934, the Knox family busy doing the Monday wash. Note the washing tub and mangle. Before the days of political correctness, the women did all the domestic chores.
(l to r): Annie Knox, Elspeth Knox, Debbie Knox and Annie Knox.
(Robert Knox collection)

Above right: Members of the Knox family gather for a family photograph in 1930 under the railway bridge which was located at the lower end of Cairntable. The entrance to Knockshinnoch Farm is on the left. The village hall can be seen in the background on the left side of the road and a man with a bicycle is patiently waiting for the photograph to be taken before coming up the hill into Cairntable.
(l to r): Robert Knox (later the Janitor at Patna Primary School and still living in Patna); Mrs Mary Knox, child in arms is Annie Knox and Debbie Knox.
(Robert Knox collection)

Moving to Dalrymple

I moved from Cairntable to Dalrymple about 1954. As older folk died or moved out of the village, younger couples moved into Cairntable. However, the rows which were established in 1914 at the start of the Great War had been totally deserted by 1963 and it was demolished shortly thereafter.

I have fond memories of Cairntable. It was very special to me. I could be here for a month telling you about what went on. In my day the village families included 'Ploxy' Smith and I remember my mother used to make suits for the Smith family for going back to school; David 'Buff' Brown; the Callaghans; the Eastons; Adam Kerr, Lindsay and McTimpany.

Memorial

I used to go up to Cairntable about three times a week and sit and reminisce. I could pass two hours with no bother, just thinking about things we did in my early years. It's strange, but it holds a special fascination for me. There were so many folk who would stop when I was sitting by the roadside there and ask me where Cairntable was. Of course it was gone. Nothing left!

One day I simply decided that it would be nice to put up a memorial stone so that former villagers, their relations and simply anyone passing by would know that between 1917 and 1963 a small community existed at this spot. I knew about a granite stone I came across years before on the Skeldon Estate. I got permission and had the stone transported to Cairntable.

I located the stone outside what had been my front door and got it concreted in place. In 2007 I arranged with Kevin Roberts, the sculptor from Patna, to put the following inscription on the stone: 'Cairntable Village 1914–1963. Erected by J Dunn'. I noticed a black mark on the stone and I asked Kevin to incorporate a wee mouse on the stone because I'm keen on the works of Robert Burns, as were many of the men of Cairntable.

I arranged for everyone I knew who was born in Cairntable to come along to officially inaugurate the stone and there was a great turnout and it was quite emotional. We were all rather proud to belong to that special wee place and still remember it with great affection.

What tho', like commoners of air,
We wander out, we know not where,
But either house or hal'?
Yet Nature's charms, the hills and woods,
The sweeping vales, and foaming floods,
Are free alike to all.

Epistle to Davie, a Brother Poet
Robert Burns

Chapter 22

Hame at Corbies
Willie McHendry

The honest heart that's free frae a'
Intended fraud or guile,
However Fortune kick the ba'
Has aye some cause to smile.

Epistle to Davie, a Brother Poet
Robert Burns

Willie McHendry is proud of his association with the Hill villages of the Doon Valley where he is well known. He now lives in Ayr, but enjoys weekly jaunts to visit friends, David and Margaret Rarity, in Patna.

Family background
I was born on 8 July 1928 in Lethanhill. My mother was Euphemia Blair, who originally came from Blantyre but her family moved through to the Doon Valley with other miners to find work in this area. My father was Alexander McHendry, who was a miner all his life and worked at Pennyvenie Nos. 2 and 3.

Lethanhill to Corbie Craigs
I was only a child when I left Lethanhill and moved to Corbie Craigs, which in some ways was even more remote than Lethanhill. I think they moved because it allowed my father to be a wee bit nearer his work at Pennyvenie. Corbie Craigs was a single row of ten houses sitting high above Dunaskin Glen. It was very remote and exposed.

I would have been four years of age when we moved there. I had a young brother, Alexander, who was actually born at Corbie Craigs. I also had one older sister, Isa, who married Sanny McDickens from Cumnock, and one older brother, Robert, better known as Rab, who later owned a popular bus company in Dalmellington. My younger brother, Alexander, is retired and lives in Annan.

I lived at Corbie Craigs until I was fifteen and started working in the coal pits. I attended Benwhat School from age five until fourteen years when I started work on a full-time basis at Pennyvenie Nos. 2 and 3.

Above: Four miners at Pennyvenie Colliery towards the end of its life. It closed in 1978.
(Photo: Courtesy of EAC Doon Valley Museum)

Opposite top: No. 1 Pennyvenie in the late 1890s. In those days the winding engine taking the cages from the pit top down to the bottom, was operated by steam, hence the large chimney. This photo seems to have been staged to demonstrate the various trades involved in the mining process.
(Photo: Courtesy of EAC Doon Valley Museum)

Opposite bottom: Last shift at Pennyvenie Colliery. All would have mixed emotions. Some pleased to be finishing working down the coal mines; others concerned about what the future held for them, but all proud miners. Several commemorative photos were taken that day when different shifts finished.
(Photo: Courtesy of EAC Doon Valley Museum)

Families at Corbie Craigs

I remember that there were other families in the row. At No. 1 there was the McCart family; the Gardiners at No. 2; No. 3 was occupied by Willie Hainey and family; No. 4 was the Ferguson family; No. 5 was our home; No. 6 was the Riley family; No. 7 was the home of the Bradley family; No. 8 was Tom 'Tam' Kirk and family; No. 9 was occupied by the McGuire family and the last house was taken by Jimmy Brown and family. Now that's more than seventy years ago, but I can still remember them fine, because in their own way, they were all part of my growing-up.

The house at Corbies was simply a room and kitchen. But we were lucky because we had an internal toilet which flushed, whereas the folk in Benwhat, about one mile away, had to go outside to a dry closet. Our toilet was just off the scullery (kitchen). There was a Dover stove in the scullery and there was a coal-fired boiler which was inside to give us hot water.

With my parents and three other family members living together, conditions were quite tight and today's generation would find it probably quite impossible if asked to live there. As I recall, there were two set-in beds in the living room and one in the bedroom.

Schooldays

When I went to school I would walk across the hillside and past Burnhead Farm just in time to play for a wee while before school began. And we ran home as quick as our feet would carry us at lunchtime for something to eat and then ran back to school. In those days it would just be a piece and jam you got, but that was fine because it was all we were used to and football with our pals was the top priority.

The headmaster at Benwhat School in my time was Frank Ferguson and the teachers included Miss Mary Hill, who later lived in Dalmellington, and Miss Wardrop, and there was a woodwork master, but I can't remember his name. School was enjoyable and at breaks we would play football.

For recreation away from Corbies, we would go to the matinee at the Doon Cinema in Dalmellington. On a Sunday we were sent to the Sunday School, held in Benwhat School. We didn't always get there, because we would occasionally get involved in playing or going bird nesting, but nobody seemed to bother too much as long as we were happy and keeping out of major mischief.

Benwhat amenities

My father would go to Benwhat store for a social drink on a Saturday night. The licensee in the pub connected to Benwhat store was David Douglas, whilst in the grocery end of the store Harry Moore was the grocer and manager. In the same building there was a doctor's surgery and Dr Campbell from Dalmellington would come up from Dalmellington to see patients. If you wanted the doctor you had to leave a line at the store and they would contact the doctor and arrange for him to come. You have to remember in those days there wasn't even one phone in Benwhat and it was an occasion to see a motor car. In fact you just stood and stared in awe at a motor car.

Robert Borland used to come up with a van from Waterside store and he sold a range of baked items and groceries. He would come along the dirt track to Corbies and he was a real blether and enjoyed meeting folk in the process of his work. Life somehow seemed much simpler then, but that might just be me wearing rose-tinted spectacles. However, all the delivery men from the Co-op or Waterside store knew all their customers by name and were on really friendly terms. They also brought us the local news about what was happening elsewhere in the valley below. That's the way it was in those days.

Pals of early days

My pals when I was young were George and Peter McCart, Jackie Gardiner, his brother Tom and Paul Riley. Tom later married the district nurse, but I can't remember her name. In the summer we would go to the Rough Burn which ran below the Corbies in the gorge and dam it to create a swimming pool and simply play about the glen. Time just seemed to fly in and we only went back home when our stomachs told us it was time for food.

Oor Rab, who was a wee bit older than me, played with David Dunsmuir who later joined the Glasgow police and was a noted boxer. We also went looking for birds' nests in the summer and ran about the moorland, sometimes being chased by peesies (lapwings) if we got too near their nests. The eggs from peesies were just wonderful and a special treat for us, because you have to remember that money was scarce and it must have been difficult for our parents to put food on the table. So, any extras such as birds' eggs were always welcomed.

Entertainment

There was, however, no great social life that I can remember at Corbies itself. You've got to remember it was only ten houses in a single row, overlooking Dunaskin Glen. I do recall that there were regular concerts at Benwhat with Paddy Stratton, George Sturgeon and the Revellers – all well-known to Benwhat folk of my era. We used to take part in cantatas in the old school building at Benwhat. This was used as a general hall, whilst the new school was located at the other end of the village.

When I came home from school and after going out to play, homework had to be done using a paraffin lamp as there was no electric light or power in the house.

William McHendry is very proud of his two grandsons, Brian and Craig, better known simply as the MacDonald Brothers, a pop group from Ayr who are proving very successful, touring the UK and abroad as well as performing on cruise ships. Their grandfather was born at Lethanhill and raised at Corbie Craigs, two of the Doon Valley lost villages.
(Photo: William McHendry collection)

Radio call

Young folk today would find it strange, but there simply were no TVs in those days and all we had was an old accumulator radio which was operated by battery. These were quite unreliable and screeched and squawked as you tried to tune in to a channel, especially when you wanted to hear a special programme.

I used to have to take the battery down the Corbies incline path that ran from Corbies down to Waterside to get the battery charged at Dunaskin power station, owned by Bairds and Dalmellington at that time. I would go back the following evening and pick it up and carry it back up the incline to my home. These batteries were heavy for a schoolboy to carry, but you just went on and did what you were asked to do by your parents, and usually a couple of pals would go along and give a hand.

At home

When my father came back from the pit, the tin bath came out and my father would get washed. This was a daily occurrence. As for myself and the family, we got washed with cold water because there was no electricity.

There was a garden at the front of the house and we grew tatties, rhubarb, kale and cabbage, so I regularly helped to dig the garden. Some of the families at Corbies kept hens, but we didn't.

Neighbours at Corbies

I remember the Bakkom family, who I think were connected in some way to the Hainey family of Corbies. The Bakkoms lived in a garden hut halfway between Corbies and the Benwhat Road. Folk will find this difficult to believe, but they really did live in a garden hut and Mrs Bakkom had two of a family – Thora and Bill – with her other children living with her husband in Canada.

They used to come to Corbies to get water because there was no spout or anything where their hut was located. They must have had a very difficult life, because ours was difficult enough and we had bricks and mortar for our building. Bill was a bit younger than me, but he did come up to Corbies to play with some of the boys. (See Chapter 14.)

Orders in

Mary Ferguson worked for Dalmellington Co-op and she would come to the Corbies and took orders for groceries and other items, and they were delivered later in the week and paid for at that time. The money was always sitting ready to pay the bill. Mary Ferguson then walked up to Benwhat and did the same and also down to Waterside, taking orders as she went. When you think about it, it was a really first-class service. Orders taken at your door and delivered to your door!

Benwhat character

One of the characters at Benwhat was Adam Bowie, whom everyone talked about. On one occasion it's said that Adam was asked to stay at Benwhat because the snow had started and a blizzard developed. He said he would stay. However, he disappeared and reappeared two hours later with his pyjamas. He'd gone home to Dalmellington to get them. That was the type of character going about in those days.

I left Benwhat School when I was fourteen years of age. I enjoyed school and in fact I was Dux Medallist, but my father always said that there was nobody else at the school!

Starting in mines

My father arranged for me to start work at Pennyvenie Nos. 2 and 3. The gaffer was a man called 'Scrabby' Moffat, and David Dodds was also a gaffer at the pithead in those days. Jimmy Pettigrew was also an oversman. The job I did was working with hutches which had to be emptied, having arrived full from the pit bottom. I did that job for two years.

Army service

I volunteered for army service in 1946 and served for two years at Fort George, Inverness and then went to Glencorse Barracks in Edinburgh, before finishing my time at Catterick Camp in Yorkshire, where I was a signaller, before serving for a period in Germany. I was demobbed in 1948 and returned to Pennyvenie, this time working down the mine.

Passing of Father

Because times were hard for mining families and money scarce, miners sometimes took risks with their own health and this was particularly true and rather poignant with my own father. I was about twenty-four years old at the time, when Father went to work at Pennyvenie one day when he was suffering from flu. He took ill down the pit, collapsed and died. A sad end for a proud miner. For my own part I worked in the coal mines for over thirty-five years all in.

Marriage

I married Sadie Carlyle of Pennyvenie in 1950 in Pennyvenie Institute and lived at 2 High Main Street, Dalmellington before moving to 76 Ness Glen Road, Bellsbank in 1952. It was great moving to a brand-new house.

Ruins of Corbies

The ruins of Corbie Craigs are still there to be seen sitting proudly above the Rough Burn and to the south of Dunaskin Glen. I always thought it was a strange place to build a row of ten houses, but apparently they were originally built to house the men who operated the Dunaskin incline and locomotives on the Hill, and that would make some sense as the coal owners always wanted the workers to be living near where they worked.

I have happy memories of living at Corbies and fondly remember those of my happy boyhood days who, like me, are no longer young.

But weel we ken oor wish is vain,
Nae mair they'll come again;
Sae while we're here, let's raise a cheer,
An' sing this mirthfu' strain;
The guid auld days, the dear auld days,
'Tis sweet tae bring tae min';
The grand auld days, the dear auld days,
The days o' auld langsyne.

The Dear Auld Days
Charles Nicol

Chapter 23

The ruins of lonely Burnhead Farm which sits just above the ruins of Corbie Craigs. It was occupied until the 1980s when open cast mining put a stop to sheep rearing in the vicinity.
(Photo: Donald L Reid)

Tom Wilson, who was born and raised at Benwhat, enjoyed meeting many old pals of yesteryear at the re-dedication service of the war memorial at this lost mining village.
(Photo: Donald L Reid)

Chapter 23

Thoughts on Benwhat

Tom Wilson

Oh! the dear auld days, the sweet auld days,
The days o' auld langsyne;
Whan we were wee, wi' spirits free,
'Tis sweet tae bring tae min'.
The funny pranks we used tae play,
Whan bairnies fu' o' glee;
An' hoo we then on ilka day,
Wad romp aboot sae free.

The Dear Auld Days
Charles Nicol

I was born on 23 May 1926 at Benwhat in a year that would become famous for the national strike, known as the strike of '26. My father, Jimmy Wilson, was a miner at Chalmerston all his days. My mother was Jean Fisher.

Family

There were ten of us in my family. Jean; John; Agnes (Mrs McWhirter); Madge, who was born during the 1921 strike; myself (Tom); David and Serena, who were twins; Mamie, who died aged ten; Nellie (Mrs Tyson); and Esther. We lived at No. 118, which was in the Laigh Row next door to the Hodgson family. I can also recall moving from the Stane Row when I was a wee boy to the Laigh Row. In those days if there was a vacant house you could apply to move. In our case we got a manager's house, because they were bigger than the normal houses and had more rooms.

In fact they were larger because it was really two houses simply knocked into one and the facilities were much better than for the smaller one-bedroom houses occupied by the miners. The other great advantage was that our house had a toilet in it, whereas the normal houses in the rows didn't have a toilet. Families had to use a dry closet toilet built in the back garden, so it could be rough in the winter time going out, but as often as not folk would use a pot which was emptied in the morning.

Living conditions

As you can imagine, with a family of ten, my mother was delighted to be moving into this bigger house, but even so it was still a strain. The three youngest boys slept in one of the bedrooms in a bed whilst the rest of us just doubled up in beds. That's the way things were in those days when you lived in such cramped conditions. Of course we weren't used to anything different, so we just got on with it, because what else could you do? Looking back on it now or telling my grandchildren about it, they find it all very strange, but you simply came to terms with the situation in which you found yourself and that was how life was for folk in Benwhat. But remember, our family were luckier than most, because we had an inside toilet, which other folk were a wee bit jealous of.

I was a wee boy growing up during the 1930s, later called the 'hungry thirties'. It must have been very difficult for my mother with ten children, looking after them, feeding them and doing the washing and ironing. It's only now as you look back that you realise just how hard she must have worked to meet the needs of all the family. But all the women were in exactly the same boat, because most of the families in Benwhat and Lethanhill were large.

No traffic jams

It was extremely rare to see a car at Benwhat. The only one I can remember seeing was one that belonging to Dr Mowat, the GP who came up from Dalmellington to tend to those in the village who were ill. It was a real occasion and all the boys and girls would be round it. Of course, I had never been in a car. As a wee boy I can also remember the railway wagons running behind the rows at Benwhat heading to and from Benbranigan Pit.

Everyone knew everyone else in Benwhat and the other small mining communities. The engine drivers I remember when I was a boy were Harry Yorston and Alex Beattie, both from Benwhat. The new school at Benwhat was built in 1926 and that was the school I attended. However, my older sisters attended the old school. Old Frank 'Bingo' Ferguson was the headmaster in my day.

The hall in Dalmellington, adjacent to the Muck Burn and near to The Path, used for a number of years by Benwhat Band. This hall had previously been the church building at Lethanhill. It was taken down and transported to Dalmellington. It was demolished in the 1970s. (Photo: Courtesy of EAC Doon Valley Museum)

I remember that I loved the outdoors. I was in my element running and playing about the moorland and out looking for birds' nests. I was really keen on nature. I also played cornet in the Benwhat Band. One memorable occasion I remember was when the band played for Robert Reid, a well-known athlete and runner, who had returned after winning some athletics event. He was led round the rows as the band played 'Hail the Conquering Hero Comes'. We were very proud of Robert Reid.

The big snow

The year 1936 was the year of the big snow. I was only about ten years old at that time. It had snowed for about two weeks and with the winds it just covered everything from roads, path, huts, and even the doors of houses had to be cleared. We were off school, because nothing was able to move and the whole Doon Valley was crippled.

The Benwhat men had to trek to Dalmellington to get supplies, because nothing could get up to the hill. I remember that, as things improved, Quintin Stirrit came up to the hill with a horse and cart with briquettes and paraffin and that was great for the villagers and he was sold out very quickly. I loved animals and that particular horse was called 'Big Paddy'.

In fact horse and cart was the main way that most things were delivered to Benwhat when I was a boy. Jimmy Carruthers, the farmer at Sillyhole, came up with his horse and cart and delivered milk from big urns. Folk would come out with cans, bottles or pans and he would fill them with milk. This was in the times before milk deliveries in bottles became common.

In our house with mother, father and ten of us, meal times were chaotic. We just stood round the table and ate the food from plates. That was just how things were done in those days.

Benwhat Heatherbell in the 1940s.
Back row (l to r): Jim 'Pim' Douglas, John Thomson, David Connell, William Barbour, Arthur O'Neil, ?
Front row: Jim Murray, Alan McCreath, Jim McCulloch with John, 'Toy' Bennett.
(Courtesy of Flora Scobie, née McCulloch)

Football

My father was a coach of Benwhat Rising Star football team along with Neilly Dempsey, and there was always a great interest by local boys in playing football or being involved with the harriers.

There were some former residents who did make their mark at football. James Arthur 'Jimmy' Murray (9 June 1880–29 October 1933) was a Scottish professional footballer who played in the Football League for Aston Villa and Small Heath. He played as a right-sided forward. Murray was born in Benwhat, Dalmellington. He played for St Augustine's and for Benwhat Heatherbell before joining Ayr in 1897. In March 1901 he moved to England and signed for the Football League champions Aston Villa; he played once in the 1900–01 season and once the following season, before joining local rivals Small Heath in November 1901. Murray scored in his only competitive outing for Small Heath, in a losing cause against Sunderland in the First Division, and was described as 'fairly fast, has capital command of the ball and can shoot excellently'. He died in Glasgow in 1933 at the age of fifty-three. And of course Robert Reid made his mark as a top-class athlete, running and later coaching with Birchfield Harriers.

Benwhat Harriers in a race with the village in the background. It was amazing just how many villagers took part in such events. Robert Reid, who later ran and became a trainer with the famous Birchfield Harriers, leads the race.
(Photo: Courtesy of EAC Doon Valley Museum)

Doon Harriers were the local athletic club based at Benwhat where this photo was taken in 1948. The club produced many fine athletes over the years.
Back row (l to r): William Currie, Walter McEwan, George Hannah, George McConnell, Neil Robertson and Addie Hannah.
Middle row: Jimmy Galloway, Jim Bigham, Robert Mullen, Richard Armour, George Mowat, Andrew Filson and Bruce Hainey.
Front row: Tommy Filson, Tom Wilson, John Wilson, Andrew Galloway and Eddie Uriarte.

Depopulation of Benwhat

In May 1940 I remember with sadness that families were beginning to move away from the village. At that time the Wilsons, Roberts and Grahams all moved to Dalmellington and our family moved shortly afterwards. I remember that for a short time I remained at Benwhat School and went up in the morning with Jackie Gardiner in the Co-op milk van. It couldn't have affected my education too much, because I was Dux Medallist at Benwhat School.

Marriage

I married Elizabeth Rollo on 6 June 1950 and we stayed in a room we rented from Mrs McGreevy in Bellsbank. Her husband was coal cutter at Minnivey and they later emigrated to Australia. We then moved in with relations, my sister and her husband, Agnes and David McWhirter, and then we got a herd's (shepherd's) cottage at Pennyvenie. That was the way things were in those days. When you got married you had to find somewhere to live until you were eventually allocated a council house. They were very scarce and usually you had to wait several years before being allocated one and that meant living in digs with someone willing to take you in locally.

At Pennyvenie I bought one of the derelict rows of houses and converted it into four deep-litter units. I used to keep some cattle and hens. I started away with a few hens and they grew and grew until I had around 1,000 at my back door. I used to go to night classes at Auchincruive College to learn farming skills. I was accompanied to these classes by two older former miners, Jimmy Black who lived at Churchill and Hugh 'Fergie' Hose of Park Crescent, both Dalmellington, and we used to help and encourage each other.

Retired

Later on I bought a smallholding in Ayr on the banks of the River Ayr and I gave up working in the coal pits to concentrate working on the smallholding. And I can honestly say that I had no regrets about that, because it was hard, dangerous work.

My wife and I have a very caring family: Jim, Tom, Jennifer, David and Alex. After years keeping cattle and thoroughly enjoying this type of outdoor life, I am now retired and still live with my wife by the banks of the River Ayr in the countryside which I so much enjoy.

I attended the war memorial re-dedication ceremony at Benwhat on 12 June 2011 and found it very moving, once again meeting so many folk of my boyhood days at this event. I hadn't seen many of them for over sixty years, so it did bring back many memories of old Benwhat. With almost 100 in attendance, not only Benwhatonians, but family members, it just goes to show that folk still remember this little community with a special pride and affection.

I think this love for Benwhat is very touching indeed and it would be my wish that 100 years hence, folk will still wonder about the miners and their families who lived high above the valley of the River Doon.

When schule was dune we aft wad rin,
Doon tae some wimplin' burn;
An' there we'd play the lee lang day,
An' ne'er think tae return.
Fu' aft we'd paidle up an' doon,
The fun tae us was fine,
We'd ne'er a thocht for ocht aroon',
In the sweet days o' langsyne.

The Dear Auld Days
Charles Nicol

Chapter 24

Dalton Avenue and Melling Terrace, Dalmellington bus outing in the late 1940s. Readers will instantly recognise many weel-kent characters of yesterday and today.
Back row (7) (l to r): 1 Tom 'Tam' Wilson, 2 Andy Wilson, 3 Rita Orr, 4 ?, 5 John McCulloch, 6 James Maltman and David Young.
Middle row (16): 1 Margaret McEwan, 2 Walter Orr, 3 William 'Wull' Currie, 4 Jim Lindsay, 5 Elizabeth Lindsay, 6 Margaret Maltman, 7 Mrs Hyde, 8 Mrs Orr, 9 Peggy Hodgson, 10 Bill Hodgson, 11 Willie Barbour, 12 Marion Maltman, 13 Mrs Young, 14 Willie Kennedy, 15 Mrs Jean McCulloch and 16 Jim McCulloch.
Front row 1 Sady Sloan, 2 Willie Newell, 3 Mamie Johnstone, 4 Mrs William Barbour, 5 Mrs Nancy McCulloch and 6 Jean Maltman.
(Courtesy of Flora Scobie, née McCulloch)

Chapter 24

Dalmellington Memories

Janet C Adams

Though he, that ever kind and true,
Kept stoutly step by step with you
Your whole long, gusty lifetime through,
Be gone awhile before,
Be now a moment gone before,
Yet, doubt not, soon the seasons shall restore
Your friend to you.

Consolation
Robert Louis Stevenson

Following the publication of one of Donald Reid's books about the Doon Valley, Janet C Adams, then residing in a nursing home in Walton-on-Thames, wrote this reflective letter to Donald highlighting some of her precious memories of Dalmellington.

I was born in Dalmellington on 9 June 1923. Although I now live in a nursing home in Walton-on-Thames, Surrey, I often think back to my early years in Dalmellington. I went to the Higher Grade school until I was fifteen and then on to Ayr Academy. I had a season ticket and travelled down the branch line by train each school day and after getting off at Ayr station I walked through the town to the Academy.

In the summer the train left Dalmellington at 7.30 a.m. but in the winter it left at 8.15 a.m. I had to walk from Burnton to the railway station in Dalmellington. I walked up the path at Sarah Hainey's wee sweetie shop, enjoyed the train journey to Ayr then it was another walk to Ayr Academy which was situated down near the harbour.

In the summer at lunch break at school we walked down to the harbour which was a mass of fishing boats. The barracks was also opposite the harbour and my friends and I would see the soldiers drilling.

Often on Sundays I went with a friend to Loch Doon. We walked up the Carsphairn Road to Mossdale then turned up the road to the loch. You can go there by car, but we used to walk another way; up past Bellsbank House and past Pennyarthur Farm and crossed the Perkelly Burn at Dalfarson then onwards to the loch. Most folk enjoyed walking in those days and the paths to Loch Doon were always busy.

When I left school I went to work in the bank in Dalmellington. At that time George T Hamilton was the agent. I also remember Mrs Wylie and her son Willie who ran the post office. Near the bank was the hairdresser, Bill Blunt was his name and everyone always thought what a comical name he had for a man of that occupation. I think his wife did the ladies' hair, but he was a barber.

In the village there was Malcolm Ross, the butcher at the Square and he had two daughters, Betty and Helen. There was also Isobel Pollock who had a newsagent and whose daughter Maisie was a good friend of mine and went to Ayr Academy with me. In those days most folk shopped at the Co-op. There was another grocer called Scott and Simpson and the chemist was Mr Fyfe and Mrs Cowan ran the library.

I do remember Benwhat, sometimes spelled Benquhat. My father came from there and I think his mother must have still lived there when I was a small child, because we used to walk up to Benwhat from Burnton on Sundays to visit her. However, I think I must have been on my father's shoulders a lot of the time.

These are just a few of my recollections. My memory is not so good on some things, but I will always have a special place in my heart for Dalmellington.

Thine be ilka joy and treasure
Peace, Contentment, Love and Pleasure

Ae Fond Kiss
Robert Burns

Two miners working underground at Pennyvenie with the metal props showing that it was probably in the 1960s or 70s. However, from the perilous position of the props and undulating ground, it's not difficult to imagine how disaster could easily strike in such tough conditions.
(Photo: Courtesy of EAC Doon Valley Museum)

Dalmellington Band at Carnegie Hall, Dunfermline, in 1969 when they won the Scottish Brass Band Championships with the test piece 'Carnival Romaine'. Hugh Johnstone was the conductor and is a lifelong band member. Hugh was a member of the band from his boyhood days and is still a brass instructor today, developing the musical talents of young bandsmen. He was awarded the MBE in 1982 for his services to the brass band movement. Dalmellington Band continues to be one of the premier bands in Scotland. The band have won Scottish championships in 1969, 1976 and 1978.

Back row (l to r): Donald Tyson, John Tyson, Hugh Uriarte, Tom Paulin, Alex Yates, William Cuthbert, Robert Dunn and Archie Hutchison.
Middle row: Edward Kerr, Robert Boyd, Bert Ritchie, Fred Galloway, David Sturgeon, Louis Uriarte, Tom Paulin (uncle of other Tom Paulin), Ian Boyle and Willie Hainey.
Front row: William Kennedy, Jim 'Jimsy' McPhail, Robert Dunn, John McCulloch, Hugh Johnstone (conductor), Peter Murray, Jim Graham, Tom Wilson and John 'Jubie' McCulloch.

Chapter 25

A Wee Boy Remembers Benwhat

John Galloway

Wit and Grace and Love and Beauty
In ae constellation shine!
To adore thee is my duty
Goddess o this soul o' mine.

Bonie Wee Thing
Robert Burns

Although John Galloway was only a young lad when he left Benwhat, the impact of living in this moorland community left a very positive impression. John now lives in Ayr, but still enjoys an occasional visit to the high moors above Dalmellington, which he still calls home.

Family

I was born at 97 Benwhat on 29 September 1935. My father was John Murphy Galloway, but he was known by one and all as J B Galloway or simply 'JB'. He was a miner, born in Benwhat in 1897, and later was an insurance agent. He was the oldest of ten of a family. My mother was Sarah Pollock. She was born in Glasgow and her mother died in childbirth. She was brought to Benwhat two days after she was born and raised there by an aunt.

I was the youngest in our family and I had a sister, Sadie (Fisher), who was the oldest, and my brother Andrew was five years older than me. He died aged fifty-four. My grandparents on my mother's side of the family also lived at Benwhat, at No. 94.

Parish Council

My father was very well known and respected. He was on the district and parish councils, served on the committees of Benwhat Heatherbell and of the Harriers, and was a joint founder of Benwhat Burns Club with Joe McKinstry and David Dunsmuir. I still have a copy of the medal he received in season 1924–25, when the Heatherbell won a trophy in the Ayr league.

Doon Harriers in season 1938/39 with their distinctive club badge. Robert Reid, a top harrier who went on to run with Birchfield Harriers where he remained all his life, is fourth from left, front row.
Back row (l to r): A Hannah, R Filson, A McHattie, J S Hannah, J B Galloway Middle row: J Wallace, S Sturgeon, W Currie, J Lindsay, Louis Scott. Front row (runners): A Travers, A Gardiner, D Wightman, Robert Reid, Louis Uriarte, William McHattie, R Campbell, J Dinwoodie, Eddie Uriarte.
(Photo: Courtesy of EAC Doon Valley Museum)

Rechabites

The Independent Order of Rechabites was very active in Benwhat and it was run by Robert Bryan and Alexander McHattie. All the children met in the school during the week and we sang songs and listened to a sermon trying to explain the evils of drink and the correct way to lead a good life.

Most of the children in Benwhat went along. In 1947 I sat one of the examinations and received a first-class pass in division 2 and I still have the certificate to this day. Once a year you would go on a trip with the Rechabites and you got a made-up parcel to take along, with Co-op buns and juice, and this was a great day out.

The McHattie family who were a well-known and popular family in Benwhat. In the early 20th century the McHatties were contractors in the coal mines and they paid the miners for their work.
(Photo: Courtesy of Doon Valley Museum)

Evacuees

During the war years we had two evacuees living with us at Benwhat. One was called Guy Deans and the other was Walter Orr, both of whom came from Glasgow. They were my mother's cousins' children. They would have been about twelve years of age. They stayed with us for about a year and they seemed to enjoy the open wild spaces of the Benwhat moor. They didn't perhaps enjoy the school as much. In 1941 my mother's Uncle George also came to stay and he didn't want to return to Glasgow and had to be hunted back home in 1945 when the war ended. As you might imagine, our house was a busy place and there never seemed to be any quiet periods.

Leaving Benwhat

We left Benwhat in 1942 to go and live at Park Crescent, Dalmellington. However, at the end of the war in 1945 my father hired a taxi from Willie Newell, who ran the taxis in Dalmellington, and we all went back up to Benwhat and joined in the celebrations marking the end of war. The Benwhat Band paraded round the rows and the beer store was opened up specially for the event and it was a time of great celebration.

Benwhat families

In my time in Benwhat the main family involved in village life was the McHatties. Adam McHattie was a great runner and Wull McHattie trained the football teams and they were also the main contractors in the local pits, so they were important people. There was also a family called McKirdy with around thirteen of a family. They all packed up and went to live in Canada. A few of them have been back over the years to visit Benwhat.

The Relly family were also very much involved in the community – David, better known as Dykes; Hugh, John and Andy. Among the older men when I was a boy were Tommy Dempsey, Tommy Kirk and Dykes Relly. There was a big family of Murrays, McKinstrys, Wilsons, Filsons, Farrells and Torbets.

As a boy at Benwhat I ran about with Adam McHattie, Willie Lindsay and Dan Wallace. We enjoyed playing football and exploring the burn and generally playing games about the village. It could be a wild and lonely place when the mist came down and in winter the weather could be ferocious.

Benwhat School circa 1910. Many of their descendants still live in the Doon Valley.
Back row (8): Agnes Fisher (Mrs Hutchison), Jock Wilson, Annie Murray, Brown, Maggie Rice, ?, ? Teacher is Miss Dunlop.
2nd B/R (9): William McBride, John Hainey, David Torbet, Tom Murray, William Dick, George Murray, Sandy Pollock, Adam McHattie and Rab McKinstry.
2nd F/R (9): Maggie Devoy, Katie Reid, Virginia Watson, Martha Dempsey, Nell Hainey, Jean Armour, Annie Hill, Lizzie Campbell and Emily Hill.
Front row (6) Jim Finlay, Sam Carlisle, ?, ?, Sam McCurdie and Pollock Neville.
(Photo: Courtesy of EAC Doon Valley Museum)

Benwhat School

When I attended Benwhat School the headmaster was Mr Jeffrey, with teachers Miss McLeod and Miss Ireland, and the cook was Mrs Campbell, the mother of Dick Campbell, who was well known in Dalmellington, having been a postman for many years. And the janitor was Scott Hannah, who was another well-known local man.

War memorial

About 1938 my grandmother, Mrs Pollock, was a very proud lady when her grandson, Robert Pollock, who incidentally was Dux at Dalmellington School in the 1930s, led the annual service of remembrance at the Benwhat memorial. She knew everyone on that memorial, so that occasion was rather special and poignant.

Bellsbank's first shop

In 1953 my Uncle Andrew built the first shop in Bellsbank as a fish and chip shop. I helped to dig the drains and the main work was done by Robbie Johnstone and Gibson the joiner from Dalmellington. He then extended and had a small post office and after some four years it was sold to John Espie. My uncle died in 1967 and I then bought the shop from my cousin, Drew, and I ran it until 1990, when I sold it. I later ran a guest house in Prestwick, but I gave that up in 1995 after I had a heart attack and I retired.

Days past

Benwhat was a great wee community but the living conditions were primitive by today's standards. Over the years I've gone back so many times, a wee bit like a salmon always returns to the same river, I suppose. However, it was my home in happy boyhood days and when I visit the ruins of the new school and walk along the foundations of the row, I quietly remember my ain folk and recall in my mind's memory, happy days that can never return.

The cheerfu' supper done, wi' serious face,
They, round the ingle, form a circle wide;
The sire turns o'er, wi' patriarchal grace,
The big ha'-bible, ance his father's pride.

The Cotter's Saturday Night
Robert Burns

Flora Scobie, née McCulloch, of Benwhat with her father relaxing on the edge of Benwhat Hill circa 1946.
(Courtesy of Flora Scobie, née McCulloch)

Chapter 26

Benwhat – The Music Plays On
Tom Filson

Content am I, if heaven shall give
But happiness to thee,
And, as wi' thee I'd wish to live,
For thee I'd bear to dee.

It Is Na, Jean, Thy Bonnie Face
Robert Burns

This interview with Tom Filson took place in January 2012. He reveals some of his happy memories of Benwhat, especially playing with the village brass band, a lifelong interest for him, which he always said greatly influenced his life. His brother Andrew was also a lifelong member of the band. The two brothers used to meet weekly at Tom's house in Bellsbank, where they enjoyed a happy blether, when Benwhat and its famous band were regular topics of conversation. Sadly, Tom passed on in February 2012, but some of his precious memories live on through this book.

Twins
Benwhat was a smashing wee place. My father was Thomas Filson and my mother Sarah Armour. The others in my family were Sadie, Jack, Jean and Willie. I was born at Benwhat in 1933, a twin of Andrew.

Our family lived first in No. 14 Benwhat, the row beside the school. We later moved to No. 52, which was slightly bigger and had an inside toilet, which our first house didn't have. However, we more or less always went up to what was called 'the privy', which was a stone dry closet toilet located in the back garden. There was running water in both houses and there was a back boiler, which enabled us to get hot water once the fire was lit.

Like two peas
The birth of Andrew and me seems to have been straightforward enough, despite it being twins. We were delivered at home by Nurse Brecknie of Dalmellington. Andrew was older than me by two minutes, according to my mother. My brother and I were so alike that for years Mother had bother distinguishing between us. As you can imagine, that caused a bit of bother when one of us had been up to no good and the other got the blame!

Benwhat Heatherbell circa 1894 with the Dalmellington Challenge Trophy snapped outside Benwhat store. The door on the left led to a room used as a surgery by the doctor on his rounds to the village.
Back row: (l to r) Willie Dick, James Allan, David 'Wheatie' McBride, Alex Orr, John Conner, Willie Orr and David McGarvie.
Front row: James 'Punch' Hainey, John Rae, David 'Dad' Torbet, James 'Lairdie' Armour, Andrew Hainey, Neil Dempsey, Adam McHattie and Alex McCall.
(Courtesy of EAC, Doon Valley Museum)

Benwhat School
Andrew and I began at Benwhat School aged five. The head teacher initially was a Mr Frank Ferguson and his replacement

was Mr Jim Jeffrey. Mr Jeffrey was a great footballer and was well respected. Her came to the school about 1943 and remained until it closed about 1951.

The teachers also had trouble sorting out who was who between Andrew and me, and that often led to the wrong twin being blamed when things went wrong. Although we still argue about it today, Andrew was most often up to no good, but he would like as not tell you different. We love each other dearly, but we still argue, but always leave on the very best of terms to argue again the next week. We've been doing this for years.

The other teachers at Benwhat during my time were Miss Rollo and Miss McLean, but I forget the names of the others. Schooldays were happy. I looked forward to going there. I wasn't clever, but did my best. Strangely enough, my favourite subject was algebra. I just loved it. I remember that there were five classes and with the lads from Corbie Craigs also attending I think there would be about twenty to twenty-five in each class.

There would be about twenty in my class at Benwhat and it was a composite class. There were five classrooms in the building and when you finished class 5, around the age of twelve, you went down the hill to Dalmellington Higher Grade school. McGuire's bus took us from Benwhat each morning and brought us back in the evening.

Pals

My boyhood pals were the McHatties and Lindsays and all of them have passed on now. Thinking back, we were all football daft and I was the goalie. We played on an area of grass known as the hearth, probably going back to the times when ironstone would be laid out and dried on these areas. It was a really good football park for a wee village. As long as there was a ball, I was there, because I loved the company and the fun of taking part.

There wasn't much trouble in Benwhat as I recall. There would be the occasional scrap, but nothing like the trouble you get in communities nowadays. It was friendly and because everyone knew one another and lived together, it probably had a controlling influence on behaviour.

The coal mines

I left Dalmellington School aged fifteen in 1948 and went to work in Chalmerston Pit and later Minnivey, where I was a coal

Chalmerston 4 and 5 Pit sat on the hill high above Craigmark. Sinking and production commenced in 1925 and in 1948 it had an output of 180 tons per day. There were 128 employees. There were pit baths and a canteen. Coal hutches ran down the incline to the coal loading point at Minnivey. It closed in 1959 and was abandoned the following year. This was the fanhouse building. Chalmerston No. 7 was sunk in 1934 and closed in 1952 and was a surface mine. Spruce trees now cover the area where the pithead was located.
(Photo: Courtesy of EAC Doon Valley Museum)

stripper working at the coal face. Although it was gruelling work, I can honestly say that I enjoyed working in the pit. There was great camaraderie among the men, although the work was very demanding. I worked in the pits for thirty-seven years, retiring from Killoch Colliery after the closure of Chalmerston. I worked with some lovely characters in the pits and got on well with most of them.

Marriage

I married Jessie Bone of Broomknowe, Dalmellington, in 1954 in the Kirk o' the Covenant, Dalmellington, with the Reverend John Morton officiating. Afterwards, we had a social in the church hall. My brother Andrew was the best man and we've always been very close, although some would have you believe we fight like cat and dog. It's always in good fun and I'm always right, anyway!

The coal loading point at Minnivey, which had an intricate system for loading wagons. The bogies that ran up to Chalmerston can clearly be seen in the background with coal wagons waiting to be loaded. Chalmerston spoil bing can be seen on the hill.
(Photo: Courtesy of EAC Doon Valley Museum)

Family

My wife and I have a son, Scott, a daughter, Norma, grandchildren Laura and Mark, and great-grandchild Leah. When first married we lived in digs, it was just a single room, with Rab McKinstry in Ness Glen Road, Bellsbank, before getting a council house in Riecawr Avenue and after twelve years there we moved to Ness Glen Road where we currently live.

I had two older brothers, Jack and Willie. Both worked at Minnivey and Chalmerston pits. Jack moved to England when he was quite young and didn't keep good health. Willie was raised in Benwhat and later Dalmellington and spent his life in the pits.

My father was a miner and worked at Chalmerston Pit. There was a gas explosion in the pit when I was about twelve years old and it badly affected his eyes and he never worked after that and passed away in 1977.

We left Benwhat to come down to Dalmellington to attend the Higher Grade School when I was about twelve (1945). We moved to Newbiggin Terrace, Dalmellington, later moving to a smaller house in Hopes Avenue.

Benwhat Band

My uncle, Jimmy Armour, was the conductor of Benwhat Band, formed in 1871. This band was born and grew in the village. The band members met and practised in the drill hall in the village school. The band was an important part of village life. There was a great but friendly rivalry between them and Dalmellington Band, in the valley below.

When I was about ten years of age, I was brought into the band by my Uncle Jimmy and I was given a bass trombone and that was my instrument throughout my banding career right until the late 1970s, when the band ceased to function. My brother Andrew joined at the same time and he was also put on the trombone and for many years was solo trombone of the band. Brother Willie played tenor horn and Jack was on cornet.

My Aunt Nellie Armour and Uncle Jimmy always had band members in their home practising, so as well as practising at home, my brothers and I were regulars at the home of the conductor, so we got more than our fair share of tuition. However, we all came to love playing brass instruments and taking part in the many and varied engagements with the band.

Benwhat was really a village of music for many of us because it dominated our lives. The band was made up mainly of men from Benwhat and the band met on a Monday, Wednesday and Friday for formal practices. We took part in Scottish brass band competitions as well as leading Sunday School trips, fetes, concerts and other events happening not only in Benwhat, but widely in Ayrshire. I had a wonderful life in the band and when I think back I am very grateful that Uncle Jimmy encouraged me to learn the trombone.

Some time after, the band moved down to Dalmellington as the village was being run down and folk were moving out. The band moved into a lovely wooden band hall situated on the edge of Dalmellington near the Path and on the far side of the Muck Burn. That remained the band's base until it eventually folded around 1978 due to a lack of players and money.

Personal reflection

Benwhat was a very happy place and it was one of those places where you never locked a door. Everybody knew everybody else and with the hills, valleys and streams right on your doorstep, it was a great place for boys to play. Mind you, the winters could be very severe and often the place was snowbound. I remember once when the snow was about 15 feet high in places with drifts, but as you can imagine, we boys really did enjoy that.

I regularly journey down memory lane to recall back to my boyhood days in Benwhat. They were great times, despite the poor living conditions, but I'm now one of the older folk and the last of a dwindling group who were raised at Benwhat. I'm very proud to say that I was a Benwhatonian and although my dear brother and I enjoy our weekly blethers on a huge range of subjects, we always agree on one thing – Benwhat was a great wee place.

In ploughman phrase, 'God send you speed,'
Still daily to grow wiser;
And may ye better reck the rede,
Than ever did th' adviser!

Epistle to a Young Friend
Robert Burns

The Wilson family of Benwhat. This photo was taken around 1956 when they had moved to Dalmellington.
Back row (l to r): Madge McCutcheon (née Wilson), Serena Shankland (née Wilson), David Wilson, John Wilson, Tom Wilson and Esther Pringle.
Front row: Agnes McWhirter (née Wilson), Jean Fisher (née Wilson), Jean Bryce (née Wilson) and Nelly Tyson (née Wilson).
(Photo: Tom Wilson collection)

Mrs Agnes Wilson sitting on the plinth of the newly built war memorial at Benwhat in 1921. Sad to say, the names of two of her sons who made the ultimate sacrifice are shown on this memorial. She would have been rather pleased that this memorial was fully refurbished in 2011.
(Photo: Tom Wilson collection)

Chapter 27

Craigmark – Water of Life
Bill Coughtrie

Leeze me on drink! It gies us mair
Than either school or college;
It kindles wit, it waukens lear,
It pangs us fou o knowledge.

The Holy Fair
Robert Burns

Bill Coughtrie, a retired police inspector, now living in Ayr and formerly of The Mill, Dalmellington, recalls popping into the Craigmark store in the days when many former miners, mostly larger-than-life characters, welcomed strangers.

I am sure the views of Benwhat and the surrounding district are much the same as when my wife Janet and I used to drive up there, and get water from Campbell's Spout. It was always pure and crystal clear. I remember going into the Craigmark store for a pint when Ian Ferguson was the licensee after he retired from the police service (mid-1970s). The store was frequented by worthies from Dalmellington and Burnton, many of whom were born in Benwhat or Craigmark and worked in the coal pits.

Ian had two bottles of water on the counter, for those who wanted water with their whisky, and each bottle had a label with Craigmark or Benwhat thereon. I saw on many occasions a customer asking for either the Craigmark Bottle or Benwhat Bottle to be passed along the bar, as they simply would not drink the water if it was not from their village of origin. It was all done in good fun and in some respects was there as a spectacle for strangers who visited.

When the bottles were emptied, Ian Ferguson refilled them from the same cold water tap under the bar, in front of the customers. Nevertheless the 'punter' would stick to the bottle of his choice and would argue on a friendly banter that they were different, the one supposedly from their former village definitely being the better of the two.

Go fetch to me a pint o wine,
And fill it in a silver tassie;
That I may drink before I go,
A service to my bonie lassie.

The Silver Tassie
Robert Burns

Craigmark Reunion in the 1960s with a number of the residents of the village coming together to reminisce. The painting of the village was the work of a man who was proud of his Craigmark and Dalmellington background – Billy Greig (second from right) and today it hangs in the pub called the Craigmark Store. Billy Greig painted this Craigmark scene in a garage lockup at Park Crescent, Dalmellington. Billy was also a stalwart member of the Dalmellington Band where he played percussion.

Chapter 28

Tongue Row Tales

Sally Robertson or Sampson

Some, lucky, find a flow'ry spot,
For which they never toil'd nor swat;
They drink the sweet and eat the fat,
But care or pain;
And haply eye the barren hut
With high disdain.

Epistle To James Smith
Robert Burns

Mrs Sampson was interviewed by Donald L Reid in March 2012, aged ninety. She lived at Polnessan, but now resides in Dalmellington Care Centre. She was one of the very few folk the writer was able to track down who experienced life at Tongue Row, occasionally called Tongue Bridge Row, yet another of the lost villages of Ayrshire's Doon Valley.

Family background

I was born on 28 April 1923 and lived at Tongue Row from 1923 until 1933. Tongue Row was a miners' row of cottages situated on the south side of the Polnessan–Rankinston road (B730) where the opencast site is now and a little way above Cairntable. There were eleven, including mother, Catherine, and father, William, in my family. From the oldest to the youngest there was Billy, Jimmy, Tom, Andrew, John, Robert, Betty, myself and Matthew. They are all dead now except my younger brother Matthew and myself.

Matthew and I now live in Dalmellington Care Centre, where we are very well looked after. In the old days we lived in a two-bedroom house at Tongue Row. The Kilpatrick family was even worse than us. They had thirteen in their family, so it couldn't have been very easy for them, living in a two-bedroom house.

My father worked in gold mines in South Africa, but when he returned here he didn't live all that long and I was only a wee girl when he died. My mother had nine of a family to look after, so times were very hard for her, especially after Father died. One thing I do remember clearly was that on a Sunday Father would get us all round the organ in the house and played hymns and we joined in with the singing.

Sally Sampson and her brother Matthew. Both spent their formative years at Tongue Row, leaving for Polnessan in 1933.
(Photo: Donald L Reid)

Kerse School

I attended the school at Kerse, about half a mile further up the brae (B730 road) towards Polnessan. The school finally closed about 1982 and the building is still there, although it's in a very bad state. The headmaster in my day was a man called David Wilson. He was a nice man and there was a Miss McArthur and Miss McConnell who were teachers during my time at that school. When Mr Wilson retired the headmistress was a Miss Ina Hynds, who later got married and became Mrs Reid. I'm ninety years old now, but I can still see them all in my mind's eye, as clear as anything, because I loved my time at school. The teachers were just great.

Kerse School 1933–34 with class teacher, Miss McConnell. The old school building, though in perilous condition, is extant. There were twenty-one houses at Kerse and forty-two at Tongue Row, a mile to the east. Many of pupils also came from Cairntable, a further 1.5 miles to the east of Kerse.
Back row (l to r): John Wilson, Jim Smith, Stuart Hay, Robert Smith, Willie Dougan and Jim Cherry.
2nd back row: Sheena McCrorie, Jean Smith, Jean McNaught, Isa Ryans, Isa McFadzean, Kate Sutherland and Mary Brown.
2nd front row: Annie Knox, Jean McFadzean, May Beaton, Nan Cook, Jean Brown, Ruby Grant, Nelly Taylor, Hannah McFadzean, Jean Colvin and Mary Taylor.
Front row: David Brown, Jimmy Mack, Bobby Brown, Willie Cole, Robert Logan, ? Cherry, Eric Chalmers and Andrew Smith.
(Photo: Courtesy of John Grant collection)

School friends

I remember that in my class there was Mary Kilpatrick and her sister Rita; Molly McCrorie, Peggy and Jessie Houston; Frank Osborne; Nelly Osborne; Margaret Murray; Jim Brown; my brother Matthew and a Cissie Brown. Everyone seemed to get on well and the community was very close-knit. There were no school dinners in these days. You took a wee tin flask and sandwiches for lunch and you went into the kitchen area and sat there and ate your lunch and then went out to enjoy some time with pals in the playground. I had very happy days at school and I often think back to my pals and wonder whatever became of them.

Leaving Tongue Row

Our family left Tongue Row and moved to the new houses at Polnessan in 1933. We thought we were in a palace, moving from Tongue Row which had absolutely no facilities that we all take for granted today, to a brand-new house at Polnessan. However, I stayed on at Kerse School until age fourteen. In these days there was nothing else for us but to go out to domestic service.

Domestic service

I went to a big house in Maybole owned by the Lees family who owned the boot and shoe factory in the town. I lived in with the family and got 30 shillings a week and my keep. Occasionally old Mrs Lees would give me an extra 5 shillings at the end of the week, but it was hard work and I really missed my family.

My village

Tongue Row and Kerse were two small mining communities near Littlemill colliery. The Kerse consisted of only twenty houses, but despite being so small it also had a provision store. This was a branch of the Dalmellington Iron Company's store headquarters at Waterside, or perhaps more properly called Bairds and Dalmellington at that time.

Kerse also had a school and the children from Kerse, Tongue Row and Cairntable all attended. When I was a wee girl the staff of the provisions store at Kerse used bicycles to make deliveries to the scattered communities in the area.

War work

During the war I went to work at Prestwick Airport. I worked on aeroplanes as an assistant to the fitter. A lot of women worked there during the war because most of the men were in the services. They taught us how to do a variety of jobs and I remember one of the male supervisors telling me that the women did the jobs far better than the men. Of course they were away fighting in the war, but when they came back, the women had to vacate the jobs for the men. I often wonder how that foreman got on with the men who took over our jobs.

Thus in memory let it steep,
And in tradition let it keep,
That those that follow get a peep,
At days gone by;
And what we do enjoy today,
Whose beauty never fades away,
If folks still try.

John S McChesney
(For many years a popular teacher at Dalmellington High School and a Dalrymple resident)

Dalmellington Co-op had a large number of horse-drawn carts which delivered a huge range of items such as baking and butcher meat to homes in the Doon Valley and travelled as far as Carsphairn and Dalry as well as to what we now call the lost mining villages of Doon. Jimmy Sadler is seen here circa 1940 with the fleshing cart at what is believed to be Dunaskin Works with the telltale chimney just visible in the background.

Andrew Wilson, a Benwhatonian who now lives in Prestwick, but has a special place in his heart for Benwhat.
(Photo: Donald L Reid)

This is "Tommy" the pit pony from the Houldsworth pit, Patna, which, as was reported in our columns last week, has been retired after nearly 20 years' underground service.

This cutting from the Ayr Advertiser of 9 January 1931 is headed 'An Old Servant Retires'. It refers to the horse, Tommy, which worked underground for twenty years at Houldsworth Colliery near Patna. There were no horses working in the Doon Valley pits after the Second World War.
(Cutting courtesy of Doon Valley Museum)

Chapter 29

Benwhat Recollections

Andrew Wilson

Contented wi' little and cantie wi' mair,
Whene'er I forgather wi' Sorrow and Care,
I gie them a skelp, as they're creepin alang,
Wi' a cog o guid swats and an auld Scottish sang.

Contented wi' Little and Cantie wi' Mair
Robert Burns

Andrew Wilson, now living in Prestwick, remembers his early days in Benwhat.

Family

I was born at No. 11 Benwhat on 5 June 1929. My father was John (Jock) Wilson and my mother was Jean Baillie. My father originated from Girvan area and my mother was from near Edinburgh. The coal pits brought them to Benwhat. I had two brothers: Tom (Tam) passed on a few years ago but he made his special mark with Dalmellington Band as a top-rank bass player. My other brother, John, now lives in Cumnock.

My grandfather, John Wilson, was employed by the council to clean the sheughs (open drains) in Benwhat and a few rats had bolted one morning as he uncovered the muck and rubbish, and afterwards he was having a breather, sitting smoking his pipe. A passing chap said, 'Its a grand morning, John.' He replied, ' Aye, it is indeed, it brings out all the vermin.' That was the kind of character he was.

Helping school and community

I was the youngest of three boys in our family. My earliest memory of Benwhat is probably going to school and helping Scott Hannah, who was the very popular janitor. He gave me a shilling a week for helping him to clean the school and set out chairs and wee jobs like that. They often had dances in the school drill hall for the Village Comforts Committee, and Wee Lizzie (Hannah), the wife of the janitor, would spread Lux soap flakes on the floor to make it slippery for the dancers and when I went to clean it on a Sunday morning it was absolutely murder to get it cleaned because it had been trampled in.

There were a few of the older villagers who were unfit to do their own gardens. Along with the janitor some of the schoolchildren would plant out their gardens. Later on we would go up to the houses with Scott Hannah and pick vegetables which were used for the school dinners by Mrs Maggie Campbell, the sister of Jimmy Armour, the village bandmaster, and the mother of Dick Campbell, who was also well known in Dalmellington, where he worked for the Co-op for years before becoming one of the postmen.

Haring about the Hill

Old Allan Dick, the father of Allan Dick, a weel-kent character about Dalmellington and a fine goalkeeper with Craigmark, was a real character in Benwhat. I remember he had an old black greyhound. One day he was wandering around the village when he came across a hare standing up and he said to the dog: 'Stand up and face your partner.' Needless to say the hare was off like a shot, but the dog didn't give chase. Allan simply said, 'Jings, dog, you're a real no-user.'

I was also a young member of Benwhat Harriers, joining when I was about fourteen. It was a very active club and we used to go out in the evening and run along the track to the Hill (Lethanhill), going through all the muck and puddles in the process. It kept us fit and was really great fun. There used to be a social each year to present prizes and you'll be amazed to learn that one of the prizes I got was a cigarette case – for a harrier!

Robert Reid was a villager who made his mark in athletics. He won many races and later moved to England and joined the famous Birchfield Harriers. They got him a job which basically went with joining the club. When he was running at Cardiff a busload from Benwhat travelled all the way down to see him run. In these days travel wasn't easy, so it just shows how proud the villagers were of his achievement and how loyal and caring they were to a son of Benwhat. Everyone knew each other well and there was a real pride in the achievements of fellow Benwhatonians.

From school to work

I left school aged fourteen and it was straight to the coal pits. There was nothing else for it in Benwhat or indeed the Doon Valley. I went to work at Chalmerston and you walked along the line from Benwhat or if you had a bike in the family, you could cycle to work along the rough tracks. I worked in the pithead at first and then down the pit and finished up as a shot-firer.

After Chalmerston closed (1959) I transferred down the hill to Minnivey. As a shotfirer I had to go down the pit on a Saturday once a month to check the pumps were working. I suppose that wouldn't be allowed nowadays for health and safety reasons, but if the pumps were to break down the pit would have flooded and that would probably mean expensive work to try to save it or it would simply have to be closed.

Entrepreneur

When I was a young lad, on a Sunday morning I used to cycle across to Lethanhill and buy the Sunday editions from the wee shop there for 1 1/2d. (penny halfpenny) and sold them when I got back to Benwhat for 2 1/2d. You could say I was a young entrepreneur. I sometimes couldn't be bothered taking the papers down to Corbies (Corbie Craigs), so I'd send young Robin Farrell to deliver them for me. In fact, sad to say, but Robin Farrell, who was very proud of his Benwhat roots, died in 2011, not long after the memorial service to re-dedicate the war memorial. However, he was a proud member of our community and he will be sadly missed.

Mining to Monsanto

I worked the pits for around twenty years and left in 1969 to work at the new Monsanto Plant at Dreghorn. I stayed there for five years before I got a job as janitor at Bellsbank Primary School and was later janitor at Ayr Academy for around twenty years, finally retiring in 1994.

Village life

The men would enjoy a drink in Benwhat store (pub) and after it closed in the afternoon, if it was a nice day, they would all go to the football field and play a game. The goalie in one team was quite drunk and when someone shot towards goal, he dived completely the wrong way, allowing a goal to be scored. When his team remonstrated with him as to why he dived the wrong way, he said that he saw three balls coming towards him at the same time and dived for the one he thought would be easiest to catch. That gave everyone a good laugh and hopefully encouraged him never to play football again after having too much to drink.

The big slide in winter at Benwhat was a great attraction. It went from the Stane Row and the Laigh Row down to the store. It was created by diverting the water from Campbell's Spout, which then froze over. Everyone enjoyed it. It was a great attraction and even the men in the village would have a go, sliding with tackety boots on.

If you needed a doctor, it was Doctor Lee or Doctor Campbell, and they would come up from Dalmellington. There were no phones in those days. You would leave a note in the village store and the doctor would pick them up and do his rounds of those who needed medical attention. When I think back, it was actually a much better service than is available today on the NHS. Now, how's that for progress?

Getting the messages

Johnny Meiklejohn, from the Co-op, would come up on a Saturday morning and go round the doors and pick up orders for groceries and other items from the villagers. This was delivered on a Wednesday by Jimmy Currie. Again, a pretty good service all those years ago.

Bawbees

Folk hadn't much money and one of the things the women tended to do was to lay out small amounts of money on the mantelpiece or sideboard, with specific amounts to pay the insurance man, grocer and butcher who would call each week.

In my opinion this was real housekeeping at work and young folk today could learn much from how it was done in wee places like Benwhat. These ways of doing things remained with folk thereafter even when money wasn't quite so scarce, so even today in our home we have amounts of money set aside ready to pay for things. Old habits die hard, but one thing was for certain. We never got into any debt and that can't be said for the present generation who seem to think they can get everything without saving for it. In our day if you wanted something, you had to save for it and I think you valued it more.

Funerals

When there was a funeral in the village we would walk behind the hearse from Benwhat all the way down to Dalmellington and it would be around 3 miles distant. But that was how we did things in those days. There was a great respect for neighbours and the passing of someone locally was always marked by attending the funeral. Of course, we all knew each other very well indeed, so a loss in a family was a loss for the entire community. One of us had passed on and we paid our respects.

Leaving Benwhat

We left Benwhat about 1947 and flitted to Finlas Avenue, Bellsbank. I married Marion Maltman of Melling Terrace, Dalmellington, in 1956. We had our family of Andrew, Morag and Alan and we eventually moved to Ayr in 1976.

I will always have a special place in my heart for Benwhat. I attended the reunion to mark the re-dedication of the war memorial on 12 June 2011 and that proved to be a very emotional occasion for everyone, meeting so many folk from my early days and recalling the sights and scenes of the past, some of which I had completely forgotten about until I was reminded by talking to a fellow villager.

As well as having a tear in the eye at the memory, I also laughed out loud. It was as if we were boys again and the rows were there and the school had come magically back to life. Benwhat was that kind of place and anyone who lived there will tell you that. It was great to look back and remember, especially as the former villagers are disappearing all too quickly and the remainder are in the autumn of their lives.

Since life's gay scenes must charm no more
Still much is left behind,
Still nobler wealth hast thou in store –
The comforts of the mind!

Inscription to Chloris
Robert Burns

Benwhat Dramatic Club 1923 showing the cast of their production of Auld Robin Gray. Benwhat, which eventually had eighty-four houses and was situated above the 1,000-foot contour, exemplified the Dalmellington Iron Company's policy of accommodating their workers as close to the mines as possible, with access roads very much a secondary consideration. There were no fewer than thirty-seven pits and ironstone mines on the plateau above the Doon Valley. By the 1870s, 'the time o' the big money', it was said that miners in Benwhat were earning £7 per week and most houses in the village had an American organ. By the 1880s times had changed dramatically and the average weekly wage had fallen to 25 shillings per week. Entertainment in villages such as Benwhat was self-made and concerts were a feature of village social life.
(Photo: Courtesy of EAC Doon Valley Museum)

Chapter 30

Memories of Cairntable

Janet Grant

Ye banks and braes o' bonny Doon,
How can ye bloom sae fresh and fair?
How can ye chant, ye little birds,
And I sae weary fu' o' care?

The Banks o' Doon
Robert Burns

Janet Montgomery or Grant was interviewed in June 2002 by Donald L Reid about her memories of Cairntable.

Love and Cairntable

I was born in Govanhill, Glasgow in 1922 and moved to Cairntable Rows in 1948 when I married Thomas McPherson Grant. He was a miner in Littlemill Colliery and worked there for fifty-one years.

I met Tom when I was in the Land Army at Kilbirnie where I lived and worked at Geirston Farm. The farmer was John Rennie, who originally came from the Old Smithston Cottage at Kerse, where he had been a shepherd.

I worked on the land during the whole of the Second World War. It was hard work because you were on the go from early in the morning until late at night. I did a whole range of jobs on the farm, from milking to general farm chores. There was always plenty to do.

Cycling to Kilbirnie

My husband and I met at this time and he cycled every Sunday for three years from Rankinston where he lived to Kilbirnie to visit me. This was no mean feat, because the weather was sometimes very bad and the roads were pretty poor, with little or no work being done on them because of the war effort. But I think it showed that he was very keen on me and I appreciated him making such great efforts.

Kerse School with some contented-looking pupils of circa 1949.
Back row: Harry McTimpany (later a police officer in Ayr), Andrew McWhirter, Catherine Campbell, Mima Smith, John Nisbet and Tom Campbell.
Second back row: Tom Smith, Iris Carey, Sheena Thomson, Peggy Paterson, Anna Goodwin, Janice Easton, Maurice Reid and Bert Wylie.
Second front row: Ella Grant, Anne McWhirter, Ruby Robertson, Minnie Robertson, Charlotte Ferguson, Betty Robertson, Vicky Wallace and Helen Wylie.
Front row: ?, Billy McCulloch, Billy Grant, Howard Ferguson, ?, Stuart Callaghan.
Sitting on ground: J Dalziel, Wallace, ?, Wylie, McTimpany and I Campbell
(John Grant collection)

Marriage

Tom and I married in 1948 in the registry office in Ayr. We had a reception in the house of Tom's mother in Rankinston. This was the way things were then, because there wasn't a lot of money about after the war. We lived in my sister-in-law's room for two years at 32 Cairntable.

You've no idea the joy it was when we eventually got our own house at 4 Cairntable. But before that I had my daughter Janet when we stayed at No. 32, so it wasn't easy, but quite a few other folk were in the same situation. There was such a shortage of council houses at that time and most young couples had to live with relatives when they were first married. That's just the way things were then. But probably young folk today would be aghast at the thought of not having their own home when married.

I remember going to Dalmellington to see the factor about getting a house. He was Mr McCormick. He was really ignorant and when I asked him when I could get a house because I had a baby, he told me it was my own fault for having a baby. I came home in tears that day and my husband was going to go back up and have words with him, but we felt that wasn't really a good idea.

Cairntable

Cairntable was situated near to Knockshinnoch Farm on the Polnessan–Rankinston road (B730). It had a row of houses on both sides of the road. All the men who lived in the rows worked at the pits, mainly Littlemill, which was nearby and within easy walking distance along the railway line. The houses had running water, but outside dry closet toilets. We kept them nice, but going out through the night was never easy, especially in the winter. But despite all these inconveniences, we were very happy and I have very fond memories of living at Cairntable.

Homely place

In fact, looking back, I would say it was a brilliant place to live. It was such a homely place. They were friendly folk who genuinely cared for each other. Everyone knew each other. It was a different type of community from Polnessan, near Patna. It was a right miners' community, that's what it was. You could leave your door open and there was no crime or bother.

There was one little shop at the top of Cairntable which sold some of the basic foodstuffs. It was owned by Bob Deans, who was very well known and respected by everyone. For our main shopping we came into Patna on the bus. At that time there was a railway station halt at Cairntable and during the winter when the snow was bad the trains would deliver the bread for the community. It used to be great going to Ayr on the train on a Saturday. You'd come back loaded with shopping, but the main shopping centre was Patna Co-op.

Fun on Whinny Hill

We used to picnic on what we called the Whinny Hill and everyone used to go there with their children. These were wonderful times and with no TV or other entertainment, that was our enjoyment. I can see them now as I talk about it.

During the winter we had great fun sledging down the hills. There wasn't a great social life, but I walked from Cairntable to Drongan every day to visit my sister. It did keep me very fit and healthy because I was not only walking, I was also pushing my daughter Janet in her pram. I did this for years and thought nothing of it. I really enjoyed it.

Beginning in 1956, the folk were gradually moved out of the village to new houses in the surrounding villages. The locals in Cairntable were really annoyed because everyone loved it there. My husband was really sad to have to move and even more sad that the houses were to be demolished. So we moved to Polnessan in 1956. My husband retired from Littlemill and sadly died in 1993. However, I can honestly say that his heart was always in Cairntable, which was demolished in 1963.

O happy is that man, an' blest!
Nae wonder that it pride him!
Whase ain dear lass, that he likes best,
Comes clinkin down beside him!

The Holy Fair
Robert Burns

A happy trio enjoy the sun at Littlemill Colliery about 1974 just when it was closing.

(l to r): Bert Smith, his grandson Brodie Smith and Jim Keirs, formerly a mining union official.
(Photo: Tom Smith collection)

Littlemill Colliery from the artistic hand of Tom Smith who was raised in nearby Cairntable which he fondly remembers with pride. (Drawing: Courtesy of Tom Smith)

Benquhat Memories

John Relly

This little poem, 'Benquhat Memories', was written by Mr John Relly, who spent his formative years in the miners' rows high above the Valley of Doon. John was very proud of his Benwhat roots.

As the reader will appreciate from this poem, the village of his birth held fond memories for him. Indeed, his happiest recollections of youth were about Benquhat and his pals of yesteryear. Importantly, the lonely windswept memorial to those who made the ultimate sacrifice in two world wars still stands sentinel overlooking Benwhat Hill, above this lost village.

The memorial, restored in 2011, is a poignant reminder that real people, family men with feelings and dreams, lived in this now tranquil land of moor and hill, where the sound of the curlew once again reigns supreme. The village was completely deserted by 1952/53 and nowadays only the sound of ongoing opencast coal operations disturbs the scene.

Gone are the days when we toddled,
Frae oor hame across tae the schule.
Gone are the days when we used to sclim,
Richt up tae the tap o' the hill.
Nae mair we'll see the Heatherbell,
Or the harriers on the run.
Nae mair for us the Sunday Schule trip,
Wi' oor tinney, oor flag and the ban'.

Gone are the days o' the char hearth,
The burn and the auld Schule brae.
Gone are the days o' the moss haggs,
And the places we used to play.
Nae mair we'll see the big snaw drifts,
Away up ower oor heid.
And the poor auld sheep at the back door,
Lookin' fur crusts o' bread.

Gone are the days o' the Reading Room,
The Meat Store, the Beer Store an a'.
Gone are the days o' oor wee bare feet,
As we skelpit along the raw.
Nae mair for us the skippin' ropes,
Or the dragons that flew in the breeze.
Or a walk along the auld hill line,
That saw mony a kiss and a squeeze.

All we like sheep have gone astray,
We are scattered all over the earth.
But with joy we sometimes meet again,
Tae remember the place o' oor birth.
Fur they came wi' the big muckle shovel,
And they levelled the place doon flat.
And a' that we've left are the memories noo,
O' that place we still ca'
BENQUHAT.

Epilogue

Ill fares the land, to hastening ills a prey,
Where wealth accumulates, and men decay;
Princes and lords may flourish, or may fade;
A breath can make them, as a breath has made.
But a bold peasantry, their country's pride,
When once destroyed, can never be supplied.

The Deserted Village
Oliver Goldsmith

O wad some power the giftie gie us
To see ourselves as ithers see us!
It wad frae monie a blunder free us,
An' foolish notion:
What airs in dress an' gait wad lea'e us,
An' ev'n devotion!

To A Louse
Robert Burns

Time does pass quicker than we think and this book is timely in that it captures the precious memories of folk, now in the autumn of life, but who proudly lived, worked and reared families in the lost mining villages of Doon Valley.

It is fitting that through this book their precious memories will live on to benefit those who follow in our footsteps, revealing a way of life that deserves to be recognised as a crucial part of the mining history of Ayrshire and Scotland. These small communities were populated by real, caring people who lived life at the sharp end, facing adversity head-on. The villages may be deserted and demolished, but a loving bond still exists between yesteryear and today that will not be easily broken.

Ghaists

A fitting way of concluding this revealing and humbling insight into personal memories of folk who experienced life in Ayrshire's Doon Valley, especially in the lost mining villages, is with yet another piece of poetry. Matthew Arnold's assertion that 'poetry is simply the most beautiful, impressive and widely effective mode of saying things' has been widely accepted and certainly touches a chord with the author.

I chose to sum up this book with poetry, in braid Scots, from the pen of one of my own favourite rhymers, Rab Wilson of New Cumnock. In my view his poem nicely encapsulates the ebb and flow of life in Benwhat and elsewhere in the Doon Valley's lost mining villages. Let's hope that, in remembering, our children's children may also from time to time reflect on these thriving small communities where now only the ghaists of the past walk.

Here, oan this blastit hillside, stuid Benwhat,
Whaur haurdy men aince mined the Ironstane,
Till it ran oot – an then they mined fir coal.
Seen frae the heichts it's lyk some Machu-Picchu;
Weird plateaus an mounds define the grunnd,
Strange promontory's grassed ower nou wi green,
As natuir slowly hains back whit's her ain.
Ower-sheddaed by the mammoth Opencasts,
The spoil-heaps o Benwhat are shilpit things;
Worm-casts, neist thae muckle mowdie-hillocks.
That lane brick wa they say wis aince the schuil,
Ah stoop tae lift a waithert block o cley,
'Dalmellington Iron Company', it reads;
The faded legend o some lang loast empire.
There's naethin left o douce, trig miners' raws,
Whaes cobbles rang wi soun o cleek n' girr,
Or scrape o tackets, thud o leather club,
The flap an whirr o racin pigeons' wings,
White-peenied weemin clashin ower the dyke;
Whaur yae road taen ye in, an taen ye oot.
Thon aiblins wis 'The Sacred Way' fir some,
Wha laucht an daffed alang it as they left –
When Ne'erday cam, their friens turnt doun a gless.
There's naethin here nou, naethin here but ghaists,
Heich oan the hill the stairk memorial stauns,
A souch o back-end wuin blaws snell an keen,
Throu brucken iron railins, whaur it steirs
The tattert remnants o a poppy wreath.

Bibliography

The books listed below are recommended to the reader wishing to learn more about Ayrshire's Doon Valley. Those interested in finding out more are advised to contact the excellent local reference libraries in Ayrshire.

Rob Close, *Ayrshire and Arran* (1992)

Peter Connon, *An Aeronautical History of the Cumbria, Dumfries and Galloway Region (Part 2: 1915 to 1930)* (1984)

Robert Farrell, *Benwhat and Corbie Craigs: A Brief History* (1983)

Alex Johnstone, *Craigmark: 1800 to 1937* (1995)

Dane Love, *Ayrshire: Discovering A County* (2004)

Dane Love, *Lost Ayrshire: Ayrshire's Lost Architectural Heritage* (2005)

T Courtney McQuillan, *The Hill: Its People and Its Pits* (1988)

John Moore (ed.), *Gently Flows the Doon* (1972)

John Moore (ed.), *Among Thy Green Braes* (1977)

Piggot's Directory Ayrshire (1837) GC Book Publishers Ltd, Wigton

Donald L Reid, *Old Dalmellington, Patna and Waterside* (2001)

Donald L Reid, *Doon Valley Memories: A Pictorial Reflection* (2002)

Donald L Reid, *Doon Valley Bygones* (2004)

Donald L Reid, *Discovering Matthew Anderson, Policeman-Poet of Ayrshire* (2009)

James Edward Shaw, *Ayrshire 1745–1950: A Social and Industrial History of the County* (1953)

David L Smith, *The Dalmellington Iron Company: Its Engines and Men* (1967)

Gavin Wark, *The Rise and Fall of Mining Communities in Central Ayrshire in the 19th and 20th Centuries* (Ayrshire Archaeological and Natural History Society Monograph No. 22) (1999)

Books by Donald L Reid

The following books have been compiled by Donald L Reid.

* *Reflections of Beith and District: On The Wings of Time* (1994)
* *Yesterday's Beith: A Pictorial Guide* (1998)
The Beith Supplement: The Story of Beith's Newspaper (2000)
+ *Old Beith* (Stenlake Publications, 2001)
In The Valley of Garnock: Beith, Dalry and Kilbirnie (2001)
+ *Old Dalmellington, Patna and Waterside* (Stenlake Publications, 2001)
* *Doon Valley Memories: A Pictorial Reflection* (2002)
Beith Bygones: A Pictorial Journey Down Memory Lane (2003)
* *Doon Valley Bygones: A Pictorial Journey Down Memory Lane* (2004)
* *Barrmill and Burns* (2004)
* *Yesterday's Patna and the Lost Mining Villages of Doon Valley* (2005)
Robert Burns' Valley of Doon: An Ayrshire Journey Down Memory Lane (2005)
Discovering Matthew Anderson: Policeman-Poet of Ayrshire (2009)
Voices and Images of Yesterday and Today. Beith, Barrmill and Gateside: Precious Memories (2011)

* *Not in print and no reprint planned*
+ *Only available from Stenlake Publishers, 54-58 Mill Square, Catrine KA5 6RD*

Author Profile

Donald L Reid is a retired police superintendent, having served in the Ayrshire Constabulary and Strathclyde Police from 1967 until 1999. He was superintendent serving mainly in Glasgow City Centre area for the last seven years of his service.

Raised in Dalmellington, he is very proud of his Doon Valley roots where his father grew up at Beoch and his mother at Craigmark, two of the lost mining villages of Doon Valley. He has lived in Beith for the past twenty-five years with his wife Kathleen and daughter Elaine. His son, Fraser, and his wife, Heather, and their sons, Taylor and Owen, live nearby.

Donald has now produced fifteen local history books since 1994 mainly about the Doon Valley and Garnock Valley areas of Ayrshire. He is the Garnock Valley correspondent for the *Ardrossan & Saltcoats Herald*, keeping locals abreast of happenings in Beith, Dalry and Kilbirnie and district. He has been correspondent for Beith since 2002. Earlier in 2012 he submitted his 500th consecutive two full pages of local news, without missing a single week – even when on holiday!

A past president of Garnock Valley Round Table, he was twice president of Barrmill Jolly Beggars Burns Club; he is also secretary and was honoured when in recognition for his services to the club he was appointed honorary president in 2008. Donald is a sought-after speaker on subjects ranging from Robert Burns and Dr Henry Faulds to the Doon Valley and Garnock Valley. With his good friend Iain D Shaw, he gives an illustrated presentation on the life and works of Robert W Service, a truly international poet with close links to Kilwinning. This is entitled 'Robert W Service – Poet of the People'.

Donald is the founder member and secretary of the Dr Henry Faulds Society, which achieved a fitting memorial in Beith in 2004 to the Beith-born medical missionary, writer and one of the early and minor pioneers of fingerprint science. Donald is a member of or assists several groups and organisations in Beith and district.

He can be contacted on:
Tel 01505-503801 or E: donaldleesreid@hotmail.com
or you can also visit the website: www.jollybeggars.org

All the world is beautiful,
and it matters little where we go.
The spot where we chance to be
Always seems the best.

John Muir, 1890

Picture Gallery

Page 96 Beoch School - additional caption
Beoch School in 1935 where the education received was said to have been first class. Back row (l to r - 7): Thomas Halbert, George McLarty, John Reid (13), Sam McLarty, Adam Rowan, David McLarty and teacher Miss Pattie Ireland. 2nd back row standing (4): teacher Mrs Park with Malcolm McLarty, George Park and Henry Halliday then continuing row of 7: Mary Given, Margarete McLarty, Ella Armstrong, Betty McArthur, Kathy Armstrong, Matt Halliday and Dan Standring. 2nd front row (8): Donald Reid (6), Betty Standring, Bessie McLarty, Betty Stewart, Jean McCabe, Robert Paxton and Jim O'Neil. Front row (8): Lewis O'Neil, Fred Standring, Willie Reid (10), David McLarty, Burney Halbert, John Stewart, Willie Given and James McLarty.
(Photo: John Reid collection)

Right: The Doon Valley miners enjoyed a pint and a laugh. The Running Dog was the name given to the pub in Craigmark in 1960s. At that time the pub regulars, mainly serving and retired miners, raised money for various charities by dressing up as cowboys and Indians and they would attend charity events such as galas and became quite well-known locally. Sam Semple, a Dalmellington character, is holding the gun. Next to Sam are Billy 'Rocky' Campbell and Alexander 'Sanny' Aitken.
(Photo: Courtesy of EAC Doon Valley Museum)

Dalmellington Band lead a parade from the school through the village to Pennyvenie Colliery with councillors, officials of the National Union of Mineworkers, and members of the public to mark the handover of the nation's collieries from private owners to the National Coal Board on 1 January 1947.

Craigengillan Dalmellington Curling Club is the oldest surviving social and recreational club in Dalmellington. This cup, still played for today, was presented to the club by Col. McAdam Cathcart who was a member in 1867. The club was established in 1841 at a meeting in the village's Black Bull Hotel.
Back row (l to r): Michael Shaw, Gavin Clyde, Jim Morrison, Gus Cochrane, Ed Bains, Gordon Neil, Craig Coulter, James Dee, Tony Bell and Kerr Alexander.
Middle row: Andrew Linn, Fiona Deans, Jinty Haddow, David Stewart, Ian Alexander, John McLeod, Anne Hay, Susanne Howie, Ruth Clyde, Edith Kerr and Jim Nisbet.
Front row: Robert White, Alex Paterson, Ian Hay, Margaret White and Kennedy (Kenny) Ferguson (secretary).
(Photo: Courtesy of Craigengillan Dalmellington Curling Club)

The MacDonald Brothers are a Scottish pop rock duo from Ayr, consisting of brothers Brian and Craig MacDonald. They first rose to prominence in the third UK series of television talent show The X Factor in 2006, and have since gone on to release four albums. As well as singing, both Craig and Brian play a range of instruments including the violin, accordion, guitar, flute, mouth organ and piano. Their grandfather is William McHendry, whose interview is included in this book.
(Photo: Courtesy of the MacDonald Brothers)

Left: Lethanhill School class of circa 1939 just at the outbreak of the Second World War when these young folk and their parents would be wondering what the future held for them.
Back row: (l to r) John McConnachie, Hugh Kirk, Alex McMurtrie, Hugh Coughtrie and Robert Knox.
Second back row: Miss Park (Teacher), Mary McNeil, Isa Gordon, Betty Roller, Mary Watson, Peggy Stevenson and Annie Kirk.
Second front row: Barbara Bowie, Mary Aitken, Annie Graham, ? believed to be an evacuee, Annie Black, Agnes Hendry and Jean McVey.
Front row: John Grant, Jim Greer, Hugh Stratton and ?
(John Grant collection)

Left: Lethanhill Primary School class of 1935. This photograph was marked '1910–35, Silver Jubilee year of their Majesties, the King and Queen.'
Back Row (l to r): Miss Hay (teacher), David Davidson, Peter Conway, Alex Gillespie, Billy Bunyan, John McFarlane, Sandy Taylor, Josie Boyce.
2nd Back Row: Jimmy Sturgeon, Jimmy Holloway, ?, Jessie McClymont, Helen McLean, Isa Gillespie, Chrissie Collins, Mary Stevenson, Ruby Coughtrie, Vera Whiteford, ?, Mary Watson and Jean Callaghan.
2nd Front Row (4):?, ?, Jean Bowie, ?.
Front Row : ?, ?, Alex Baillie, Jim Bryce, Jim McRoberts, Tom McCartney, ?, ?, ?, ? and Jim Baillie.
(Photo: Courtesy of EAC Doon Valley Museum)

Below: Lethanhill School class of circa 1939. The Teacher is Mr Geddes who many folk will recall later in his career became head teacher at Bellsbank Primary School, Dalmellington.
Back row: (l to r) Jimmy Sturgeon, John McFarlane, Sandy Taylor, Jim Bowie and Sandy Smith.
Middle row: Jenny Knox, Mary Stevenson, May Craig, Nellie Kelly, Cathy Cockburn, Nettie Stevenson and Jean Callaghan.
Second front row: Dorothy Holloway, Lottie Graham, Anna Onions, Mary Campbell, May Lafferty, Mary Gilmour and Nettie Sturgeon.
Front row: Willie McBride, Robert Ferguson and Robert McConnochie.
(John Relly collection)

Above: Lethanhill School class of circa 1943.
Back row: (l to r) Robert Ferris, Jim McVey, Bob Finlay, Bobby Kirkland, Edgar Ireland and Cecil McCormack.
Front row: Jean Brown, Nan Kirkland, Margaret Winning, Betty Wallace, Margaret Bowie, Ina Reid, Nettie Curry, Annie Conway, Jean McCulloch and Margaret Stevenson.
(William Stevenson collection)

Above: Lethanhill School in 1956. The entire population of Lethanhill and Burnfoothill, known simply as 'the Hill', had been removed to Patna and Dalmellington in 1955, but the school remained open and the pupils were bussed there until 1959. Little sign of the village remains today and trees cover the area where the rows formerly stood.
Back row: Billy Bryden, Jim Guthrie, Billy Brown, M Auld, Margaret Mulholland, Madge Bain, Charlotte McClymont, Ann Robertson, ?, Margaret McDermont, May McHattie, J Givens, Agnes Knox, Elizabeth Laughlan, John McLeod, Alex Kirk and Francie Bryce.
Second back row: Andrew Brown, Irene Gillespie, Elizabeth Murray, Margaret Johnstone, Mary Muir, Jean Grant, Mamie McCormack, Rita Wylie, Christine Coughtrie, Margaret Ferguson, Margaret Gillespie, Jessie Wilson, Ann Graham, Marjorie Fawcett, Helen Mitchell, William Walker and W Campbell.
Second front row: John Dunn, William Bryce, Betty Orr, Betty McCubbin, B Brown, S Ballantyne, Jean Findlater, Ella Knox, Helen Boyle, Mary McDougall, Jessie McLeod, Nancy Brolley, Janice Bradford, Marion Bryden, A McDougall, Agnes Fyvie, Annie Ferguson, Jim Stevenson, James Whiteford and James Spiers.

High Pennyvenie with No. 4 Pennyvenie, otherwise known as the Big Mine, seen in the background. This was where the railway system terminated, albeit a bogey line ran onwards to Beoch Mine.

Dalmellington Bowling Green, pictured in the foreground, was established in 1875 while the open ground on the right became the King George V football park, used by local schoolboy and amateur teams. In the centre background above Dalmellington can be seen Benbranigan with Chalmerston Pit just to the left in front. By 1930 some 250 miners were winning coal at Chalmerston Nos. 4, 5 and 6. Nos. 4 and 5 were opened in 1924 and continued until 1959, while No. 6 opened in 1925 and closed in 1935. On the upper left of the photograph can be seen Burnton rows, which were built by the Dalmellington Iron Company between 1924 and 1926 and consisted of eighty-eight houses. The Doon Valley Cinema is the large building between the church and Burnton and it was demolished in the 1970s.

An early photo of Patna, probably around 1906. The houses in the immediate foreground no longer exist, nor does the market garden with greenhouses. Patna Auld Brig can be clearly seen and there are no housing developments at this time. The railway station building can be seen on the left, but the line closed to passengers in 1964, although it is still open for coal workings between Chalmerston loading point and Killoch. On the hill to the high left can be seen the rows at Burnfoothill, and to the right Lethanhill, with the rough road outline leading from the valley to the Hill, can also be seen.
(Photo: Scott J Rarity collection)

A sombre scene at Lethanhill which was by then a village in the process of being demolished. However, if you look closely you will see children playing happily in the school playground. The Hill was abandoned in 1954 yet children were bussed up to the school, which remained open until 1959.
(Photo: Courtesy of Ann MacLean collection)

Craigmark, like the other ghost mining villages of the Doon Valley, Lethanhill, Burnfoothill, Corbie Craigs, Beoch and Benwhat, is remembered with pride by a dwindling number of former residents. Most of those surviving today (2012) would have been children at Craigmark. The village was established in the 1840s and eventually abandoned around 1936. The construction of Burnton, close to Craigmark, began in 1924 and over the next few years the villagers moved to Burnton and Dalmellington. The author's mother, Mary McCulloch Hose, with her parents and family moved from Craigmark to Park Crescent in 1934.

Kerse Store in the early 1900s with staff standing outside.
(Photo: Scott J Rarity collection)

Danny Crockett was under-manager at Pennyvenie and here he marks the closure of the pit in 1978.
(Photo: Courtesy of EAC Doon Valley Museum)

Andrew Galloway and James McKinstry who were mine driving at Chalmerston in 1939. This was a very dangerous part of mining, the danger of roof falls always lurking in the background. Props had to be securely positioned to ensure safe working and these can be clearly seen.
(Photo: Courtesy of EAC Doon Valley Museum)

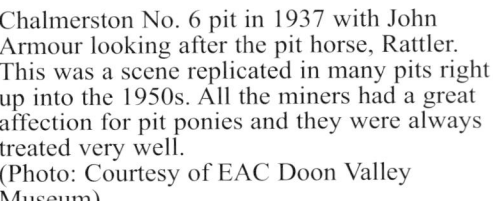

Chalmerston No. 6 pit in 1937 with John Armour looking after the pit horse, Rattler. This was a scene replicated in many pits right up into the 1950s. All the miners had a great affection for pit ponies and they were always treated very well.
(Photo: Courtesy of EAC Doon Valley Museum)

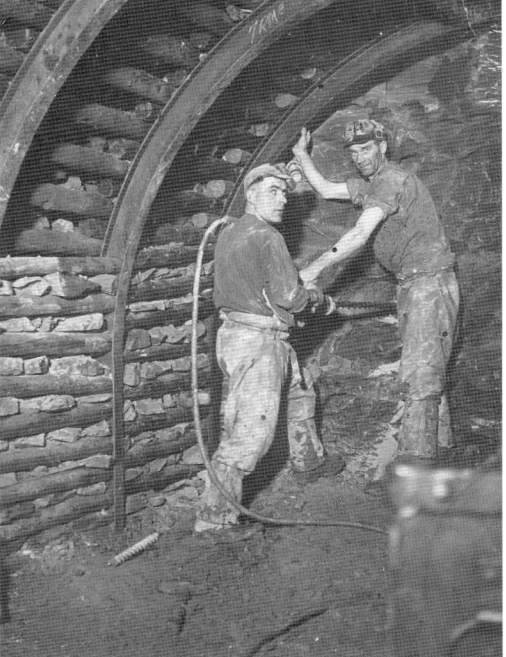

Underground at Pennyvenie Pit in the 1960s showing the dress of the miners and the hutches used to move the coal along the underground workings.
(l to r): John Craig, Sam McLarty, George Sturgeon and Hugh Rogers.
(Photo: Courtesy of EAC Doon Valley Museum)

Workers underground in Clawfin Mine which was situated near to Benbeoch Craig in 1931. This photo clearly illustrates the conditions in which the miners had to operate. Health and safety was not high on the agenda of the coal owners prior to nationalisation of the mines in 1947. The supporting wooden prop looks very suspect according to miners who have examined this photograph.
(l to r): Tommy Knox (father) and his three sons, Tom, Matthew and Frank of Patna.
(Photo: Courtesy of EAC Doon Valley Museum)

Opposite: Littlemill Colliery near Cairntable before it closed in 1974. The towers of Killoch Colliery can be seen in the background.
(Photo: Tom Smith collection)

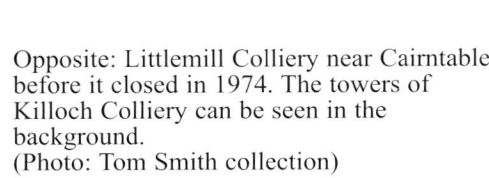

Appendix

Families of Yesteryear from the Lost Mining Villages of Doon Valley

Selected information from Valuation Roll of County of Ayr, Parish of Dalrymple 1892/1893

Kerse
(Valuation Roll, page 94)

House No.	Tenant
Store at Kerse	Dalmellington Iron Company (owners)
1 Kerse	Alexander McCartney, collier
2	John Blane, miner
3	Archibald Campbell, engineman
4	Robert Stark, miner
5	William McSeffney, collier
6	John Young, collier
7	John Hill, engineman
8	James McLannachan, miner
9	John Watt, collier
10 & 11	William Dougan, miner
12	James Mullholland, miner
13	Robert Henderson, storeman
14	Alexander Bell, miner
14	Archibald McCulloch, collier
15	Quintin Watt, collier
16	Peter Paterson, collier
17	William McCulloch, collier
18 & 19	Alexander Lyle, teacher

Tongue Row, Kerse (1892/1893)

1 Tongue Row	James Gates, miner
2	John O'Hair, miner
3	Francis Lafferty, miner
4	Charles Knox, miner
5	Andrew Montgomerie Jun, Miner
6	Thomas Hawthorn, miner
7	John Gates, miner
8	Robert Gibson, miner
9	Robert Irvine, miner
10	John Irvine, miner
11	Robert Lafferty, sen, miner
12	Maurice Mullholland, miner
13	John Templeton or Townsley, miner
14 & 15	Robert Kirkwood, miner
16	William Watson, labourer
17	Henry Waters, miner
18 & 19	John Osborne, pitheadman
20 & 21	Richard Campbell, miner
22	empty
23	empty
24 & 25	Matthew Knox, miner
26	empty
27	William Wilson, miner
28	empty
29	Alexander Adams, miner
30	empty
31 & 32	William O'Hair, miner
33	Andrew Montgomerie, sen, Labourer
34	empty
35	empty
36	John Beattie, miner
37 & 28	James Hawthorn, miner
39	empty
40	empty
41	empty

Bowhill

1 Bowhill	Hugh Murray, labourer
2	Alexander McCulloch, miner
3	James Ferguson, engineman
4	David Young, labourer

Selected information from Valuation Roll of County of Ayr, Parish of Dalrymple 1901/1901

Kerse
(Valuation Roll, page 102)

Store, Kerse	Dalmellington Iron Company
1 Kerse	Alexander McCartney, collier
2	John Blane, miner
3	John Watt, collier
4	William Dougan, jun, miner
5	John Young, collier
6	John Young, collier
7	John Hill, engineman
8	Stewart Blane, miner
9	James Blane, collier

10 & 11	William Dougan, sen, miner	34 Craigmark	Alexander McLean, jun., collier
12	Robert Stark, miner	35 Craigmark	John Murray, collier
13	James Mullholland, miner	36 Craigmark	Archibald Biggans, collier
14	Alexander Kirkwood, miner	37 Craigmark	John Murray, brusher
14	Archibald McCulloch, collier	38 Craigmark	Robert White, sen., collier
15	Quintin Watt, collier	39 Craigmark	Thomas Newall, engineman
16	George Moore, miner	40 Craigmark	George Calderwood, collier
17	William McCulloch, collier	41 Craigmark	James Griffen & Thomas Prindergast (colliers)

Selected information from Valuation Roll of County of Ayr, Parish of Dalmellington 1909/1910

Craigmark

(Valuation Roll 1909–1910, pages 77 and 78)

Sillyhole	Robert McCreath, jun., collier	42 Craigmark	Hugh Hose & Hugh Spiers, colliers
Sillyhole	Alexander Rantine, storeman	43 Craigmark	Robert Findlay, collier
Store, Craigmark		44 Craigmark	Alexander Murphy, collier
1 Craigmark	John Boyle, miner	45 Craigmark	John Bigham, collier
2 Craigmark	John McLelland, miner	46 Craigmark	William Buchanan, collier
3 Craigmark	Thomas Hastie, miner	47 Craigmark	Thomas Anderson, collier
4 Craigmark	Adam Dixon, collier	48 Craigmark	Robert White sen., collier
5 Craigmark	Mrs Wilson, widow	49 Craigmark	William Allan, collier
6 Craigmark	James Torbit, collier	50 Craigmark	James Findlay, borer
7 Craigmark	John Greig, collier	51 Craigmark	John McClement, collier
8 Craigmark	George Park, collier	52 Craigmark	John Calderwood, jun., collier
9 Craigmark	David Watson, jun., miner	53 Craigmark	Francis Graham, collier
10 Craigmark	Robert Wilson, collier	54 Craigmark	Frank Small, collier
11 Craigmark	James Boyle, miner	55 Craigmark	James Small, collier
12 Craigmark	Robert Leitch, miner	56 Craigmark	James Murray, collier
13 Craigmark	Patrick Leitch, collier	57 Craigmark	Patrick Milligan, collier
14 Craigmark	Alexander McCracken, miner	58 Craigmark	Dennis Scally, collier
15 Craigmark	James McLelland, miner	59 Craigmark	James Robertson, collier
16 Craigmark	William Shaw, labourer	60 Craigmark	James Telfer, collier
17 Craigmark	David McCulloch, labourer	61 Craigmark	William Johnstone, collier
18 Craigmark	William Newall, engineman	62 Craigmark	William Kerr, miner
19 Craigmark	John Wilson, miner	63 Craigmark	John McCulloch, collier
20 Craigmark	Alexander Smith, bricklayer	64 Craigmark	John Murphy, brusher
21 Craigmark	Robert Campbell, collier	65 Craigmark	Andrew Halbert, sen., collier
22 Craigmark (& 25)	David Smith, bricklayer	66 Craigmark	William Campbell, collier
23 Craigmark	Robert Lawson, miner	67 Craigmark	James Buchanan, collier
24 Craigmark	John Smith & Robert Neil, colliers	68 Craigmark	William Buchanan, collier
26 Craigmark	Alexander McLean, sen., collier	69 Craigmark	James Bennett, collier
27 Craigmark	Alexander Brown, collier	70 Craigmark	John Johnstone, collier
28 Craigmark	James Conway, miner	71 Craigmark	John Leitch, collier
29 Craigmark	Arthur James, miner	72 Craigmark	James Hose, collier
30 Craigmark	Thomas Leitch, collier	School do	Ayr County Education Authority

Corbie Craigs

(Pages 78 and 79 Valuation Roll 1920–1921)

31 Craigmark	John Greig, collier
32 Craigmark	James Whelan, collier
33 Craigmark	John Calderwood, collier
1 & 2 Corbie Craigs	Adam McHattie, miner
3 do	James McKnight, collier
4 do	Alexander McHattie, mason
5 do	Emmett Ainsworth

6	do	Robert Kerr, collier	41	do	James Adams, collier
7	do	Peter McMurray, miner	42	do	Mrs McFarlane, widow
8	do	Thomas Newall, labourer	43/44	do	David Dick, miner
9	do	Henry Rice, miner	45	do	Alex McHattie, jun., collier
10	do	Alexander Johnstone, collier	46	do	Malcolm McPhail, collier

Benwhat

(Valuation Roll 1920–1921, pages 79, 80 and 81)

1	Benwhat	William Cochrane, labourer	47/48	do	William Campbell, miner
2	do	Hugh Baillie, miner	49	do	Robert Bryan, sen., miner
3	do	Robert McKnight, boiler fireman	50	do	William Fisher, charfiller
4	do	John Baillie, collier	51/52	do	John Philson, miner
5	do	empty	53/54	do	John Hannah, miner
6	do	Samuel Ayre, plasterer	55/56	do	John Hill, engineman
7	do	Mrs Wilson, widow	57/58	do	Malcolm Hannah, miner
8	do	Andrew Armour, collier	59/60	do	William McCurdie, miner
9	do	Robert Neville, collier	61/62	do	Robert Hill, miner
10	do	Andrew Currie, miner	63/64	do	Samuel Falconer, miner
11	do	Andrew Wilson, miner	65	do	William Dick, collier
12	do	John Wilson, labourer	66	do	Hugh Riley, collier
13	do	empty	67/68	do	John Riley, collier
14	do	James Harkness, miner	69/70	do	Archibald Campbell, collier
15	do	empty	71/72	do	Arthur H Gear, teacher
16	do	Charles Fisher, collier	73	do	John Philson, oversman
17	do	Samuel Wilson, miner	74	do	John Philson, oversman
18	do	empty	75	do	Andrew Hannah, collier
19	do	Robert Morrison, collier	76	do	Charles Hannah, miner
20	do	Edward Hainey, collier	77	do	Thomas Hudson, miner
21	do	Thomas Gordon, miner	78	do	David McBride, miner
22	do	Mrs Hudson, widow	79	do	David McBride, miner
23	do	John McFarlane, collier	80	do	James Gourlay, blacksmith
24	do	Andrew Galloway, miner	81	do	Simpson Allan, collier
25	do	Neil Dempsey, miner	82	do	William Gourlay, engineman
26	do	William Kennedy, miner	83	do	William Gourlay, engineman
27	do	Robert Kirk, collier	84	do	James Allan, hammerman
28	do	Henry Hogson, miner	85	do	Alexander Reid, collier
29	do	Robert McFarlane, collier	86	do	Alexander Reid, collier
30	do	Daniel Parker, miner	87	do	William Hay, collier
31	do	Samuel Piper, engineman	88	do	William Hay, collier
32	do	William Torbet, miner	89	do	Thomas McEwan, collier
33	do	Thomas Allan, collier	90	do	Robert Watson, miner
34	do	Hugh Murray, miner	91	do	Robert Watson, miner
35	do	John Fisher, collier	92	do	Andrew Connell, miner
36	do	Joseph Park, collier	93	do	Andrew Connell, miner
37	do	Mrs Moffat, widow	94	do	Robert Pollock, miner
38	do	Mrs Miller, widow	95	do	Robert Pollock, miner
39	do	Thomas Fisher, collier	96	do	James Campbell, collier
40	do	John Robertson, miner	97	do	Thomas Dougan, miner
			98	do	Samuel Falconer collier
			99	do	George Liddle, manager

100/101 & 102		Reading Room Benwhat	12	do	James Fraser, joiner
School, Benwhat		Ayrshire Education Authority	13	do	Malcolm Ross, jun., blacksmith
103	do	James Wilson, collier	14	do	Malcolm Ross, jun., blacksmith
104	do	Mrs Mary Hainey, widow	15	do	Robert Park, collier
105	do	Robert McCurdie, jun., collier	16	do	William McConnell, miner
106	do	George Murray, miner	17	do	Gilbert Park, collier
107	do	George Murray, miner	18	do	William Bryden, miner
108	do	John McCurdie, miner	19	do	Andrew Gilmour, miner
109	do	John McCurdie, miner	20	do	Mrs Moore, widow
110	do	James McKinstray, miner	21	do	Hugh Park, weigher
111	do	James McKinstray, miner	22	do	William Grant, labourer
112	do	William Donnan, miner	23	do	James Dalziel, miner
113	do	William McFadzean, fireman	24	do	Mrs Barnes, widow
114	do	William McFadzean, fireman	25	do	James Robertson, miner
115	do	John Barr, pitheadman	26	do	Samuel Harkness, miner
116	do	George Long, miner	27	do	Thomas Fowler, miner
117	do	George Long, miner	28	do	James McDermont, miner
118	do	George Long, miner	29	do	Matthew Ravie, collier
119	do	John Hudson, collier	30	do	Robert Bates, residenter
120	do	Thomas Corbett, collier	31	do	Archibald Ballantyne, collier
121	do	James Hutchison, collier	32	do	James Baillie, miner
122	do	David Scobie, miner	33	do	James Sodan, engineer
123	do	David Scobie, miner	34	do	Hugh McClymont, collier
124	do	James Martin, collier	35	do	Robert Findlay, collier
125	do	Robert McCartney, miner	36	do	Robert McDermont, collier
126	do	Robert McCartney, miner	37	do	Thomas Ballantyne, miner
127	do	Alexander Gourlay, miner	38	do	James Martin, labourer
128	do	Patrick Murray, collier	39	do	Benjamin Moffat, miner
129	do	William McCurdie, jun., miner	40	do	James Grant, collier
130	do	James Murray, miner	41	do	William Gillespie, miner
131	do	James Murray, miner	42	do	Stewart Bryden, boilerman
Store	do	Alexander Orr, storeman	43	do	John Wightman, collier

Lethanhill
(Valuation Roll 1920–1921, pages 81, 82, 83 and 84)

Store, Lethanhill		DICo	44	do	empty
House	do	Allan McDougall, storeman	45	do	Martin Callow, collier
1 Lethanhill		James C Lawson, police constable	46	do	David Denham, labourer
2	do	Archibald McKie, miner	47	do	Peter Reid, labourer
3	do	Edward Courtney, miner	48	do	William McClymond, labourer
4	do	Mrs Fraser, widow	49	do	Robert Bates, foreman
5	do	Robert Murphy, collier	50	do	Thomas Bryden, collier
6	do	James Hampson, miner	51	do	Thomas Bryden collier
7	do	George Gillespie, miner	52	do	William Bryden, miner
8	do	James Gibson, miner	53	do	William Bryden, miner
9	do	Joseph Mathieson, collier	54	do	Robert Baillie, collier
10	do	James Stewart, teacher	55	do	William Boyle, collier
11	do	Henry McTimpany, miner	56	do	Henry Landsborough, collier
			57	do	James McFadzean, labourer
			58/59	do	George Ballantyne, miner

60	do	John Moore, miner	109	do	Robert Hosie, labourer
61	do	William McEwan, labourer	110	do	empty
62	do	James Moffat, collier	111	do	empty
63	do	Archibald Ballantyne, miner	112	do	John Gavin, miner
64	do	David Picken, miner	113	do	James McClymont, miner
65	do	James McEwan, labourer	114	do	David Grant, collier
66	do	Hugh McLelland, miner	115	do	Hugh Reid, miner
67	do	Hugh Bunyan, collier	116	do	John McKie, jun., miner
68	do	James McEwan, labourer	117	do	John Grant, collier
69/70	do	William Park, collier	118	do	Albert Smith, labourer
71	do	Joseph Gillespie, miner	119	do	Thomas Currie, miner
72/73	do	empty	120	do	Robert Conn, collier
74	do	David Campbell, miner	121	do	Hugh Kirk, collier
75	do	David Campbell, miner	122	do	Thomas Knox, jun., collier
76	do	Campbell Bryden, collier	123	do	William Reid, miner
77	do	Henry McTimpany, collier	124	do	Henry Graham, guard
78	do	Matthew Bunyan, miner	125	do	Matthew Knox, miner
79	do	Robert McTimpany, miner	126	do	James Tait, collier
80	do	James Bunyan, collier	127	do	Hugh Nugent, collier
81	do	Peter McDermont, collier	128	do	John Gilmour, collier
82	do	William Muir, labourer	129	do	empty
83	do	James Black, collier	130	do	empty
84	do	Joseph Thomson, collier	131	do	James Cook, slater
85	do	Mrs Ferguson, widow	132	do	Patrick Staiton, miner
86	do	John McRoberts, collier	133	do	William Irvine, miner
87	do	Philip Dunn, labourer	134	do	Hugh Robertson, miner
88	do	John Bunyan, collier	135	do	David Tait, collier
89	do	William McGuckin, miner	136	do	Hugh Hainey, miner
90	do	William Drain, miner	137	do	John McKie, miner
91	do	Andrew Wilson, miner	138	do	William McConnachie, collier
92	do	empty	139	do	John Jones, miner
93	do	Samuel Alexander, labourer	140	do	John Hogarth, surfaceman
94	do	Robert McLean, miner	141	do	Alexander Beattie, guard
95	do	empty	142	do	Peter Roberts, collier
96	do	John Thomson, collier	143	do	William Fawcett, collier
97	do	James Bunyan, collier	144	do	George McQuillan, miner
98	do	James Bunyan, collier	145	do	William Ferres, collier
99	do	John McCall, blacksmith	146	do	John Ferris, miner
100	do	John Hamilton, labourer	148	do	James Whiteford, residenter
101	do	David Simpson, boiler fireman	149	do	David McLelland, collier
102	do	William Bell, labourer	150	do	Roderick Fraser, labourer
103	do	Thomas Kirk, collier	151	do	William Clark
104	do	David Lang, miner	152	do	George Findlay, miner
105	do	empty	153	do	William McKie, miner
106	do	John Clark, engineman	154	do	Richard McQuillan, miner
107	do	Samuel Tait, miner	155	do	William McCoombe, labourer
108	do	Robert Simpson, miner	156	do	James McRoberts, miner

157/158		James Anderson, contractor
159/160		John McConnachie, collier
161	do	John Gillespie, miner
162	do	Joseph Gillespie, miner
163	do	William Dempsey, storeman
164	do	Robert Stark, miner
165	do	John Brown, miner
166	do	John Brown, miner
167	do	Hugh McTimpany, miner
168	do	Hugh Ferguson, miner
169/170		Hugh McClymont, miner
171	do	Frank McKie, collier
172	do	William Boyle, miner
173	do	Archibald Campbell, platelayer
174	do	John Sturgeon, miner
175	do	Thomas Ballantyne, collier
176	do	Thomas Ballantyne, collier
177	do	Alexander Kirkland, miner
178	do	James McReady, labourer
179/180		Robert Campbell, foreman
181	do	John Bannantyne, collier
182	do	John Bannantyne, collier
183/184		Samuel Piper, miner
185/186		John Hainey, collier
187	do	Andrew McCormack, labourer
Lethanhill School		Ayr County Education Authority
188	do	Robert Gibson, labourer
189	do	James McTimpany, labourer
190	do	empty
191	do	Samuel Caughtrie, miner
192	do	empty
193/194		Samuel Caughtrie, senior, miner
195	do	John McDermott, collier
196	do	John McDermott, collier
197	do	James Boyle, miner
198	do	James Boyle, miner
199/200		Frank McCormick, miner
201	do	James McMurtrie, labourer
202	do	Mrs Geates, widow

Burnfoothill
(Valuation Roll 1920–1921, page 84)

1	Burnfoothill	in ruins
3	do	in ruins
4	do	In ruins
5	do	In ruins
6	do	In ruins
7	do	In ruins
8	do	In ruins
9	do	In ruins
10	do	In ruins
11	do	In ruins
12	do	In ruins
13	do	Thomas Hood, miner
14	do	James McMurtrie, miner
15	do	David Stevenson, miner
16/17 Reading Room		Dalmellington Iron Company
18	do	James Stevenson, guard

Selected information from Valuation Roll of County of Ayr, Parish of Dalrymple 1922/1923

Kerse
(Valuation Roll, page 113)

Store, Kerse	Dalmellington Iron Co
1 Kerse	Andrew Craig, drawer
2	Quintin Blane, miner
3	John Watt, collier
4	James Blane, miner
5	James Blane, miner
6	John Young, collier
7	William Gill, collier
8	Joseph Gillespie, jun, collier
9	Robert Logan, collier
10	James McCartney, collier
11	James McCartney, collier
12	Gibson Simpson, miner
13	Gibson Simpson, miner
14	Robert Landsborough, collier
14a	George McTimpany, collier
15	Robert Watt, collier
16	Robert Stark, collier
17	William McCulloch, collier
18	Joseph Howatson, storeman
19	James Logan, collier
20	William Dougan, collier
21	James Dalziel, collier

Tongue Row (1922/1923)

1 Tongue Row	Frank Osborne, collier
2	John Hair, miner
3	John Hair, miner
4	Charles Knox, miner
5	Maurice Mulholland, miner
6	Thomas Lafferty, labourer
7	Thomas Knox, miner
8	Robert Brown, collier
9	Robert Irvine, miner

10	Mrs Ramage, widow	20	George Irvine, miner
11	Thomas Knox, miner	21	Quintin Young, miner
12	William Robertson, collier	22	Robert McLean, miner
13	William Robertson, collier	23	James Craighead, fireman
14 & 15	James Murray, collier	24	Joseph Johnstone, miner
16	Alexander Gillespie, collier	25	Robert Dean, miner
17	Thomas Fisher, collier	26	John Reid, miner
18 & 19	David Reid, collier	27	Robert Brown, miner
20 & 21	Mrs Hawthorn, widow	28	John Rodger, miner
22 & 23	Mission House Tongue Row	29	Richard Kirkham, miner
24	William Sutherland, miner	30	Thomas Cushnie, police constable
25	Mrs Findlay, widow	31	Thomas Cushnie, police constable
26	empty	32	William Aitken, engineman
27	Hugh Scott, miner	33	Henry Walters, oncostman
28	empty	34	James Kilpatrick, labourer
29	James Spiers, collier	35	Archibald McPike, miner
30	John Hamilton, miner	36	William Clifford, fireman
31 & 32	empty	37	Robert McMurtrie, miner
33	William Brown, collier	38	Robert Kirkwood, miner
34	William Logan, miner	39	Frank McGlasson, pitheadman
35	William Grant, collier	40	William Smith, miner
36	Campbell Hawthorn, collier	41	Andrew Lindsay, miner
37, 38 & 39	empty	42	Thomas Cunningham, fireman
40	Robert Brown, miner	44	John Nisbet, miner
41	empty	45	Andrew Smith, miner

Cairntable (1922/1923)

House, Rowanbank	Coylton Coal Company	46	George Hay, under manager
	Robert P Roberts, manager	47	William Lindsay, miner
No. 1 Cairntable Terr	Andrew Davidson, miner	48	Hugh Simpson, electrician
2	George McKelvie, roadman		
3	William Lambert, fireman		
4	John Gilchrist, engineman		
5	Thomas Cunningham, fireman		
6	Henry Muir, miner		
7	Matthew Williamson, miner		
8	William Devoy		
9	William McLean, fireman		
10	Joseph Nutt, jun.		
11	John McNeil, joiner		
12	Edward Cunningham, oncostman		
13	William Dunlop, miner		
14	empty		
15	Patrick Madden, miner		
16	John Kelly, labourer		
17	James Kelty, miner		
18	Peter Batton, miner		
19	William Brown, miner		